The Story of
OKLAHOMA

The Story of
OKLAHOMA

W. David Baird
Danney Goble

University of
Oklahoma Press
Norman and London

Written or edited by W. David Baird

Peter Pitchlynn: Chief of the Choctaws (Norman, 1972; 1986)
The Osage People (Phoenix, 1972)
The Choctaw People (Phoenix, 1974)
The Chickasaw People (Phoenix, 1975)
A Dictionary of the Osage Language, by Francis La Flesche
   (Phoenix, 1975)
The Quapaw People (Phoenix, 1975)
Years of Discontent: Doctor Frank L. James in Arkansas, 1877–
   1878 (Memphis, 1977)
Medical Education in Arkansas, 1879–1978 (Memphis, 1979)
The Quapaw Indians: A History of the Downstream People
   (Norman, 1980)
A Creek Warrior for the Confederacy: The Autobiography of
   Chief G.W. Grayson (Norman, 1988)
The Quapaws (New York, 1989)

By Danney Goble

Progressive Oklahoma: The Making of a New Kind of State
   (Norman, 1981)
With James R. Scales, *Oklahoma Politics: A History* (Norman,
   1982)
With Carl Albert, *Little Giant: The Life and Times of Speaker*
   Carl Albert (Norman, 1990)

Library of Congress Cataloging-in-Publication Data

Baird, W. David.
   The story of Oklahoma / W. David Baird, Danney Goble.
      p.   cm.
   Includes index.
   ISBN 0-8061-2650-7
   1. Oklahoma—History—Juvenile literature. [1. Oklahoma—
History.] I. Goble, Danney, 1946–   . II. Title.
   F694.3.B35   1994
   976.7—dc20   93-47075
                                                           CIP
                                                           AC

The paper in this book meets the guidelines for permanence and durability of the Committee on Production Guidelines for Book Longevity of the Council on Library Resources, Inc. ⊗

1   2   3   4   5

6   7   8   9   10

For
Angela Baird Cheves and Tony Baird
and
Codie, Geoffrey, and Hannah Goble

Contents

Maps

Preface

This book's own history began a long time ago. Both of us are products of the public schools of Oklahoma. In fact, we attended the same high school (Edmond High School), although at slightly different times. We both also have graduate degrees from the University of Oklahoma and have spent years teaching in the state's higher education system. Each of us has written scholarly books dealing with various aspects of the state's long past. Two other things that we share is that both of us have taught Oklahoma's history at the college level and both of us have worked closely with Oklahoma secondary teachers in a variety of programs.

For all of those reasons it was natural that our conversations eventually would come around to the need for a modern history of our state, one that would put the best of recent academic scholarship to use in Oklahoma classrooms. Many summers ago we agreed that we would do that. We also agreed on something else. Recently we read that the American Historical Association awarded a special prize to a book written as a text for secondary students in Alabama. Before we started our own, we bought copies of that book, Virginia Van der Veer Hamilton's *The Story of Alabama*. It turned out to be the best decision that we made.

The Story of Oklahoma—starting with its title— draws upon Professor Hamilton's model. As she did, we wanted to make our state's story come alive. This is a history that places people at the forefront. Much that is in older textbooks is not here because we believe that too many dates and trivial events only obscure the vitality and the importance of the history that Oklahoma's people have made. What is here is the story of our state and its people.

And by "people," we mean all of Oklahoma's people. Thus if we have deprived our readers of the details of a few treaties that are now forgotten, or of legislative acts that ought never to be remembered, we have included the experiences that have shaped the lives of countless Oklahomans. These include women and men (and children, too), red people and white (and blacks and others, too), the prominent and the poor (and a lot in between, too). As groups, they are here. As individuals, many are as well.

This is a people's history, with people at the center of its narrative. But the book is more than the narrative. Photographs and other illustrations are as important to its mission as are any of our words. The sidebars and other inserted items are there for reasons—to illustrate, to personalize, even (we dare dream) to entertain. When we list places that students can visit to see history for themselves, usually we have been there. We have used and enjoyed our suggested readings. Altogether, this book—in all of its parts—represents the history that we have learned and the history that we wish to share with our readers.

It represents, too, the *way* that we have learned Oklahoma's history. Because we have been students ourselves, we include the necessary building blocks of historical knowledge: names, dates, places and events—often with tables to ease their way into our reader's consciousness. Because we are historians, we also discuss how we know these things, how others have understood them, and why we think they are important. For such subjects there are fancy words (like *epistemology* and *historiography*), but such words do not appear in this book. What should appear—if just beneath the surface—is our own intellectual quest to learn history and to make it worth learning.

As is true for every author, we can do so only because we ourselves have profited from others' earlier efforts. In our case, it happens that we have separately learned from many of the same individuals. These include high-school teachers that we both had (Lelia Hall, who taught us American history at Edmond High, for example), college professors who taught us both (for example, Arrell Morgan Gibson, who introduced us to scholarship at the University of Oklahoma), and friends that we have known (starting with Angie Debo, who gave us the example of a life well lived).

This work only has enlarged our circle of mutual obligation. John Drayton and the staff at the University of Oklahoma Press have greeted this project with an enthusiasm for it as valuable as has been their patience with us. John R. Lovett and others with the University of Oklahoma's Western History Collections provided us materials, most notably many of the photographs that show Oklahoma's history. John Lovett also prepared unit four, "Oklahoma History on Glass—a Photographic Essay," which adds to the primary sources in the book. Bob Blackburn and the professionals of the Oklahoma Historical Society once again have extended their own contributions to preserving our state's history. We are both indebted to all of them.

Finally, we share one other thing. Each of us is Sooner born and Sooner bred—even if neither of us prefers to be Sooner dead. Not all of our children have been so lucky: the Baird children happen to have been born in Arkansas. Through the veins of all of them, however, run several generations of Oklahomans' blood. The book dedication is to our children. For them—and for those others who read it—it is our hope that it will show them how very strong that blood truly is.

W. DAVID BAIRD

Pepperdine University
Malibu, California

DANNEY GOBLE

University of Oklahoma
Norman, Oklahoma

Unit 1: NATURAL OKLAHOMA

Introduction

Because it became a state only in 1907, Oklahoma is one of the youngest American states. Its history, however, is much longer than that might imply. The historic era begins when humanity introduces writing, making it possible to create records that its descendants may later discover and ponder. Oklahoma's history runs back that far and even further. In fact, it runs back to the beginnings of human history on this continent, even beyond that to the ancient geological ages when the earth itself was forming.

If humankind had existed then, no one would have used or heard the word "Oklahoma." Still, the groanings and roars of the ancient earth have left echoes that sound down through the ages. Those with the ears to hear may still find that true in this state and in the lives of the people who live here. The humans who have known Oklahoma's broad prairies, its fertile soils, its worn mountains, its meandering streams, and its mineral resources, have touched Oklahoma's history at its very origins.

In this section is the story of those origins and of the first people who dealt with their consequences.

Chapter 1: **Prehistoric Oklahoma**

Some 400 million years ago the surface of Oklahoma was flat and almost completely covered by a shallow sea. For 100 million years, geologists tell us, it remained beneath the water. Any exposed land was empty and colorless, but not so the sea. Warmed by the sun, it was a thick soup, teeming with all kinds of living plants and creatures. The trilobite was the predominate form of marine life. Its body could grow thirty inches long.

Over time (and very much of it), the skeletons and shells of countless billions of these prehistoric creatures settled to the bottom of the sea. As they slowly accumulated, the remains formed thick deposits of dolomite and limestone, sometimes as much as a mile deep. You can see the evidence along Interstate 35 as it passes through the Arbuckle Mountains north of Ardmore. Modern Oklahomans use this fossilized ma-

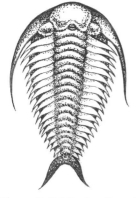

Above: Trilobite fossils, millions of years old, may still be found in Oklahoma.

Right: Kiamichi Mountains in southeastern Oklahoma as seen from near Talihina.

terial in a variety of ways. It provides stone blocks to construct buildings, as well as the cement that joins those blocks together. It also is used in the production of quicklime and the manufacture of glass.

Oklahoma's Mountains Form

About 300 million years ago pressure within our planet pushed violently at the surface. The earth shook and volcanoes erupted. Whole sections of the sea's bottom rose majestically from beneath the water to be tilted, folded, and fractured to form great mountain chains. In Oklahoma small remnants of this dramatic process are apparent in the scenic Ouachita, Arbuckle, and Wichita mountains. There is also a good chance that you can see them in rock ledges around your home. If you can, notice that almost all of them are tilted in one direction or another.

Gold and Granite in Oklahoma

Not the least consequence of these revolutionary events was the gold left behind in some of Oklahoma's mountains. It took humankind long to find it—but, of course, it took humanity long even to appear. In the 1890s prospectors discovered deposits in the Wichita Mountains near present Fort Sill. When they did, the *Oklahoma State Capitol* newspaper at Guthrie reported, "GOLD! GOLD! Five Hundred People on the Ground!" Because the land belonged to the Kiowas and the Comanches, active mining was delayed until 1901. Some 2,000 to 3,000 miners rushed to boomtowns like Golden Pass, Camp Homestead, and Poverty Gulch. On the streets of one town, a visitor wrote that, "trouble [was] hanging around waiting for everyone." Doubtless, trouble found many. Almost certainly, trouble found more than found gold. In ten years of frenzied digging no one discovered more than just a little gold in the Wichitas. When disappointed miners moved on, Oklahoma's gold rush ended.

The heat and pressure that formed gold also produced Oklahoma's granite. There are two locations of granite in our state today. One is in Johnston County, from which stone was taken to construct the first floor of the Oklahoma State Capitol in Oklahoma City. The other is in Jackson and Greer

Gold and granite were formed in Oklahoma millions of years ago. About 1904 in the Wichita Mountains near Snyder (*left*), miners lift buckets filled with quartz rock, or ore, from which they later extracted small amounts of gold. Blocks of granite (*right*) are drilled and then removed from an early quarry near present Granite in Greer County.

counties. Pink, grey, blue, and black in color, granite from those locations is often fashioned into cemetery and historical monuments. The *Cimarron Cowboy* in Woods County, the *Great Men of the Plains* memorial in Greer County, and many of the state's major historical markers come from a quarry just north of one of Oklahoma's most perfectly named towns: Granite.

Geological Basins Develop

As the mountains pushed up, adjacent regions dropped down, forming huge basins. Two of these are found in Oklahoma, the Anadarko Basin in the west and the Arkoma Basin in the east. These massive depressions then filled with water that teemed with marine life. Over the next 200 million years sand and silt also flowed into the basins. It washed down from nearby and distant mountains, eroding their peaks to only one-sixth of their original size.

The sand and the mud lay in thick layers at the bottom of these inland seas. The skeletons and shells of numberless marine creatures formed another layer. It included the remains of the fusulinidae, microscopic animals that secreted a protective covering and often measured two inches long. There also were the bryozoa, creatures that looked like growing moss or seaweed and reached two feet in diameter. These deposits were then buried, compressed, and cemented together to form shale, sandstone, limestone, and even flint.

Swamp Treasure

At the outer edge of the water-filled basins lay extensive swamps and marshlands. They existed in Oklahoma for at least 30 million years. Life in them was lush and dynamic, with huge plants, colorful flowers, strange insects, and large reptiles abounding. When these plants and creatures died, their remains also collected beneath the swamp waters.

From time to time, the tremendous pressure within the planet caused these water-filled basins and adjacent swamps to sink even farther. As they did, mud, sand and gravel washed in to cover the swamps, sealing the material there into deposits and preserving it from decay. Millions of years later, these ancient swamp and marshlands provide us with vital sources of energy that we know as coal, petroleum, and natural gas.

Thus swamp treasure lies buried beneath, often times far beneath, the soil of Oklahoma. Finding, retrieving, processing, and selling such "black gold" is one of the enterprises that has helped determine the state's history. It contributed to the demise of tribal government in Indian Territory. It brought incredible wealth to a few and jobs to many. It provided tax revenues for schools and other government functions. It made Tulsa the "Oil Capital of the World." Not least, it helped produce a state of mind that has both enriched and bedeviled Oklahoma's social life.

In many years Oklahoma has led the nation in oil

One of several similar facilities in Oklahoma, the Sinclair oil refinery, tank farm, and terminal near downtown Tulsa contributes significantly to Oklahoma's economy.

production, and it consistently is among the five leading oil-producing states. About 5 percent of the barrels produced in the United States come from our state. For all that Oklahomans have removed over the years, geologists tell us that more than 25 billion barrels of petroleum still lie buried beneath the state's surface. Although oil has been found in sixty-six of our seventy-seven counties, the five largest producing areas are near Ardmore and Healdton, in Carter County; near Enid, in Garfield County; near Lindsey, in Garvin County; and near Guymon, in Texas County.

Natural gas is almost as important to Oklahoma as petroleum. We produce 10 percent of the national total; only two states produce more. The known reserves total about 12 trillion cubic feet, although undiscovered resources easily could be six times that much. Like petroleum, natural gas is produced widely in Oklahoma. The largest fields are located in Texas and Beaver counties in the west and Haskell county in the east. Discovery of natural gas five miles down in the Deep Anadarko Basin near Elk City suggests the presence of an even-larger field.

Oklahoma contributes only a small fraction of the nation's total coal production. There are 2.3 billion tons of recoverable coal reserves. Most of that is situated in nineteen counties in the Arkoma Basin and along a north-south line that links McAlester with the Kansas border. The coal is bituminous (soft) in grade and particularly suitable for electric power generation. Today the state's coal is produced entirely from strip mines, with the greatest activity in Craig, Rogers, and Haskell counties.

The value annually of Oklahoma's swamp treasure is more than double the value of agricultural products, the state's second leading industry. Refineries process crude oil into a variety of products including gasoline, jet fuel, fuel oil, lubricating oils, asphalt, and petrochemicals. Used as a fuel to produce heat and light, natural gas is delivered to consumers through pipelines that connect Oklahoma to the rest of the nation. It is also processed into carbon black, ammonia, plastics, and other materials. Much of Oklahoma's coal is sold to fuel electrical generators in states as far away as Tennessee and Ohio.

HOW IT WORKS: AN EARLY OIL DRILLING RIG

Oklahoma's first commercially successful oil well "blew in" at 1,320 feet on April 15, 1897, near what is now Bartlesville. Known as Nellie Johnstone No. 1, it launched the rush for black gold that had such a profound impact on the history of the state. The rig that drilled the historic well was not new in concept or design. It was of a kind that was first used to dig for water, but since 1859 had been employed in the production of petroleum. Of course, the Nellie Johnstone had benefited from forty years of technological improvements.

The Bartlesville rig employed what oilmen called the cable-tool or percussion method of drilling. The wood-frame derrick was four-sided and stood seventy-five feet high. At the top of the derrick was a pulley over which ran the cable used to hoist and lower the tools, casing, and bailer. Central to the rig was a walking beam (like a teeter-totter in appearance), which was lowered and raised by a motor-powered crank attached to one end. At the other end of the beam a cable was connected to metal links, called "jars," which in turn were connected to the long, cylindrical, steel "drill stem" that was connected to the "bit." This string of cable tools was thirty to forty feet long and weighed several thousand pounds.

The drill bit was made of steel and was about eleven feet long, somewhat wider than it was thick. The end of the bit was shaped like a chisel. As the walking beam was raised and lowered by the engine-powered crank, the bit was raised and dropped on the rock at the bottom of the hole. Periodically it was sharpened and the cuttings were bailed out of the shaft.

Drilling continued until the rock showed signs of petroleum. The Nellie Johnstone pushed down to 1,320 feet before that occurred. When it did, drillers "shot" the well with nitroglycerin, creating an explosion at the bottom of the bore that released the swamp treasure and permitted it to "gush" to the surface. Thereafter natural gas brought fifty to seventy-five barrels of petroleum to the surface daily.

Cable-drilling rigs were used in Oklahoma until the mid-1920s. Then they were replaced by rotary drilling rigs, which bore holes by revolving or rotating a steel bit at the end of a string of pipe. The new rigs were more efficient and permitted oilmen to drill much deeper holes. In the late 1920s the Oklahoma City field came in at 6,455 feet. By the 1980s drillers were pushing to 20,000 feet, or almost four miles, in the Anadarko Basin in western Oklahoma.

The Nellie Johnstone #1 (*left*) blew in on April 15, 1897. Compare the wooden rig of Oklahoma's first commercially successful oil well with the modern, high-tech Rig 201 of the Parker Drilling Company (*right*).

Oklahoma's Aquifers Are Charged

The creative pressures that turned ancient swamps into petroleum and natural gas also trapped something else every bit as precious—billions and billions of gallons of fresh water that now lie deep beneath the surface of the earth. The mainly limestone and sandstone rocks, alluvial deposits, and other formations holding that water are known as aquifers. From them many Oklahoma towns and cities pump their municipal water supplies. At least 70 percent of the water that farmers use to irrigate their crops comes from these living stones as well.

The Ogallala aquifer is the most important source of ground water (in contrast to surface water) in Oklahoma. Lying deep beneath the Panhandle, it provides "underground rain" to a very thirsty land, enabling the Panhandle to be one of Oklahoma's most productive agriculture areas. So huge is that massive aquifer that, raised to the surface, it would cover all of Oklahoma to a depth of seven feet. Conservative estimates place the value of the water still in the Ogallala aquifer beneath the Panhandle at more than $1 billion.

Rainfall percolating beneath the surface continuously "recharges" the aquifers. Although that is true, the water that gently falls as rain does not even approach the volume that is sucked out by powerful irrigation pumps. This is particularly

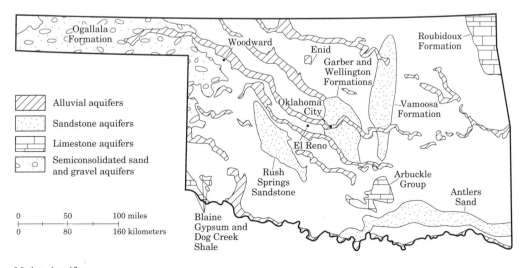

Major Aquifers

true in the dry, parched Panhandle region. Oklahomans drain even the mighty Ogallala far faster than nature can replenish it. In some areas of the Panhandle the water level already has dropped in excess of 100 feet in just a few decades.

Gypsum Hills and Salt Plains

When the great geological basins were filling, such concerns lay far ahead. For millennia, warm winds stirred the surface of the seas. In time the sea water began to evaporate, leaving behind thick deposits of gypsum and salt. Today we see evidence of that activity in the Gypsum Hills of Blaine and Major counties and in the large salt flats in Alfalfa and Woods counties. From gypsum, Oklahomans manufacture plasterboard. From salt deposits, they produce water softeners, stock feed, and deicing compounds. Reserves are vast. A few spots in Oklahoma contain enough gypsum to plaster the entire world. Some springs in the state are eight times more salty than sea water.

The Age of Reptiles

From time to time an Oklahoma farmer's plow turns up an odd bone. In some cases these are the remains of huge dinosaurs that once roamed the land that is now Oklahoma. Among them was the apatosaurus. The apatosaurus had a small head on the end of a long neck, a body that weighed fifty tons or more, and a long tapering tail. It fed on leaves and needles from the tops of trees. In contrast, the camptosaurus measured only two to seventeen feet in length and looked something like an upright lizard with a long tail and short front legs. A plant eater, the camptosaurus generally traveled in herds. Skeletons of these creatures are in the Oklahoma Museum of Natural History in Norman. If you are lucky, you may find one of their footprints closer to home, on some flat sandstone surface.

For reasons that we do not understand, all species of dinosaurs disappeared from the Oklahoma landscape about 65 million years ago. The prevailing theory is that a giant meteor struck the earth, sending forth shock waves and huge clouds of dust and debris that rendered the atmosphere incapable of

Archaeologists find evidence of the presence of dinosaurs in Oklahoma in different settings. *Left:* Near Optima, Texas County, researchers find bones ten or more feet beneath the earth. *Right:* Dinosaur footprints in a riverbed in the Panhandle.

supporting the great creatures. Surely, future scientists will propound more theories. Just as surely, the dinosaurs will neither reappear nor lose their fascination.

The Water Recedes

About 70 million years ago pressures within the earth moved the surface of the land upward, in time pushing it well above sea level. The waters drained from the basins, and the sea retreated far to the south. The landscape of Oklahoma still had some changes to make, but its uplift to the sun, for the moment, was progress enough. Its birth had been millions of years in the making. The addition of color, texture, and personality would not take so long.

See History for Yourself

For excellent exhibits on Oklahoma's prehistoric development, visit the Oklahoma Museum of Natural History in Norman and the Museum of the Great Plains in Lawton. Hike the Arbuckle Mountains parallel to old Highway 77 and examine the rock layers embedded in the ground. They provide a trip into the heart of the planet. Look for fossils three miles south of Lake Ardmore, at Big Canyon east and south of Dougherty, and on the shore of Lake

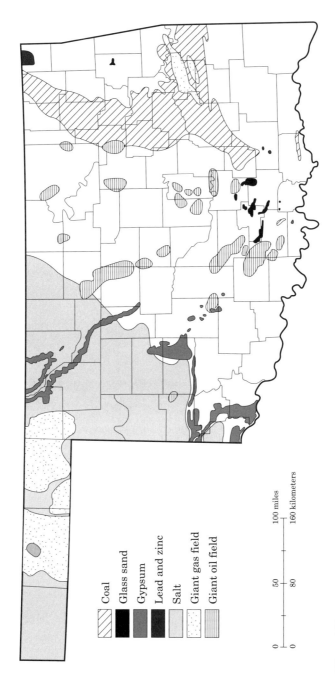

Coal

Glass sand

Gypsum

Lead and zinc

Salt

Giant gas field

Giant oil field

0   50   100 miles

0   80   160 kilometers

Mineral Resources

Apatosaurus

Camptosaurus

Okmulgee. Explore an old gold mine site in the Wichita Mountains and the granite quarry north of Granite. Visit the wood-framed Nellie Johnstone No. 1 oil well at Bartlesville, the steel-framed well on the grounds of the Oklahoma Historical Society in Oklahoma City, and one of Oklahoma's many oil refineries.

Suggestions for Further Reading

Reference

Bell, Robert E. *Prehistory of Oklahoma.* New York: Academic Press, 1984.

Franks, Kenny A. *Oklahoma Natural History Map.* Oklahoma City: Oklahoma Heritage Association, 1990.

——. *The Oklahoma Petroleum Industry.* Norman: University of Oklahoma Press, 1980.

Morris, John W., ed. *Drill Bits, Picks, and Shovels: A History of Mineral Resources in Oklahoma.* Oklahoma City: Oklahoma Historical Society, 1982.

Morris, John W., et al. *Historical Atlas of Oklahoma.* 3d ed. Norman: University of Oklahoma Press, 1986.

Oklahoma Geographical Survey. *Geology and Earth Resources of Oklahoma.* Educational Publication 1. Oklahoma City: Oklahoma Geological Survey, 1981.

Opie, John. *Ogallala: Water for a Dry Land.* Lincoln: University of Nebraska Press, 1993.

Pettyjohn, Wayne A., et al. *Water Atlas of Oklahoma.* Stillwater: Oklahoma State University, Center for Water Research, 1983.

Sattler, Helen Roney. *Dinosaurs of North America.* New York: Lothrup, Lee, and Shepard Books, 1981.

General Histories of Oklahoma

Debo, Angie. *Oklahoma, Foot-loose and Fancy-free.* Norman: University of Oklahoma Press, 1949, 1987.

Faulk, Odie B. *Oklahoma, the Land of the Fair God.* Northridge, Calif.: Windsor Publications, 1986.

Gibson, Arrell Morgan. *Oklahoma: A History of Five Centuries.* 2d ed. Norman: University of Oklahoma Press, 1981.

Milligan, James C. *Oklahoma: A Regional History.* Durant, Okla.: Mesa Publishing, 1985.

Morgan, Anne Hodges, and H. Wayne Morgan. *Oklahoma: A Bicentennial History.* New York: W. W. Norton, 1977.

Stein, Howard F., and Robert F. Hill. *The Culture of Oklahoma.* Norman: University of Oklahoma Press, 1993.

The WPA Guide to 1930s Oklahoma. Lawrence, Kans.: University Press of Kansas, 1986.

Chapter 2: **Natural Features**

The lifting, tilting, cracking, and eroding that accompanied the birth of Oklahoma left it with flatlands, hills, and mountains. Geologists and geographers have studied this diverse landscape and have identified ten distinct regions. Look at the map below to find their names. Try to identify the area in which you live. If the map is of no help, just look around.

Is your home on a huge, rolling prairie where your vision is obstructed only by a few low ridges? Are the soils and rocks reddish? Do the principal rivers flow west to east through broad beds, but with little water? Along those rivers are you likely to find post oak and blackjack trees? Can you find both tall

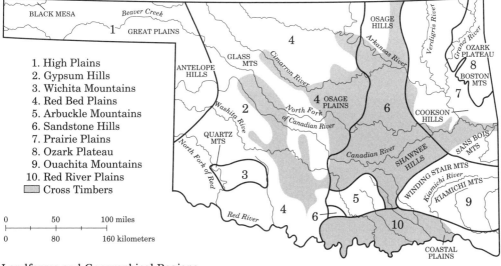

1. High Plains
2. Gypsum Hills
3. Wichita Mountains
4. Red Bed Plains
5. Arbuckle Mountains
6. Sandstone Hills
7. Prairie Plains
8. Ozark Plateau
9. Ouachita Mountains
10. Red River Plains
▨ Cross Timbers

Landforms and Geographical Regions

bluestem and short buffalo grass in pasture areas? Is winter-wheat farming a principal occupation, along with cattle raising, horse breeding, cotton planting, and petroleum production? Do you get about thirty-two inches of rain annually, far more sunny days than cloudy ones, and snow only occasionally? If so, you live in central and southwestern Oklahoma on the Red Bed Plains.

Your home region may be similar to that just described except that deep red mesas filled with gypsum glisten on the horizon. Moreover, the amount of moisture is six inches less, temperature extremes are a little greater, the rivers are a little dryer, and they tend to flow in deeper channels. The soil also tends to be a bit sandier. Should that be the case, then you live in the Gypsum Hills.

Perhaps there is absolutely no obstruction to your vision except along the edges, or "breaks," of the rivers. Perhaps where you live is higher, dryer, and cooler than anywhere else in Oklahoma. Short buffalo grass prevails on the flat uplands; juniper and piñon trees thrive on the mesas. Wheat, petroleum, and cattle provide people their principal occupations—an economic mix that gives your area the highest per-capita income in our state. If these are your surroundings, then you live on the High Plains of the Panhandle.

Or is your part of the state mountainous, with peaks rising over 2,000 feet from their base? Is your area known for unique rock formations, springs, and even waterfalls? Do rivers run clear, full, and

Captured on film early in the twentieth century, this typical ranch scene on the High Plains of Oklahoma shows wide-open spaces and short-grass vegetation, enjoyed equally by both cattle and men.

swift? Are the ruins of an old gristmill within driving distance? Are your forests filled with oak and hickory trees or oak and pine trees? Does your area get forty to fifty inches of rain yearly, more than anywhere else in Oklahoma? Are coal mines or pulpwood plants nearby? Do cattle graze in the valley meadows? If so, then you live in the Ouachita Mountains, or on the Ozark Plateau, in the eastern part of the state. Excepting the coal and a few inches of rain, you may even live in the Arbuckle Mountains of south-central Oklahoma.

Are there low cuestas—sandstone ridges with a steep slope on the east and a gentle slope on the west—where you live? Do the principal rivers run north to south through gentle prairies that are covered by tall bluestem grass? Is coal strip-mined and oil produced in the area? Is hay a principal crop, and are cattle raising and horse breeding major economic activities? If that is the case, then you probably live in what has been described as the Prairie-Plains region.

Perhaps your home is where the land is hilly and much of the sandy soil is covered with tall prairie grass or scrub oak trees? Can you see in nearby fields evidence of heavy erosion because of poor farming practices earlier in this century? Is one of Oklahoma's more famous oil fields close by? Are most of the towns near you rather small? If this is familiar, then you live in the Sandstone Hills.

Or it may be that you live where the land is generally flat, where pine trees are abundant and cyprus trees can be found, where the soils are sandy, where elevations are lower, and where the growing season is the longest in Oklahoma. Can you find evidence nearby of old plantations where cotton was once grown with slave labor? In addition to cotton, are cattle raised near your home? Do you find soybean fields and hay meadows in the countryside? If so, then you probably live on the Coastal Plains near Red River.

A tributary to the Illinois River in Delaware County created this classic scene in eastern Oklahoma of a delicate waterfall, a reflecting pool, carved rocks, and dark green foliage.

The Cross Timbers

The geographical term for the region in which you live is important to students of history only if the qualities described had some influence on the development of the region. In one way or another all the regions of Oklahoma have had significance, but none more than a unique vegetation zone that cuts across several geographical regions—the Cross Timbers. The noted American author Washington Irving described the area in 1832 as "forests of cast iron" that tore "the flesh of man and horse." Actually they were post oak and blackjack oak trees that grew so close together that they formed a natural barrier between Oklahoma's western plains and eastern prairies and mountains. You can see the western edge of the Cross Timbers when you drive along Interstate 35 between Ponca City and Ardmore.

Early travelers and settlers found them difficult to penetrate. Plains Indian peoples like the Comanches and the Cheyennes almost always stayed west of them, as did Texas cowboys who drove cattle north to Kansas markets. The first railroads built their lines either east or west of the Cross Timbers, while the routes of modern interstate highways generally avoid them. The largest cities of the state lie outside their borders.

The earliest farmers could cultivate only the intermittent, small meadows in the Cross Timbers. They found the sandy soil fertile but unstable; it eroded easily and quickly once plowed. In less than a generation most of the farms were unproductive and most of the farmers were poverty stricken. This heritage of broken dreams explains partly why many of Oklahoma's radical political and religious traditions have centered in the Cross Timbers. This same area that once gave the state an army of socialist organizers later produced a host of faith-healing evangelists.

Physical characteristics have also produced significant economic and political rivalries as well as different lifestyles within Oklahoma. The treeless uplands and rich soils of the western plains promoted large-scale farming, cattle ranching, and identification with a cowboy culture. The cast-iron forests and eroded soils of the Cross Timbers restricted farmers to small tracts of land, to crops of cotton and corn, and to a Southern yeoman style of life. Since statehood the two areas have fought each other for political power. This east-west rivalry is still evident today. One sees it everywhere from high-school football fields to the floor of the state legislature.

AN EYEWITNESS ACCOUNT:
WASHINGTON IRVING IN OKLAHOMA, 1832

In 1832, Washington Irving, whom we know best for his stories about Rip Van Winkle and Ichabod Crane, accompanied an official expedition to Indian territory. With a party of United States Rangers, he toured the area between Fort Gibson and present Oklahoma City. His observations, first published in 1835 as *A Tour on the Prairies,* (Norman: University of Oklahoma Press, 1956), give us a glimpse of Oklahoma when it was still "natural."

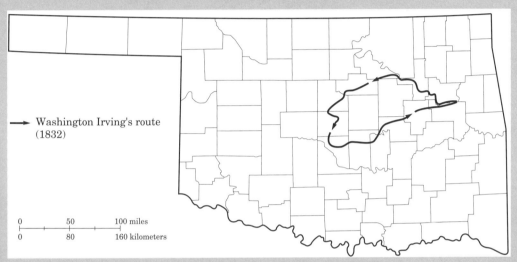

→ Washington Irving's route (1832)

| 0 | 50 | 100 miles |
| 0 | 80 | 160 kilometers |

Area of Oklahoma explored by Washington Irving in 1832

THE FOREST
We were overshadowed by lofty trees, with straight smooth trunks, like stately columns; and as the glancing rays of the sun shone through the transparent leaves, tinted with the many-colored hues of autumn, I was reminded of the effect of sunshine among the stained windows and clustering columns of a Gothic cathedral. (41)

ABUNDANCE OF WILDLIFE
The game killed at this camp consisted of six deer, one elk, two bears, and six or eight turkeys. (93)

We came in sight of six wild horses, among which I especially noticed two very handsome ones, a gray and a roan. They pranced about, with heads erect, and long flaunting tails, offering a proud contrast to our poor, spiritless, travel-tired steeds. (137)

THE PRAIRIE
Here one of the characteristic scenes of the Far West broke upon us. An immense extent of grassy, undulating, or, as it is termed, rolling country, with here and there a clump of trees, dimly seen in the distance like a ship at sea; the landscape deriving sublimity from its vastness and simplicity. (106)

THE CROSS TIMBERS
The Cross Timber is about forty miles in breadth, and stretches over a rough country of rolling hills, covered with scattered tracts of post-oak and black-jack. . . . It is much cut up by deep ravines. . . . I shall not easily forget the mortal toil, and the vexations of flesh and spirit, that we underwent occasionally, in our wanderings through the Cross Timbers. It was like struggling through forests of cast iron. (124–25)

Tornado Alley

Have you noticed that Oklahomans are committed weather watchers? Every radio and television station in the state broadcasts lengthy segments several times a day describing current conditions and forecasting future ones. In the spring neighbors spend many evening hours observing large clouds boil in from the west, prepared to run to the "cellar" if a twister is spotted. Storm watching, someone has said, is Oklahoma's largest spectator sport. Sometimes it becomes a participant sport.

Why all the interest? For one thing, Oklahoma's weather is so variable. A norther can turn a warm spring day into a bone-chilling blizzard. Late "Indian summers" have pushed temperatures above 90° F. in January. Hot, dry daytime winds in the summer are followed by gentle evening breezes. Thunderstorms possess such power that they produce baseball-size hail, dazzling displays of lightning, and sheets of rain. Nothing, however, is as awesome as the funnel-shaped tornado that dips out of the sky and devastates all that it touches.

Since 1950, Oklahoma has experienced an average of 53 tornadoes annually. In 1957 alone, some 107 were reported. These storms do millions of dollars' worth of damage each year. Even worse, they kill an average of six people annually. This helps explain why Oklahoma is often known to the nation and to the world as Tornado Alley. It also explains why the federal government operates the National Severe Storms Laboratory in Norman.

What accounts for the variety in Oklahoma's weather? It is because we live in a zone where three climatic regions—humid, subhumid, and semiarid—meet and mingle. There are only two other states in the union (Kansas and Texas) where that happens. Mixing cool, dry air from Canada and warm, moist air from the Gulf of Mexico under continental conditions produces, on the whole, very pleasant weather. There are almost as many days of clear sunshine as there are days with cloudy or partly cloudy skies. The average annual temperature is about 60° F., although usually there are several days during each summer that exceed 100° F. and several days each

The unpredictability and severity of Oklahoma's weather are captured in this dramatic photograph of an 1895 tornado that struck Oklahoma City.

winter when temperatures below 0° F. are recorded. The growing season, or length of time between killing frosts, averages 207 days. The range is great, running from 180 days in the Panhandle to 340 days in the extreme southeast of Oklahoma.

The distribution of precipitation (rain and snow) across our state varies even more than the temperature. The Panhandle's Black Mesa receives an average of only fifteen inches of rainfall a year. The Ouachita Mountains in the southeast are drenched with more than fifty-two inches annually. In the Panhandle that moisture comes primarily in the summer and spring; in other parts of the state it is rather evenly distributed throughout the year, although spring is the wettest season. In general, western Oklahoma, because of higher evaporation rates, gets less moisture than it needs, while the eastern part of the state receives more than it requires.

Our Productive Soils

It is worth knowing that Oklahoma has soils that are among the world's most productive. The podzolic soils in eastern Oklahoma are the least fertile, primarily because heavier precipitation there leaches, or drains, them of nutrients. The reddish prairie soils elsewhere are naturally fertile, and with the right amount of moisture they can be very productive. The problem is that on the western plains moisture is generally scanty. Successful agriculture there depends on supplemental supplies of surface or ground water.

How do climate and soils affect our history? Because Oklahoma has rich soils, adequate rain, and a long growing season, agriculture long remained a major source of Oklahomans' income. Today far more work in nonfarm than farm occupations, but agriculture, horse breeding, and cattle raising continue as major activities. Some observers argue that the climate and the soils have also helped to shape the personality of those of us who live in the state. They detect qualities of resignation and tenacity in the typical Oklahoman, which, they feel, are what Oklahomans are left with after confronting the power of a tornado, the devastation of a drought, or the destruction of a flood.

Riches of the Forest

More than 130 different species of trees are native to Oklahoma, and they cover just over one-fifth of the state's land surface. The trees range from the red bud—the state tree—to the pecan, from the dogwood to the walnut, and from the elm to the cottonwood. Hardwoods (like oak and hickory) and softwoods (like pine, loblolly pine, and cypress) once grew especially dense in the eastern part of our state. Because of the lack of sunlight and the occasional fire, few plants grew on the forest floor.

After the Civil War, Oklahoma residents began to harvest the forests for commercial purposes. This harvest accelerated as railroads came to Oklahoma and opened markets for the products of the forests. Within fifty years lumbermen virtually exhausted the virgin stands of hardwoods, pines, and cypress on the Ozark Plateau, in the Ouachita Mountains, and on the Red River Plains. A "cut out and get out" method of harvesting jeopardized the future of Oklahoma's timber industry. It was saved by a conservation movement that began in the 1920s. Introduction of fast-growing varieties of pine and use of contour

Portable sawmills made it easy to harvest Oklahoma's forests after the Civil War. This one, located in Atoka County, operated with both mechanical and horse power.

plowing helped restore the forests. Modern foresters, recognizing the value of a diverse ecosystem, now harvest the timber by selective- rather than clear-cutting methods. The result is a thriving lumber industry that produces goods valued at millions of dollars annually from 5 million acres of land.

The western borders of the Ouachita National Forest extend into Oklahoma in Le Flore and Mc-Curtain counties. These are public lands managed by the Forest Service of the United States Department of Agriculture. Rangers seek to achieve a balance between timber production, water resources, wildlife protection, and recreation.

Natural Wonders

To appreciate Oklahoma completely, you should see its spectacular prairies, remarkable rock formations, ever-flowing springs, and blue mountain peaks. People have known of these natural wonders for many centuries. Most of these places have played a role in our history.

Unique Plains and Prairies

The Great Salt Plains in Alfalfa County are probably our state's most historically significant salt flat. Covering 120 square miles, one early explorer described it as a "lake of white water." It is less a lake than deposits of pure salt that are several feet thick in some places but only a few inches in others. The deposits occur when fresh water flowing through thick beds of rock salt deep within the earth comes to the surface as brine (heavy salt water). When the surface is dry, it appears crystal white to the eye; if it is wet with rain, it looks no different than any other barren piece of ground.

For untold centuries the Great Salt Plains were an important source of salt for both people and animals. Migratory birds used the surrounding marshlands on their journeys north and south. To preserve its natural state, in 1930 the federal government secured the property and created the Great Salt Plains Wildlife Refuge. Eleven years later it dammed the nearby Salt Fork River as a flood control measure, creating a reservoir that covered the plains completely and established wetlands that attract thousands of ducks and geese annually. Along with seven similar reserves in Oklahoma (Optima, Black Kettle, Washita, Wichita Mountain, Tishomingo, Little River, and Sequoyah), the refuge is administered by the Fish and Wildlife Service of the United States Department of the Interior.

Other notable salt springs and flats exist near Freedom, in Woods County; close to Erick, in Beckham County; and southeast of Southard, in Blaine County.

Prairies are large expanses of grassland with a nearly level landscape. They occur where soils are dark and deep and the climate is warm and relatively wet. Early on, grasses often grew as tall as a man, and they were intermixed with a variety of flowers, including the black-eyed Susan. The tallgrass prairie of North America once extended like a great triangle from Illinois to Alberta, Canada, to Oklahoma. Today only the small part in Oklahoma—in present-day Osage County—retains its natural grasses. Its existence is partly a consequence of luck. The land's Indian and white owners happened to use it for ranching rather than farming purposes. In the late 1980s a portion of the area was incorporated into the Tallgrass Prairie Preserve managed by the Nature Conservancy, a private organization seeking to preserve our natural heritage.

Natural Springs and Waterfalls

Water has always been a precious commodity in Oklahoma. Where it boils to the surface from some hidden source in small or great quantities, it attracts both beasts and humans. Some of Oklahoma's more notable springs are at Sulphur in Murray County near the Arbuckle Mountains. Because they contain minerals (sulphur, iron, and bromide) believed to have medical benefits, they were long used by individuals who hoped to restore or retain good health by drinking or bathing in the waters. To protect them and make them more widely available, in 1902 the federal government purchased the area from the Chickasaw Indians and organized it as Platt National Park. With the advent of antibiotics, and because of its small size, in 1976 national officials reclassified the property, grouped it with other nearby lands, and renamed it the Chickasaw National Recreation Area. Today it is managed by the National Parks Service of the United States Department of the Interior.

Just north of Watonga in Blaine County are other significant springs. Situated in a canyon in the Gypsum Hills and producing 800 gallons of water per minute, the springs were a favorite camping site for the Cheyenne Indians, who named them Springs of Everlasting Water. Cheyenne chief Henry Roman Nose, who had taken part in the battle of the Washita (1868), selected his allotment and built his home just above them. The springs now are a part of the state park named for him.

Oklahoma has fifty-six state parks and resorts. Almost certainly there is one near your home. Like Roman Nose State Park, they are properties purchased, owned, and supported by and for the taxpayers. Most are adjacent to one of Oklahoma's natural wonders or man-made lakes. Managed by the Oklahoma State Tourism and Recreation Department, the park system is designed to preserve natural resources, protect wildlife, and provide recreational facilities.

The state's most noted waterfall is Turner Falls near Davis in Murray County. Rising in the Arbuckle Mountains, Honey Creek falls seventy-seven feet at this point before it enters the Washita River. In the last century the site was a favorite camping and recreational area for Wichita and Comanche Indians. Chickasaw citizen Mazeppa Turner, after whom the falls was named, built his cabin there in the 1870s. Today the property is owned by the city of Davis and maintained as a recreational site.

Mesas and Hills

Mesas and hills are common features in most sections of Oklahoma. They were formed as water and wind slowly eroded the surface of sandstone, shale, and clay uplifts. Several of these formations are particularly important historically. Black Mesa, in the northwest corner of the Oklahoma Panhandle, is the highest point in the state, about 4,973 feet above sea level. Covered by a thick lava cap, the mesa has been a major landmark for centuries. Scientists have located nearby the skeletal remains of dinosaurs and prehistoric human beings. Within sight of the mesa are wagon ruts left by the thousands of travelers who crossed from Missouri to New Mexico on the Santa Fe Trail between 1822 and 1875. Along those ruts are the ruins of Fort Nichols, built in 1865 to guard the trail.

The Antelope Hills in northern Roger Mills County are six gypsum peaks that tower several hundred feet above the surface. Vegetation is sparse, although the South Canadian River winds around the northern slope of the hills. From earliest times Plains Indian peoples used the Antelope Hills as a camp and council ground. The hills also marked the Canadian River route that many migrants followed to the California goldfields in the 1850s.

Mountains

Rainy Mountain, situated southwest of Mountain View in Kiowa County, guards the northern approach to the Wichita Mountain chain of granite and rhyolite peaks. Looming large on an otherwise level landscape, it is a sacred place to the Kiowa people, who found refuge on the surrounding plains from their northern enemies early in the nineteenth century. Between 1896 and 1922 the federal government operated a school there for Kiowa children. N. Scott Momaday, an award-winning Kiowa author, has explained the special significance of the area to his people in a moving little book, *The Way to Rainy Mountain*. The Kiowa tribe maintains the property today.

Sugar Loaf Mountain near Poteau is one of the highest peaks in the Ouachita mountain chain. With a sandstone cap and a shale base, it towers 2,100 feet above the valley floor. Geologists tell us that the scenic Ouachitas are a western extension of the Appalachian Mountains, which extend from the Canadian province of Newfoundland to Alabama. Sugar Loaf marked the way for the earliest Indian residents and European explorers in the area. When the Choctaws were removed to our state in the 1830s, it was the focus of many of their settlements.

Oklahoma's Rivers

If you are a fisherman, or if you enjoy canoeing, you have some idea of what rivers and creeks meant to Oklahoma's early inhabitants. At the very spot you throw in your hook, Indians may also have fished. As one paddles along a quiet stretch of water it is easy to imagine meeting the dugout of a French coureur de bois (fur trader) filled with guns, axes, knives, and cloth to swap for valuable furs. Had you lived in the nineteenth century you might

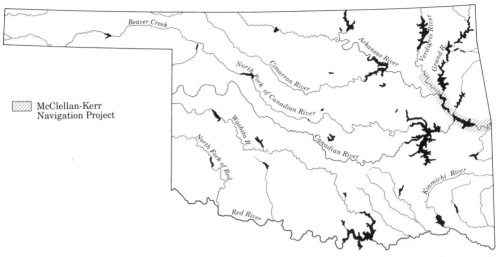

McClellan-Kerr
Navigation Project

Principal Rivers and Reservoirs

have seen a flatboat or a keelboat loaded with buffalo hides, deerskins, cotton, grain, and manufactured merchandise. And along the Arkansas and Red rivers, you might have witnessed the passing of a paddle-wheel steamer with smoke billowing from its stacks and its whistle screeching from the deck.

The first steamboat struggled up the Arkansas River to Fort Gibson in 1828. Thereafter boats were the preferred means of transportation for both freight and passengers until railroads were constructed in 1876. Man-powered keelboats took almost five times longer to come upriver than did the steam-powered paddle wheelers. Steamboats transported beef hides, buffalo robes, deerskins, and pecans down the river. They returned with cloth, canned goods, and other

Although it operated eighty years after the first steamboat struggled up the Arkansas River to Oklahoma, the *City of Muskogee* looked very much like its predecessors. Note that the steamer is a stern-wheeler.

manufactured items for local merchants, as well as supplies for military posts and the Indian agencies. Passengers went both ways, as did gamblers and prostitutes from New Orleans.

Although the advantages were obvious, travel could be hazardous. Low water prevented navigation between July and December. Tree stumps and submerged rocks often smashed hulls and sunk the vessels. Explosions from overpressured steam boilers could and did rip boats apart. There were more obstacles to navigation on Oklahoma rivers than on the other streams flowing into the Mississippi River from the west.

Steamboat navigation on the Red River was delayed by the "Great Raft," a 150-mile natural accumulation of tightly packed trees and stumps that prevented even keelboat travel below Fort Towson. In 1838 the United States Army Corps of Engineers, commanded by Colonel Henry Miller Shreve, removed this massive obstruction. From then on paddle wheelers made their way up the Red River as far as the Washita (to present Lake Texoma).

In the twentieth century the federal government has spent nearly $2 billion to ensure that Oklahoma has navigable rivers. It has built large dams to conserve water, dug channels, and constructed locks. As a consequence huge barges pushed by stout tugs have replaced the romantic steamboat.

The Arkansas River is the largest of Oklahoma's two drainage systems, carrying two-thirds of all the water that flows in the various rivers of the state. In addition to the Verdigris, tributaries from the north include the Illinois and Grand River. Entering from the west are the Salt Fork; the Cimarron, or Red Fork; and the Canadian. The North Canadian, known as Beaver River in the Panhandle, enters the Canadian at historic North Fork Town (present Eufaula).

The Red River is our state's other drainage system. Forming the southern boundary of Oklahoma, it is fed principally by the North Fork (once considered the Red itself), the Washita, the Blue, the Boggy, and the Kiamichi.

From the map on page 27 you will note that Oklahoma's rivers generally flow from west to east. This is because western Oklahoma is at least 1,500 feet higher than the eastern part of the state. The difference in elevation also explains why enough water

THE McCLELLAN-KERR NAVIGATION SYSTEM

The Verdigris River was only a small, sleepy stream flowing south out of Kansas into the Arkansas River. It provided water for animals and prime fishing for fishermen, but not much else. Near Claremore the Osages had a major hunting camp on its banks, but they were horsemen rather than rivermen. As a boy Will Rogers herded cattle on adjacent prairies. Winter and spring rains could turn the Verdigris into a raging torrent, destroying everything in its path.

The Arkansas River was navigable to the mouth of the Verdigris, but only when there was water in it. That did not happen except for the first six months of the year, and even then navigation was difficult. Sandbars were always a problem, and the three-foot-high waterfall near present Webbers Falls represented a challenge to the best of river pilots. The Arkansas could go on a rampage, too, if the rains were heavy upstream. Over time such floods buried even the waterfall under silt.

River navigation ceased to be significant in the late 1870s after railroads pushed into Oklahoma. But the pe-

riodic flooding in the Arkansas River watershed continued, making worse an even more difficult problem—poverty. Outside of the larger communities, the northeastern part of Oklahoma had struggled unsuccessfully to develop its economic potential. At the beginning of the Great Depression of the 1930s, it was the poorest region in Oklahoma and one of the

poorer regions in the nation.

When Robert S. Kerr became governor in 1943 he envisioned a long-range solution to the region's problems. He proposed that the federal government build a navigation system via the Arkansas and Verdigris rivers that would link Catoosa, near Tulsa, with the Mississippi River and the Gulf of Mexico. With direct

(continued on next page)

It was floods like that which devastated Bartlesville, probably in about 1943 (*above*), that caused Robert S. Kerr to propose a series of dams and locks to control flood waters and permit navigation on the Arkansas River. The dam and lock at Webbers Falls (*below*), constructed in 1965, helped make his dream a reality.

THE McCLELLAN-KERR NAVIGATION SYSTEM—continued

access to world markets and cheaper transportation rates, Kerr believed that the development of eastern Oklahoma was only a matter of time. Working with Senator John L. McClellan of Arkansas, he succeeded in getting the project authorized by the Congress and the president in 1946.

Elected to the United States Senate two years later, Kerr made the navigation system his principal legislative goal. Getting the required appropriations required all of his abundant political skills. The United States Army Corps of Engineers supervised the work on the 448-mile channel (398 miles along the Arkansas; 50 on the Verdigris). Five locks and dams (W. D. Mayo, Robert Kerr, Webbers Falls, Chouteau, and Newt Graham) and three lakes (Eufaula, Keystone, and Oologah) in Oklahoma, and thirteen in Arkansas, were required to stabilize the water flow in the channel. At a total cost of $1.2 billion, the system was the largest civil works project ever undertaken by the federal government with the exception of the Panama Canal and the space program.

Economic benefits from the McClellan-Kerr Navigation System came slowly. The first commercial barge, carrying about 650 tons of newsprint, arrived at the Port of Catoosa, now Oklahoma's window on the sea, on January 18, 1971. Tonnage has increased annually since then, exceeding 6 million tons a year on the Oklahoma portion of the system by the 1990s. Kerr's vision of eastern Oklahoma as a region of small factories remains unfulfilled, although the promise persists. Other benefits have been realized. Destructive flooding is no longer a major problem, hydroelectric power is generated, recreational facilities abound, new habitats shelter fish and wildlife, and tourism has become a major industry.

to cover the state ten inches deep runs right on through it to Arkansas and Louisiana annually. That run-off is likely to be largest after spring rains, during which flooding causes millions of dollars of crop and property damage. In more normal times, said historian Angie Debo, "it runs blood-red to the sea . . . drain[ing] the very life of Oklahoma."

A Land of Many Lakes

Because more water leaves the state than comes into it, Oklahomans have long favored "water banking." The objective is to intercept and store water where it will do the most good, saving it for drought years. There are about 1,800 man-made lakes in Oklahoma that have more than ten acres of surface area, plus thirty-four major federal reservoirs. For the location of the larger lakes consult the map on page 27. As you can see, Lake Eufaula is the largest. It covers 105,000 acres. Lake Texoma is the second largest, covering 88,000 acres.

The major lakes and reservoirs were constructed by the United States Army Corps of Engineers, the U.S. Bureau of Reclamation, or the Grand River Dam Authority. They cover more than 900 square miles, and their combined shorelines exceed the total of the Atlantic Ocean and Gulf of Mexico coastlines. You probably have gone swimming, boating, or fishing in one of these lakes; more than likely, you have drunk water from and used electricity generated by them. If you live along one of Oklahoma's rivers, you have felt their presence because, if your home has not flooded, it probably is because of one of the reservoirs.

Although there are a lot of big dams in the state, Oklahomans have long argued that water is best banked where it first falls, specifically behind terraces in the fields and small dams in the creeks. For that reason the state constructed the first upstream flood-control structures in the nation on the Sandstone Creek watershed northwest of Elk City in 1953. Since then Oklahoma has remained very active in this kind of program. Well over 1,500 such structures have been built by local conservation districts with the assistance of the Soil Conservation Service of the United States Department of Agriculture.

Wildlife

If you like to hunt, hike, or camp, you have some idea of what wildlife meant to Oklahoma's early inhabitants. When you are sitting around a campfire, it is easy to imagine what a freshly killed buffalo was to an Indian or white hunting party. Zoologists tell us that the range of native Oklahoma animal species is probably greater than that in any equal area in the United States. It is because the prairies, the plains, and the Rocky Mountains meet in the state to produce a wide variety of habitats. At least 400 species of birds have been identified. These range from song birds like the scissor-tailed flycatcher (the state bird), the robin, and the mockingbird, to game birds like the wild turkey, the bobwhite quail, and the tragically extinct passenger pigeon. Game birds were significant historically because they furnished so much food for Oklahoma's Indians and European American settlers.

HOW IT WORKS: HUNTING PIGEONS IN EASTERN OKLAHOMA

In 1832 a single flock of wild, or passenger, pigeons, roosting near Frankfurt, Kentucky, was estimated to include, incredibly, more than 2 billion birds. Eighty-two years later the last of the species died at the Cincinnati Zoo.

One of the last sanctuaries for the wild pigeon was eastern Oklahoma. In the 1870s and 1880s large pigeon roosts were frequently reported throughout the area "where millions . . . flock by night." Why were such large congregations in the state when the pigeons were extinct everywhere else but Pennsylvania? Primarily it was because Oklahoma was relatively isolated from the rest of the United States, and the hunters here killed game only for their own tables or for sport, not for profit.

The coming of the railroad in 1876 changed all that, bringing whites who hunted for profit, and connecting the territory with eastern poultry markets. The new kind of hunter, long active in other states, captured and crated the pigeons, or killed them and packed them in barrels. The perishable merchandise was then shipped quickly via railroad to consumers in St. Louis or Chicago.

"Harvesting" the pigeons was not difficult. They flew low at speeds up to sixty miles per hour in flocks of millions. They were heard before they were seen, when they blocked out the sky and hid the sun. Rather than shoot them, hunters generally netted them. The birds flew into upright nets, or the nets were placed on the ground, baited with some sort of grain, and when the birds moved onto them, they were drawn together by ropes and springs. Hunters used a stool pigeon (a tame pigeon tied to the end of a long pole) to lure the flock onto the net. In this way they could capture thousands of birds a day.

Another successful hunting method was to rob the roosts where the birds nested after feeding during the day. Some of the roosts were known to be several miles wide and at least forty miles long. At night hunters threw rocks or clubs at the birds, or knocked them from their perches with long poles. In this way they also destroyed the nests and their contents: eggs and hatchlings.

It is not clear how many pigeons were killed after the railroad came to Indian Territory. Yet the number had to be staggering. Near Muskogee in 1879 one journalist noticed "upon a ware-room floor four thousand pigeons, which were being packed for freightage to St. Louis and New York." In 1887 two teams of Cherokee men bet on which could catch the most pigeons in one day. One team killed 1,000; the other killed 1,005. Early Oklahomans believed that the pigeons were so numerous "that they would exist for an indefinite period of the future." They were wrong.

Further Reading: Daniel F. Littlefield, Jr., "Pigeoners in the Indian Territory," *Chronicles of Oklahoma* 47 (1969): 154–59; and two articles Littlefield wrote with Lonnie E. Underhill, "Wild Turkeys in Oklahoma," and "Quail Hunting in Early Oklahoma," *Chronicles of Oklahoma* 48 (1970–71): 376–88, and 49 (1971): 315–33.

Early explorers in our state always commented on the abundance of game animals that were important both to the diet and spirit life of Indian people. These included the buffalo, the white-tailed deer, the elk, the black bear, the antelope, the beaver, and even alligators. The buffalo, or American bison, was by far the most significant. Some 20 million of

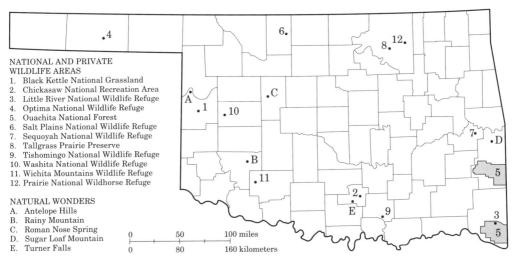

NATIONAL AND PRIVATE
WILDLIFE AREAS
1. Black Kettle National Grassland
2. Chickasaw National Recreation Area
3. Little River National Wildlife Refuge
4. Optima National Wildlife Refuge
5. Ouachita National Forest
6. Salt Plains National Wildlife Refuge
7. Sequoyah National Wildlife Refuge
8. Tallgrass Prairie Preserve
9. Tishomingo National Wildlife Refuge
10. Washita National Wildlife Refuge
11. Wichita Mountains Wildlife Refuge
12. Prairie National Wildhorse Refuge

NATURAL WONDERS
A. Antelope Hills
B. Rainy Mountain
C. Roman Nose Spring
D. Sugar Loaf Mountain
E. Turner Falls

Wildlife Areas and Natural Wonders

them once roamed the Great Plains, including all sections of Oklahoma.

Yet by the end of the nineteenth century they were almost extinct. To preserve the buffalo, in 1905 the federal government established the Wichita Mountains Wildlife Refuge northwest of Lawton and stocked it with fifteen animals imported from a New York City zoo. They prospered in the protected but natural environment, later stocking other herds across the nation. The refuge is managed by the Fish and Wildlife Service of the United States Department of the Interior.

See History for Yourself

Cave dwellers, American Indians, French and American explorers, early traders, California gold seekers, and soldiers discovered Oklahoma's natural wonders many years ago. It is your turn now.

Using the Oklahoma Historical Society's roadside markers and the map on page 19, try to locate part of the trail followed by Washington Irving more than 150 years ago. Wander through the Cross Timbers at Little River State Park near Norman or Arcadia Lake near Edmond, and see if the blackjacks are like cast iron. Hike in the Ouachita National Forest in Le Flore County, or in the Great Salt Plains Wildlife Refuge in Alfalfa County, to get a sense of what Oklahoma was like in its natural state.

Visit some of the other natural wonders described in this chapter, especially the new Tallgrass Prairie Preserve in Osage County.

Visit one of the many dams constructed on Oklahoma's rivers by the United States Army Corps of Engineers, the United States Bureau of Reclamation, or the Grand River Dam Authority. Tour one of the five locks along the McClellan-Kerr Navigation System. Hike through the Wichita Mountain Wildlife Refuge northwest of Lawton and contemplate the survival of the buffalo and the extinction of the passenger pigeon.

Suggestions for Further Reading

Reference

Baumgartner, Frederick M., and A. Marguerite Baumgartner. *Oklahoma Bird Life.* Norman: University of Oklahoma Press, 1992.

McCoy, Doyle. *Roadside Trees and Shrubs of Oklahoma.* Norman: University of Oklahoma Press, 1981.

Morris, John W., ed. *Geography of Oklahoma.* Oklahoma City: Oklahoma Historical Society, 1977.

Settle, William A., Jr. *The Dawning: A New Day for the Southwest: A History of the Tulsa District Corps of Engineers, 1939–1971.* Tulsa: U.S. Army Corps of Engineers, Tulsa District, 1975.

Related Reading

England, Gary. *Those Terrible Twisters and the Weather of Oklahoma.* Oklahoma City: Globe Color Press, 1987.

Fifty Years Remembered: The First Fifty Years of the Tulsa District, U.S. Army Corps of Engineers. Tulsa, Okla.: U.S. Army Corps of Engineers, Tulsa District, 1989.

Irving, Washington. 1835. *A Tour on the Prairies.* Edited with an introductory essay by John Francis McDermott. Norman: University of Oklahoma Press, 1956.

Momaday, Scott. *The Way to Rainy Mountain.* New York: Harper and Row, 1968.

Chapter 3: **Earliest Inhabitants**

The first human inhabitants of Oklahoma arrived a long, long time ago. From where they came, and just when, are matters of dispute. Many American Indians believe that the Life Force of the World created their ancestors at some special place here on this continent. A prominent religious group holds that the first native Americans were ancient Hebrews who migrated to this land across the South Pacific Ocean. Scholars, who have to work with observed data rather than tradition or revelation, tell a different story. This is that one.

North America's first human residents came to North America from Asia. Thousands of years ago, during the Ice Age, small bands of them walked from one continent to the other through an area that geologists call Beringia. Known as Paleo (old or first) Indians, these people hunted large animals and used stone and bone tools.

From Beringia these early hunters pushed slowly southward as they followed herds of such prehistoric animals as the mammoth, the mastodon, the bison, the horse, and the camel. Several thousand years later the earth warmed and much of the ice melted. The runoff slowly raised the level of the sea and flooded the land bridge, creating what we now call the Bering Strait. The hunters, deep within the interior of the continent, probably took no notice of the event. They were too busy finding food. Isolated in a new land, they truly had become the first Americans.

A hanging for a necklace, this shell illustrates some of the beliefs held by the Spiro Mound Builders of eastern Oklahoma. The entire shell represents our earth, or This World, with the internal cross suggesting the four points of the compass. The Spiro people themselves occupied the center circle, to which they are tied with beaded belts and fringed skirts. Note that the human figures wear earspools and have diamond-shaped eyes surrounded by zig-zag lines.

A CHRONOLOGY OF PREHISTORY

You need not memorize the chronology set out below. It is after all only a rough approximation; moreover, not all scholars will agree with it. Think of it only as a reference tool that will help you place the changes in prehistoric society in the proper sequence.

1.	Paleo Indians	22,000 B.C.–15,000 B.C.
2.	Big-Game Hunters	15,000 B.C.–5000 B.C.
3.	Foragers	5000 B.C.–1 A.D.
4.	Early Farmers	1 A.D.–1000 A.D.
5.	Golden Age of Prehistory	
	A. Plains Village Farmers	800 A.D.–1400 A.D.
	B. Caddoan Mound Builders	1000 A.D.–1500 A.D.

Big-Game Hunters

Big-Game Hunter cultures are generally defined by the type of projectile points they used. The longer Clovis point identifies a people that lived some 11,000 to 12,000 years ago. We associate Folsom points with a people who hunted on the Great Plains some 10,500 years ago.

Archaeologists are certain that the Big-Game Hunters had reached Oklahoma by 11,000 years ago, if not well before. Their evidence comes from near Stecker in southern Caddo County. In a nearby canyon archaeologists discovered a place where ancient hunters trapped and killed their game. Digging carefully through layers of dirt, they uncovered the skeleton of a mammoth, which they named Domebo. Embedded within its bones were three large, man-made spearpoints, known as Clovis points. They later had a sample of the bones dated by the radiocarbon method. That test established the 11,000-year-old date. Archaeologists have found the distinctive Clovis point at other sites in Oklahoma, as well as the smaller, and almost as old, Folsom points. Their discoveries give us assurance that in the western part of our state men and women feasted on roasted meat and slept snugly by the side of an open fire some 6,000 years before the fabled Odysseus wandered the shores of the Mediterranean Sea.

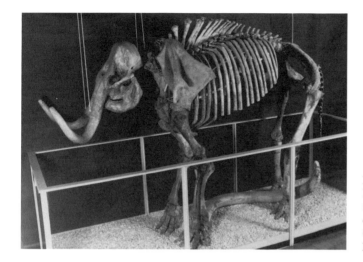

Paleo-Indians hunted elephant-like mammoths with bone structures similar to this one now exhibited in the Oklahoma Museum of Natural History.

Foragers

Once in Oklahoma, the early hunters stayed. Over time, their descendants developed a society more complex than that of the Big-Game Hunters, based on foraging. Hunting remained very important, but the Foragers no longer followed the animals as they migrated from range to range. Instead they limited their hunting to a smaller area, returning to certain sites again and again. Anthropologists define this practice as "centrally based wandering." On such a circuit the Foragers camped during the spring and summer along creeks and rivers, usually near freshwater springs. In the fall and winter months they lived in caves and under rock ledges.

Archaeologists have excavated some Forager camps on Fourche Maline Creek in Le Flore County, in the Ozarks of northeastern Oklahoma, and near Kenton in the Panhandle. The material they have found tells us much about the Foragers. Bone fragments indicate that they hunted modern species of buffalo and deer instead of mammoths and mastodons. Bones of smaller animals suggest that they were also more effective hunters than the Big-Game Hunters. Scholars attribute their greater skill to invention of the atlatl, a wooden throwing stick, which made it possible to hurl a spear or a dart farther and with greater accuracy than ever before.

We know that Foragers supplemented their meat

diet with nuts, berries, sunflower seeds, and roots gathered from the forests, streams, and grasslands. Some of this bounty they stored in pits lined with leaves or stone slabs; some they cooked in rock-lined pits. They also began to manufacture baskets, nets, and string. These items made transportation of food and personal goods much easier. In a cave near Kenton, Foragers left wall paintings (known as petroglyphs) that suggest an appreciation of the fine arts.

HOW IT WORKS: CARBON DATING

Dating prehistoric material was a matter of educated guesswork until 1949. Then a University of Chicago chemist, Willard Libby, discovered a new and revolutionary dating method based on radioactive carbon, or carbon 14.

Formed in the upper atmosphere, carbon 14 is absorbed by all living things, plant and animal. After an organism dies the amount of carbon 14 begins to decrease at a measurable rate. A sample 1,000 years old, for example, will have more carbon 14 in it than one 2,000 years old. After nearly 6,000 years a skeleton will contain only half the radioactive carbon it did when alive. Nineteen thousand years later all carbon 14 will have disappeared. Therefore, to determine the age of a mammoth skeleton, we need to establish how much carbon 14 remains in it. We do this by sending tissue samples to a laboratory where they are measured by a sophisticated Geiger counter.

Early Farmers

About the time of the birth of Christ, Oklahoma's foragers became farmers. Maize (or corn), a plant native to the western hemisphere, had first been domesticated in central Mexico and had been cultivated there since about 5000 B.C. Some 2,000 years later Indian peoples were growing corn in New Mexico and Arizona. From there, the cultivation of corn spread eastward to transform other Native American societies.

At first agricultural activity was limited in Oklahoma. In small fields located along rivers and creeks, Early Farmers raised a few hills of corn along with beans, pumpkins, and squash. The need to watch their fields caused them to leave their rock ledge and cave shelters and to build semipermanent houses nearby. Generally they constructed these houses with a frame of poles driven into the ground and covered with grass thatch or cane matting. In the Panhandle they used rock slabs for walls. There were usually two or three dwellings at each settlement.

Excavations of these hamlets, especially along Fourche Maline Creek and the Red River, make clear that these early agriculturalists did not totally abandon their former lifestyle. They continued to hunt and to gather in the forest and prairies near their fields. In their trash pits are remnants of atlatls, spearpoints, animal bones, and seeds. But something new is there too: pottery fragments, or shards. Probably made by women, Early Farmer pottery is distinctive for its coil technique and oval bottom.

HOW IT WORKS: MAKING A COILED POT

Oklahoma's first farmers were also its first potters. They made their pots by using the coil technique, by which clay is rolled in the hand to form wormlike coils. The coils are built up layer by layer on the base to the desired height. Then they were smoothed over by gently pressing them with the fingers and by rubbing them with a smooth implement such as a shell. During this process the fingers and the shell are kept wet so that the clay will not dry too quickly. Designs are added with a small pointed stick, a sharp rock, or a mussel shell. The pot is dried by the sun or by a fire.

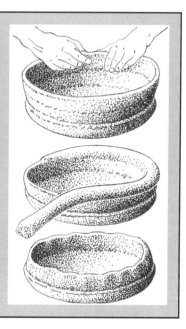

Pottery revolutionized Indian society in Oklahoma. It aided food preparation and storage, and it made it easy to carry water. Above all, it provided a means of artistic expression. For their makers pots were containers for food and water; for us they are the first evidences of personality in these early Americans.

The Golden Age of Prehistory

About 1,100 years ago (900 A.D.) the early agricultural societies in Oklahoma became much richer and more complex. They entered what some have called the Golden Age of Prehistory, of which there were two different expressions in our state. If you remember the natural features of Oklahoma discussed in chapter 2, you probably can guess where they centered. One group was on the plains in the west, the other in the woodlands and on the prairies in the east.

Plains Village Farmers

A striking development in both places was that the people became social, that is, they began to live together. Along the Washita River and its tributaries, archaeologists have found the sites of more than two hundred villages, each containing at least twelve different dwellings. The houses were square. Their stick walls were plastered with a mixture of clay and grass, and their roofs were of grass thatch. The sites also have yielded artifacts that were not local in origin, telling us that the villagers were trading with other people who lived in distant communities.

It is clear that the farmers along the Washita and other western rivers were much more proficient agriculturally than their ancestors had been. They planted a greater variety of crops, including tobacco, and tended them with improved bone, stone, and wooden tools. Large storage pits indicate that the villagers had bountiful harvests.

They also were more effective hunters, primarily because they had mastered the bow and arrow. The greater accuracy of this method permitted hunters to stalk not only the bigger game (bison, deer, elk, and antelope) but smaller animals as well (rabbit, squirrel, wolf, raccoon, beaver, opossum, turkey, duck, and crow). Of these the bison was the most important, judging from the large amount of remains found. Its skin furnished raw materials for clothing, bedding, fibers, and containers. Its bones could be fashioned into tools, implements, and other household equipment. The villagers also fished, collected mussels and shellfish, and increased the range of the plants they gathered for foods, dyes, and medicines (including hickory nuts, walnuts, hackberry seeds, wild cherries, plums, and persimmons).

Clearly, Plains Village Farmers also began to both celebrate and contemplate the mysteries and meaning of life. Archaeologists have discovered that they manufactured undecorated pottery and that

A

B

C

D

Plains Village Farmer artifacts: (A) Huffaker projectile points, 1000–1500 A.D.; (B) drills from eastern Oklahoma, 1300–1400 A.D.; (C) projectile points from Reed Mound in eastern Oklahoma 500–1500A.D.; (D) a ceremonial knife found in Arkansas but made from Kay County chert quarried in northeast Oklahoma and traded to sites in Arkansas 1300–1400 A.D.

they fashioned small figurines. They also have found "grave goods" in cemeteries located next to village sites. These small objects, which the living believed the dead would need in the next world, suggest a spiritual life of increasing sophistication. At the same time their simplicity makes clear that these people did not have highly developed ceremonies or a society separated by classes. Nor did they have any mounds.

The satisfying and productive life of the Plains Village Farmers lasted 600 years, or until 1400 A.D. About that time Oklahoma experienced a dryer climate, and one crop after another failed. The villagers abandoned farming altogether, and with it their former way of life. They became full-time bison hunters instead. Their homes and fields were soon forgotten and quickly covered. We know of these early villagers now only because they left behind some "diaries in the dirt."

Caddoan Mound Builders

Meanwhile, on the other side of Oklahoma, native people organized a more complex society. It was part of a culture that had developed in the Mississippi River valley and spread both east and west. These people are popularly called Mound Builders because of the huge earthen mounds that dominated some of their communities. Generally these earthworks were foundations for temples, public buildings, or the homes of chiefs. They served similar functions in Oklahoma, but here they were also burial sites for wealthy leaders of the community.

If you visit these mounds, you may wonder how they were constructed by a people who lacked both bulldozers and dump trucks. Craig Mound at Spiro is thirty-three feet high and more than four hundred feet long. Williams Mound on Fourche Maline Creek is only five feet tall, but it covers a 17,000-square-foot area. The first Spanish explorers to the southeastern part of the United States saw some Mound Builders at work. They carried dirt to the construction site one basketful at a time!

Archaeologists have identified numerous sites in eastern Oklahoma constructed by a group known more precisely as Caddoan Mound Builders. The most important of these is Spiro, a great ceremonial center of eleven mounds located on the Arkansas River in northeastern Le Flore County. Excavations there earlier in this century yielded a fabulous treasure of artifacts including basketry and objects made of wood, cloth, copper, shell, and stone. These materials reveal much about the lives and culture of the Spiro people and their neighbors between 900 and 1450 A.D.

The Caddoan Mound Builders lived near streams and rivers in villages that surrounded their mounds or were some distance away. The number of permanent houses in these settlements ranged from several dozen to several hundred. In small communal fields the inhabitants planted and grew essentially the same crops as the Plains Village Farmers had,

Craig Mound with snow on the ground in 1913 before archaeologists found its rich treasure troves.

An artist's conception of a Spiro farmer house.

cultivating them with the same kinds of tools. They even hunted the same animals with the same weapons, although they were less dependent on the buffalo than were their western neighbors.

But the Mound Builders were much more than farmers and hunters. They were industrious traders too. Relics found at Spiro came from as far away as northern Wisconsin (copper), southern Florida (conch shells), central New Mexico (cotton cloth), and northwestern Nebraska (painted pottery). These items suggest that Spiro, located strategically on the Arkansas River, was the gateway for an extensive commerce that linked people in the Mississippi valley with those on the Southern Plains. Some of Spiro's leaders acted as middlemen for and profited from that trade.

Caddoan Mound Builders were talented artisans who influenced the works and ideas of people living elsewhere. Shell and copper jewelry, pottery, and stone pipes recovered at Spiro are elaborately decorated with scenes of dancing and gaming and images of warriors and mythological creatures. Archaeologists have found such early Caddoan designs as the feathered serpent, the horned serpent, the spider and a catlike monster, on objects recovered from sites east of the Mississippi River. Craftsmen there probably saw the Spiro designs, liked them, and copied them.

No doubt the foreigners understood and believed what the designs represented. They even passed those beliefs on to their descendents among south-

This shell necklace piece reflects the artistic skills of the Spiro people. Note the cross-in-circle design in the palm of each hand. What point do you think the artist was trying to make?

eastern United States Indians. The Cherokees, for example, believed in the existence of a horrible monster that had the body of a snake, the horns of a deer, and the wings of a bird. Known as Uktena, it had been ordered to kill the Sun, the most sacred god of the Cherokees. When it failed in its mission, it became angry at all human beings and spent its days creating trouble for them. We know from objects decorated by them that members of the Spiro community were fascinated by a similar creature well before the Cherokees existed as a historical people.

Some of the designs used by the Spiro artisans (feathered serpent, cross in a circle, and the human eye highlighted by a zigzag) are often associated with the Indians of Mexico. When scholars found them there and elsewhere in the American Southeast, many understandably concluded that they indicated some kind of contact with Mexico. Recently scholars have challenged that conclusion and argue instead that the designs and the beliefs they represented were native to North America.

The Spiro treasures reflect that the Oklahoma Mound Builders were a fervently religious people. The images on the jewelry they wore expressed their faith much as the star of David and the symbol of a fish express the faith of others today. The objects they buried with their dead indicate that they believed in an afterlife. Because the relics in certain graves are so elaborate and are associated principally with one particular mound, it is clear that the Spiro community also honored and followed a wealthy class of priests.

For two or three centuries Spiro and its satellite villages flourished as centers of trade and religion. But by about 1250 A.D. the drought that had transformed the Plains Village Farmers into nomadic hunters impacted the Mound Builders as well. The large community around the mounds dispersed, although the mounds themselves continued to be ceremonial centers and burial sites for the priestly leadership during the next two centuries. Smaller communities also were abandoned. By 1500 A.D. the people whose sophisticated culture had once influenced the entire Southeast were congregated in small hamlets along the Grand and Arkansas rivers,

A pipe in the form of a human figure manufactured by the artisans of Spiro.

HOW NOT TO EXCAVATE A PREHISTORIC SITE

As early as the nineteenth century Spiro was recognized as a prehistoric Indian site. In 1914, Joseph Thoburn, a noted Oklahoma historian and archaeologist, excavated one of the smaller mounds. Beneath the soil he found a house with four centerposts and two sets of graves. On the basis of the relics that he had discovered, Thoburn quickly recognized the importance of the site and its relationship to the prehistoric cultures of the Mississippi valley.

In 1933 a group of men living in eastern Oklahoma organized the Pocola Mining Company. From the owners of the property they leased the largest burial mound on the Spiro site, Craig Mound. For the next two years they haphazardly dug into the four lobes of the mound. They discovered rich troves of spectacular relics, the most exotic and best-preserved materials from any Mississippian ceremonial center.

Unfortunately, the diggers were not concerned with preserving the significance of their discovery; they were interested only in finding and selling the artifacts for profit. Irreplaceable information about Oklahoma's past was lost forever, or as one archaeologist has written, "like pages ripped from a rare book." It was equally unfortunate that the treasures were sold to buyers outside Oklahoma. As a consequence, if you want to see the best of the Spiro material, you have to go to Chicago, New York, or Europe.

There was one positive benefit to come from this tragedy. In 1935 the Oklahoma state legislature passed an antiquities-preservation law. Revised several times since then, the law makes it illegal to disturb prehistoric sites containing skeletal remains or burial material. Such sites must be reported to both law-enforcement officers and the director of the Oklahoma Archaeological Survey at the University of Oklahoma. If you ever find skeletal remains near your home, contact the police department and the survey office at Norman. Do not be guilty of destroying irreplaceable information as did the pot hunters of Craig Mound.

In sharp contrast to the diggings of pot hunters a few years earlier, the Works Progress Administration excavates Craig Mound in about 1938 using scientific methodology.

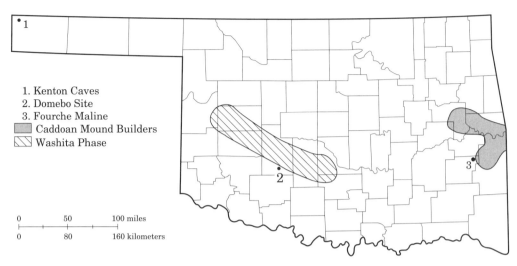

1. Kenton Caves
2. Domebo Site
3. Fourche Maline
▨ Caddoan Mound Builders
▨ Washita Phase

Prehistoric Sites

living in small, less-substantial houses, and supplementing their meager harvests with meat from buffalo hunts.

Today the site of the Spiro Mounds is Oklahoma's only National Historic Landmark. The United States Army Corps of Engineers leases the property to the Oklahoma Historical Society, which operates it as the state's only archaeological park. If you visit it, you will see exhibits on how the mounds were excavated, of relics taken from the more than 700 burials in Craig Mound, and on the trading network that radiated east and west from Spiro. A self-guided tour will lead you by the mounds themselves and to a reconstructed version of a house typical of the time.

See History for Yourself

To appreciate the culture of Oklahoma's Mound Builders, visit the Spiro Mounds Archaeological Park near Spiro. Stand at the base of Craig Mound and imagine how long it took for workers carrying one basket at a time to complete such a project. Also imagine yourself in a crowd of people who have gathered to witness the burial of one of their priests. You can find artifacts taken from the Spiro burial sites at Woolaroc Museum southwest of Bartlesville and at the Oklahoma Museum of Natural History in Norman. Gilcrease Museum in Tulsa also has an excellent collection of prehistoric relics. Although many exist, other mounds in eastern Oklahoma have not yet been developed as parks and museums.

If you live near the Washita River in western Oklahoma, search along its banks for prehistoric spearpoints. Stand at the edge of one of many nearby canyons and imagine yourself going down the side with only a spear to kill a huge mammoth trapped in the mud below. At the Museum of the Great Plains in Lawton there is an excellent exhibit on the Domebo site. Near Freedom, in Woods County, you may visit the ranch of Vic Burnham, where archaeologists have made exciting finds that may push the date of the first occupation of Oklahoma back another 10,000 years.

Make an atlatl and try to throw a spear 100 feet to a still target. Then try the same thing trying to hit a rabbit. Also try your hand at making a spearpoint by chipping a piece of stone with a rock or a deer antler.

Suggestions for Further Reading

Reference

Bell, Robert E. *Oklahoma Indian Artifacts*. Norman: Stovall Museum, University of Oklahoma, 1980.

——, ed. *Prehistory of Oklahoma*. New York: Academic Press, 1984.

Brooks, Robert L. "The Last Prehistoric People: The Southern Plains Villagers," *Chronicles of Oklahoma* 67 (Fall 1989): 296–319.

Fagan, Brian M. *Ancient North America: The Archaeology of a Continent*. New York: Thames and Hudson, 1991.

Galloway, Patricia, ed. *The Southeastern Ceremonial Complex: Artifacts and Analysis; The Cottonlandia Conference*. Lincoln: University of Nebraska Press, 1989.

Holmes, Mary Ann, and Marshal Hill. *The Spiro Mounds Site*. Norman: Stovall Museum of Science and History and the Oklahoma Archaeological Society, 1976.

Phillips, Phillip, and James A. Brown. *Pre-Columbian Shell Engravings from the Craig Mound at Spiro, Oklahoma*. Cambridge, Mass.: Peabody Museum Press, 1978.

Wedel, Waldo H. *Prehistoric Man on the Great Plains*. Norman: University of Oklahoma Press, 1961.

Related Reading

Lyttle, Richard B. *People of the Dawn*. New York: Atheneum, 1980.

Rhoades, Roxanne. *Diaries In the Dirt: Archaeology and the Plains Village People: A Teacher's Guide*. Oklahoma City: Oklahoma Foundation for the Humanities and the Oklahoma Museums Association, 1990.

Wyckoff, Don G., and Dennis Peterson. *Educational Aid for the Spiro Mounds: Prehistoric Gateway, Present-Day Enigma*. Norman: Stovall Museum of Science and History and the Oklahoma Archaeological Survey, 1983.

————. *Spiro Mounds: Prehistoric Gateway, Present-day Enigma*. Norman: Stovall Museum of Science and History and the Oklahoma Archaeological Survey, 1983.

Chapter 4: **Historical Peoples**

As we have learned, Oklahoma was inhabited long before the first Europeans arrived. Well before the first whites appeared on the horizon, the native peoples of our state had economies that combined farming, hunting, gathering, and commerce. They lived in fortified towns, constructed architecturally unique houses, made functional pottery, and designed beautiful body tattoos. Their social and belief systems were remarkably complex. The Europeans, who dared to believe that they had "discovered" these early Oklahomans, called them by different names. Among those used—and not always widely—were Wichita, Tawakoni, Waco, Kichai, Panipiquet, Taovaya, and Jumano. The Indians, who with equal justice could have claimed to have discovered the wandering Europeans, preferred

George Catlin, noted American explorer and artist, sketched this large village of Oklahoma's First People, the Wichita, in 1834. The community of beehivelike grass houses was situated a few miles southeast of the present-day Lake Altus dam.

Tawenhash or Kitikitish. Either name meant the same thing: "First People."

We know them collectively today as the Wichita and Affiliated Tribes, most of whom live near Anadarko in Caddo County. As direct descendents of the Plains Village Farmers, the Wichita tribe is Oklahoma's oldest historical community. Because these truly were our First People, our understanding of the beginnings of our state demands an appreciation of them.

The "First People" in Oklahoma

Anthropologists organize Indian peoples into major language stocks, or groups. This helps them study migration patterns and relations among tribes. Wichitas are members of the Caddoan language family. In early historic times other tribes in that group were distributed over the Great Plains, including the Arikaras in North Dakota, the Pawnees in Nebraska, and the Caddos in Texas and Louisiana. Because their languages and cultures have common characteristics, those three tribes are considered as if they were close cousins of the Wichitas.

In the sixteenth century Oklahoma's First People lived in small-to-large villages along the Arkansas, Canadian, Washita, and Red rivers. A village or cluster of villages generally considered itself independent of the others, even identifying as a separate tribe. Thus the First People were merely a loose confederation of different tribes, of which the Wichitas were only one. A common language, lifestyle, and tradition united this confederation and its estimated 20,000 or more people.

Economy

Farming

The Wichitas were primarily agriculturalists. They cultivated fields of corn, beans, squash, gourds, and tobacco in the rich bottomlands adjacent to their villages. According to historic sources, they even irrigated some of these fields. Corn was usually planted in the late spring, and the main harvest took place in the early fall after it had dried. Some corn was eaten green during the early summer. The dry corn was shelled and ground into meal for stor-

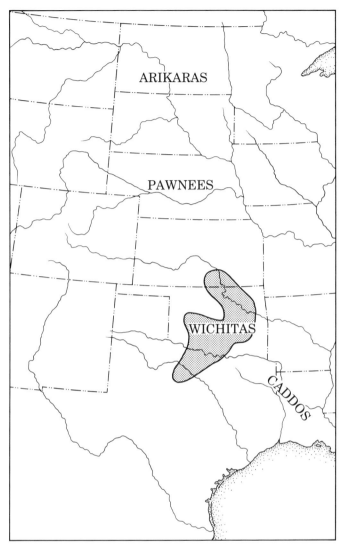

Linguistic Cousins of the Wichitas, circa 1500

age. Squash and pumpkin were planted in early spring and collected throughout the summer. Some of the squash was cut into strips, then dried and woven into mats before storage.

The entire village turned out to clear fields for cultivation. According to one witness, men constructed the fences that enclosed the fields, but the planting, the initial tending, and the weeding of the crop were the responsibility of women and children.

HOW TO MAKE IT: WICHITA FRY BREAD

Corn was the staple of the Wichita diet. Sometimes it was eaten green, as it is when we buy it in grocery stores to prepare corn on the cob. Generally it was roasted over a fire and laid out to dry in the sun. In time it was shelled and placed for storage in large bags made of buffalo hide. Wichita women used kernels of dried corn in meat or corn soups. Usually they ground it into meal using a stone mano and metate. From the cornmeal they prepared various kinds of bread, usually a thin cornbread but possibly an early variety of a hush puppy deep fried in animal fat.

The Wichitas still make fry bread, but from wheat flour rather than cornmeal. It is eaten as a snack, dipped in soup or stew, or covered with jelly for a dessert. Below is their recipe for fry bread. Try it; you'll like it.

3 cups sifted flour
3 teaspoons baking powder
1 teaspoon salt
1 heaping teaspoon sugar
1 one cup lukewarm water

In a large bowl, mix well the flour, baking powder, salt, and sugar. Slowly add the water. If the dough is too sticky, add more flour. On a floured board, roll the dough to ½ inch thickness. Cut into 2" x 3" rectangles; also cut a small slit in the center of each rectangle. Fry in hot, deep oil or fat. Once it is crispy brown, drain the bread on a paper towel. Note: If using self-rising flour, eliminate baking powder and salt from the recipe.

Hunting

The First People also hunted and killed buffalo for meat, hides, robes, and tallow. During the winter months the entire village left on an annual bison hunt. Before setting out, the women carefully hid their family's food supply and other valuables in underground pits to prevent theft by marauding neighbors. On the hunt, which lasted from four to six weeks, the Wichitas, like other Plains tribes, lived in tipis made of buffalo hide erected on a frame of poles. Finding the buffalo herd and chasing and killing the animals were the responsibilities of the men.

The buffalo was never as important to the Wichitas as to other tribal peoples who later arrived on the Southern Plains. It was more a source of food than the representation of the Life Force. The First People also hunted deer, elk, antelope, rabbit, and squirrel, usually in areas close to their villages.

From the forests and prairies, the Wichitas gathered a variety of edible wild plants, roots, seeds, and berries. They harvested the tasty sand plums that grew in thickets on the banks of most rivers. During the autumn, they collected the seeds of such plants as goosefoot and pigweed, which they used much as we use sunflower seeds.

Commerce

The Wichitas were skilled traders even before the Europeans arrived. They exchanged ground corn, dried squash mats, and cured tobacco for meat and skins from neighboring tribes. In time they exchanged their agriculture products and processed buffalo hides for horses and guns. In the middle of the eighteenth century they were the middlemen who commanded the vital trade linking the French in the Mississippi River valley with the tribes of the Southern Plains.

HOW TO MAKE IT: A SQUASH MAT

To make a squash mat, Wichita women began with a fully matured squash, which they cut into long strips that they hung on a wooden rack to dry in the sun. During the drying time the women often took the strips from the rack and pounded them flat with a mallet. When the squash was completely dried, they wove the strips into mats of various sizes, which were folded and stored for later use. Sometimes the strips were twisted into braids. Visitors to Wichita villages often reported seeing the brightly colored mats or braids hanging in brush arbors.

Women used the mats to flavor soups or to add to other dishes. Squash mats were also important trade items. They were favorites of hunting tribes like the Comanches and the Kiowas.

Settlement

Houses

Wichita lodges were remarkable examples of what architects call environmental adaptation. They used local materials in construction and responded to natural and social conditions like climate and cost. The houses were dome-shaped and manufactured by covering a wooden frame with a heavy thatch of bluestem grass. Willow rods, cut from nearby trees,

Photographed early in the twentieth century, this Wichita campsite features structures we would have seen hundreds of years before: the grass lodge, the brush arbor, and the tipi.

held the thatch in place. The houses averaged thirty feet in diameter at their bases, stood twenty feet high, and had doorways on the east and west sides. They could accommodate a family as large as ten to fifteen people. Along the inner walls the Wichitas constructed raised beds, which often were concealed behind a curtain of hide. Situated at the very center of the lodge was the fire pit, from which the smoke escaped through a hole near the top of the roof.

Wichita villages also included brush arbors. Through their open sides, cooling breezes circulated. There corn and meat could dry, and a family could gather to work or rest. The distinctive woven mats of dried pumpkin strips were often stored in these arbors.

Coalesced Villages

Anthropologists describe the typical settlement of Oklahoma's First People as a coalesced village. In other words, smaller villages often joined together to form a larger one. This process produced settlements with populations that ran into the thousands, most notably along the Arkansas River in present Tulsa County. The Wichitas merged their villages primarily for defensive purposes. That also explains why they favored high terraces or ridges as settlement sites. By the 1700s many Wichita villages had either a defensive earthworks or ditch in a central location or around the perimeter.

Technology

In the sixteenth century the technology of the Wichitas differed little from that of their Plains Village Farmer ancestors. Their major hunting weapons remained the bow and stone-tipped arrow. The Wichitas used stone knives and scrapers to butcher animals. With other stone tools (the mano

The First People of Oklahoma used tools fashioned from flint rock to scrape excess flesh from animal hides that they processed into clothes.

and metate), they ground dried corn into meal. From the broad, strong bones of buffalo they created digging sticks, hoes, and rasps. Turkey and deer bones yielded pins and awls. The First People used wood, especially cedar, to construct the frames of their houses. Deer and bison hides furnished the materials from which they made clothing.

Art and Crafts

The Wichitas used local clay to make pottery and small figurines. Their pots served as vessels rather than objects of art, and thus were usually undecorated. From bones and stone, Oklahoma's First People created attractive personal ornaments such as pendants and gorgets (ornamental collars). But they were most creative when it came to body decorations. Both men and women covered their faces and bodies with elaborate tattoos, generally for cosmetic purposes but also to record a warrior's personal history in combat and on the hunting trail. They created the tattoos by cutting the skin and filling the wound with charcoal. When the wound healed, the color was permanent.

Social Organization

The Wichitas traced their relationships through women. We call this system matrilineal (tracing descent through the mother's line). Houses and other structures were the property of the oldest married woman in the household. In them lived an extended family of ten to twelve persons that included the wife and her mother along with her sisters, husband, unmarried children, married daughters, and those daughters' own husbands and children. A young boy living in this household looked not to his biological father but to his mother's brother, or maternal uncle, for both advice and discipline.

Among most Indian tribes kinship was the basis of a wider association known as a clan. Members of such a group believed themselves to be blood relatives on the mother's side of the family or, in some cases, on the father's side. On those grounds, members of the same clan were forbidden to marry each other. Clans were associated with and took the name of an animal or natural phenomenon such as thunder. Tribes that would later challenge the Wichitas for control of the land that is now Oklahoma were much influenced by these kinship organizations. But for reasons that we do not fully understand, the First People themselves had no clan structure.

In the absence of a clan tie, men and women were free to marry whomever they pleased beyond the extended family. Young men secured their mates by purchasing them from an uncle or brother of the bride. In 1808 a witness recorded that the going price was one or two horses if the man was known to the woman's family. If he was a stranger, he had to pay with blankets, vermilion (red pigment), and beads. On the whole, purchasing a bride was less an economic exchange than a method of showing honor to the bride's parents. Men often had more than one wife and (if some observers are to be believed) willingly shared them with visitors to the tribe.

Here a Wichita man and woman hold ears of corn and pipes that are symbolic of those bestowed upon the First People at the beginning of the world.

They also tell us that marriages were terminated with equal ease by either the husband or the wife.

Political System

The matrilineal social organization of the Wichitas did not mean that women controlled society beyond the household. So far as we know, the men held the political power. Each village had a chief and a sub-chief, who were chosen for their qualities of generosity, kindness, and bravery. They were assisted by a council of warriors who served as an advisory and rule-making body for the band. The several chiefdoms that comprised the Wichita people as a whole generally acted independently of each other.

Religious Beliefs and Practices

Basic to Wichita traditional religion was the belief that powerful creative forces in the universe directed individual and tribal destinies. These powers had bestowed the gift of corn on women with instructions on planting, cultivating, and processing it. To men they had given both the bow and arrow and wisdom—the one to make the hunt and warpath successful, the other to make men effective in the councils of the chiefdom. Such blessings put the Wichitas under an obligation to please these powerful forces with meditation, prayer, and ceremony.

The Corn Dance was the most important ceremonial event of the Wichitas. It took place when the corn crop ripened sometime in the late summer. Much like our Thanksgiving, it was a time when individual Wichitas sought to purify themselves as well as their community. Men repaired public struc-

Wichita men participate in the concluding ceremony of the Corn Dance on their reservation near Anadarko in 1893. Note the frame of a sweat lodge in the right foreground.

tures, fasted, and cleansed their bodies by sweating and vomiting. Women cleaned houses and cooking utensils. The culmination of the Corn Ceremony was the lighting of a new sacred fire, a ceremony in which only men participated. The Wichitas believed that the old fire had become polluted as people violated the rules of the village. A new fire symbolized a new beginning.

Games

Shinny was such a popular game that most Wichita men and women had their own stick.

One of the Wichitas' oldest customs was a ball game known as "shinny," presumably given to them by Having the Power to Carry Light, the first man on earth. It was a game of competition between opposing teams played with a hide ball and a stick. Among the Wichitas, the ball was somewhat flattened and buckskin covered, with a leather thong attached. It was also painted with red, green, white, yellow, and black rings. The wooden stick held by each player was about three feet long and had a knob at the end. With the stick players drove the ball toward the opposing goals.

Both men and women of all ages originally played shinny, but it eventually became a women's game among the Wichitas. The point limits and the length of the game were set before hand. Matches were played on fields of varying sizes with no holds barred. Players hit and tripped the opposition as was deemed necessary. The Wichita women came to prefer double-ball shinny, in which two balls were tied together with a thong and were batted or kicked from goal to goal.

War

When we think of war, we often think of one nation trying to conquer the people of another and forcing them to become part of an empire. Certainly, that was how Europeans experienced war. Conquest, however did not characterize warfare involving the Wichitas before the arrival of Europeans. One would do better to compare their wars to feuds between rival urban gangs such as the Crips and the Bloods. Conflicts usually began when members of one extended family or village killed someone from another family or village. Blood revenge rather than conquest was the main reason for tribal warfare, although personal status and honor were important motives too.

Usually Wichitas went to war in small groups of no more than thirty. The object of any one raid was to kill or capture the enemy in an unexpected attack. If that was not possible, the attackers might not fight at all. The Wichitas did not judge the success of the raid on the basis of how many enemy were killed or captured. It was considered a victory if the party merely surprised the enemy and returned without losing any of its members.

If they made captives during their raids, how did Wichita warriors treat them? Apparently not very well. Eighteenth-century accounts tell us that they ate them in public feasts. Reports indicate that adult captives were still being beaten to death in the nineteenth century. While they were tied to a stake, their bodies were dismembered, and the pieces were hung as trophies in different parts of the village. A Wichita warrior victorious in battle also cut pieces of flesh from the body of a slain enemy and distributed them to favored friends whom he wished to honor.

On their raids Wichita warriors carried bows and arrows as their principal weapons. They had learned at an early age to shoot small animals. By the time they were adults, their skills were awesome. Most warriors could fire five or six arrows before Europeans could reload their crossbows once. Their bois d'arc bows delivered arrows with such force that they could pass completely through a buffalo.

Except perhaps for the shield, Wichita warriors had dress and equipment similar to those of Hisoosanches, a Comanche warrior painted by George Catlin in 1834. Note the bois d'arc bow and long lance.

Indian Intruders

For 500 years the First People possessed without serious challenge the western part of the land that is now Oklahoma. For reasons that we do not fully understand, other native people appeared in the fifteenth century to contest that occupation. Drought conditions or similar natural catastrophes may have driven the intruders to seek a new homeland. Or perhaps they had been pushed out of their own homeland by tribespeople who had themselves—in a chain reaction—been pushed out of their ancestral domain. Whatever the reason, the Wichitas

soon found themselves locked in a life or death
struggle with people alien to the land.

Plains Apaches

Among the earliest intruders were the Athapascan-
speaking Plains Apaches. They represented the
easternmost fringe of a mighty invasion that had
swept down from the far north to vanquish the
splendid old Anasazi cultures of the American
Southwest. By 1500 the Lipan, one of the Apache
subgroups, roamed the Southern Plains following
the buffalo, which provided their food, shelter, and
clothing. Dried buffalo dung even furnished them
fuel. Two things made them memorable to the earliest
European observers. First, they used the portable
tipi, which later became the characteristic dwelling
of most buffalo-hunting tribes. Also, they used dogs
hitched to their tipi poles to transport their possessions from one hunting ground to another.

In search of buffalo, some Lipan bands wandered
into what is now western Oklahoma. The Antelope
Hills were a favorite rendezvous site. The Wichitas
immediately saw the newcomers as threats to their
own food supplies and security and resisted the invasion. The strife that followed may have caused
the First People to remove some of their villages
from along the Washita River northeast into the Arkansas River valley, a migration that took them into
what is now south-central Kansas and northeastern
Oklahoma. The animosity lasted for several centuries, involved other tribes, and ultimately forced
the Lipan Apaches to remove their villages deep
into present South Texas.

Yet one Plains Apache group remained to carry
on the struggle. These were the Ka-ta-kas, better
known as the Kiowa Apaches because of their long
association with the Kiowa people. Few in number,
they too were buffalo hunters, and once mounted on
horses and armed with rifles, they could hold their
own in any battle. With their Kiowa friends, they
annually celebrated the Sun Dance, a world-renewal
ceremony. Although they arrived in our state relatively late (that is, in the eighteenth century), and
they were opposed by the Wichitas and other tribes,
the Ka-ta-kas never left after they got here. Today
they are organized as the Apache Tribe of Oklahoma
with headquarters at Anadarko in Caddo County.

Comanches

The Comanches represented an even greater threat to the security of the Wichitas than did the Apaches. The Comanches were Uto-Aztecan speakers who once had lived west of the Rocky Mountains in the Great Basin area. They abandoned their ancient homeland to their Shoshone cousins and migrated south and east to the edge of the Great Plains, where they became buffalo hunters.

In the late seventeenth century the Comanches acquired the horse from the Spanish settlements in New Mexico. With greater mobility, they ranged over a wider area, periodically plundering Indian pueblos and Spanish outposts for grain, horses, and captives. In search of the bison, they pushed as far east as the Cross Timbers in central Oklahoma. As they went, the Red Raiders (as they subsequently were known) attacked and subdued most local tribes, including the Wichitas. By 1725 they were masters of the Southern Plains.

They were supreme, but they were not self-sufficient. The Comanches needed corn and squash to supplement their diet. They also needed guns and ammunition to conquer their enemies. They had no ready access to those products, but the Wichitas did—in their cornfields and in their trade relationships, in this case with the French. Thus in the 1740s the Comanches and the Wichitas negotiated an alliance of friendship and commerce, ending their half-century of conflict. Thereafter the Wichitas supplied the Comanches with foodstuffs and French

George Catlin captured the boldness of the Comanche warriors in this 1834 sketch. Notice that they approached their adversary in single file.

guns. In return, the Comanches provided the Wichas with buffalo hides, horses, and captives who could be sold to the French. The by-product of the alliance was a lasting peace that has permitted the Comanche invaders to live harmoniously with Oklahoma's First People until this very day. If you live in the Lawton area, you probably know a large number of Comanches. You may be one yourself.

Osages

Unlike the Comanches, the Osages did not want to work out their problems with the Wichitas. They were Dhegian Sioux speakers who in the late sixteenth century had migrated from the Ohio River valley to the area that is now southwestern Missouri. There they continued to plant extensive fields of corn and squash and to live in permanent wood-frame longhouses. They also maintained a complicated social system and practiced a very complex ceremonial life. Located on the edge of the plains, they ventured out each spring and fall to hunt buffalo. When they did, they encountered hunters from the Wichita villages.

Initially, Oklahoma's First People did not consider these Woodland Indian intruders major threats to their security. Yet considerable tension surfaced after the Osages acquired Spanish horses in the 1680s. Horses became such status symbols in their society that ambitious young men were quite willing to steal them from the nearby Wichitas. Being closer to New Mexico, the First People had gotten the horse earlier and had subsequently gathered herds of substantial size. The Osage raids engendered a lot of hostility, even bloodshed, but they apparently caused no permanent rupture between the two neighbors.

Guns changed all of that. Subjected to repeated attacks by well-armed tribes on their northern border, the Osages needed guns to defend themselves. French traders would provide them, but the traders demanded in exchange furs, horses, or Indian slaves. Only among the Wichitas were these items readily available to the Osages. To obtain the guns and ammunition that would permit them to protect their homes from eastern invaders, the Osages raided the First People for horses and captives. They also launched large-scale commercial buffalo hunts on herds in the Wichita domain.

The war that followed was not pretty, and it was long (lasting at least a century). During the course of it perhaps one-half of the total Osage population moved to Oklahoma, establishing villages on the Verdigris River between Fort Gibson and Claremore. From there they carried out constant raids on the Wichitas, whose losses in life and property were immense. The First People fought back heroically, but by 1800 they had retreated to new villages along and south of the Red River, leaving their ancient homeland in the control of the Osages.

As we will see, Osage hegemony did not last long. Let us note, however, that, with the exception of some thirty years in the nineteenth century, the Osages have been contesting for control of or have been residents in Oklahoma for nearly 300 years. Most Osages today live in and around Osage County. If by chance you have not met any of them, make a special trip to Pawhuska, Fairfax, or Hominy, so that you can.

A Distinctive State

One of the things that makes Oklahoma so distinctive as a state is the long and continuous presence of Native American peoples. Europeans arrived only in 1541. By that date the Wichitas had been here for 500 years, developing a distinctive lifestyle and complex social system that harmonized with the natural environment. Before Europeans came in considerable numbers (after about 1720), the Plains Apaches, the Comanches, and the Osages had joined the First People. The coming of the immigrants was not always peaceful, but the ultimate result was a native population varied in its languages and diverse in its cultures.

That variety has continued to characterize our state's Indian population. In the nineteenth century the United States government made Oklahoma a special resettlement zone for native people, relocating here tribes from all sections of the country. By the end of the process part or all of sixty-seven different tribes resided in Oklahoma. Virtually every culture type identified by anthropologists was represented, as well as nine different language groups. According to the United States Census, there were 252,468 Native Americans living in

Oklahoma in 1990. Oklahoma had the largest Native American population of any state in the union. Indeed, 13 percent of all United States citizens who claim an Indian heritage live here.

INDIAN LANGUAGE GROUPS IN OKLAHOMA

According to anthropologists, nearly 300 different languages were spoken by Indian tribes north of Mexico at the time of the arrival of Europeans in 1500. After nearly a century of study, scholars of the Bureau of American Ethnology of the Smithsonian Institution finally formulated a system for classifying the Indian tribes by language. Specifically, they identified fifty-six different linguistic families or stocks into which they categorized the languages of the hundreds of tribes. Anthropologists then studied the various groupings to make generalizations about common cultures and settlement patterns.

New schemes of language classification have emerged since the 1950s; however, the principle of categorizing tribes into language groups has not changed. The Oklahoma language groups reflect the great cultural variety in the state's Native American population in the twentieth century. The list provided is arranged chronologically to show the order in which the groups appeared in Oklahoma.

Caddoan: Wichita, Caddo, Pawnee
Athapascan: Apache
Uto-Aztecan: Comanche
Siouian: Osage, Quapaw, Kansa, Missouri, Ponca, Iowa
Tanoan: Kiowa
Muskogean: Choctaw, Chickasaw, Creek, Seminole
Iroquoian: Cherokee, Wyandot, Seneca, Cayuga, Erie
Algonkian: Arapaho, Cheyenne, Delaware, Fox, Kickapoo, Miami, Potawatomi, Sac, Shawnee
Tonkawan: Tonkawa
Shahaptian: Nez Perce

Conclusion

Oklahoma's history begins with the social development and interactions of Wichitas, Apaches, Comanches, and Osages. They maintained sophisticated and self-sufficient societies that lived in harmony with the land—if not always with each other. Sadly, the Europeans who came to Oklahoma failed to assess the level of the Native Americans' social development or the nature of their interactions. Instead they saw these peoples as resources to be used, their lands as a region to be exploited. Much tragedy—and much history—would begin with those mistakes.

See History for Yourself

To glimpse the lifestyle of Oklahoma's first historic residents, visit Indian City USA and the Southern Plains Indian Museum and Craft Center in Anadarko, the Museum of the Great Plains in Lawton, the Osage Tribal Museum in Pawhuska, and the Museum of the Red River in Idabel. Visit the tribal offices of the Wichita and Apache tribes at Anadarko, of the Comanches at Lawton, and of the Osages at Pawhuska. Contrast the people you meet there with the ones you read about in this chapter. How do you explain the difference?

Attend a powwow hosted by the Wichita, the Apache, the Comanche, or the Osage tribe to appreciate the role that ceremony still plays in the life of the tribespeople. View the exhibits "From Generation to Generation: The Plains Apache Way" and "Wichita Memories," both available from TRACKS, Oklahoma Museums Association, Oklahoma City, Oklahoma.

Suggestions for Further Reading

Reference

Dorsey, George. *The Mythology of the Wichitas.* Washington, D.C.: Carnegie Institution, 1904.

Fehrenbach, T. R. *Comanches: Destruction of A People.* New York: Alfred A. Knopf, 1974.

Mathews, John Joseph. *The Osages: Children of the Middle Waters.* Norman: University of Oklahoma Press, 1961.

Newcomb, W. W., Jr. *The Indians of Texas, from Prehistoric to Modern Times.* Austin: University of Texas Press, 1961.

Noyes, Stanley. *Los Comanches: The Horse People, 1751–1845.* Albuquerque: University of New Mexico Press, 1993.

Schilz, Thomas F. *Lipan Apaches.* El Paso: Texas Western Press, 1987.

Wallace, Ernest, and E. Adamson Hoebel. *The Comanches: Lords of the South Plains.* Norman: University of Oklahoma Press, 1952.

Wedel, Mildred Mott. *The Wichita Indians, 1541–1750: Ethnohistorical Essay.* Lincoln, Nebr.: J and L Reprint, 1988.

Related Reading

Brant, Charles S. *Jim Whitewolf: The Life of a Kiowa Apache Indian.* New York: Dover Publications, 1969.

Baird, W. David. *The Osage People.* Phoenix: Indian Tribal Series, 1972.

Cash, Joseph H., and Gerald Wolff. *The Comanche People.* Phoenix: Indian Tribal Series, 1974.

Educational Aid for "Wichita Memories." Norman: Oklahoma Humanities Committee and the Stovall Museum of Science and History, 1982.

Newcomb, W. W., Jr. *The People Called Wichita.* Phoenix: Indian Tribal Series, 1976.

Unit 2: **THE DISCOVERY OF OKLAHOMA**

Introduction

Oklahoma's earliest inhabitants may have thought of themselves as the First People, but they certainly were not going to be the last. Even as the First People sat in their wood-and-grass homes or tended their fields of corn, squash, and tobacco, wooden ships were heading west across the Atlantic Ocean. In time, the sailors' weary eyes would spot land on the horizon. Beginning precisely at that moment, a "New World" was conceived. It replaced not one "Old World" but many. These were worlds—as separate from one another as are the planets—in which human beings had lived ignorant and independent of others.

The future lives of all of those humans and all of their descendants would be made in what we know as the New World. People came from every corner of the globe to the western hemisphere. The Europeans were followed by Africans. Later came others from the same continent, Asia, that originally had spawned Oklahoma's First People. Some eventually made their way to Oklahoma. They were both the creators and the products of this new world. They were Oklahoma's next people. And this is their story.

Chapter 5: The European Discoverers

To say that Columbus "discovered" America in 1492 is not quite accurate. As we know, Indian peoples had discovered it long before and had lived there in sophisticated societies for centuries. Also, Vikings from Norway knew of this continent as early as the eleventh century. Some of those

Found on a large stone slab near Heavener in Le Flore County, these eight "runes" have been translated to mean "sun dial valley" or "November 11, 1012." Whether they are the work of early Vikings or later European settlers will probably never be known.

Norsemen, if local historians are to be believed, traveled to Oklahoma and left puzzling markings on the "runestone" near Heavener in Le Flore County. Still, it is true that not until the voyages of Christopher Columbus, sponsored by Spain at the close of the fifteenth century, did the attention of Europe's Old World focus on the "New World."

Spain in Oklahoma

For the Spaniards, America was both an opportunity and an obstruction. It promised treasures of gold to those who persevered in looking for them, but it was also a major barrier to reaching Cathay, the oriental source of spices that Columbus had sought. To take advantage of the opportunity and to overcome the obstruction, adventuresome Spaniards rushed to the New World. Their vessels explored every mile of coastline between Florida and Yucatán. Moreover, in 1521 a Spanish army, led by

VIEWING HISTORY IN CENTURIES

Dates are to history what dribbling is to basketball. You have to have them. They are the mileposts of history. If you do not have these markers, it is easy to confuse the sequence of events that make up a story. When that happens, the story does not make sense and often conveys the wrong impression.

It doesn't help to *memorize* dates as you would memorize irregular verbs. You must *understand* why one event leads to another. Sometimes it is easier to comprehend sequences of events if you place them in broader chronological categories. For example, the evolution of Oklahoma from self-sufficient Indian communities to statehood is best understood in terms of centuries rather than years or decades. The chart below is organized that way. Use it as a reference.

15th century:	Wichitas dominate Oklahoma.
	Voyages of Columbus, 1492.
16th century:	Spanish explorations in Oklahoma.
17th century:	No Europeans in Oklahoma.
18th century:	French authority (1719–63) and Spanish authority (1763–1802).
	Osages dominate Oklahoma.
	American Revolution, 1776–83.
19th century:	Oklahoma becomes part of the United States after the Louisiana Purchase (1803); established first as a settlement zone for Indians (1825), it was organized as a territory (1890).
20th century:	Oklahoma becomes a state in 1907.

SPAIN AND FRANCE IN OKLAHOMA DURING THE SIXTEENTH AND EIGHTEENTH CENTURIES

All of the Spanish explorations that impacted Oklahoma took place in the sixteenth century after the voyages of Columbus. All of the French explorations took place in the eighteenth century. Below is an outline of the expeditions arranged by nation. Use it for reference purposes instead of trying to memorize it. It will encourage you to see the Spanish and the French explorations as distinct enterprises that are related to each other.

Nation	Year	Leader	Area
Spain	1541	Francisco Vásquez de Coronado	Panhandle
	1542–47	Andres do Campo	Cross Timbers
	1601	Juan de Oñate	Antelope Hills and north
France	1719	Bénard de La Harpe	Kiamichi and Arkansas rivers
	1719	Claude-Charles Du Tisné	Verdigris River (in Kansas)
	1740	Pierre and Paul Mallet	Canadian River
	1741	Fabry de La Bruyère	Canadian River

the daring conquistador Hernán Cortes, invaded Mexico and conquered the Aztec empire.

Mexico yielded dazzling treasures for the Spaniards. So too did the Inca kingdom of Peru. Those discoveries lent credability to rumors that had surfaced from time to time about the fabulous Seven Cities of Cíbola where houses had walls of solid gold and doors of turquoise. Spanish authorities sent many expeditions to Mexico's northern frontier in search of the fabled kingdom. The one led by Francisco Vásquez de Coronado was of particular importance to Oklahoma.

Coronado's Story

Coronado was governor of New Spain's most-northern province, New Galicia. At only twenty-seven years of age he was already a wealthy man who had made a name for himself as an able administrator and capable military leader. The royal authorization to search for the Seven Cities of Cíbola he saw as an honor. Not incidentally, it also was an opportunity to enrich himself further.

The governor gathered his command at Compostela on the west coast of Mexico. When he set out for Cíbola, his column consisted of 240 mounted men, 60 foot soldiers, more than 800 Indians, a very long baggage train, at least 1,000 horses, and large herds of cattle, sheep, and hogs (none of which were native to the American Southwest). Over the next several months his men traveled through much of Arizona and New Mexico looking for the fabled cities. All they found were humble Indian villages built of mud rather than gold.

During those maneuvers Coronado and his men showed little respect for the lives and rights of the native people they encountered. He took chiefs as hostages, he robbed the villagers of their food, he insisted that Indian men act as porters for his army, and he demanded women who would sleep with his soldiers. Increasingly frustrated by his failure to find Cíbola, he was absolutely ruthless in battle.

On the Rio Grande in New Mexico, Coronado's luck changed. He heard from a Pawnee Indian captive that there existed on the east a land of incredible wealth, known as Quivira, where even common folk ate their meals off silver plates and drank from golden bowls. The Indian, who was named "The Turk" because "he looked like one," offered to guide the Spaniards to it. There were good reasons to be suspicious, but Coronado ignored them. He and his men followed The Turk eastward onto the High Plains of Texas, where they eventually turned north and east across Oklahoma into Kansas. There on the Arkansas River near present Wichita, Coronado found Quivira.

Coronado's march to and from Quivira in 1541 was not a happy one. From *Drawings by Frederic Remington* (1894).

It was far from what he had expected. There were no golden bells in the shade trees. Indeed, there were not many trees at all. But there were a lot of yapping dogs and dome-shaped grass houses occupied by people whose bodies were covered by tattoos. Quivira was not a city of great wealth, but merely a village of the Wichita Indians, Oklahoma's First People.

The governor was bitterly disappointed. He demanded an explanation of The Turk, who reluctantly admitted that his description of Quivira was just a hoax to get the Spanish out of the Rio Grande settlements. Coronado was not amused. His soldiers were outraged, and one of them put a rope around the ex-guide's neck and choked him to death. The governor then assembled the Wichita chiefs and demanded that they swear an oath of allegiance to the king of Spain. They did so—maybe even knowing what they were doing. With that accomplished, Coronado assembled his weary command and went back to the Rio Grande pueblos, following a route that took him southwest through the Oklahoma Panhandle.

Two fundamental goals motivated Spain in America, gold and God. Coronado embodied the one, while Friar Juan de Padilla, a chaplain assigned to Coronado's expedition, personified the other. Padilla was so impressed with the Wichita people that he, two Mexican Indian lay brothers, and Andres do Campo, a Portuguese-born soldier, returned to establish a Catholic mission among them. After a few months' labor the Spaniards decided to move on to more promising fields farther east. Somewhere in south-central Kansas, the Kaw Indians ambushed the party, Padilla died, and Do Campo and the two lay brothers were taken captive for almost a year. When they finally escaped, they traveled south by a route that took them across central Oklahoma into Texas, and on to the Gulf Coast of New Spain.

It took the Do Campo party months, if not years, to cross our state, five years in all to reach the Gulf Coast. What slowed it was a heavy wooden cross that the two lay brothers carried by turns on their backs to mourn the death of their teacher, Padilla. It was an act of piety not matched many times since in Oklahoma. The trail it marked between Quivira and the Spanish settlements, moreover, was much more direct than the one followed by Coronado. Thereafter, Mexico City officials recommended the Do Campo route as the preferred link to Spain's newest northern province. Today if you drive on Interstate 35, you are not far from this "trail of the cross."

Friar Padilla was not the only one who saw the northern frontier as a fertile ground for Christian missions. So too did other chaplains on the Coronado expedition. It took almost sixty years, but they and later church leaders persuaded Spanish officials to establish a mission and settlement on the Rio Grande in what is now New Mexico. Juan de Oñate, rich from Mexican silver, was appointed as governor of the new colony. The settlement he established near present Santa Fe took root and survived—before there was either a Jamestown or a Quebec.

The day-to-day tasks of a regional administrator

Going east along the Canadian River in 1601, Oñate turned north-northeast at the Antelope Hills to Quivira. Somewhere near present-day Gage he encountered Plains Apache villages.

soon bored Oñate. He left those to others and turned to his real interest, which was to complete Coronado's quest for Quivira. One of his trips took him eastward to the headwaters of the Canadian River, down it to the Antelope Hills on Oklahoma's western border, then north and east through the villages of the Plains Apaches to the Arkansas River in present Kansas. Oñate found there what Coronado had found: the villages of several thousand Wichitas. Since they retained a clear memory of the earlier visit, the Indians gave the Spaniards free access to their villages and willingly told them about their country. But they soon tired of all the questions. Their irritation, perceived as hostility, caused Oñate and his men to leave Quivira as they had come.

The Spanish-Oklahoma Connection

Given their limited objectives, both Coronado and Oñate correctly judged their two expeditions as failures. They found no gold and concluded therefore that the extensive areas they had traversed were useless. Nor did either of them make any friends for the Spanish king. Yet both expeditions were extremely important to Oklahoma.

The written reports of Coronado's and Oñate's expeditions give us our first glimpses of what life was like in our state five centuries ago. For the first time native peoples have faces and take on personality for us. This is true not only of the Wichitas but also of the Plains Apaches, whom Coronado and Oñate both encountered on their way to and from Quivira. We also learn something about the land. The Spaniards encountered "humped-backed cows" on the plains, for example, and they rode through grass so tall that you had to be on a horse to see over it. Quivira itself was "fat and black, and . . . well watered by rivulets and springs and rivers."

Coronado's council with the Wichita chiefs also had political significance for Oklahoma. Because of it, Spain could claim dominion over the western side of the Mississippi River valley. Probably that did not mean a lot to the chiefs, although they surely had a vague sense that something was different. Sixty years later they received Oñate as a friend, and subsequently they sent a mission to Santa Fe to ask Spanish help in subduing their Apache enemies.

Among the kings of Europe, Coronado's claim had substantial meaning. During the sixteenth century the Europeans were all engaged in a worldwide contest for empire. Because of Coronado, Spain had won the prize of a vast domain that included Oklahoma. Revised maps of North America now showed Quivira as the northern province of New Spain.

Did the designation of Oklahoma as one of its provinces mean anything to Spain, or was it just a chip in the great poker game of empire? Coronado probably had determined that the region would not be important. "There is not any gold nor any other metal—nothing but villages," he had written. Oklahoma's First People were curiosities with little human potential. With such publicity, is it any wonder that in the next 250 years only two official Spanish expeditions visited Oklahoma? Clearly Spain had no real interest in the state or its people.

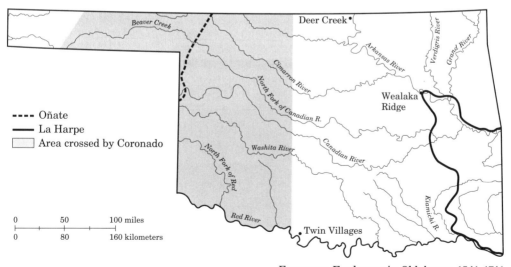

European Explorers in Oklahoma, 1541–1741

France in Oklahoma

Oklahoma was on the Spaniard's map, but it was in the heart of the French. In the early seventeenth century France launched its bid for a share of the emerging new world, making its first settlements in Canada. In 1682, Robert Cavelier, sieur de La Salle, canoed down the Mississippi River to claim it and the western lands it drained for the king of France. Naming the prize Louisiana, La Salle saw it as the center of a great new commercial empire based on trading for furs with the local Indians. He anticipated focusing the trade in a series of settlements and military posts along the Mississippi River and its tributaries. La Salle died trying to establish one of these posts, but others succeeded, pioneering Mobile, New Orleans, Arkansas Post, and Natchitoches, among other settlements.

Neither La Salle nor his successors expected the Indians to be Louisiana's only trading partner. They also hoped to begin a commercial relationship with the Spanish settlements on the Rio Grande, where communities like Santa Fe presumably hungered for trade goods that Louisiana could easily supply. To tap those markets, the French needed only to follow the great western rivers that emptied into the Mississippi. Significantly, the rivers that linked the Mississippi most directly with Santa Fe all went through Oklahoma—the Red, the Arkansas, and the Canadian.

Much of the success or failure of Louisiana as a trading center therefore depended on circumstances in our state. Would the Wichitas and the Osages be open to trading relationships? Would the rivers themselves be suitable channels of commerce to Santa Fe? Would the Indian people living along those rivers grant safe passage to trading parties? French authorities sought answers to those questions early in the eighteenth century.

La Harpe's Story

Jean-Baptiste Bénard, sieur de La Harpe, had made and lost one fortune in South America while still a young man. He hoped to recoup some of his losses in Louisiana, where French officials had authorized him to explore, trade with the Indians, and establish

a commercial link with the distant settlements of
New Mexico. He established his headquarters near
present Texarkana, Texas, from which he began to
explore the area. He sent his friend, the geographer
Gaston Du Rivage, 180 miles up the Red River to
identify Indian tribes and evaluate prospects for
trade with the Spaniards. La Harpe himself led a
party northward through the very heart of eastern
Oklahoma. Included in his group were three Indian
guides, two gentlemen, three enlisted soldiers, and
two blacks (probably slaves).

Historians have disputed the route of La Harpe's
expedition through Oklahoma. Yet a careful reading of his original journal indicates that he went
north across present McCurtain, Choctaw, Pushmataha, Latimer, and Pittsburg counties. He then
crossed the Canadian River near present Eufaula
and struck north through McIntosh, western Muskogee, and western Wagoner counties to southern
Tulsa County. Along the Arkansas River on what we
now call Wealaka Ridge, near Leonard, La Harpe
encountered nine villages of some 6,000 Wichitas.

La Harpe was considerably impressed with the
country he traversed. There were beautiful prairies enclosed by mountains. Rivers were filled with
fish and with mussels that contained pearls. The
climate was mild, and the land was both fertile and
rich in minerals. He saw coal and rocks with grains
resembling gold. There were large buffalo herds,
abundant deer, and great numbers of wolves (which
were "little and not all bad"). La Harpe even killed a
"very large bear." In the land also were partridges,
woodcocks, plover, and geese.

We-ta-ra-sha-ro, sketched
here by George Catlin in
1834, was probably a direct
descendent of Wichitas who
greeted La Harpe in 1719. It is
not clear from the drawing,
but the facial lines may represent tattoos.

The Wichitas greeted the French party enthusiastically. Chief Touacara, leader of the principal
village, and other chiefs made clear they would welcome a trading partnership with the French. Such a
relationship would bring them guns, by which they
could defend their villages from their enemies, and
other manufactured goods. They were willing also
to give safe passage to French convoys going up the
Arkansas and Canadian rivers to trade with the
Spanish settlements. The formalities of an alliance
were quickly concluded, and a wooden post, on
which Du Rivage had carved the arms of the king of
France, was erected to commemorate the event.

La Harpe had intended to leave three of his men

among the Wichitas to establish a permanent trading facility on Wealaka Ridge. He abandoned that idea when he learned that the Wichitas left their villages for six months each winter to hunt buffalo. What kind of a commercial relationship the French would establish with the Wichitas he thus left to others to determine. He and his party returned to his fort on the Red River, which he soon left for New Orleans. La Harpe remained prominent in Louisiana affairs for the next several years, but he never again returned to Oklahoma.

The Fur Trade

La Harpe's expedition confirmed Oklahoma's economic potential to Louisiana officials. So too did the simultaneous and subsequent expeditions to Wichita villages in Kansas by Claude-Charles Du Tisné and, along the Canadian River, by Pierre and Paul Mallet and by Fabry de La Bruyère. To the French, Oklahoma was obviously neither a trackless wasteland nor part of any Great American Desert. It sat astride a promising although dangerous route to Santa Fe. Most important, its native people represented future partners in commercial ventures that would help determine whether France was a success or a failure in North America.

The French quickly involved the Oklahoma Indians in these ventures. To both the Wichitas and the Osages, they took guns, ammunition, knives, hatchets, axes, hoes, cloth, blankets, beads, mirrors, and paint. At a glance, most tribespeople saw the value of such products. They willingly exchanged for them the hides of buffalo and deer and the skins of beaver, otter, mink, and muskrat. They also offered, and the French gladly accepted, horses (even stolen ones) and Indian captives who could be sold as slaves.

The Wichitas and the Osages quickly became dependent on the trade goods. The obsession had tragic consequences, altering fundamental economic and social habits. They once had hunted only for food and clothes, and they had made war only for revenge. With the onset of the fur trade they hunted for hides and skins and fought for horses and captives. Put differently, they became not only commercial hunters but commercial warriors as well.

Who were the Frenchmen who carried on the trade? They were the famous coureurs de bois, generally nameless young men who enjoyed the freedom and challenges of life in the woods. They were a loose and happy group, willing to live with the Indians, to learn Indian ways and languages, and to take Indian women as their wives. In the mid-eighteenth century probably a hundred or so coureurs de bois were active in Oklahoma Indian villages.

Deer Creek Village

Archaeologists are helping us learn more about the relationship between some coureurs de bois and Indian people. They have done considerable work on the site of a Wichita village located where Deer Creek enters the Arkansas River just east of Newkirk in Kay County. There they have discovered twenty-five or more circular mounds from fifteen to twenty inches high. These are middens (a plainer name is trash heaps) composed primarily of buffalo bones but also including large numbers of chipped-stone hide scrapers. Additionally there are ditches that appear to be man-made. Archaeologists have identified at the site such French-manufactured items as gun parts, metal tools, kettles, ornaments, and glass beads.

There has been no systematic excavation of Deer Creek Village so far. Yet careful evaluation of both the materials that have been randomly collected and the known historical sources enables scholars to draw some rather-definitive conclusions. It is clear, for example, that the site was occupied by the Wichita Indians as a village as early as 1720 (if not before) and remained in use until the late 1750s. We can be certain also that the center of the village was fortified with something that resembled a dry moat. The residents of the village obviously felt the need to protect themselves from enemy attacks, probably by Osages.

Doubtless French trade goods came through the village on a regular basis. Since only small quantities of these have been found, researchers have concluded that Deer Creek was not the site of a permanent French trading post. The large presence of animal bones also suggests that the principal activities of the village were to process buffalo hides; to smoke, dry, or salt meat; and to rend tallow and oil.

DEMYTHOLOGIZING HISTORY: THE CASE OF FERNANDINA

In May or June 1926, Joseph B. Thoburn of the Oklahoma Historical Society learned of a map with the name "Fernandina" printed in the general region of the Deer Creek archaeological site east of Newkirk. Examination of the map revealed that it had been published in London, England, in the 1860s by "Lloyds," presumably the famous insurance company. Impressed by the age of the map and its publication in Europe, Thoburn decided that the "Fernandina" of the 1860s and the Deer Creek site of the 1750s were one and the same.

Thereafter Dr. Thoburn and other historians made extravagant claims for "Fernandina." Some asserted that it was the first white settlement in Oklahoma, known to early cartographers in England and Scotland. Others claimed it was a French fort where Frenchmen lived and traded with the Wichitas. Dr. Thoburn himself concluded that "Fernandina" was named after King Ferdinand VI of Spain, who reigned between 1746 to 1759, and that the proper spelling for the French fort should be "Ferdinandina." (He never explained why the French would name a post after a Spanish king.) For two generations Oklahoma historians and geographers accepted these interpretations uncritically and incorporated them into their texts and atlases.

Not until the late 1970s did anyone bother to examine the documents that presumably confirmed the existance of "Ferdinandina."

Then ethnohistorian Mildred Mott Wedel learned that the actual map Thoburn used no longer existed, only a picture of a part of it. Using that small clue, she was able to determine that the original map was in fact a copy of "Lloyd's Topographical Railway Map of North America, or the United States Continent," which was published in 1868 by J. T. Lloyd of New York and London. Dr. Wedel established that "Fernandina" does appear on this map as a site in northern Indian Territory, although not at the exact location of the Deer Creek village.

Dr. Wedel conducted an extensive search of international archives to locate other maps or documents that might show "Fernandina." She found no refer-

So what was Deer Creek? The evidence suggests that it was a typical Wichita village and that it became the headquarters of thirty to forty Frenchmen who were there as professional hunters to supply Louisiana with meat. The villagers worked for these men as hunters themselves and as meat processors, being paid in European merchandise. Contrary to historical legend, there was no thriving commerce at Deer Creek in which the Wichitas served as crafty brokers between the coureurs de bois and the Plains tribes. The evidence collected from the trash mounds may not be terribly romantic, but it is persuasive. Deer Creek was an early-day stockyard and meat-processing plant, where the Indian people worked as laborers.

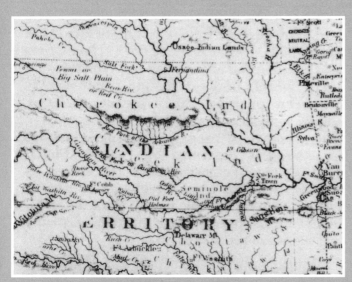

Published in 1868, a copy of "Lloyd's Topographical Railway Map of North America, or the United States Continent" launched the myth of Fernandina.

the time when a fort of that name was supposed to have existed. She found three maps from the 1850s that used the designation, but all three placed it differently. One put "Fernandina" in Kansas near the Santa Fe Trail.

Wedel concluded that "Fernandina" as a geographical place-name dated only from the 1850s. As such, it was never used during the 1740s to designate the Deer Creek site. Moreover, that location was not a French fort, and therefore not the first white settlement in Oklahoma. Instead it was a hunting and meat-processing operation that supplied meat for French Louisiana. To use the term "Ferdinandina" to identify the Wichita village at Deer Creek is to perpetuate a historical myth.

ence to the name on any source from the 1740s and 1750s when Deer Creek was an active hunting and meat-processing site. Indeed, she discovered that "Fernandina" as a place-name was not used in manuscripts or printed sources until the 1850s, a full century after

Relocation to Red River

Operations at Deer Creek continued into the mid-1750s, when the villagers joined with other Wichitas in a general relocation of their communities to sites along the Red River. This general departure took about twenty years, and it was due in large part to the full-fledged war that had broken out between the Wichitas and the Osages. The better-armed Osages launched raid after raid against Oklahoma's First People, seeking to terrorize them into abandoning their homeland, and thereby to open it up to Osage hunting parties and permanent villages.

To defend themselves, the Wichitas tried different strategies. They consolidated and then fortified their villages. They secured guns from the French,

Tal-lee (Tally), sketched by George Catlin, was one of the principal chiefs of the Arkansas Osage band in the early nineteenth century.

but they never had enough, nor were they proficient with the ones they had. The Wichitas also succeeded in 1747 or 1748 in negotiating an alliance with the Comanches, a remarkable union that produced some important victories. But such successes were few.

While the Osages pushed, other factors pulled the Wichitas to the Red River. One was the desire to be nearer the more stable supplies of French trade goods that came up the Red River through Natchitoches. The southern location also put them closer to herds of Spanish horses, which they could trade for or steal; and to the Plains Apaches, who were old enemies with few guns who made good captives. Also, the Wichitas may have moved southward at the invitation of French officials who were anxious to erect an Indian barrier to possible Spanish expansion from Texas.

Twin Villages

The Wichitas established several villages along the Red River. Most famous were the so-called Twin Villages on either side of the river, one in modern Jefferson County, Oklahoma, the other in Montague County, Texas. The village on the north bank was fortified with a log stockade and a moat, inside of which was a horse corral. Centered in the villages was a remarkable commerce in which the Wichitas did act as shrewd brokers between the Southern Plains tribes and resident French traders. Horses, hides, meat, and Apache and Spanish captives were exchanged for guns, ammunition, pots, blankets, and other manufactured items.

From the Twin Villages, the Wichitas and their Comanche allies also launched joint raids against Apache villages in Texas. Attempts to protect the Apaches by assembling them near the mission of San Saba northeast of San Antonio were futile. In 1758 some 2,000 raiders swooped down on the mission, drove off the defenders, sacked and then burned its buildings, and forced the Apaches to seek refuge elsewhere.

The next year, Colonel Diego Ortiz Parrilla set out with an army of five hundred men and two cannon to punish the so-called Nations of the North. He should have stayed in the south. He ultimately located the Twin Villages, but their fortifications, over which flew a French flag, were much more formidable than he had expected. Eleven cannon shots had so little effect that the defenders laughed. Moreover, a daring Wichita chief led his comrades out of the fort and assaulted Spanish positions time after time. That night the Wichitas held a great fire-light celebration inside the fort, which unnerved the Spanish army. Before dawn arrived, Parrilla had ordered a retreat.

France Loses Oklahoma

The battle of Twin Villages was an effort on the part of Spain to curtail France's influence along her northern border. As it turned out, the effort was unnecessary. Farther east France had been defeated by England in what we call the French and Indian War. In the Treaty of Paris in 1763, France withdrew entirely from North America, relinquishing all of its claims west of the Mississippi River to Spain. Translated so that the Wichitas and the Comanches could understand it, the treaty meant that the French flag no longer flew in Oklahoma.

The French-Oklahoma Connection

For nearly 150 years the French controlled the destiny of our state. Unlike the Spanish before them, they publicized it as a land of promise and opportunity. They recognized the abundance of its natural resources, the fertility of its soil, and the beauty of its landscapes. Above all, they treated native people as equals, seeing them as necessary allies in their commercial and diplomatic plans for Louisiana.

Over the years thousands of Frenchmen came to Oklahoma. Evidence of the French is seen today in geographical place-names. Take a state highway map and notice the French words: Poteau, Illinois, Sallisaw, Verdigris, Sans Bois, Fourche Maline, Kiamichi, Chouteau, and Salina. Look at detailed county maps that show rivers and creeks and see even more. The French legacy is also seen in the surnames of many Oklahoma Indian families, whose members often take leadership roles in tribal affairs.

In other states where French influence was strong there is an architectural legacy (as in Louisiana and Missouri). Why is there none in Oklahoma? Largely because the French did not come to Oklahoma to settle or to build. They came instead to exploit natural resources and the people through the fur trade. Their agenda was to take and not to give. They left behind not architectural monuments but native peoples who had lost many of their traditional skills, who had slaughtered their own food supply for profit, and who now made vicious war on each other.

Spanish Louisiana

Between 1763 and 1800, Oklahoma was a province of Spanish Louisiana. During that period of time the English colonies on the Atlantic coast of North America declared independence, fought a revolution, established the United States, and adopted a constitutional form of government. With those momentous events going on outside of Louisiana, it is no wonder that what took place in Oklahoma was never a matter of priority for Spanish officials at New Orleans. Still, two problems simply would not go away: the Wichitas and the Osages.

Over a period of years Spain was able to humble the Twin Village Wichitas by limiting their access to guns and by outlawing their trade in horses and slaves. These policies soon reduced Oklahoma's First People to poverty and helplessness. On the other hand, not even Spain could control the Osages. A large band, led by Clermont, settled permanently in the Verdigris River valley in today's Rogers County on lands from which the Osages had recently driven the Wichitas. From there they launched raids that extended their control over Oklahoma and even took them deep into Texas. The horses and captives taken in these attacks, traded to the English, made them wealthy and haughty.

Oklahoma Returns to France

In 1800, pressured by Napoleon Bonaparte, Spain returned Louisiana to French control at the Treaty of San Ildefonso. Napoleon envisioned the province as the breadbasket of a restored French empire in North America. Problems in Europe and in the Caribbean Sea caused the abandonment of that plan, making Louisiana surplus property. Always short of cash, Napoleon offered the whole of the province to the young United States for a mere $15 million.

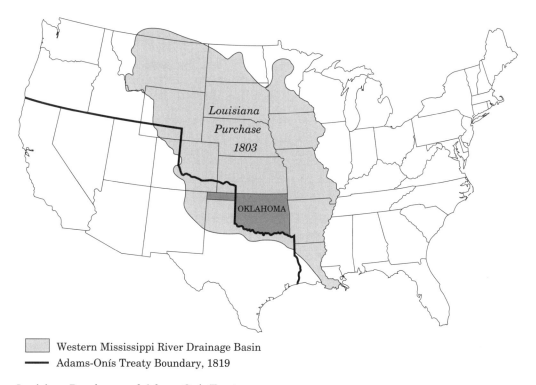

[ ] Western Mississippi River Drainage Basin
— Adams-Onís Treaty Boundary, 1819

Louisiana Purchase and Adams-Onís Treaty

The new republic purchased the territory in 1803.
With that transaction, the flag of the United States
rose over Oklahoma.

See History for Yourself

Visit the Heavener Runestone Recreation Area and
see what some believe are messages left by Viking
explorers.

   On the map on page 75 you will see that La Harpe's
1719 expedition passed through nine different counties. If you live in those counties, try to trace the
course of his route. Currently the best guides to
consult are articles by Anna Lewis, "La Harpe's
First Expedition in Oklahoma, 1718–1719," *Chronicles
of Oklahoma* 2 (1924), and by Mildred Mott Wedel,
"J. B. Bénard, Sieur de La Harpe: Visitor to the Wichitas in 1719," *Great Plains Journal* 10 (1971). Both articles should be in your library. Try to identify the
major landmarks mentioned by La Harpe, particularly the Wichita Indian village. Is Wealaka Ridge
the site of the nine villages visited by La Harpe?

Students in western Oklahoma might like to follow the route of Oñate. The best reference to it is Herbert E. Bolton, ed., *Spanish Exploration of the Southwest, 1542–1706* (New York, 1916).

To get a feeling for how Indians placed and defended their eighteenth-century villages, walk over the Wichita village site at Deer Creek near Newkirk, or the Twin Village (known as Longest) site in Jefferson County south of Ryan. Before you go, make arrangements with property owners, and once you get to the site, do not disturb it by doing any digging.

Suggestions for Further Reading

Reference

Bolton, Herbert E. *Athanase de Mézières and the Louisiana-Texas Frontier, 1768–1780.* 2 vols. Cleveland: Arthur H. Clark, 1914.

———. *Coronado, Knight of Pueblos and Plains.* Albuquerque: University of New Mexico Press, 1949.

———. *Texas in the Middle Eighteenth Century.* Berkeley: University of California Press, 1915.

Brandon, William. *Quivira: Europeans in the Region of the Santa Fe Trail, 1540–1820.* Athens: Ohio University Press, 1990.

John, Elizabeth Ann Harper. *Storms Brewed in Other Men's Worlds: Confrontation of Indians, Spanish, and French in the Southwest, 1540–1795.* College Station: Texas A & M University Press, 1975.

Rollings, Willard H. *The Osage: An Ethnohistorical Study of Hegemony on the Prairie-Plains.* Columbia: University of Missouri Press, 1992.

Wedel, Mildred Mott. *The Deer Creek Site, Oklahoma: A Wichita Village Sometimes called Ferdinandina, An Ethnohistorian's View.* Oklahoma City: Oklahoma Historical Society, 1981.

Chapter 6: American Explorers in Oklahoma

On finalizing the agreement to purchase Louisiana, United States Commissioner Robert Livingston asked his French counterpart to define the boundaries of the province. The reply was, "You have made a noble bargain, Mr. Livingston. Make the most of it!" From the very beginning President Thomas Jefferson and his administration intended to make the most of it. That determination had important implications for Oklahoma.

For President Thomas Jefferson, locating the Great Salt Plains in present-day Cherokee County was a priority. George Sibley was the first American explorer to visit them.

Territorial Government

After some experimentation, in 1805 the United States Congress divided Louisiana into two territories: Orleans in the south and Louisiana in the north. The Territory of Louisiana, with jurisdiction over what is now Oklahoma, had its administrative center at Saint Louis. General James B. Wilkinson served briefly as the governor of Louisiana and then was succeeded by William Clark of the famous Lewis and Clark expedition. Clark continued as governor when northern Louisiana became the Territory of Missouri in 1812. Seven years later Oklahoma was attached to the Territory of Arkansas, which eventually had its administrative capital at Little Rock. The territorial governors of Arkansas frequently had to deal with events occurring in the state.

However it was organized administratively, President Jefferson believed that Louisiana would provide the foundation for a great American empire. In that role it could supply needed natural resources, living room for an expanding population, a barrier against foreign aggression, and space for the resettlement of eastern Indians. Yet Jefferson recognized that effective use of Louisiana's resources required better knowledge of its topography, its flora and fauna, its rocks and minerals, and its people. His desire for that kind of information caused him to dispatch a series of military expeditions to undertake scientific exploration of Louisiana once it passed into the possession of the United States.

Scientific Explorers

The earliest and probably the best known of the scientific expeditions was commanded by Meriwether Lewis and William Clark. Between 1804 and 1806 it went up the Missouri River, crossed the Rocky Mountains, and followed the Columbia River to the Pacific Ocean. Along the way Lewis and Clark gathered incredible amounts of information about the northern reaches of Louisiana, in addition to impressing the Indians with the power and might of the "Great Father" in Washington. What the two commanders had done in the north, Jefferson hoped other army officers could do in the south.

CHRONOLOGY OF AMERICAN EXPLORATION

Below is a chronology of the American exploration of Oklahoma. Consult it from time to time as you read to help you keep straight the sequence of the different expeditions.

Date	Explorer	Region
1806	Richard Sparks	Red River
1806	James B. Wilkinson	Arkansas River
1808	Anthony Glass	Red River
1811	George C. Sibley	Great Salt and Big Salt plains
1819	Thomas Nuttall	Poteau and Kiamichi rivers, Three Forks, Cimarron
1820	John R. Bell	Arkansas River
1820	Stephen H. Long	Canadian River
1821	Hugh Glenn	Arkansas and Canadian rivers
1821	Thomas James	North Canadian and Canadian rivers
1822	Thomas James	North Canadian River
1822	William Becknell	Panhandle

These were dispatched almost immediately after Lewis and Clark completed their expedition.

The Sparks Expedition

Early in 1806 the president ordered Captain Richard Sparks to proceed up the Red River by boat to the Twin Villages of the Wichitas and from there to go overland by horseback to the Rocky Mountains. He was to take careful notes on the country he saw and the people he met. Sparks put together a company of twenty-four soldiers and moved upriver in a small flotilla of canoes. But his party barely made it into present-day Oklahoma—if it made it at all. A Spanish cavalry unit of several hundred men overran its camp and ordered the captain to return to the American settlements or face arrest. Sparks went back. Obviously the Spanish were very sensitive about any United States party exploring southern Louisiana when boundaries were still indefinite.

The Pike-Wilkinson Expedition

Since southern Louisiana remained a mystery, military authorities next dispatched Captain Zebulon M. Pike to search out the origins and course of the Red River. In July 1806, Pike departed from St. Louis with twenty-three men on a route that took him up the Missouri River to the Osage villages. There he obtained horses and, dodging Spanish patrols, made his way to the Great Bend of the Arkansas River in west-central Kansas. By prearrangement, he divided his command at that point, ordering Lieutenant James B. Wilkinson and five men to go east down the Arkansas while he and the rest of the troop went west up the river to its sources. Pike's party pushed on to the Rocky Mountains, where he climbed the peak now named after him. Later he and his men were arrested by another Spanish patrol and subjected to a long imprisonment before returning to the United States.

Meanwhile, in November and December, Lieutenant Wilkinson's party worked its way down the Arkansas River in two elm bark canoes. Shallow water soon forced them to march along the riverbank. By the time they had reached Oklahoma in northeast Kay County, they were able to navigate the river in two dugout canoes, but only barely. Winter came early and hard in 1806. The Arkansas filled with ice, and snowstorms limited visibility. Wilkinson and his men suffered greatly, losing their supply of food and ammunition and experiencing severe frostbite. What relief they found came from Osage hunters camped along the river's edge.

Wilkinson celebrated New Year's Day, 1807, by leaving Oklahoma. His had been a brutal crossing, not leaving much time for observation. Yet his journal shows that he had learned a good deal. The Osages were numerous and in "a constant state of warfare" with any Cherokees, Creeks, and Choctaws who ventured into the area. Wilkinson heard about a prairie that was encrusted with salt and about lead mines "northwest" of the Osages, and he passed over a seven-foot waterfall (Webbers Falls) on the Arkansas River. He also documented that American hunters and trappers were already working the Poteau River. President Jefferson, no doubt, found his official report extremely interesting, especially the part about an entire prairie of salt. Earlier comments by him about a "salt mountain" in Louisiana had drawn ridicule from the eastern press.

The Sibley Expedition

It was the prospect of salt that brought the third official expedition to Oklahoma in 1811. Salt, of course, was an important commodity on the frontier, necessary for meat preservation and food seasoning. George C. Sibley led the expedition, which included interpreters, Osage Indian guides, and Sibley's Irish valet. Sibley, who was a subagent at Fort Osage rather than a military officer, was given the primary mission of negotiating peace alliances between the Osages and western Kansas tribes. But he also used the occasion to lead his party into Oklahoma to look at the storied deposits of salt.

Sibley first visited the Great Salt Plains on the Salt Fork of the Arkansas in present Cherokee County north of Jet. The wafer-thin sheets of salt on the vast flat glistened "like a brilliant field of snow." The sight so excited Sibley's imagination that he pressed on to the salt deposits mentioned by Lieutenant Wilkinson five years earlier. Situated near Freedom in present Woods County, the Big Salt Plain was equally impressive, although recent rains had washed away most of the surface deposits. Near the brine springs, salt accumulated to the depth of sixteen inches. The "beautifully white" rock salt, Sibley wrote, was "unquestionably superior to any that I ever saw." Altogether, there was in northern Oklahoma an "inexhaustible store of ready made salt" just waiting to enter "into channels of commerce."

The Long-Bell Expedition

No military expedition yielded more information about our state than did that commanded by Stephen H. Long. Yet it was an accident. A major in the elite Corps of Topographical Engineers, Long was assigned to search out the sources of the Red and Arkansas rivers and to descend each to the Mississippi River. In July 1820 he led his command west from Omaha along the Platte River to the Rocky Mountains. After hiking up the peak now named for him, Long turned south to the headwaters of the Arkansas River. There, as had Pike before him, he divided his column, sending Captain John R. Bell and twelve men down the Arkansas while he continued south to the headwaters of the Red River.

Like Wilkinson fourteen years earlier, Captain Bell found the Arkansas route tough going. Only this time the problem was not cold temperatures but hot ones. When Bell and his party got to Oklahoma in mid-August, ninety-degree temperatures had worn out the animals and men and made game difficult to find. For food they were reduced to eating skunks, a fawn taken literally from the jaws of a wolf, hawks, turkeys, turtles, mussels, and boiled corn. An occasional deer, and grain and melons taken from abandoned Osage campsites, restored their strength and kept them going. On September 9, Bell and his men arrived at Fort Smith.

Thomas Say, the father of America zoology, was a member of Bell's command. His task was to make and record observations on the plants, animals, minerals, and native peoples the party encountered along the Arkansas. Unfortunately his five large journals were lost when three soldiers deserted and took those valuable materials with them. A reward of $200 was offered for the return of the papers, but to no avail. From the few remaining notebooks, Say later published our only account of the expedition.

In the meantime Major Long continued southward from the Arkansas looking for the headwaters of the Red River. His party also included a noted

Stephen H. Long, here in full military dress, commanded the U.S. Army expedition that explored the Canadian River in 1820. Long also picked the site of Fort Smith.

TRIAL BY SEED TICKS

We would expect exploring parties across Oklahoma to confront rugged terrain, wild animals, and angry Indians. That is what explorers were supposed to do. Yet those were exceptional activities. Most of their days were given over to mundane matters like setting up camp and fighting off insects. Edwin James of Major Stephen Long's expedition across Oklahoma in 1820 has left a marvelous description of his daily battle with seed ticks:

We found, however, the annoyance of innumerable multitudes of minute, almost invisible seed ticks, a sufficient counterpart to the advantages of our situation. These insects unlike the mosquitoes, gnats, and sandflies, are not to be turned aside by a gust of wind, or an atmosphere surcharged with smoke, nor does the closest dress of leather afford any protection from their persecutions. A person no sooner sets foot among them than they commence in countless thousands, their silent and unseen march; ascending along the feet and legs, they insinuate themselves into every article of dress, and fasten, unperceived, their fangs upon every part of the body. The bite is not felt until the insect has had time to bury the whole of his beak, and in the case of the most minute and most troublesome species, nearly his whole body seems hid under the skin. Where he fastens himself with such tenacity, . . . he will sooner suffer his head and body to be dragged apart than relinquish his hold. It would perhaps be well . . . to suffer them to remain unmolested, but they excite such intolerable itching that the sufferer cannot avoid aggravating the evil by his efforts to relieve himself from the offending cause. (Edwin James, comp., *Account of an Expedition from Pittsburgh to the Rocky Mountains* 2:143–44)

scientist, Edwin James. Eventually Long encountered a broad stream which he took to be the Red River, an assumption he held for nearly seven weeks. Actually it was the Canadian, that fabled waterway the French had followed to Santa Fe. Riding horses in the bed of the river, Long and his party reached the Antelope Hills and Oklahoma on August 17. Botanist James was impressed with the wildlife he saw: "Herds of bison, wild horses, elk, and deer, are seen quietly grazing in these extensive and fertile pastures." A prairie-dog colony, a mile square in area, filled him with awe, as did flocks of white pelicans, egrets, and snowy herons, and the occasional bald eagle, not to mention tarantulas.

These natural wonders aside, Dr. James was even more impressed by the scorching heat and the dry bed of the Canadian River. Deep holes in the river sand produced no more than a mere cup of water. As he saw it, there was only a "wide sandy desert" between what is now Indianola in Pittsburg County and the Rocky Mountains: "The traveller who shall, at any time, have traversed its desolate sands will, we think, join us in the wish that this region may

The lack of water in the bed of the Canadian River caused Stephen Long to include Oklahoma in what he termed the "Great American Desert."

forever remain the unmolested haunt of the native hunter, the bison, the prairie wolf, and the marmot." But the parched land did have a purpose. It would prevent undisciplined expansion over the entire continent, or as James said, "ruinous diffusion" of the American people.

When Major Long and his party arrived at the Arkansas River on September 10, 1820, they recognized to their "mortification" that they were not on the Red River, but the Canadian. Both Long and James were embarrassed and disappointed, even more so because they knew that they had not the energy, the time, or the means to go back and do the job right. Instead they pushed on to Fort Smith, where three days later they were reunited with Captain Bell and other members of the original party.

The Long expedition did not meet its declared objective, yet it had important consequences. It generated, despite the loss of Say's journals, an impressive quantity of scientific data on Oklahoma's flora, fauna, geology, geography, and native peoples. More important, the expedition confirmed a general impression that the Southern Plains were a sandy wasteland unsuitable for general agriculture. Thereafter, maps of the American West usually labeled the area as "the Great American Desert." If Major Long and his colleagues had had their way, Oklahoma and the surrounding area would have remained in its natural state.

Thomas Nuttall in Oklahoma

The most useful and complete information assembled about the resources and people of Oklahoma did not come from government-sponsored expeditions. Rather it was gathered by the internationally

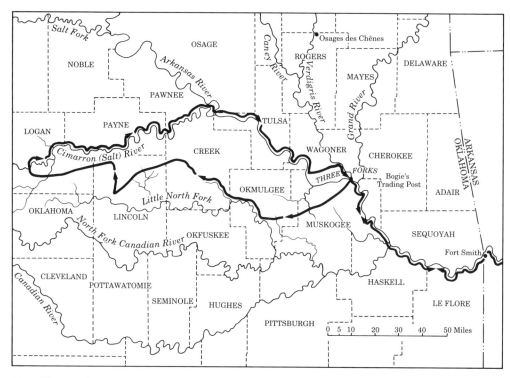

Nuttall's Expedition West of Three Forks

In 1819, Thomas Nuttall assembled more information on the people and resources of Oklahoma than did any other nineteenth-century explorer.

famous English botanist Thomas Nuttall. In 1819 he spent several months in the state gathering botanical samples. He arrived at Fort Smith early in the spring and promptly joined Major William Bradford and a company of riflemen on an expedition to the Red River. The army unit had orders to eject white squatters (illegal settlers) from lands claimed by the Osages.

The expedition followed a route up the Poteau River to the dividing ridge and then down the Kiamichi River. Along the way Nuttall marveled at the wildlife he saw (bears, bison, panthers, and snakes) and the loveliness of the prairies and mountains. "Nothing could at this season exceed the beauty of these plains," he wrote, "enamelled with such an uncommon variety of flowers of vivid tints, possessing all the brilliancy of tropical productions."

The two hundred or so families squatting near the mouth of Kiamichi had planted substantial fields of corn, cotton, and wheat. Their wheat had yielded eighty bushels per acre and brought $3.50 per bushel. They were wholly unprepared for their eviction

NUTTALL ON OKLAHOMA'S MOCKING BIRD

The father of western American botany, Thomas Nuttall wrote some of the best descriptions of Oklahoma's wildlife in existence. Consider his account of the mocking bird. The creature so common in the skies of our state takes on almost divine attributes.

In my solitary, but amusing rambles over these delightful prairies, I now, for the first time in my life, notwithstanding my long residence and peregrinations in North America, hearkened to the inimitable notes of the mocking-bird (*Turdus polyglottus*). After amusing itself in ludicrous imitations of other birds, perched on the topmost bough of a spreading elm, it at length broke forth into a strain of melody the most wild, varied, and pathetic, that ever I had heard from any thing less than human. In the midst of these enchanting strains, which gradually increased to loudness, it oftentimes flew upwards from the topmost twig, continuing its note as if overpowered by the sublimest ecstasy. (Thomas Nuttall, *A Journal of Travels into the Arkansas Territory during the Year 1819*, p. 178)

notices. Nuttall sympathized with their protests, but he thought the policy of honoring commitments to the Indians was admirable. Besides, the offenders had "the worst moral character imaginable, being many of them renegadoes [*sic*] from justice, and such as have forfeited the esteem of civilized society."

On the return trip to Fort Smith, Nuttall missed connection with Bradford's party. He finally persuaded three of the settlers to accompany him back to the fort. From there he was able to take a boat up the Arkansas River to the Verdigris. The boat was just barely able to navigate the falls of the Arkansas, which now were only three feet high. From the Three Forks area, Nuttall explored up the Grand River. Near present Mazie in Mayes County, he examined a commercial saltworks and walked west and south through the Great Osage Prairie, a treeless expanse where native grasses grew three feet tall. With a guide, he also went west on a route that took him overland to the Cimarron River near present Guthrie in Logan County. Nuttall followed that stream back to Three Forks.

Commercial Explorers

While some Americans sought scientific knowledge about our state, others sought primarily to make a profit from it. In the tradition of the French coureurs de bois, they ventured up the Arkansas and Red rivers to trade with the Indians for furs, livestock, and captives, or to trap and hunt for the skins themselves. Some hoped to realize the old French dream of opening a trade with the Spanish settlements along the Rio Grande. Many of these "expectant capitalists," as one historian has called them, became trailblazers and explorers in their own right.

Red River Traders

The quest for economic success of Anthony Glass, a resident of Natchez, Mississippi, took him up the Red River only two years after Captain Sparks had been turned back. With the approval of the United States Indian agent at Natchitoches, Glass and ten other men set off in July 1808 to participate in a trade fair hosted by the Wichitas and involving all of the Southern Plains tribes. Because of Spanish apprehensions regarding American intentions, Glass was supposed to follow the north bank of the Red River to the Twin Villages. Actually he followed a route parallel to the river on the Texas side, crossing into Oklahoma when he reached Love County. There he turned west to the Twin villages.

Glass presented the greetings of the president of the United States to the Wichitas and expressed his own desire to trade with them and their Comanche allies. He remained in the area for six months swapping for horses and tracking down a meteorite revered by the Indians. His final report to John Sibley tells us much about Wichita cultural habits. Particularly important were his observations that the Wichitas were a people under siege and held virtually as captives in their own villages by the Osages. (Three years later the Osages caused the Wichitas to abandon the Twin Villages permanently.) Also significant was Glass's report that an American trading party had already passed though the villages on its way to Santa Fe.

Glass was able to ascend the Red River when two United States military expeditions (Sparks and Long) had failed. Other commercial explorers would follow him to the Twin Villages and beyond, but most focused their activities in what is now southeastern Oklahoma. These hunters and trappers are nameless to us, but we do know that they were an independent lot who had little respect for the needs and rights of Indian people. The army tried to expel them from the area in 1819—but with little success.

Three Forks Traders

American traders and trappers along the Arkansas tended to concentrate in the Three Forks area where the Arkansas, the Verdigris, and the Grand River merge just north of Muskogee. Near there the Arkansas band of the Osages resided. After having driven the Wichitas from the area, they had occupied it first for hunting camps (in the 1760s) and then in permanent villages (in the 1780s). The talented warrior Cashesegra, or Big Track, led this splinter group, although Clermont, a noted hereditary chief, joined it before 1800. French traders out of Arkansas Post frequented the Osages' Verdigris River villages from the time they were established.

With the onset of the American period, there was even more commercial activity at Three Forks. The Chouteau brothers accounted for much of this. Pierre and Auguste Chouteau had made fortunes trading with the Osages along the Missouri River. The brothers had lost their monopoly of that trade, granted by the Spanish, and in 1802 they relocated their considerable operation among the 3,000 members of the Arkansas Osage band. Historians once assumed that the Chouteaus, in retaliation for losing their monopoly, had caused Clermont's people to leave their homeland and to follow them to Oklahoma. We know now that just the opposite was the case. The Chouteaus came to Oklahoma because the Osages were already there and had been for thirty years.

Clermont II, sketched in 1834 by George Catlin, was the leading Osage chief in the Three Forks area after 1800.

Joseph Bogy was another early Three Forks trader. Of French extraction, he had operated trading establishments earlier at Kaskaskia in Illinois and at Arkansas Post. On the Verdigris he constructed a post of picket logs (driven vertically into the ground) and traded extensively with the Osages. That commerce in part accounted for his loss of a boatload of trade goods to a Choctaw war party in 1807. The leader of the party, the great Pushmataha, justified the raid because the goods were destined for his Osage enemies.

With the general westward movement of the American people after the War of 1812, both the population and the range of activity in the Three Forks area increased. Joining Joseph Bogy—the Chouteaus were temporarily absent—were merchants, hunters, salt manufacturers, and even farmers.

Among the newcomers was Nathaniel Pryor, a member of the famous Lewis and Clark expedition and a captain in the late war. Pryor, a native of Virginia, came to the Three Forks country after going bankrupt operating a trading house at Arkansas Post. He opened a small establishment near the mouth of the Verdigris, took an Osage woman as his wife, learned the Osage language, and won the confidence of the tribe. He was never a very successful merchant, but late in life he received an appointment as subagent for the Arkansas band of Osages. In that position he did much to mediate many of the Osages' disputes with their Indian neighbors.

Another notable resident at Three Forks was Hugh Glenn of Cincinnati. Glenn had made and lost a fortune as a banker and steamboat owner before opening a trading house on the Verdigris. George W. Brand, of Tennessee, and Captain Henry Barbour, of New Orleans, did business there as partners too. They brought with them considerable capital and constructed an elaborate property known as Verdigris Landing. It consisted of ten or twelve houses, several warehouses, a ferry, and thirty acres of cleared land. Profits from the fur trade were never as grand as Brand and Barbour hoped, however.

The Chouteau interests returned to the Three Forks area when Colonel A. P. Chouteau, the son of Pierre and a graduate of West Point, opened a post on Grand River at Salina in present Mayes County in 1817. Colonel A. P. had just completed a prison term in Mexico, his reward for taking trade goods across the plains to Santa Fe without Spanish authorization. Joseph Revoir managed the post for Chouteau admirably and even attempted (without success) to open a branch near Bogy's and Pryor's operations on the Verdigris.

When Revoir was killed in 1821 by a Cherokee raiding party, Colonel Chouteau came from St. Louis to assume management of the Grand River post. He immediately purchased the interests of Brand and Barbour near the mouth of the Verdigris, expanded them, and even added a keelboat construction operation. Fluent in the Osage language and the husband of "two or more" Osage women, for the next decade Chouteau reigned as the merchant prince of the Three Forks area.

In 1824, Chouteau shipped 38,000 pounds of furs

Colonel A. P. Chouteau dominated the Indian fur trade in early Oklahoma with posts at Three Forks on the Verdigris and at present-day Salina on the Grand River.

to New Orleans markets. Seven years later he sent only 14,684 pounds. The difference illustrated the changes that were taking place in eastern Oklahoma. The Osages and other Indian hunters were finding game scarce in the Three Forks region. Also, products other than furs were being shipped downriver, namely grain, salt, lead, beeswax, and pecans. Obviously the Three Forks economy was changing from hunting to agriculture.

Tom Slover illustrated the change. He had made his living as a commercial hunter at first. Then he had brought his family to eastern Oklahoma and built a log cabin, cleared a field, planted a crop, and bought a horse and cow. When Thomas Nuttall visited him in 1819 near Mazie, Slover had a "finely elevated and productive farm . . . well suited to the production of small grain." So Slover did not take furs to market anymore, just the grain he harvested from his own fields. And what was happening to Slover was happening to others in the Three Forks area and the Red River valley.

Santa Fe Traders

In 1819 the United States negotiated the Adams-Onís Treaty with Spain. This agreement finally defined the southern boundary of the Louisiana Purchase from the Gulf of Mexico to the Pacific Ocean. It was especially important to Oklahoma because it drew the common boundary between Spanish Texas and our state. Specifically, it set Oklahoma's southern boundary as the south bank of the Red River and its western boundary as the 100th meridian (see map on page 85). The language of the treaty was later very important in determining a complicated lawsuit with Texas during Governor William Murray's administration in the 1930s.

Spain negotiated the Adams-Onís Treaty in part to help ensure continued control of its Mexican provinces. The idea was to protect them from North American aggression by a well-defined boundary. But Spain's problem in Mexico was not external; it was internal. Two years after the Adams-Onís Treaty, Mexico declared its independence from Spain and made it stick. This had important implications for the traders and merchants at Three Forks and St. Louis because it offered hope that the new government might liberalize its trade policies and per-

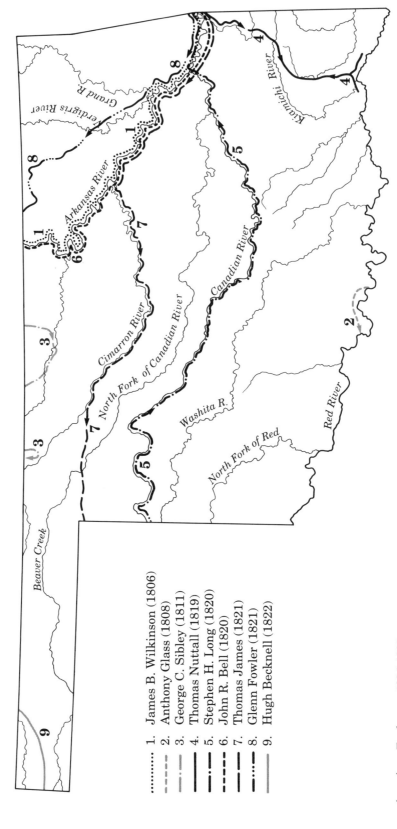

Grand R.

Verdigris River

Verdigris River

Arkansas River

Kiamichi River

Cimarron River

North Fork of Canadian River

Canadian River

Washita R.

North Fork of Red

Red River

Beaver Creek

1. James B. Wilkinson (1806)
2. Anthony Glass (1808)
3. George C. Sibley (1811)
4. Thomas Nuttall (1819)
5. Stephen H. Long (1820)
6. John R. Bell (1820)
7. Thomas James (1821)
8. Glenn Fowler (1821)
9. Hugh Becknell (1822)

American Explorers, 1806–1822

mit Americans to trade with Santa Fe and other Rio Grande settlements.

Peter Baum, a St. Louis trader, confirmed that something was afoot. Like Colonel A. P. Chouteau, he had been imprisoned in Mexico for importing trade goods to Santa Fe. Baum had escaped from his prison and had finally worked his way eastward along the Canadian River. Early in 1821 he arrived at Three Forks, told his story at Glenn's post, and then went on to St. Louis, where he told it again. His account encouraged the traders both at St. Louis and Three Forks to test whether or not new policies in Santa Fe would admit Americans.

Thomas James, an Indian trader with experience on the upper Missouri River, led the eleven-man St. Louis party. He took cloth, biscuits, flour, powder, lead, and whiskey as trade goods. Going in a keelboat, they reached Three Forks late in the summer of 1821. There they purchased horses and mules, intending to make the final crossing to Santa Fe overland.

The James company arrived at Three Forks just as Hugh Glenn and his partner, Nathaniel Pryor, were putting the finishing touches on their preparations to send a trapping and trading party to New Mexico. They had recruited twenty men from the Three Forks area (including Tom Slover), and they also had gathered horses, mules, and supplies. A member of their group was Jacob Fowler, a surveyor from Kentucky, who brought his brother and a black slave with him. Fowler kept the only journal of the expedition, and as a consequence historians usually refer to it as the Glenn-Fowler party.

Both the James company and the Glenn-Fowler party left the Three Forks area for New Mexico in September. Each followed different routes west. The Glenn-Fowler party went northeast from Three Forks through the Great Osage Prairie into what is now Kansas. There they followed the Arkansas River into present southeastern Colorado, stopping in the Pueblo area to trade with the Indians and to trap for beaver. Business was so brisk, and hunting was so good, that the Oklahomans soon had more pelts and furs than they could transport. Rather than going on to Santa Fe, in the following spring they recrossed the plains and sold their hides in St. Louis. From there they returned to Three Forks.

The James party followed the Cimarron River to some point in Major County and turned due west, crossing the North Canadian River near present Woodward. Along the way the column suffered much from lack of cooking fuel and drinking water. Fortunately the buffalo provided both: dried chips for fuel and blood to drink. In western Oklahoma, James and his party also encountered a large band of Comanches, who invited him to return the next year to trade with them. The Missourians pushed on west, ultimately encountering a Mexican army patrol, who informed them that new government policies had indeed opened Santa Fe for trade. In December they set up shop in Market Square. The following spring, they too returned to St. Louis, traveling for a time with the Glenn-Fowler party.

MAKING FIRE ON THE TRAIL

Finding fuel for fire on the treeless plains was an unexpected challenge for American explorers and trappers. Like the Thomas James party, they often resorted to the use of dried buffalo chips, or manure. Josiah Gregg, a trader along the Santa Fe trail, recorded that using "dry ordure" for fuel had both up and down sides:

On the night after the first buffalo scamper, we encamped upon a woodless ravine, and were obliged to resort to "buffalo chips" (dry ordure) for fuel. It is amusing to witness the bustle which generally takes place in collecting this offal. In dry weather it is an excellent substitute for wood, than [which] it even makes a hotter fire; but when moistened by rain, the smoldering pile will smoke for hours before it condescends to burn, if it does at all. The buffalo meat which the hunter roasts or broils upon this fire, he accounts more savory than the steaks dressed by the most delicate cooks in civilized life. (Josiah Gregg, *Commerce of the Prairies*, 237)

The Three Forks expedition reached Santa Fe only days after William Becknell, a livestock dealer out of Franklin, Missouri. Becknell, therefore, won the honor of being the father of the Santa Fe trade—but for more reasons than just being the first American to trade successfully in the Rio Grande settlements. In the following year, in 1822, he returned with large wagons filled with merchandise. The overland trail he pioneered cut across the Panhandle of our state. Over the next thirty years tens of thousands of Americans followed it to northern Mexico as merchants or settlers. If you visit Cimarron County today, you can still see the ruts of their wagons.

Meanwhile, life at Three Forks had nearly returned to normal. Neither of the Santa Fe expeditions had been very profitable. Hugh Glenn and Nathaniel Pryor focused their attention on their Verdigris trading posts. Thomas James and his partners orga-

Every American explorer who visited Oklahoma commented on its large herds of wild horses, and traders out of Three Forks and along the Red River wanted to capture and sell them. George Catlin captured the beauty and spirit of those animals in this 1834 drawing.

nized a trading expedition to the Comanches in the fall of 1822. They took $5,500 worth of merchandise by keelboat to the North Canadian River. Where the water was too shallow for navigation, the twenty-man party loaded its goods onto horses and into dugout canoes. James was much impressed with central Oklahoma. Near Spring Valley (probably northeast of Banner) in Canadian County he and his party erected a fort, but heavy rains caused them to move on upriver into present Blaine County. From the stockade they constructed there, James and his partners had a very successful trading season, taking in four hundred horses and mules and more buffalo hides and beaver pelts than they could carry to market.

What Is the Meaning?

In 1803 when the flag of the United States rose over Oklahoma very little was known of its resources. Official and unofficial scientific expeditions discovered much about the state, especially along the Arkansas, Cimarron, Canadian, and Poteau rivers. Hunters and traders operating out of Three Forks and along the Red River discovered even more. By 1825 the "nature and extent" of the land that is now the state—what Jefferson had set out to find—were reasonably well known, if not officially, then unofficially. Adjoined to "the Great American Desert" and bounded on two sides by the Republic of Mexico, the area was not likely to attract even the energetic American farmers. Given those prospects, Oklahoma was ideal as a resettlement zone for eastern Indians who, federal officials assumed, wanted to escape the pressures of civilization.

See History for Yourself

To get a sense of what American exploring parties saw when they followed Oklahoma's rivers, canoe the Arkansas River below Kaw Dam, the Cimarron between Guthrie and Perkins, and the Canadian between Taloga and Thomas (when it has water in it). Get a copy of Nuttall's journal (see "Suggestions for Further Reading") and retrace his ramblings between Little River and the Cimarron River.

Visit the Great Salt Plains at Jet in Alfalfa County and the Big Salt Plain west of Freedom in Woods County to see why they fascinated each explorer who saw them. Near Mazie in Mayes County visit the saltworks mentioned by Nuttall in his journal. Visit the Chouteau Memorial at Salina in Mayes County. Organize an exploring party to try to find the site of Thomas James's fort in Spring Valley (northeast of Banner) in Canadian County.

Suggestions for Further Reading

Reference

Flores, Dan L., ed. *Journal of an Indian Trader: Anthony Glass and the Texas Trading Frontier, 1790–1810.* College Station: Texas A & M University Press, 1985.

Foreman, Grant. *Pioneer Days in the Early Southwest.* Cleveland: Arthur H. Clark, 1926.

Fowler, Jacob. *The Journal of Jacob Fowler.* Edited by Elliott Coues. 1898. Lincoln: University of Nebraska Press, 1970.

Fuller, Harlin M., and Le Roy R. Hafen, eds. *The Journal of Captain John R. Bell, Official Journal for the Stephen H. Long Expedition.* Glendale, Calif.: Arthur H. Clark, 1957.

Goetzmann, William H. *Army Exploration of the American West, 1803–1863.* New Haven: Yale University Press, 1959.

———. *Exploration and Empire: The Explorer and the Sci-*

entist in the Winning of the American West. New York: Alfred A. Knopf, 1966.

James, Edwin, comp. *Account of an Expedition from Pittsburgh to the Rocky Mountains, 1819–1920.* Vol. 2., 1822–1823. Reprint. Ann Arbor: University Microfilms, 1966.

James, Thomas. *Three Years among the Indians and Mexicans.* 1846. St. Louis: Missouri Historical Society, 1916.

Nuttall, Thomas. *A Journal of Travels into the Arkansas Territory during the Year 1819.* Edited by Savoie Lottinville. Norman: University of Oklahoma Press, 1980.

Stout, Joseph A., Jr., ed. *Frontier Adventurers: American Exploration in Oklahoma.* Oklahoma City: Oklahoma Historical Society, 1976.

Related Reading

Gregg, Josiah. *Commerce of the Prairies.* Edited by Max L. Moorehead. Norman: University of Oklahoma Press, 1954.

Chapter 7: The Southeastern Indians

The name of our state, Oklahoma, is a Choctaw Indian word. The seals of five Indian nations—the Choctaws, the Chickasaws, the Creeks, the Seminoles, and the Cherokees—appear on the great seal of Oklahoma. From Atoka to Wewoka, countless place-names in the state originate with the Five Tribes. Today, nearly two-thirds of all the Indian people in our state are members of the Five Tribes.

How do we explain this close connection between Oklahoma and the Choctaws, Chickasaws, Creeks, Seminoles, and Cherokees? Primarily, it is because people of those tribes dominated the history of our state for most of the nineteenth century. They were the first to develop the land rather than just exploit it. They organized Oklahoma's earliest schools and churches, as well as its first constitutional government. In sum, the real pioneers of modern Oklahoma were not Spanish, not French, not European American; our pioneers were people of those Southeastern tribes. To help us appreciate their contribution, we need to know something about them before their arrival in Oklahoma.

Southeastern Indians

The Choctaws, the Chickasaws, the Creeks, the Seminoles, and the Cherokees lived initially in the southeastern United States. The map on page 107 will give you a sense of their general location about 1800. The Cherokees spoke a language similar to

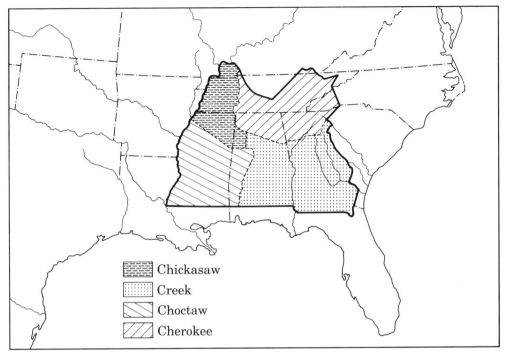

Homelands of Southeastern Indians, 1789

that of the Iroquois Indians of New York. The other four tribes belonged to the Muskogean linguistic family. Although their languages differed, all of the tribes held many beliefs and customs in common at the time of the arrival of Europeans.

Belief System

The Southeastern Indians believed that all living creatures and spiritual beings in the universe existed together in harmony. Everything—even directions, colors, and numbers—had purpose and significance. If tragedy occurred, Indians concluded that things were no longer in harmony.

There were three worlds in the universe. The perfectly harmonious Upper World was the residence of gods like the Sun, the Moon, Thunder, and Corn. Monsters and witches lived in the Under World, which was filled with chaos. Southeastern Indians lived in the third world, or "This World," which they conceived of as a flat island floating on water and hanging on four cords. This World benefited from fire, which was a gift of the Sun, but it was often troubled by the activities of spiritual beings from the Under World. These visitors from the Under World had to be treated carefully. If they were slighted, they might strike the offender with disease or even death.

The Southeastern Indians believed that ghosts were the source of great misery. When a person died, friends and relatives shouted and made noise to frighten the dead person's ghost up into the western sky. Unfortunately, the ghost did not always stay away but might return when it was lonely and haunt its relatives. In contrast, spirits known as the Immortals were friendly beings, who looked after tired hunters and helped defend villages from enemy attack. They were invisible except when they wanted to be seen. The Immortals lived on high peaks where no timber grew.

Ceremony

Five Tribes Indians believed that the universe was well ordered and that everything in it had a place and a role. So long as that delicate balance was maintained, things would go well for the individual and the community. If people or objects became polluted, then that order could turn into chaos. To avoid chaos and to restore harmony was the aim of ceremony. Certainly that was the purpose of the Green Corn Ceremony, the most important annual event for the Southeastern Indians.

The Green Corn, or Busk, festival was both a thanksgiving celebration and a quest for purity. As among the Wichita Indians, men fasted and purged their bodies by drinking a liquid, known as the black drink, that stimulated their central nervous system and might make them throw up. The climax of the ceremony was the lighting of a new sacred fire in the village plaza. From this flame women then kindled a new fire in their own home.

After dancing and feasting, everyone painted themselves with white clay. Then in a solemn procession led by the priests and chiefs, all walked to the nearest stream and washed themselves in the water. This symbolic cleansing marked the end of the Green Corn Ceremony. It signified also the purification of the people and the restoration of harmony.

Fashioned into a human figure, this Choctaw pipe was used on special ceremonial occasions when its tobacco smoke was blown toward the three divisions of the world or in the four cardinal directions.

CORN: A GIFT OF THE SPIRIT

As among other Native Americans, corn was sacred to the Southeastern Indians. The annual Green Corn, or Busk, ceremony illustrates its importance. Also, all of the Five Tribes preserved an account of how their people first got corn. The Choctaw story is set out below. Can you think of any stories in our culture that compare to it?

In the beginning the Choctaw people were hungry. "We have nothing to feed our little ones," cried the mothers. "And our old people are starving. They cannot chase the deer." The men of the council spoke: "We do not want to go with the buffalo. We have found the place where Choctaw Spirits can dwell and wish to be able to build our homes here."

The Spirits heard the Choctaws. The Indian had always followed the animals and had eaten the flesh of the beasts and birds. The Choctaws dreamed of a new way, a way which even the Spirits did not know. The food which the Choctaws wanted would be unlike any that the Indian had ever known.

One day birds came from the south. They flew over the place where the Choctaws were camped. What the birds carried in their claws and beaks was truly remarkable. This was unlike anything the Choctaws had ever known. The birds dropped this thing into the Choctaw fields.

Soon a beautiful and mysterious plant began to grow. Because of the long stalks, the green coating, and the silken covering, some said it was brought by a lovely woman. Others thought it was evil, sent by a wicked witch. But the wise men knew that it was corn, a gift of the Spirits brought on the wings of the birds.

And soon the Choctaws had a new life. They were no longer hungry. They no longer had to chase the beasts. Their journey was over and they could live in the place where the Choctaw Spirits had bought them. (Jack Gregory and Rennard Strickland, *Choctaw Spirit Tales* [Muskogee, 1972], 9)

Social Organization

The Southeastern Indians traced their relationships through women. As among the Wichitas, this meant that women owned the houses and land and it was their male relatives who disciplined the children. Matrilineage also dictated clan membership, since children became members of their mother's clan. Kinship even determined who your enemies were, who your friends were, and whom you would marry.

Young men and women could not marry someone within their own clan or kinship group. Marriages were often arranged by the mother's sister, but they were never forced on the couple. Ceremonies were quite simple. The young man went to the woods and killed a deer or bear to show that he could provide meat. The woman presented him with an ear of corn that she had cooked to show that she could provide vegetable food. With those exchanges, the couple was considered married.

Southeastern Indian men often had more than one wife. But they took another wife only with the permission of the first one and on the assumption they could afford the second one.

Political Organization

The Southeastern Indians lived in political units known as chiefdoms. The territory of a chiefdom could extend over several miles and contained at least one village, where residents would gather to discuss matters of common concern, play games, and participate in religious ceremonies. Often several chiefdoms joined together to form larger political units. These units might be divisions of tribes or tribes themselves. The Choctaw chiefdoms coalesced into three to five divisions that together comprised the tribe as a whole. Among the Creeks, however, some fifty or more chiefdoms, known as "towns," were virtually autonomous. Cherokee chiefdoms were independent too, although a National Council, composed of representatives from the chiefdoms, had some influence when the interests of all were involved.

A council of leading men chose the head of the chiefdom, generally from one of the more important clans. At their meetings each member of the council, seated according to his rank, listened politely to all speeches. The purpose of the council was to achieve a consensus of opinion and harmony of action. The objective was the same in district or national councils.

Economic System

Indian boys and girls never agonized about what they would do as adults. Men would clear land, construct buildings, make tools and weapons, hunt with a bow and arrows, and fish with spears, traps, nets, and hooks. They would also be warriors. Women would cultivate fields of corn, squash, and beans, gather wild foods, cook, manufacture baskets and pottery, tan hides, and make clothing. They would also bear the children. Women owned the food they produced and controlled the fields they worked. They did not, however, own the land. That belonged to everyone, or, more precisely, it was held in common by the chiefdom.

There was no money system among the Southeastern Indians. Goods changed hands in barter transactions where one Indian might swap grain for the meat of another Indian. Products also moved from person to person as gifts. Members of the Five Tribes were more impressed with generosity than individual wealth. They chose their leaders because of their willingness to share their possessions with the rest of the chiefdom. In turn, the leaders had an obligation to be generous, especially in the distribution of the fruits of a common hunt or harvest.

Games

All Southeastern Indians enjoyed playing games. The recreation they most enjoyed was a ball game. The ball was made of deerskin. Ball sticks were fashioned from hickory with a pocket at one end made of deerskin. The object of the game was to throw the ball through two goal posts at either end of a field. (See chapter 13 for an eyewitness account of a Choctaw ball game.)

Individual Choctaws played their unique brand of ball with a stick in each hand.

Chunkey was another popular game. It was played with a disc-shaped stone and a wooden lance. Two men played at a time. Each in turn rolled the stone and then, as it was just about to stop, threw his lance at it. The winner was the one whose lance struck closest to the stone.

War

War among the Southeastern Indians had similarities with war among the First People of Oklahoma. It was like a feud between rival clans, primarily motivated by revenge. They also went to war in groups of twenty to forty, their object being to kill by surprise attack. Five Tribes raiding parties usually went out in late spring, summer, or early fall. At other seasons the men were too busy hunting game to go to war. No parties were sent until the council of the chiefdom, district, or tribe had approved.

Most warriors were volunteers. Before leaving on raids, they purified themselves by fasting and purging their bodies. They painted themselves with red and black colors, signifying conflict and death. On the raid they wore only moccasins and a loin cloth, carrying with them a bag of cornmeal, a knife, a war club, a bow, and arrows. With a bow and arrow they were as proficient as the Wichitas.

When warriors killed an enemy, they sometimes cut off part of his scalp. This was later tied to a small hoop, painted red, and hung from the end of a long pole much like a trophy. Raiding parties often brought back captives, who were made slaves or tortured.

European Invasion

The Southeastern Indians remained uncorrupted in their natural ways until 1539. In that year Hernando de Soto and his expedition landed at Tampa Bay, Florida, and plundered their way across much of what is now the southeastern United States. In the course of his journey De Soto encountered all of the peoples we know now as the Five Tribes. He treated them all alike: with contempt and disrespect, demanding food, porters, and women. The Choctaws and Chickasaws fought bloody battles with the Spanish to force them to leave their lands.

De Soto left little permanent impression on the Southeastern Indians. That was not true of his fellow countrymen. In 1565, Pedro Menéndez de Avilés founded St. Augustine in Florida as a base from which to protect the Spanish treasure ships on their way from Mexico to Spain. Over the next 250 years St. Augustine became the center of Spanish activity in the domain of the Southeastern Indians. From there Franciscan missionaries established a vast network of missions that extended into Georgia and South Carolina. By 1650 these Catholic outposts ministered to 26,000 Indians, who in turn helped Spanish Florida defend its northern border from any hostile attack.

In due time other European powers challenged

Spain's domination of the American Southeast. England was the first to arrive. In 1670, British citizens settled what is now Charlestown, South Carolina, and moved immediately to take advantage of the fur trade. Trading parties made their way first to the Creeks and then as far west as the Chickasaws. They bartered the usual European goods for deerskins and Indian captives who could be sold as slaves. The British traders were remarkably successful. In 1707 alone, Southeastern Indians produced 121,000 deerskins for shipment to England.

The principal competitor of Britain in the fur trade was France. As we have seen, La Salle and other Frenchmen pushed into the lower Mississippi River valley in the late seventeenth century to claim it for their king. By 1699, France had permanent settlements on the Gulf of Mexico and was engaged in a fierce contest with both England and Spain to win control over the lands occupied by the Southeastern Indians. The struggle continued for a century.

Southeastern Indians as European Allies

In the international war for empire the Southeastern Indians were always major players. The competing powers needed them as both trading partners and auxiliary troops. In one capacity they made the quest for empire profitable; in the other, they made it possible. As matters sorted themselves out, both the Chickasaws and the Cherokees generally supported the British interests. The Choctaws lined up with first the French and then the Spaniards, always favoring whichever nation occupied New Orleans. The Creeks and Seminoles never chose one side over the other, but flirted with all three.

To win support of one chiefdom or another, Europeans used various techniques. A favorable trade arrangement was particularly important, but so too was the giving of gifts. Presents to a single chief won more than just one friend, for under obligations of generosity, he redistributed them through the chiefdom.

Properly staged diplomacy was equally effective. Negotiations with tribal delegations at New Orleans, Augusta, or elsewhere were always accompanied by the elaborate ceremony usually reserved for a king

Chickasaw warriors like Tishomingo repelled the French invasion of their homeland in the 1730s.

visiting a European court. A part of this was the presentation of medals two to four inches in diameter to symbolize the perpetual alliance with France, England, or Spain.

After a chief had been wooed and won with promises of trade, gifts, and medals, what did it mean to be an ally of one of the competitors for empire? Primarily it meant two things. First, trading activities were limited to allies alone. The Chickasaws, for example, admitted to their domain only traders out of South Carolina once they committed to Britain. Second, the Indians would support their allies with military assistance should the need arise. Unfortunately, that need arose almost constantly during the eighteenth century, and as a result the tribes were almost always fighting one another.

During the American Revolution (1775–83), the Southeastern Indians made peace among themselves and joined the British in opposing American independence. Cherokees, led by Dragging Canoe, attacked American settlements in eastern Tennessee, but then suffered devastating reprisals by troops from Virginia and South Carolina. The Chickasaws launched daring raids along the Mississippi River, attacking positions held by America's ally Spain. The Creeks carried out raids along the Georgia and South Carolina frontier, while the Choctaws attacked Pensacola for the British.

William McIntosh, the son of a Scotch trader and Creek Indian mother, was a successful cotton planter and tribal leader.

The involvement of the five Southeastern Tribes in the European quest for empire had costly consequences. The white-tailed deer, which once had supplied their villages with meat, no longer inhabited surrounding forests. They were killed off by greedy Indian hunters seeking hides to exchange for trade goods. Also, tens of thousands of warriors lay dead or injured because of participation in the century of imperial warfare. Thousands more were lost to the slave traffic and to diseases imported from Europe.

The European quest for control of North America worked as well to change the skin complexion and tribal power structure of the Southeastern Indians. Many of the European traders took Indian wives and fathered large mixed-blood families. These included the Hicks, Ross, Vann, Rogers, and Martin families among the Cherokees; the Le Flore, McCurtain, Pitchlynn, Folsom, and Harkins families among the Choc-

THE FRENCH-CHICKASAW WAR, 1736–1739

The Mississippi River valley was a crucial area of dispute in the wars for empire that raged in North America during the eighteenth century. To carry their flag in that area, England looked to the Chickasaws, while the French looked to the Choctaws. Better armed and more committed as warriors, the Chickasaws successfully dominated the Choctaws and made French commerce on the Mississippi extremely hazardous. In 1735 the governor of Louisiana, Jean Baptiste Le Moyne, sieur de Bienville, wrote to his superiors in Paris that "the entire destruction of [the Chickasaws] becomes every day more necessary to our interests and I am going to exert all diligence to accomplish it."

True to his word, Bienville made plans to send two large military expeditions into the Chickasaw domain. He would lead an attack from the south, while Major Pierre d'Artaguette of the Illinois country would attack from the west. In preparation for the campaign he stockpiled supplies, sent spies into the Chickasaw country, and ordered construction of a fort in the Choctaw Nation to provide cover for the attacking army. On April 4, 1736, Bienville left Mobile with a 600-man force that included French and Swiss regulars, local militia, volunteers, and 45 black slaves. Marching north-northwest

he reached the Choctaw Nation sixteen days later. There he added 600 warriors to his column.

In the meantime Major Artaguette had assembled an army of 400 men in the Illinois country. After gathering supplies, he took his command down the Mississippi River in boats to Chickasaw Bluffs at the site of present Memphis, arriving in early February. For twenty-one days he attempted to make a connection with Bienville's forces, who, unknown to him, had not yet left Mobile. Failing to do so, he determined to make good use of his army and to attack the Chickasaw town of Chocolissa. He would have been better advised not to have done so. The Chickasaws cut his command to ribbons. Only twenty escaped. The remainder, including the major and Father Antoine Sénat, were burned alive.

Unaware of this disaster, Bienville pushed on into the Chickasaw domain, arriving at the tribal town of Akia, near present Tupelo, Mississippi, in late May. After studying the Indian defenses, he ordered an attack on the afternoon of May 26. With flags flying and drums rattling, the French marched toward the Chickasaw defenders in classic European formation. Although they carried a forward palisade, a deadly cross fire checked any further advance. Three hours of bloodletting was

all that Bienville could stand, and he ordered his decimated army to retreat to the safety of the Choctaw Nation. The governor blamed his defeat in part on his Choctaw allies, who he said hid under the cover of a hill until the outcome of the battle of Akia was clear, "then rose and fired several volleys."

Three years later Bienville tried again to bring the Chickasaws to terms and to expel their British allies. He mustered an even larger army of 1,200 regular and militia troops and 1,500 northern and southern Indian auxiliaries (including Choctaws). He put together a small arsenal of cannon, grenades, and guns, as well as a large herd of packhorses. In all it was the largest military force ever assembled to meet an Indian adversary in the West. But it was to no avail, for the grand army got bogged down in mud at Chickasaw Bluffs. To salvage something from the expedition, Governor Bienville prevailed on the Chickasaws to accept a cease-fire and to exchange prisoners. Ignoring that the Chickasaws had chewed up three French armies, he claimed victory in the French-Chickasaw War— and then retreated downriver to Mobile.

For further information, refer to Arrell M. Gibson, *The Chickasaws* (Norman, 1971).

taws; the McIntosh, Grayson, Stidham, Porter, and Barnett families among the Creeks; and the Colbert, Pickens, Love, Harris, and Cheadle families among the Chickasaws. The intermarried white men usually opted for a European style of existence, established plantations, and introduced Negro slaves. In due time they came to exert more influence in the affairs of the chiefdoms than their number warranted.

New Masters

The Treaty of Paris (1783) ended the American Revolutionary War and established United States independence. One of the early challenges of the new national government was to make peace with the five Southeastern tribes. Early in 1786 it sent commissioners to meet with the leaders of the Cherokee, Choctaw, and Chickasaw nations at Hopewell in South Carolina. The Creek chiefs refused to participate in the negotiations because they were bitter at Georgia officials over previous treatment.

In the treaties concluded at Hopewell, tribal leaders agreed to peace with the United States and to recognize its dominion over them. The treaties also defined tribal boundaries and authorized cession to the United States of small tracts as sites for military and trading posts. In 1790 in New York City, Creek leaders agreed to essentially the same terms.

Civilization Program

The United States government dealt with the Indians much as it would have dealt with a European nation. It recognized each tribe as a sovereign community that conducted its internal affairs by traditional methods. If a change in relations between a tribe and the United States was required, a treaty was negotiated with tribal leaders by representatives of the president, and it was ratified by the United States Senate.

Congress gave the task of supervising Indian affairs to the secretary of war. That official in time assigned those responsibilities to a Bureau of Indian Affairs, headed by a commissioner. The commissioner had his offices in Washington, D.C., and left the daily interactions with the various tribes to field agents who actually lived among the Indians. The first of these agents, Benjamin Hawkins, was assigned to work among the Southeastern Indians in general and the Creeks in particular.

In relationships with the Indians, the goal of United States was quite simple. Its leaders wanted to transform the tribespeople so that they behaved like white Americans. The Indians were to set aside their natural life in the wilderness for one dependent on agriculture and domestic arts (spinning and weaving), facilitated by reading, writing, and arithmetic, and redeemed by the truths of the Christian religion. In other words, United States officials wanted to civilize the Indians and then assimilate them into American society.

Government leaders never questioned whether Native Americans could recast themselves into the images of white men and women. Indians and whites were equal "in body and mind," Thomas Jefferson insisted. Native society had not progressed to the same level as Anglo-American society because of environmental differences, not because of any genetic deficiencies. Civilization was just a matter of changing the environment, Jefferson believed, and changing the environment was just a matter of education.

United States Indian policy at the beginning of the ninetenth century was essentially an educational policy designed to "civilize" native Americans. Federal officials funded agricultural demonstration programs and encouraged Christian mission groups to establish schools and churches. Agents counseled the tribes on the importance of law and order and the need to formalize tribal governments.

Southeastern Indians and American Civilization

Native Americans responded to the civilization program differently. Some made it clear that they did not want any part of it. Others welcomed it, but not because they wanted to be assimilated into American society. Instead, they saw it as a way of preserving their tribal independence, for "civilized" people got more respect from the whites than did "savages." Certainly this was the response of the Southeastern Indians to the government's civilization program.

To win the respect of the outside world, the leaders of the Five Tribes set for themselves and their people a course of change. They proposed rapid adoption of the customs and habits of the Anglo-Americans (known as "acculturation"), they encouraged acceptance of Christianity, and they proposed centralization of tribal governments. The members of prominent mixed-blood families, of course, were most receptive to the changes. Indeed, they made up the leadership that proposed them. Yet support was not limited to the mixed-blood community. "Progressives," as they have since been labeled, came from every level of tribal society.

The transformation of the customs and habits of the Southeastern Indian peoples was readily apparent by 1830. As we look at the extent of some of those changes, compare and contrast them with the lifestyles that prevailed among their ancestors as described earlier in this chapter.

Economics

Early in the nineteenth century the economies of the Southeastern tribes changed from hunting and subsistence farming to herding and plantation agriculture. Indian families like the Pitchlynns (Choctaw) grazed large herds of cattle on pastures once covered by white-tailed deer. The McIntoshes (Creek) cleared large fields and planted cotton. The cattlemen and planters sold their calves and cotton crops to buyers in adjacent states. A substantial number reinvested the money they received in black slaves. George Waters (Cherokee), for example, possessed 100 slaves, while the Gunter family (Cherokee) owned 104.

As United States currency began to circulate within the tribal domains, Indians opened their own stores and trading posts. One of the most successful merchants was James Vann (Cherokee). Still others, like John Ross (Cherokee), built and operated ferries at crucial river crossings.

In the household, the introduction of spinning wheels and weaving looms changed the work patterns of many women. No longer did wives and daughters labor in the fields planting and tending the corn crop. Rather their days largely were spent in the house manufacturing cloth and sewing clothes.

James Vann, a successful Cherokee merchant, built this three-story brick house in northern Georgia in 1804.

Lifestyles

The pressure to "civilize" affected the lifestyles of most Southeastern Indians. The basic form of housing became the log cabin with either one or two rooms. If the structure had two rooms, the units were usually separated by a breezeway, or large hallway, and were covered with a gable roof. Such successful planters as James Vann (Cherokee) had houses that rivaled the mansions of wealthy white southern planters.

Clothing fashions also changed. Cotton shirts and pants generally replaced those made of deerskin. Moccasins were almost wholly abandoned in favor of shoes. Both men and women continued to wear their hair long, but many covered their heads with hats of felt and other materials. At the same time, many Cherokees, Creeks, and Seminoles continued to wear turbans as headgear.

Reading, Writing, and Arithmetic

Of all the Southeastern Indians the Cherokees were the most receptive to proposals from Christian missionary groups in the United States to establish schools among them. The Moravian fellowship founded Spring Place as early as 1804, beginning a mission work that lasted a century. Even more active was the American Board of Commissioners for Foreign Missions (known as ABCFM), a joint venture of the Congregationalists, Presbyterians, and Dutch Reformed Church.

The ABCFM began its work among the Cherokees in 1816. The following year it organized the Brai-

This image of George Lowrey, a prominent Cherokee leader in the 1820s and 1830s, reflects the changing fashions among the Five Tribes. Note both the cotton hunting shirt and the head turban.

nerd School and model farm in present Tennessee, where missionaries Daniel S. Butrick and Samuel A. Worcester became principal teachers. Within two more years Cyrus Kingsbury had opened the Mayhew and Eliot missions among the Choctaws in what is today Mississippi, and Cephas Washburn had established Dwight Mission among the Western Cherokees in present Arkansas. At its peak the ABCFM operated as many as eighteen schools among the Southeastern Indians and enrolled as many as six hundred students.

Methodist and Baptist organizations in the 1820s established schools among the Creeks, the Chickasaws, and the Cherokees. The Baptists also operated the famous Choctaw Academy in Blue Springs, Kentucky.

The objective of the mission schools was to teach students to read and write in English. That proved difficult to do, although there were notable exceptions. Students learned much faster if they worked with materials in their own language. That became possible for the Cherokees because of Sequoyah's creation of an alphabet, or syllabary (see chapter 14). Sequoyah's "letters" were used not only in instructional materials for the schools but also in the columns of the *Cherokee Phoenix*, a tribal newspaper launched in 1828. Later Samuel Worcester translated and published the Bible in Cherokee.

Religion

The Southeastern Indians, as a general rule, had little interest in the spiritual opportunities presented by the Christian missionaries. At first the Cherokees permitted missionary societies to open schools only if the teachers kept their religious convictions to themselves. Until 1822 the Creeks kept missionaries out of their domain. The Choctaws were so impressed with the Presbyterian gospel that ten years passed before there was a single convert among them!

The removal crisis of the 1820s and 1830s both helped and hurt the cause of Christianity among the Southeastern Indians. In despair Choctaws by the thousands attended both Methodist and Presbyterian camp meetings and professed belief in Christianity. On the other hand, the Creeks became stridently anti-Christian, attributing some of the

Cyrus Kingsbury established the first two schools and Christian missions, Mayhew and Eliot, among the Choctaws when they still resided in Mississippi.

pressure for removal to the missionaries. There was a similar feeling among the Cherokees.

In none of the Five Tribes did Christianity replace traditional Indian religion. The sacred fires continued to burn in most villages. What the Indians took from the missionaries they took on their own terms and adapted to their own needs and perspectives.

Government

The forms and functions of tribal government changed dramatically under the pressures of white civilization and the encouragement of a small group of wealthy mixed-blood Indians. In 1808 the first written law of the Cherokees established a police force that was to find, try, and execute criminals as well as assure the descent of property through the father's line. To make government more efficient, the Cherokees in the following year established an executive committee of thirteen members, and by 1817 the National Committee had become a powerful and independent executive body. Ten years later the Cherokee Nation adopted a written constitution modeled on that of the United States, creating a government with legislative, executive, and judicial branches.

The Cherokees even established a capital at New Echota, in northwestern Georgia. There they built a two-story log council house, a two-story clapboard supreme-court building, and a small log house for the printing press. The capital also featured a two-acre public square and a hundred building lots for homes, stores, and taverns. Streets were sixty feet wide.

The Cherokee Supreme Court building, restored at New Echota, Georgia, reflects the increasing commitment of the Southeastern Indians to constitutional government.

Meanwhile, in the summer of 1826, the Choctaws wrote their first constitution. It provided for a central government with an executive of three district chiefs and a council of elected representatives. Among its first laws were those ordering the construction of a national council house, providing for inheritance through the father's line, and discouraging plural wives. The Chickasaws began adopting written laws in 1829. The Creeks and the Seminoles did not enact written codes of law and establish constitutional governments until after removal to Oklahoma.

Resistance to Civilization

Not all Southeastern Indians embraced the civilization program, nor did they all see a need to change traditional habits. They preferred instead to continue in the old paths, planting small patches of corn, hunting whatever game they could find, maintaining the traditions of the clan, and remaining faithful to the sacred fire. Historians often call these people "traditionalists" and associate them with Indians who had no white ancestors, that is, with the "full-bloods." There were "mixed-blood" traditionalists, but they usually were aspiring leaders who adopted traditionalists' points of views mainly to win their political support. Chief John Ross of the Cherokees was one of those. Another was Alexander McGillivray of the Creeks.

The pressure to "civilize" met particularly strong resistance among the Creeks. Their traditionalists looked to William Weatherford for leadership and called themselves Red Sticks. In 1811, when the great Shawnee warrior Tecumseh came among the Southeastern Indians with the call to resist whites, the Red Sticks were receptive. Their common cause with Tecumseh involved them in the War of 1812 as an ally of Britain. American and Southeastern Indian troops defeated the Red Sticks at the battle of Horseshoe Bend in present Alabama. Thereafter, the opposition of the Creek traditionalists to the civilization program was more internal than external.

Although they were less militant, there was also strong resistance among the Cherokees to rapid "civilization." As early as 1794, The Bowl so objected to the new regime that he took several hundred followers and crossed the Mississippi River into Arkansas. Subsequent opposition expressed itself in the so-called Ghost Dance movement in 1811, and again in 1827 with the noted White Path Rebellion. White Path and his followers were particularly troubled by the constitutional government instituted by progressives like John Ross and The Ridge.

What Is the Meaning?

The Southeastern Indians had developed a remarkably sophisticated culture and lifestyle well before the arrival of the Europeans. Their three hundred years of interaction first with Spain, then with England and France, and finally with the United States caused the Indians to make dramatic changes in their traditional patterns of behavior. Some tribes, namely the Cherokees and the Choctaws, changed more than others, but all were affected. By 1830 it was difficult to tell the difference between a typical Indian farmer and a typical white frontier farmer.

The changes that had occurred among the Southeastern Indians were recognized widely in the United States. Everywhere there were references to the "Five Civilized Tribes." Today scholars are inclined to think that expression either belittles other Indian people in Oklahoma or implies superiority of European cultural traditions. Perhaps it does. Nonetheless, the phrase is useful because it reflects the healthy vitality of Choctaw, Chickasaw, Creek, Seminole, and Cherokee societies during the early nineteenth century. Incredibly they were able to make dramatic changes in their communities yet retain their identities as distinct peoples.

See History for Yourself

To glimpse the lifestyle of Oklahoma's Southeastern Indians in the seventeenth century visit the reconstructed Tsa-La-Gi Ancient Village at the Cherokee Heritage Center near Tahlequah and the Museum of the Red River at Idabel. On your summer vacation visit the southern Appalachian Mountains and see the reconstructed Cherokee capital at New Echota in north-central Georgia and the Museum of the Cherokee Indian and Oconaluftee Indian Village at Cherokee, North Carolina.

Suggestions for Further Reading

Reference

Berkhofer, Robert F., Jr. *Salvation and the Savage: An Analysis of Protestant Missions and American Indian Response, 1787–1862.* Lexington: University of Kentucky Press, 1965.

Cotterill, R. S. *The Southern Indians: The Story of the Civilized Tribes before Removal.* Norman: University of Oklahoma Press, 1954.

Henri, Florette. *The Southern Indians and Benjamin Hawkins, 1796–1816.* Norman: University of Oklahoma Press, 1986.

Hudson, Charles. *The Southeastern Indians.* Knoxville: University of Tennessee Press, 1976.

McLoughlin, William G. *Cherokees and Missionaries, 1789–1839.* New Haven: Yale University Press, 1984.

———. *Cherokee Renascence in the New Republic.* Princeton: Princeton University Press, 1986.

———. *Champions of the Cherokees: Evan and John B. Jones.* Princeton: Princeton University Press, 1990.

White, Richard. *The Roots of Dependency: Subsistence, Environment, and Social Change among the Choctaws, Pawnees, and Navajos.* Lincoln: University of Nebraska Press, 1983.

Wright, J. Leitch, Jr. *Creeks and Seminoles: Destruction and Regeneration of the Muscogulge People.* Lincoln: University of Nebraska Press, 1986.

———. *The Only Land They Knew: The Tragic Story of the American Indians in the Old South.* New York: Free Press, 1981.

Related Reading

Baird, W. David. *The Chickasaw People.* Phoenix: Indian Tribal Series, 1974.

———. *The Choctaw People.* Phoenix: Indian Tribal Series, 1973.

Caughey, John W. *McGillivray of the Creeks.* Norman: University of Oklahoma Press, 1938.

Green, Donald E. *The Creek People.* Phoenix: Indian Tribal Series, 1973.

Chapter 8: **Indian Removals**

President Thomas Jefferson, as we have seen, believed that the American Indian should be "civilized" and then assimilated into white society. Yet he also recognized that some Indian people would not or could not change their traditional lifestyles. In those cases—and there were far more than he thought there would be—Jefferson believed the group in question should relocate to some distant and protected region until it was ready to adopt new customs and habits. The place the president had in mind for this resettlement was Louisiana. Indeed, that was one of the reasons why he wanted the United States to purchase it in 1803.

During his administration Jefferson took every opportunity to encourage traditional Indians to remove to Louisiana. Several hundred Delawares and Shawnees, at his urging, moved from Ohio to northeastern Arkansas and from there to our state, establishing villages along the Canadian River near Allen in present Pontotoc County. Perhaps as many as 1,000 Choctaws crossed the Mississippi River to settle in the Red River valley and hunt as far west as Oklahoma. Chief Tahlonteskee and 300 Cherokees relocated in Arkansas, joining kinsmen who had been living there for more than a decade. By 1817 an estimated 6,000 Cherokees lived west of the Mississippi River, or approximately one-third of the entire tribe.

In urging eastern tribes to move west, President Jefferson did not recognize that other Indian peoples had prior claim to Louisiana. Among those, of course, were the Wichitas, the Apaches, the Comanches, and the Kiowas (recent arrivals) in the western part of Oklahoma, and the Osages in the eastern part of the state. These resident tribes viewed the emigrant Indians as intruders at best and as deadly enemies at worst. Competition for control of the same space quickly devolved into a full-scale war.

The Red War for the West

The Osages felt the brunt of the Indian invasion more than did any other western tribe. The several thousand emigrant Indians, although they claimed to be farmers, hunted for bear, deer, and other game in the Ozark Plateau of northwest Arkansas. When Osage hunting parties encountered these intruders, they attacked, robbed, and killed them. The reception was no different if the emigrants were found on the prairies hunting for buffalo. The Western Cherokees responded to these attacks in kind, but they also appealed to the federal government to provide protection for their settlements.

For United States officials the conflict was a matter of serious concern, as it threatened to undermine all efforts to get eastern Indians to remove west. By treaties in 1808 and 1816 (Lovely's Purchase) the United States was able to pacify the Osages, who ceded large tracts of land for the exclusive use of the emigrants. Consequently the Osages received gifts, cash payments, and cancellations of debts, which were meant to compensate them for the deaths of warriors lost in their clashes with the emigrant Indians.

Satisfying the Western Cherokees proved more difficult. They insisted that no treaty or payment would atone for the deaths of their kinsmen. What was required was blood revenge. Accordingly, in October 1817 some 500 Cherokees, joined by Choctaws and Chickasaws, marched on Clermont's village near present Claremore. There they found that the Osage warriors were away on their fall hunt. Undeterred, the Cherokees attacked the settlement, killing 83 Osages and taking 103 women and children as captives. Before leaving, the raiders stole what they could carry, destroyed caches of food, and set fire to the village. The Cherokees had taken their revenge.

INDIAN REMOVAL TO OKLAHOMA

Here is a chart to help you follow the events surrounding the removal of the Five Tribes to Oklahoma. It is best used as a reference if you need to check a date and follow chronology.

1803 President Jefferson purchases Louisiana as a potential home for eastern Indians.

1808 Osages cede most of Arkansas and Missouri.

1816 Lovely purchases land from the Osages to provide hunting grounds for the Cherokees.

1818 Osages formally cede Lovely's purchase. Quapaws cede to the United States all of southern Oklahoma below the Arkansas and Canadian rivers.

1820 Treaty of Doak's Stand: the Choctaws cede part of Mississippi and get all of southern Oklahoma below the Arkansas and Canadian rivers.

1825 Osages cede claims to all of Oklahoma above the Arkansas and Canadian rivers. Choctaws cede back the southwest quarter of modern Arkansas.

1826 Treaty of Washington, D.C.: Creeks cede Georgia lands in exchange for territory in central Oklahoma.

1828 Western Cherokees cede their Arkansas domain for one in northeastern Oklahoma, including the Outlet to the Plains.

1830 Treaty of Dancing Rabbit Creek: Choctaws cede all of their remaining Mississippi lands and remove to Oklahoma.

1832 Treaty of Pontotoc: Chickasaws cede all of their remaining Mississippi lands and remove to Oklahoma. Treaty of Washington, D.C.: Creeks cede all of their remaining Alabama lands and remove to Oklahoma. Treaty of Payne's Landing: Seminoles cede Florida lands for a home in Indian Territory.

1833 Fort Gibson Agreement: Seminoles agree to make their home with the Creeks.

1835 Treaty of New Echota: Cherokees agree to cede their eastern homeland and remove to the West. Treaty of Camp Holmes: Wichitas, Comanches, and Apaches agree to peace with the emigrant tribes.

1837 Kiowas agree to peace with the emigrant tribes. Treaty of Doaksville: Chickasaws find a home with the Choctaws.

Although not entirely unhappy with the massacre at Claremore Mound, the United States realized such Osage retaliations could be swift and general and that they would further impede eastern Indian emigration. To try to prevent more bloodshed, the secretary of war ordered the United States Army to move quickly with their plans to construct a fort on the Arkansas River near the Osage boundary. By

December 1817, Major William Bradford had begun construction of Fort Smith.

The establishment of Fort Smith did not end the Osage-Cherokee War. Despite another treaty in 1818

Aerial view of Fort Gibson, carefully restored according to the 1824 construction plans.

and promises of peace, the conflict continued, with isolated and general attacks involving both sides. To monitor Clermont's people more closely, the United States Army constructed Fort Gibson on the Neosho River in 1824 and assigned there five companies commanded by Major Matthew Arbuckle. Such a display of force impressed the Osages. Bowing to the inevitable, in the following year they ceded their claim to all land in Oklahoma and agreed to remove their villages to Kansas. Although Clermont's people lingered in our state for fourteen more years, the worst of the Osage-Cherokee War was over.

Anglo-American Infiltration

Conflict between resident and emigrant tribes was not the only hindrance to the Indian removal program. Anglo-American infiltration into the resettlement zone was also a major problem. The Western Cherokees, much to their dismay, found themselves incorporated into another territory of the United States in 1819. This time it was Arkansas. Choctaws and other potential emigrants found that white squatters, robbers, murderers, and moonshiners already controlled much of the Red River valley. Not until 1824, when the United States Army built and garrisoned Fort Towson in present Choctaw County, were these "banditti" forced from the region.

Not all white infiltrators were riffraff. Some came to provide European American forms of education and religion to both resident and emigrant tribes. In 1820 the United Foreign Mission Society of New York sent Epaphras Chapman and seventeen co-workers to establish a Protestant mission among the Osages. Known as Union Mission, it was situated near Mazie in Mayes County. The school opened there was the first in Oklahoma. The society subsequently organized a second mission a few miles farther north, known as Hopefield. Both were abandoned in 1837.

Simultaneously the ABCFM established Dwight Mission among the Western Cherokees in Arkansas. Under the supervision of Cephas Washburn, it was so well received that the board soon opened a second church and school, known as Mulberry Mission. When the Western Cherokees relocated into what is now Oklahoma in 1828, Washburn reestablished Dwight Mission at a site northwest of Sallisaw in Sequoyah County. Mulberry Mission was renamed Fairfield Mission and opened just southwest of present Stilwell in Adair County.

Removal by Enticement

While the United States Army struggled in Oklahoma to eliminate obstructions to the removal program, government officials elsewhere labored to implement it. Like President James Monroe, most had concluded that the civilization of the Indians could not be accomplished in the territories where they resided. Yet few wanted to forcefully eject the tribes from their ancestral homes because that would be, said the president, "revolting to humanity, and utterly unjustifiable." Rather, they would prefer to entice the Native Americans to take up homes voluntarily in the West.

How do you induce eastern Indians to move west of the Mississippi? Monroe and his associates would begin with an exchange of land whereby eastern tribes would cede a portion of their domain and receive in return a larger estate in the West. By and by, they believed, traditional tribespeople would naturally migrate to those lands because they were beyond the influence of white authority. Their progressive kinsmen would then be free to assimilate into "civilized" society and open the ancestral domain to Anglo-American settlement.

Cherokees

Removal by enticement was first tried on the Cherokees. The several thousand of their number who had migrated to Arkansas at the encouragement of the United States lived on lands to which they had no legal claim. Government officials were able to assign a clear title to them in 1817, but the Western Cherokees never had undisturbed possession of the land. Although it was included in the Territory of Arkansas two years later, daily disputes with land-hungry white settlers occurred afterward. A new centralized government led by Principal Chief John Jolly, the brother of Tahlonteskee, enabled the Western Cherokees to defend themselves effectively in these controversies. Yet it was a frustrating struggle, and one not calculated to entice Eastern Cherokees to remove to the West.

United States officials sought to address the problem in 1828. In that year the Western Cherokees exchanged their Arkansas lands for territory that now encompasses thirteen counties in northeastern Oklahoma. In addition, they received a perpetual outlet fifty-seven miles wide that extended to the 100th meridian, that is, to the modern western border of Oklahoma except for the Panhandle. This new domain was to belong to the Cherokees "forever" and was never to be "placed . . . [under] the jurisdiction of a Territory or State."

The Treaty of 1828 provided other benefits. The United States promised to remove all white persons from the new Cherokee Nation, compensate the Western Cherokees for their Arkansas improvements, and pay for the general inconvenience of moving. The government also agreed to buy the nation a printing press with Sequoyahan type and to grant the Western Cherokees money for ten years to support tribal schools. Finally, the treaty provided that, for any Eastern Cherokees who wished to migrate west, the United States would pay the cost of removal and subsistence for one year.

Upon settlement in Oklahoma in 1828, the Western Cherokees established their capital at Tahlonteskee just east of Gore. The reconstructed courthouse near the site of the original structure reminds us of the political sophistication of the Western Cherokees and reflects the architectural style of the 1820s and 1830s.

Most of the 3,000 or so Western Cherokees moved to northeastern Oklahoma within a year. They took up homes along the Illinois River and established their capital at Tahlonteskee just east of present Gore. Sam Houston joined them there and for a while lived with a Cherokee woman before he moved on to Texas. Sequoyah also came, to share with them the good news of his "talking leaves." Other Eastern Cherokees came for visits or short stays, although only a few were enticed to remove to Oklahoma permanently.

Choctaws

In the meantime federal officials were trying to induce the Choctaws to exchange a part of their eastern domain for a tract in the West. In 1820 they finally succeeded. Tribal leaders at the Treaty of Doak's Stand agreed to exchange 5 million acres of their Mississippi lands for 13 million acres in what is now the southern half of Oklahoma and the southwest corner of Arkansas. In addition to educational benefits and funds to support the light horse, a mounted police force, the treaty provided for a resident agent in the West and promised assistance to those Choctaws who would emigrate to the new domain.

The treaty outraged the citizens of Arkansas. The portion of their state assigned to the Choctaws was already heavily settled by white frontiersmen and even organized into counties. Intense political pressure caused federal officials to renegotiate the eastern boundary of the Choctaws' domain in 1825, setting it at a line due south from the Arkansas River beginning at a point 100 paces west of Fort Smith.

In the following year, the federal government appointed an agent for the Choctaw Nation West. He constructed buildings for his agency about fifteen miles southwest of Fort Smith at what was later known as Skullyville, in Le Flore County. He and other officials encouraged scattered bands living in Louisiana and Arkansas to reassemble in the new tribal domain. By 1829 only about 150 Indians had responded to the invitation.

Creeks

Removal officials had better success with the Creeks. Initially, the Creek leadership rejected all proposals that they exchange eastern for western lands. Indeed, in 1824 the National Council of the Creek confederation adopted a law imposing the death penalty on any person who signed away tribal lands without the approval of the council. But pressure to do so was intense, especially in Georgia. In response, William McIntosh, a chief of the Lower Creek towns, convened a tribal council at Indian Springs in 1825, where United States commissioners proposed again that the Creeks exchange their Georgia lands for ones in Oklahoma.

Again the chiefs of the Upper Creek towns, led by Opothleyaholo, rejected the proposal. McIntosh, however, and other "progressive" chiefs of the Lower Towns signed the treaty. They argued that the salvation of the tribe depended on its moving west. But "traditionalists" were deeply offended, and the law was clear. On April 29, 1825, about 100 warriors surrounded McIntosh's home, set it on fire, and when heat and flames forced the chief to the door, shot him to death.

When he learned of McIntosh's execution, President John Quincy Adams refused to proclaim the controversial treaty. Instead, in 1826 he called a Creek delegation to Washington to renegotiate the matter. This time the National Council authorized its delegation, led by Opothleyaholo, to cede the Georgia lands if necessary. Perhaps a land exchange would avert a civil war between the supporters of McIntosh and those who opposed him. At least it would encourage the McIntosh faction to remove, which would leave the rest of the tribe in peace. The delegates, therefore, agreed to exchange all Creek lands remaining in Georgia for new ones situated in Oklahoma between the Arkansas and Canadian rivers. Those who removed west would do so at federal expense, receive an additional $100,000 in compensation, and be assisted on arrival by a full-service agency.

Because of the tension among the Creeks themselves, removal to the West moved quickly. Within two years nearly 2,400 emigrants, primarily from the Lower Towns, had taken up settlements near present Tullahassee in Wagoner County. The government purchased A. P. Chouteau's trading post on the Verdigris River to house the agency. But the goods promised to the Indians by the treaty were not delivered for two years, causing unnecessary hardship among the emigrant party.

Andrew Jackson and Indian Removal

By 1830 the government's program of removal by enticement had attracted no more than 6,000 members of the Five Tribes to Oklahoma. That response was not what federal officials had anticipated nor what white settlers in the southern states had demanded. A new president, Andrew Jackson of Tennessee, determined to address the problem. In 1830 he had Congress pass legislation known as the General Removal Act, which provided for the relocation of eastern tribes to new homes in the West. It made no difference to the president that the Cherokees, the Choctaws, and others of the Five Tribes were rapidly adopting the lifestyles and institutions of the whites. Assimilation of the Indians was no longer the goal; acquisition of their ancestral land was.

David Folsom, a prominent Choctaw leader, opposed tribal removal until pressure from federal and state governments forced him to consent.

Choctaw Removal

President Jackson applied the provisions of the General Removal Act first to the Choctaws. Under the leadership of David Folsom and other mixed-bloods, the Choctaws had adopted European-American lifestyles, opened schools, centralized their government, and introduced Christianity. But Mississippi authorities saw all of that as a challenge to their authority, and they acted to abolish the tribal government and subject the tribespeople to the laws

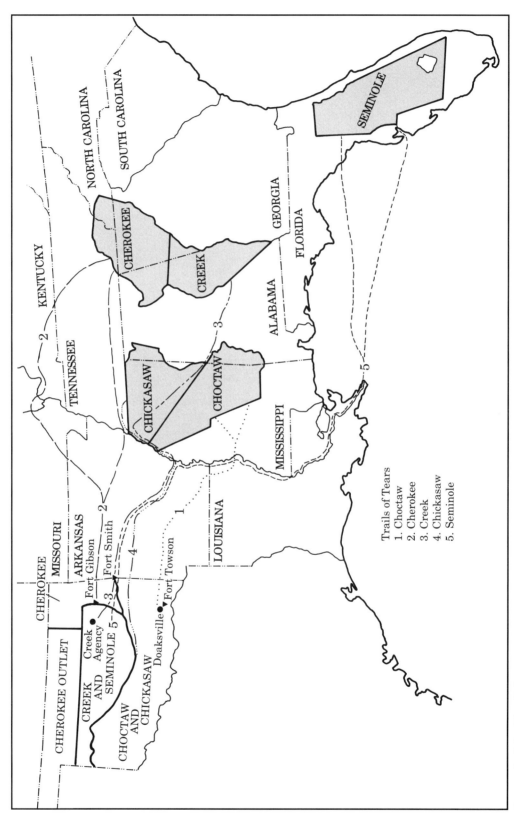

Removal of the Five Tribes

of the state. Weary of Mississippi's harassment, the Choctaw leadership agreed to meet with United States commissioners at Dancing Rabbit Creek in 1830 to discuss removal.

The result of the negotiations was predictable. The Choctaws agreed to cede all of their remaining ancestral lands and remove to the Choctaw Nation West in Oklahoma. They received no payment for the cession, but the government did promise to compensate them for improvements, to pay the cost of transportation to the West, to provide subsistence for a year after removal, and to give additional support for education. The United States also guaranteed that in the West the Choctaws would never be included within the limits of any state or territory and would be free to govern themselves.

The principal Choctaw removals to Oklahoma took place during 1831, 1832, and 1833. Under the direction of government agents and contractors, the Choctaws made their way to the Mississippi River by wagon, horseback, or foot. There they were put on steamboats and taken to points on the Arkansas, Ouachita, and Red rivers from which they proceeded overland to Fort Smith or Fort Towson. Low water and cold weather plagued the first party of emigrants; limited transportation, insufficient food, and cholera decimated the second group. In all, the estimated 11,000 Choctaws who removed during the three years suffered immeasurable misery, uncounted loss of lives, and ruinous destruction of property.

Chickasaw Removal

United States commissioners did not reach agreement with the Chickasaws on a removal until 1832. Then by the terms of the Treaty of Pontotoc the tribe ceded its domain to the United States government, which would in turn survey and sell it, paying the proceeds to the tribe. The Chickasaws would remove to the West at their own expense, but only after they located a suitable new home. Although it took five years, they found that home among the Choctaws, who, for a payment of $530,000, agreed to admit the Chickasaws to full citizenship in their nation. They also set aside a district for the newcomers in the western portion of their domain, the title to which would be held by both tribes.

INDIAN RESPONSES TO REMOVAL

A Creek response:

When we left our homes the great General Jesup told us that we could get to our country as we wanted to. We wanted to gather our crops, and we wanted to go in peace and friendship. Did we? No! We were drove off like wolves . . . lost our crops . . . and our people's feet were bleeding with long marches. . . . We are men . . . we have women and children, and why should we come like wild horses? (Grant Foreman, *Indian Removal: The Emigration of the Five Civilized Tribes*, 176)

A Choctaw response:

We have gone to the West
You will say tis for the best,
We shall never think it so
We shall never think it so.

(W. David Baird, *Peter Pitchlynn: Chief of the Choctaws* [Norman, 1972], 48)

A Cherokee response:

We are now about to take our final leave and kind farewell to our native land[,] the country the Great Spirit gave our Fathers. . . . We are forced by the authority of the white man to quit the scenes of our childhood, but stern necessity says we must go. . . . We know that it is a laborious undertaking, but with firm resolutions we think we will be able to accomplish it, if the white citizens will permit us. (Gary Moulton, ed., *The Papers of Chief John Ross* 1:687 [Norman, 1985])

A Chickasaw response:

With the exception of the Creek nation I expect there never has been such frauds imposed on any people as the Chickasaws, but we look with confidence to the President of the United States to see that every treaty stipulation is complyed with. (Grant Foreman, *Indian Removal: The Emigration of the Five Civilized Tribes*, 202)

Two Seminole responses:

I concluded to die, if I must, like a man.

Give me a jug of whisky for I have lost sight of the last hummock on my land.

(Virginia Bergman Peters, *The Florida Wars*, 137 and 135)

Removal of the Chickasaws began almost immediately. At least two groups crossed the Mississippi River at Memphis and, because of the large amount of stock (including 5,000 horses in one herd), went overland to the Choctaw Nation. One large party went by steamboat up the Arkansas River to Fort Coffee. By early 1838 almost all of the 4,900 Chickasaws and their 1,150 slaves had relocated in Oklahoma. There they took up new homes along the western border of the Choctaw Nation near present Boggy Depot.

Creek Removal

Federal officials had long harassed the Creeks to cede their remaining lands in Alabama. Fed up and disheartened, Opothleyaholo and other Creek leaders negotiated the Treaty of Washington in 1832 with United States commissioners. The terms of the treaty dissolved the Creek Nation in Alabama and gave tribal members the option of either joining their kinsmen in Oklahoma or staying in Alabama. If they

The Trail of Tears as painted by Doug Maytubbie, a Choctaw artist.

went west immediately, the government would pay removal and subsistence expenses. If they stayed in Alabama, they would live under state law on specific land allotments. The Creeks could sell those tracts whenever they wished and remove at their own expense. By staying on them for five years, they would receive full title. The treaty also granted the Creeks an annuity of at least $10,000 for twenty years.

Most Creeks elected to take allotments and stay in Alabama. It was a disastrous decision. Not understanding what it meant to own land individually, they were soon dispossessed of it. After four years of abuse, eighty-four-year-old Chief Eneah Emarthla led a protest rebellion that left some white settlers dead and a lot of property destroyed. To bring peace to Alabama, President Jackson sent the United States Army.

The so-called Creek War of 1836 lasted only a few months. The rebels quickly surrendered or joined the Seminoles in Florida. Those that gave up were then placed in chains and with their families were marched ninety miles to where they could board steamboats bound for Oklahoma. At dockside, one man cut his throat in despair. The remainder of the Creeks, none of whom had supported the rebels, were told they had to remove to Oklahoma too.

No tribe suffered more than the Creeks on the trek west. Some went in chains, and all suffered from extreme heat and cold, from inadequate clothing, from dysentery and cholera, from shortages in food, and from overcrowded conditions. One small boat sank, with the loss of 311 Creek lives. Perhaps 3,000 others died during the course of the removal process.

A JOURNAL OF EVENTS

United States Marine Corps Lieutenant J. T. Sprague had responsibility for conducting a party of 2,287 Creeks of the Kasihta and Coweta towns to Oklahoma in the fall of 1836. The party set out from Chambers County, Alabama, on September 5; it arrived at Fort Gibson on December 10. Including 45 wagons and 500 ponies, the train covered 800 miles by land and 425 by water. Along the way 29 people died, one-half of whom were small children. Sprague's final report of his assignment is a compelling document. What follows are excerpts from it:

The necessity of their leaving their country immediately was evident to every one; although wretchedly poor they were growing more so every day they remained. A large number of whitemen were prowling about robbing them of their horses and cattle and carrying among them liquors which kept up an alarming state of intoxication. . . .

The marches for the first four or five days were long and tedious and attended with many embarrassing circumstances. Men, who had claims upon these distressed beings, now preyed upon them without mercy. Fraudulent demands were presented and unless some friend was near, they were robbed of their horses and even clothing. . . .

Our marches were long, owing to the great scarcity of water; no one time, however, exceeding twenty miles. The Indians in large numbers straggled behind, and many could not get to Camp til after dark. . . .

At Memphis we remained from the 9th of October until the 27th. The assembling of thirteen thousand Indians at this one point, necessarily made our movements slow. This detention was of advantage to the Indians as it gave them rest and afforded the sick and feeble an opportunity to recover. . . .

A mutual agreement was effected . . . to take the party up the Arkansas river to Little Rock. . . . The boats stopped at night for them to cook and sleep, and in the morning, resumed the journey.

The sufferings of the Indians [after leaving Little Rock] were intense. With nothing more than a cotton garment thrown over them, their feet bare, they were compelled to encounter cold, sleeting storms and to travel over hard frozen ground. . . .

We arrived at Fort Gibson on the 10th inst. By the order of Brigadier General Arbuckle I encamped the party in the vicinity of the Fort. . . . After the Indians had received their blankets in compliance with the treaty, I proceeded with the larger portion of them to the country assigned them. Thirty five miles beyond Fort Gibson I encamped them upon a prairie and they soon after scattered in every direction, seeking a desirable location for their new homes. (Grant Foreman, *Indian Removal: The Emigration of the Five Civilized Tribes*, 166–75)

Nearly 15,000 Creeks made it to Oklahoma in 1836. They were met by as many as 2,500 McIntosh, or Lower, Creeks who had established their farms along the Arkansas River northwest of Muskogee. The newcomers, mostly Upper Creeks, made their homes along the Canadian River and consented to integrate themselves into the existing political and social structure.

Seminole Removal

The same year that Creeks and Chickasaws signed treaties of removal, so too did the Seminoles. The

Seminoles were closely related to the Creeks and probably once were a part of the Creek confederation. Residing in Florida, southern Georgia, and Alabama, they were town dwellers with chiefs and councils. Each town usually had adjacent to it a settlement of "black Indians" whom the Seminoles claimed as slaves but treated as equals. In 1832, thirteen years after they first came under the jurisdiction of the United States, federal officials persuaded them to sign the Treaty of Payne's Landing. Its terms obligated the tribe to remove to Oklahoma when a suitable home could be found, but within three years. The federal government agreed to compensate the tribe $15,400 for the land they surrendered in Florida and pay their removal costs, a year's subsistence, and a $3,000 annuity for fifteen years.

Micanopy, principal chief of the Seminoles.

A delegation of Seminole chiefs and headmen went to Oklahoma the following year. The McIntosh Creeks, prodded by the Stokes Commission (see below), invited the Seminoles to make their home along the western border of their nation. The delegation agreed that the land was satisfactory, although it apparently had no intention of committing the Seminoles to remove to it. The marks of the members on a vague Fort Gibson agreement, however, were interpreted by federal officials as a firm commitment to make the desired move. The majority of the Seminoles did not see it that way.

Osceola, for example, had no intention of leaving Florida. He and his followers killed one of the signers of the Fort Gibson agreement and later ambushed a United States Army patrol, killing 110 soldiers. In so doing, Osceola triggered a general Seminole War that lasted until 1842. During the course of it, he was taken prisoner in violation of a truce agreement and died in chains. Wildcat and Billy Bowlegs continued the struggle, but to no avail.

Between 1836 and 1842 some 3,500 Florida Seminoles, both black and white, removed to Oklahoma. Under Chief Micanopy, who was assisted by his shrewd black interpreter, Abraham, the Seminoles settled in villages near Fort Gibson. It was nearly a decade before they moved out to what are now western Hughes and Okfuskee counties.

Cherokee Removal

The last of the Five Tribes to sign a treaty of removal was the Cherokees. The mixed-blood leadership of the tribe—John Ross, The Ridge, Charles Hicks—had hoped to avoid tribal removal by recasting the tribe into the image of white society. The rapid acculturation failed to impress the Georgians; in fact, it irritated them. Their legislature responded by abolishing the tribal government and declaring all Cherokees subject to state law. Moreover, it required all white people residing among the Cherokees to hold permits from state authorities. But none of this caused the Cherokees to consider removal.

In 1831, Georgia arrested ABCFM missionaries Samuel A. Worcester and Elizar Butler for not having the proper permits to teach and preach among the Cherokees. The state court quickly convicted and imprisoned them, whereupon the missionaries appealed their case to the United States Supreme Court. The next year Chief Justice John Marshall issued his famous *Worcester* v. *Georgia* decision vindicating both the missionaries and the Cherokees. The state, said Marshall, had no authority to execute its laws within an Indian nation protected under the treaty clause of the Constitution. Since the decision of the court put an Indian tribe beyond the reach of a state law, President Jackson refused to enforce it. The Cherokees were heartsick, but they still refused to consider removal.

Ignoring the decision of the U.S. Supreme Court, the state government of Georgia surveyed the Cherokee domain and then disposed of the choice properties by a lottery. Tribal leaders lost their homes to lucky ticket winners. The Georgia militia also marched to the offices of the tribal newspaper, *Cherokee Phoenix*, and smashed the printing press. With those outrages, some Cherokees began to consider removal.

Leaders like The Ridge, his son John, and his nephews Elias Boudinot and Stand Watie decided that the Cherokees could not survive as a people under the continued harassment of Georgia and the United States. "We can never forget these homes," The Ridge told the National Council, "but an unbending, iron necessity tells us we must leave them . . . and go beyond the great Father of Waters."

Major Ridge (*left*) and John Ross (*right*) were the principal leaders of the Eastern Cherokees. Ridge came to accept removal to Oklahoma as necessary for the preservation of the Cherokees; Ross always opposed it.

On December 29, 1835, The Ridge and nineteen of his supporters signed the Treaty of New Echota. The Cherokees agreed to sell their eastern lands for $5 million, they were given joint ownership with the Western Cherokees in the tribal estate in Oklahoma, and they were obligated to remove within two years. The treaty required the federal government to pay the cost of removal and subsistence on arrival. It also directed the purchase of a strip of territory in present southeastern Kansas to be known as the Cherokee Neutral Lands.

Chief John Ross and his full-blood followers considered the treaty a work of treason and refused to recognize it. Even when some 2,000 members of the Ridge party, or so-called Treaty party, migrated peacefully to Oklahoma, Chief Ross told his supporters that they would not have to go. As the two-year deadline approached, therefore, the Ross party had made no preparations to remove. At that point President Martin Van Buren ordered United States troops to round up the Indians and forcibly relocate them in Indian Territory.

Gathering the Indians into stockades at three collection points was a nasty business, both for the army and the Cherokees. Not until then did Chief Ross and other traditionalist leaders accept that the federal government was deadly serious about removal. Ross hastened to propose that the Eastern Cherokees assume responsibility for their own relocation to Oklahoma. Even though the costs would double and the government would lose control of expenditures, the army granted the request and stepped out of the picture. Thereafter Ross organized the 13,149 Cherokees into thirteen travel parties of approximately 1,000 each and dispatched them sequentially overland to Oklahoma. Most left in September 1838.

For the Eastern Cherokees the march west was truly the "Trail of Tears." Along the way they were harassed by whites, they suffered much from lack of food and clothing, and they were ravaged by sickness. About 13 percent died on the journey itself, primarily the very old and the very young. The greatest loss of life occurred in the year after removal, however, as the Eastern Cherokees struggled to reestablish themselves in a new and not always friendly land. But that ordeal was not unique to the Cherokees. The Choctaws, the Creeks, the Seminoles, and to a lesser extent even the Chickasaws had also followed trails of tears to Oklahoma.

The Stokes Commission

Making Oklahoma a resettlement zone for Eastern Indians was not always a tidy undertaking for the federal government. Boundaries between the different tribes were often fuzzy, the Plains tribes were not enthusiastic about having thousands of emigrants as neighbors, and Clermont's Osages still refused to abandon their villages on the Verdigris. To address some of those problems and to smooth the ongoing removal process, President Jackson appointed a three-member commission in 1832 and sent it immediately to Indian Territory.

Chaired by Montfort Stokes of North Carolina, the commission arrived at Fort Gibson early in 1833. There it found that the United States Army had placed at its disposal three companies of Mounted Rangers commanded by Major Henry Dodge. One of the companies had just returned from a reconnaissance of the Cimarron and Canadian rivers. Unknown to the commissioners, that particular patrol would receive world attention because of the published accounts of three civilians who accompanied it: the noted American writer Washington Irving and two prominent Europeans, Charles Latrobe and Count Albert-Alexandre de Pourtalès. For the time being, the Stokes Commission left the Rangers in their barracks and turned their attention to other matters.

Among these was the question of the overlapping borders of the domains granted by treaty to the different tribes. The Senecas and the Shawnees, two Ohio tribes, had been assigned lands that actually fell within the Cherokee Nation. The commission renegotiated their earlier treaties and allocated them lands in what is now the northeastern corner of Oklahoma. It also concluded a treaty with the Quapaws, natives of Arkansas, which granted them lands north of the Senecas and the Shawnees. The commission was able as well to persuade the Cherokees and the Creeks to define their common boundary to the satisfaction of both parties.

It was much more difficult to work with the Osages. Despite the provisions of earlier treaties, Clermont's people refused to join their kinsmen in Kansas. Their continued presence irritated the Cherokees and the Creeks, who complained that the Osages stole their horses and vandalized their property. Every attempt on the part of the Stokes Commission to get them to commit to removing to Kansas was scorned. Indeed, in the midst of the discussions, the Osages nonchalantly packed their belongings and went west to hunt buffalo.

On their hunt they took more than meat. Intersecting a Kiowa trail, Osage warriors followed it to Cutthroat Gap in the Wichita Mountains in northwest Comanche County. There they found an undefended village with only women, children and old men present. The warriors ransacked and burned the village, and then killed and scalped 100 Kiowas, putting their decapitated heads in brass kettles. Others they took captives.

The success of their Kiowa raid did not make Clermont's people any more willing to leave their Verdigris homes. Yet it did provide the Stokes Commission with an opening to the tribes on the Southern Plains. The commission purchased a Kiowa captive girl, Gunpandama, as well as a Wichita boy, with the intention of returning them to their tribes. That gesture of goodwill, the commission hoped, would encourage the Kiowas, the Wichitas, and the Comanches to sign treaties of peace with the United States and the emigrant Indians.

To emphasize the seriousness of its mission, the commission determined to deliver the captives in the company of a large military column. The troop would be made up of a new kind of mounted infantry unit, known as dragoons, and commanded by

The First U.S. Dragoon Regiment, 1836–51, stationed at Fort Gibson, helped broker a peace between resident and emigrant tribes in Oklahoma during the 1830s.

General Henry Leavenworth. The unit was impressive in both appearance and leadership. Its blue and grey uniforms were highlighted with gold epaulets and braid, patent leather belts, and plumed hats. Henry Dodge, Stephen Watts Kearny, Nathan Boone, and Jefferson Davis served as Leavenworth's junior officers.

Five hundred young troopers, the pride of the United States Army, rode out of Fort Gibson in June 1834. The scorching heat quickly took its toll. By the time the column had reached the Washita River in present Marshall County nearly one-half of the command was ill, including General Leavenworth. Leaving the sick behind, some 250 troopers pushed on under the leadership of Colonel Dodge. On July 21 they finally reached the large village of the Wichita Indians at Devils Canyon, southeast of Lake Altus in Kiowa County.

The Wichitas, Kiowas, and Comanches were impressed by the dragoons, even though the command had shrunk to less than 200. They were overjoyed when Dodge ceremoniously returned to them the two captives he had brought. After further negotiations, the leaders of the three tribes promised to maintain the peace and to come to Fort Gibson for formal treaty negotiations. That pledge made the mission a success, but it had been achieved at a high price. Some 150 dragoons had died in the Oklahoma heat, including General Leavenworth.

The Wichitas and the Comanches, true to their promises, came to Fort Gibson in the fall. Yet treaties with them and other Plains tribes were not signed until the next year at Camp Holmes, near present Lexington in Cleveland County. By those agreements, the Plains tribes agreed to live in peace with their new neighbors, the five Southeastern tribes, and to allow free passage of persons crossing the buffalo range on their way to New Mexico. The Kiowas signed the same treaty two years later.

The task of the Stokes Commission and the officers and men of Fort Gibson was to make Oklahoma a safe zone for the peaceful resettlement of Indians from east of the Mississippi River. When Clermont's

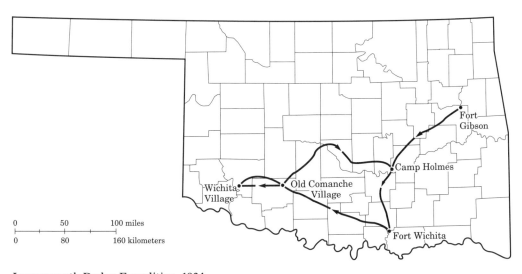

Leavenworth-Dodge Expedition, 1834

people finally dismantled their lodges and moved northward into Kansas in 1839, it could be said that the commission had completed its task.

What Does It Mean?

From the vantage point of one and one-half centuries, it is difficult to look at the removal epoch and not see it as anything other than an example of man's inhumanity to man. In Oklahoma history it is that, but also much more. Every society has at least one creation account, a story that helps define it to itself and to others. The removal epoch is Oklahoma's creation account. From it we mark the beginning of many of those qualities that characterize us as a people: greed, fraud, and insensitivity as well as generosity, resiliency, and hope.

The removal epoch also speaks to how Oklahoma is perceived by the world at large. United States officials saw it as a place that could serve the interests of the national government by providing a resettlement zone for eastern Indians. Oklahoma was a resource to be used, in much the same way that England used the American colonies.

Seeing History for Yourself

Visit the Cherokee Courthouse complex near Gore in Sequoyah County to get a sense of the architecture and the government of eighteenth-century Indian emigrants to Oklahoma. Explore Claremore Mound in Rogers County and see if you can identify where Clermont's village was situated. Visit Old Fort Smith, in Fort Smith, Arkansas; the reconstructed Old Fort Gibson, in Cherokee County; and the ruins of Fort Towson, in Choctaw County, to appreciate the work and lifestyle of army troops stationed in Indian Territory. Hike into Devils Canyon southeast of Lake Altus to the location of Major Dodge's council with the Wichita Indians, and up to Cutthroat Gap in northwest Comanche County, where the Osages took revenge on a Kiowa camp.

Suggestions for Further Reading

Reference

Agnew, Brad. *Fort Gibson, Terminal on the Trail of Tears.* Norman: University of Oklahoma Press, 1980.

Bearss, Edwin C., and Arrell M. Gibson. *Fort Smith, Little Gibraltar on the Arkansas.* 2d ed. Norman: University of Oklahoma Press, 1979.

De Rosier, Arthur H., Jr. *The Removal of the Choctaw Indians.* Knoxville: University of Tennessee Press, 1970.

Foreman, Grant. *Indians and Pioneers.* Norman: University of Oklahoma Press, 1936.

———. *Indian Removal: The Emigration of the Five Civilized Tribes of Indians.* Norman: University of Oklahoma Press, 1932.

Green, Michael D. *The Politics of Indian Removal: Creek Government and Society in Crisis.* Lincoln: University of Nebraska Press, 1982.

Peters, Virginia Bergman. *The Florida Wars.* Hamden, Conn.: Archon Books, Shoe String Press, 1979.

Prucha, Francis Paul. *The Great Father: The United States Government and the American Indian.* Abridged ed. Lincoln: University of Nebraska Press, 1986.

Thornton, Russell. *The Cherokees: A Population History.* Lincoln: University of Nebraska Press, 1990.

Wilkins, Thurman. *Cherokee Tragedy: The Ridge Family and the Decimation of a People.* 2d ed., rev. Norman: University of Oklahoma Press, 1986.

Woodward, Grace Steel. *The Cherokees.* Norman: University of Oklahoma Press, 1963.

Related Reading

Gibson, Arrell Morgan, ed. *America's Exiles: Indian Colonization in Oklahoma.* Oklahoma City: Oklahoma Historical Society, 1976.

Irving, Washington. *A Tour on the Prairies.* Edited by John Francis McDermott. Norman: University of Oklahoma Press, 1956.

Latrobe, Charles Joseph. *The Rambler in Oklahoma: Latrobe's Tour with Washington Irving.* Edited by Muriel H. Wright and George Shirk. Oklahoma City: Harlow Publishing Company, 1955.

Van Every, Dale. *Disinherited: The Lost Birthright of the American Indian.* New York: William Morrow, 1966.

Unit 3: **THE DEVELOPMENT OF OKLAHOMA**

Introduction

The great majority of the people who lived in Oklahoma after 1830 had not chosen to live there voluntarily. To them Oklahoma was less a home than just a place to be—and not a terribly favorable place at that. That it became a home at all is due to their remarkable efforts. It became home, and therein is a story, one with two sides. On one side was the tragedy of racism and removal; on the other, the triumph of persistence and courage.

The people who experienced both soon found themselves confronting yet another story that also had two sides. This time the two sides made war on each other, and Oklahoma's new population took part in that. The peace that brought an end to one war seemed only to begin another one—a whole series of wars, in fact. When those ended, Oklahoma gained still more people. They too had not chosen to live there voluntarily.

These are the stories that we now are ready to tell.

Chapter 9: **The Five Republics**

Thomas Farnham was impressed. In 1839 he had left his native England to explore the vast expanses of North America and to be amused by its "savages." His trip had gone according to plan until he got to Indian Territory and was given a copy of the Choctaw Nation's new constitution. What he saw moved him almost to poetry: "At the time when the lights of religion and science had scarcely begun to dawn upon them . . . they read on all the holy battlements, written with beams of living light, 'all men are, and of right ought to be, free and equal.' This teaching leads them," he concluded, "to rear in the Great Prairie wilderness a sanctuary of republican liberty."

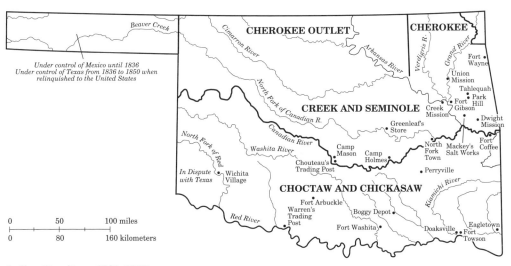

Indian Territory, 1830–1855

Governmental Reconstruction

The English romantic probably read too much into the document, but Farnham's basic assumption was correct: the Choctaws and others of the five Southeastern tribes cherished their right to govern themselves. They had no more than arrived in Indian Territory, as a matter of fact, before they were at pains to reorganize their tribal governments along lines similar to those that existed in the East.

Choctaw National Government

Young and ambitious, Peter Pitchlynn was one of the principal authors of the Choctaw constitution of 1834, which was Oklahoma's first constitution.

The nearly 13,000 Choctaws wrote a constitution that was the second for them but Oklahoma's first. On June 3, 1834, tribal representatives gathered at Nanih Waiya near Tuskahoma in present Pushmataha County to draft a document that envisioned a government with three branches. It delegated legislative authority to a unicameral, or single, council of ten representatives who came from each of three districts and met annually. It vested executive power in three district chiefs who were elected for four years and sat together. Three appointed judges composed the judiciary, while eighteen elected light horsemen had responsibility for law enforcement. The constitution also contained a bill of rights and extended suffrage to all males sixteen years of age and over. All things considered, it was an impressive piece of work, and once implemented, it restored political authority west of the Mississippi to the Choctaws themselves.

Chickasaw National Government

The Chickasaws benefited from the Choctaws' governmental experience. The 4,900 Chickasaws who came to Indian Territory after 1837 expected to become citizens of the Choctaw Nation. They were assigned a specific district in which to settle and given the right to participate on an equal basis in the established Choctaw government. But within a decade they found this minority status restrictive. In 1855 they negotiated a treaty with the Choctaws that permitted them to create an independent nation of their own. In the following year they drafted their own constitution, creating a government almost identical to that of the Choctaws and establishing their capital at Tishomingo in Johnston County.

Cyrus Harris was elected as the first governor of the Chickasaws.

Cherokee National Government

Establishing constitutional government was relatively easy for the Choctaws and the Chickasaws, but not for other tribes. When the 11,500 Cherokees led by John Ross arrived in Indian Territory early in 1839, they were met by John Jolly and other leaders of the 5,000 Western and Treaty-party Cherokees, who invited the newcomers to participate fully in the established government that centered at Tahlonteskee. Ross declined and insisted that the old settlers should join with the emigrants to write a new constitution. When the Western Cherokees demanded that their government should take precedence, Ross and the Eastern Cherokees blamed their obstinacy on the hated Treaty party.

What followed was almost predictable. Apparently unknown to John Ross, his supporters invoked the law of blood revenge. On June 22, 1839, Major Ridge, John Ridge, and Elias Boudinot—all signers of the Treaty of New Echota—were brutally assassinated. Stand Watie immediately organized members of the Treaty party to avenge the deaths of his uncle, cousin, and brother. For seven long and exhausting years a blood feud existed between the two factions.

Although Ross had contributed to the disorder, he desired unity for the tribe rather than division. At his call, the Cherokees gathered in July to organize a new government for all the tribe. Not many Western Cherokees came, but the venerable Sequoyah took a leadership role. On July 12, 1839, the convention adopted a formal "Act of Union," which declared that the Eastern and Western Cherokees were "one body politic." The following September another convention drafted and adopted an organic law similar to the constitution of 1827. In June 1840 a third convention, this time with the Western Cherokees participating, ratified the document and set Tahlequah as the tribal capital. Significantly, this constitution remained in place for the next sixty-six years.

Educated in New England, a brilliant linguist and the editor of the *Cherokee Phoenix*, Elias Boudinot (Buck Watie) was assassinated on June 22, 1839, for having signed the Cherokee removal treaty of New Echota.

Creek National Government

The Creeks had no tradition of constitutional government when they arrived in Indian Territory.

Like the Cherokees, they too had come in two different groups—the treaty party, or Lower Creeks, in 1826 and the Upper Creeks ten years later. But unlike the Cherokees, the more than 15,000 late arrivals agreed to defer to the leadership of the 2,500 Western Creeks, namely, to Roley McIntosh. Moreover, they also consented to take up homes in a more remote district of their new homeland, assuring the continuation of the dual division of the tribe.

Government among the Creeks was decentralized, reflecting the importance of the nearly fifty towns that comprised the confederation. Each town recognized a hereditary principal chief, or "king," and a second chief. In addition to local duties, the king represented the town in the regional Upper Town or Lower Town council as well as at the National Council. The chiefs of both the Upper Town and the Lower Town districts presided over their separate councils but sat together during National Councils. Organized in 1840, the National Council met at "High Spring" just north of Hitchita in McIntosh County.

In 1859 representatives of both the Upper and the Lower Creeks joined to produce the tribe's first written constitution. It perpetuated the two-part division of the tribe, including the dual executive, but departed dramatically from tradition by making the positions of chief—town and divisional—elected. As principal chief, the Lower Creeks elected Motey Kennard, while the Upper Creeks selected Echo Harjo.

Seminole Tribal Government

Of all the Five Tribes, the Seminoles had the least organized government—and for a very good reason. Federal officials intended that the 4,000 or so Florida natives who were removed to Indian Territory would become a part of the Creek Nation. But the Seminoles refused to cooperate with the plan, fearful that the Creeks would rob them of their slaves and of their identity as a people. Eventually, in 1845, the Seminoles won permission to settle as a group on Little River and to live according to their own laws.

For them, as among the Creeks, the basic governmental unit was the town, of which the Seminoles had twenty-five. Towns had their own chiefs and councils of warriors and often acted independently of each other. Chief Micanopy spoke for the Seminole Nation as a whole, advised by an annual summer meeting of the town chiefs and leading men.

The little autonomy that the Seminoles exercised did not satisfy all of them. In 1849 national councilor Wildcat and former slave John Horse organized a party of Seminole, Creek, and black warriors to establish an Indian colony south of the Rio Grande in Mexico. Anxious to prevent a mass exodus, especially by their slaves, the Creeks finally consented to Seminole independence in a treaty signed in 1856. By its terms, the smaller tribe was given its own domain in the West, to which it promptly moved. Under the leadership of a new chief, John Jumper, the Seminoles reestablished their towns and constructed a national council house near present Trousdale in Pottawatomie County.

Economic Reconstruction

As the Five Tribes reestablished their governments in Indian Territory, they also sought to reconstruct their economies. For the traditionalists that meant selecting a new farm site, clearing small fields out of the timber, and planting patches of corn, beans, potatoes, peas, pumpkins, and melons. Many also planted fruit trees. It was difficult labor, especially when floods one year and drought another wiped out the crops. Most did not plant for the commercial market, but these farmers were so proficient that they often produced surpluses that were sold to military garrisons (from Fort Smith to Fort Washita) and in border towns.

Other tribespeople selected farm sites in the lowlands along such major rivers as the Red, the Washita, the Arkansas, the Canadian, and the Verdigris. With the help of slave labor, they cleared and cultivated the fields, which they promptly planted to cotton. The harvest from those fields was then marketed in New Orleans and sometimes in Cincinnati, on steamboats owned by the Indian planters. Robert M. Jones of the Choctaws was one of the more successful cotton growers. He controlled five large Red River plantations, owned more than 500 slaves, and operated his own steamboats.

Choctaw Robert M. Jones was one of Indian Territory's most successful planters and merchants.

A Different Kind of Slavery

Slavery had been introduced among the Five Tribes well before they were removed to Indian Territory. At the time of removal the Cherokees owned more slaves—nearly 1,600 in all—than any other tribe. In the West the institution grew rapidly among all the tribes, so that by 1860 there were more than 8,300 slaves in Indian Territory, representing 14 percent of the total population. Less than one out of every ten Indians owned slaves, however.

Among the Five Tribes slavery was different from what it was elsewhere in the American South. It rested more easily on the bondsmen held by the Creeks and the Seminoles, whose slaves lived on individual farms, accumulated personal property, acted as interpreters, and moved about with relative freedom. Often there was intermarriage between the African Americans and the Indians despite laws forbidding it. The peculiar institution was more restrictive for Cherokee, Choctaw and Chickasaw slaves, but for them too it was less demeaning than among white plantation owners.

Slavery may have been easier in Indian Territory, but it still meant the absence of freedom for those involved. In 1842, thirty-five Cherokee slaves belonging to Joseph Vann and other slave holders ran away from their quarters and fled west toward Mexico. They were captured and returned to their plantations before reaching freedom. "Uncle" Wallace Willis and "Aunt" Minerva, slaves of Choctaw owners, expressed their longing for freedom by composing the spirituals "Swing Low, Sweet Chariot" and "Steal Away to Jesus." The freedom for which they longed did not come until 1865.

$20 REWARD.

RANAWAY on the 21st September last, from the subscriber, living on Grand river, near the mouth of Honey creek, Cherokee Nation, a negro man named ALLEN, who is about 25 years old; about 5 feet 2 or 3 inches high; very black; has very white eyes; rather a stoppage in his speech when speaking; and a wen under his thigh. When he left he had on a plaid shirt and copperas colored pantaloons; and also, marks of the whip, inflicted before he came into my possession.

Any person arresting and returning the said negro to me or lodging him in jail so that I can get him, will receive a reward of twenty dollars.

PETER HILDEBRAND.
Cherokee Nation, Oct. 22—2w.

The offer of a reward for the capture of Allen, a run-a-way slave, should remind us that slavery was essentially a denial of freedom. The advertisement was published in the *Cherokee Advocate* on October 23, 1845.

Ranching

In addition to subsistence and plantation agriculture, the Five Tribes engaged in significant amounts of stock raising. On the prairies of their domain the Creeks ranged large herds of both cattle and hogs. In 1846 they sold 1,000 of the latter as far away as Indiana. The Chickasaws were famous for their distinctive horses, and for the large herds of cattle, sheep, and goats that grazed their open fields. In 1859, Cherokee stockmen pastured 24,000 head of cattle and 20,000 head of horses and mules.

Some Five Tribes people depended on the hunt for part of their food. Fortunately for them, the forest was filled with white tailed deer and smaller animals. For larger game, some even journeyed to the plains in search of buffalo, although that effort was more for sport than for food.

Commercial Development

Simultaneously with the revival of agriculture, a thriving commerce evolved. Annuity payments and the profits from agriculture were used to purchase goods imported by enterprising Indian merchants and licensed white traders. These included Elijah Hicks among the Cherokees, G. W. Stidham among the Creeks, Robert M. Jones among the Choctaws, and Benjamin Franklin Colbert among the Chickasaws. Some tribespeople, like Cherokee Jesse Chisholm, traded regularly with the different tribes that roamed the western side of our state.

Indian merchants centered their operations in towns that grew up at strategic locations. The list of these commercial centers is long, but among the most important were Tahlequah in the Cherokee Nation, North Fork Town in the Creek Nation, Doaksville in the Choctaw Nation, and Pontotoc in the Chickasaw Nation. Most shops were located on a single main street; small houses were clustered behind. Each town had its own United States post office, and two had their own newspapers (the *Cherokee Advocate* at Tahlequah and the *Choctaw Intelligencer* at Doaksville).

Transportation Network

No systematic transportation network connected these commercial centers in Indian Territory. Goods and people followed the wagon roads and trails constructed by the United States military in the 1820s and 1830s, which linked the different forts, especially Fort Smith with Fort Towson. Even heavier traffic flowed along the famous northeast-southwest Texas Road (currently U.S. Highway 69 and the Missouri, Kansas, and Texas Railroad tracks). Most of those who followed those roadways were headed

ON GROWING WITH THE LAND

Charles Fanning Stewart was born in Connecticut in 1814. When he was sixteen years old he left New England for New Orleans, where he took a position working for a firm of wholesale merchants, remaining with it for five years. In 1841 he was in Doaksville, Choctaw Nation, clerking for one of the merchants in that community. His salary was $1,200 per year and also included board and room. The following year he married Tryphena Wall, a member of a very prominent Choctaw mixed-blood family, who had been educated in ABCFM mission schools. By virtue of his marriage to Tryphena, Charles became a citizen of the Choctaw Nation. Mr. and Mrs. Stewart moved to Mayhew, a hamlet just north of Boswell in Choctaw County, and opened a general merchandise establishment.

The Stewarts prospered in their new location on the road between Fort Towson and Fort Washita. He built a fine house, "one of the handsomest places in this District," and a new store. Within a year he was able to purchase two slaves for $1,100, and a herd of seventy-five cattle, fifty-five hogs, and ten horses. He was sorry, he wrote his mother, that he had not married sooner, "for when I was single I sought every means but the right to make me happy without success." In 1845 the Stewarts owned, in addition to their store, a tavern, five slaves, and 400 to 500 head of cattle, horses, and hogs. He was, he said, "a tolerable big bug for this country."

In July 1849, Tryphena Stewart died, leaving four small children and a deeply bereaved husband. He buried her in the Doaksville cemetery under a slab with the simple marking "Tryphena's Grave." Four months later Charles Stewart married again. His business continued to prosper. Two years later he was able to buy the steamer *Sun* to carry his own freight upstream from New Orleans. Then about 1855 tragedy struck again. The Stewart Store at Mayhew caught fire, and Charles rushed to save his safe from the fire. He never recovered from the exertion, and he died within the year.

south toward Stephen Austin's Texas rather than to a destination among the Five Tribes.

In the 1850s two new trails were established to accommodate people and goods passing through Oklahoma. One of these was the familiar east-west route that followed the Canadian River. Marked clearly by Josiah Gregg, a prominent Santa Fe trader, in 1839, it was surveyed officially on two subsequent occasions by the United States Army. Captain Randolph B. Marcy first evaluated it as an overland route to California goldfields, and in 1853 Lieutenant A. W. Whipple assessed it as a possible route for a transcontinental railroad. This interest on the part of the government made the so-called California Trail a major east-west thoroughfare across the domains of the Five Tribes before the Civil War.

Another road passing through our state to California was the Butterfield Overland Mail route. Established

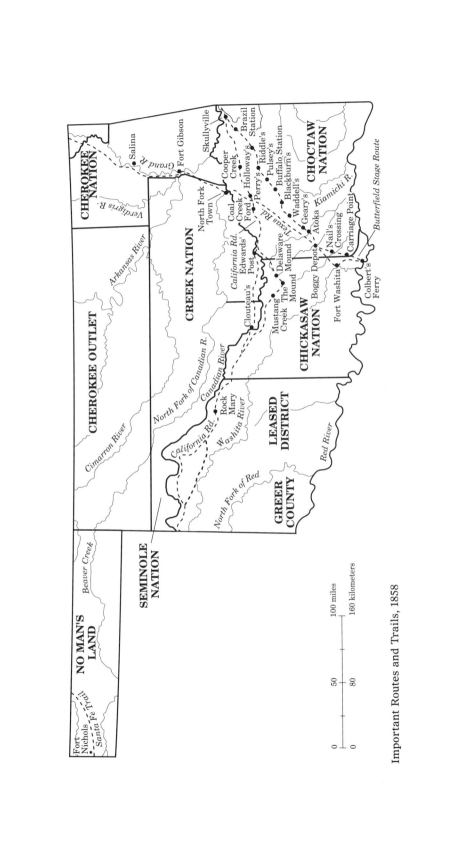

Important Routes and Trails, 1858

in 1859 to connect St. Louis with Los Angeles, this road entered Oklahoma at Fort Smith and made its way southwest to Colbert's Ferry on the Red River. Along it horse-pulled Concord coaches carried passengers and the United States mail twice each week, stopping at fourteen different stations within the Choctaw Nation to change horse teams and to give weary travelers some rest. The trip across Oklahoma took forty-five hours. When the Civil War broke out, the stage company closed its operations in Indian Territory, but the route itself continued as a major transportation artery linking Arkansas and Texas.

But overland traffic was not nearly as important to the commercial life of the Five Tribes as was

Steamboats became the preferred method of commercial transportation to and from Indian Territory after 1828. They remained important through the 1880s, as this photograph of two stern-wheelers at Webbers Falls indicates.

river transportation. Only the Red and the Arkansas River were actually navigable, although larger craft could occasionally get into some of the deeper tributaries. The goods destined to go up-river to the Indian nations after 1820 came first in keelboats and ultimately in steamboats. In 1828 four stern-wheeler riverboats—the *Velocipede*, the *Scioto*, the *Catawba*, and the *Highland Laddie*—reached Fort Gibson, making it the head of navigation on the Arkansas River. Between Fort Gibson and Fort Smith the boats stopped at twenty-two different landings. On the Red River successful navigation required removal of a 150-mile logjam (the "Great Raft"), but in the 1840s stern-wheelers pushed regularly to the mouths of the Kiamichi and Wichita rivers.

HOW IT WORKS: MOVING A KEELBOAT UPSTREAM

Keelboat men moved their craft up the Arkansas and Red rivers in a variety of ways. If the wind was right, and it seldom was, sails were hoisted to propel the boat. Where the current was slow, the crew used oars,

and where the bottom was firm, they could pole the boat. But the current was often swift and the bottom was often soft, and the crew spent most days cordelling—which was more like skinning a mule than piloting a boat.

To cordel a boat, as many as twenty men stepped ashore and pulled the vessel upstream with a towline—the cordelle. The line was tied to the top of the mast to lift it clear of bushes along the bank. The men on shore did not have the benefit of paths. They crashed through underbrush, scrambled across steep bluffs, and slopped through muddy shallows.

When both banks were impassable, they resorted to warping: a small skiff would take the cordelle upstream several hundred feet, where the cordelle would be anchored to a tree, and then the crew on the keelboat would reel it in, pulling the craft to the tree.

By cordelling and warping, keelboats could cover about ten to fifteen miles per day, but it was "a distinctly pedestrian mode of navigation."

(Paul O'Neil, *The Rivermen* [New York, 1975], 64)

Manufacturing

In their western domains the Five Tribes engaged in limited yet significant industrial activity. Dynamic members of the tribe operated grist- and sawmills, while others established saltworks and cotton gins. Some even entered into contracts to manufacture spinning wheels and looms for government distribution among the Indians.

Reestablishment of Religious Life

As the Five Tribes rebuilt their economy, they also sought to resume a meaningful social life. The religious observances and guidance that took place before their removal to Indian Territory continued in their new homelands. Traditionalists rekindled sacred fires and retained their faith in the power of secret medicines. At least annually they gathered to renew clan ties, to honor their elders, to participate in sacred dances, to take "medicine," and to light new fires. These gatherings were widespread and involved substantial numbers of Oklahoma's newest residents. What we know about them, however, is minimal, primarily because participants were reluctant to commit their faith and practices to the writing system of whites.

Because its adherents left written records and because it was the victor in the battle of religions, we know much more about Christianity. Among the most influential missionaries were those sent by the American Board of Commissioners for Foreign Missions. As we have seen, the ABCFM sent its first missionaries among the Five Tribes when they still lived in the East. With removal, its workers followed their converts to Oklahoma, reestablishing Presbyterian congregations and organizing new ones. By 1860 some 500 ABCFM workers had served in Indian Territory.

Two of the most noted missionaries in American history served in ABCFM stations in Indian Territory. One of these was Cyrus Byington, who worked among the Choctaws at Stockbridge Mission near present Eagletown in McCurtain County. The other was Samuel A. Worcester, who ministered to the Cherokees at Park Hill just southwest of Tahlequah. Byington converted the Choctaw language to written form, while Worcester printed millions of pages of material in both the Cherokee and the Choctaw language. Other venerable ABCFM missionaries included Cyrus Kingsbury at Pine Ridge near Fort Towson in Choctaw County and Alfred Wright at Wheelock just east of Valliant in McCurtain County. Wright was Byington's coworker in learning the

Wheelock Church, organized in 1832 among the Choctaws, is Oklahoma's oldest Christian church. The building (*below right*) was constructed in 1846. Harriet Bunce Wright (*below left*) was the partner of her husband, missionary Alfred Wright, who ministered to the congregation at Wheelock, in the task of providing the Choctaws with a written language.

Choctaw language. The Presbyterian church he organized in 1832 is the oldest in our state; the stone building constructed in 1846 still stands.

The Foreign Mission Board of the Presbyterian Church also was active among the Five Tribes. Robert M. Loughridge and William S. Robertson, along with their wives, served as both ministers and educators among the Creeks at Koweta (now Coweta) and at Tullahassee, just north of Muskogee, while John Bemo, John Lilly, and J. Ross Ramsey and their families did similar work among the Seminoles at Oak Ridge, southeast of Holdenville. The board also administered and staffed major schools among both the Choctaws and the Chickasaws.

Sponsored by their Foreign Mission Board, the Baptists were almost as active in Indian Territory as the Presbyterians. Evan Jones was the dean of Baptist missionaries. He had begun his work among the Cherokees before removal and had followed them to Indian Territory in 1839. Appealing to full-blood traditionalists, Jones established a large station north of Westville that included a church, a school, and a print shop. Jones and his foremost disciple, Dennis Bushyhead, published religious tracts, a newspaper, and books of the Bible in both English and Cherokee. Unlike most Presbyterian missionaries, Jones strongly opposed slavery and often preached against it.

Other noted Baptist missionaries included H. F. Buckner among the Creeks, Joseph S. Murrow among the Seminoles (and the Choctaws), and Ramsey D. Potts among the Choctaws.

Methodist missionary work among the Five Tribes had begun well before removal, and it continued in Indian Territory afterwards. Unlike those of other denominations, the Methodist missionaries were commissioned by regional conferences to work among the Indians as circuit-riding preachers. In 1844 a Methodist Indian Conference was organized at Riley's Mill near Tahlequah with eleven different stations in Indian Territory. Samuel G. Patterson worked among the Quapaws and other northeastern tribes; Thomas B. Ruble preached among the Creeks; and William H. Goode worked among the Choctaws.

The Moravians had sent their first missionaries among the Cherokees as early as 1801. They reestablished their missions in Indian Territory following removal near Oaks in Delaware County. Al-

Only this simple stone recalls the ultimate sacrifice that Ms. C. M. Belden made as a missionary teacher at Goodwater in the Choctaw Nation.

together the Moravians ministered to the Cherokees for 100 years, but with less than 200 converts.

All of the missionary societies commissioned an unusually large number of women to serve in Indian Territory. One authority has counted at least 190 who worked in Oklahoma before 1860. Some of them were the wives of men who had appointments as ministers, teachers, or farm managers. But many were unmarried and came simply to teach in one of the several schools supervised by the missionary agency. The contribution of these women to the religious and educational life of the Five Tribes is often overlooked. On the tombstone of one who died after only two short years in the service of the Choctaws is a very simple but eloquent epitaph: "Here sleeps a Missionary."

With Presbyterian support and administration, Tulla-hassee (*above*), just north of Muskogee, opened in 1848 for the benefit of Creek Indian children. The Baptists and Choctaws opened Armstrong Academy (*below*), near Bokchito, in 1845. Between 1863 and 1883 the building served as the capitol of the Choctaws.

Whatever their denomination, the Christian missionaries among the Five Tribes had similar responsibilities. Fundamental, of course, was to preach the gospel. For most this meant long and frequent trips to preach at different places. It also meant organizing churches, training leaders, and counseling members. But missionaries also served in a variety of other ways. Many acted as physicians, dispensing medicine and making house calls. They organized Bible, tract, and temperance societies. They advised tribal leaders on constitutional forms as well as specific laws.

Especially important was their work in converting all of the Five Tribes' languages—except Cherokee, for which Sequoyah had already created a syllabary— to written form. This helped the missionaries to teach Christianity, but it also helped preserve the Indian languages. Since language and culture are nearly inseparable, preserving the languages of the Five Tribes contributed to the preservation of their culture.

Educational Reconstruction

The missionaries made their greatest contribution in the area of formal education. As they reestablished their churches in Indian Territory after removal, they also reestablished their schools. Almost every mission station had some kind of school associated with it. Usually it was a day school where students were taught to read and write in English. Eleven such schools existed among the Choctaws in 1836; tribal annuity funds supported eight others where the teachers were not missionaries.

The missionaries also cooperated with the Indians in providing more advanced educational opportunities. In 1842, for example, the Choctaws created a system of boarding schools financed by treaty annuities and staffed by different Christian mission boards (ABCFM, Presbyterian, Baptist, and Methodist). Among the eight schools established before 1860 were Spencer, Fort Coffee, Wheelock, and Armstrong.

The Chickasaws and the Creeks had similar experiences. The Chickasaws opened five schools during the 1850s: Chickasaw Manual Labor Academy, Bloomfield, Colbert Institute, Wapanucka, and

Burney Institute. The Creeks established three: Koweta, Tullahassee, and Asbury Manual Labor School.

All the boarding schools had essentially the same curriculum. In addition to reading and writing in English, students received instruction in arithmetic, history, Latin, Greek, philosophy, biology, astronomy, and the Bible. Each was given vocational training also. Boys learned to care for animals, how to grow a crop, and how to do carpentry and other mechanical art; women learned about cooking, sewing, child care, and other domestic activities. In short, the curriculum was designed to educate the head, hands, and heart of each Indian after the fashion of white Americans.

There was little difference in the curriculum, but the organization and staffing of boarding schools among the Cherokees did differ from elsewhere. The schools at Park Hill and Dwight were both constructed and staffed by the ABCFM. The architecturally magnificent Cherokee Male Seminary and Female Seminary, however, were built in 1846 with tribal funds and operated strictly under tribal authority. Cherokee-funded day schools also functioned without direct missionary participation. The Cherokees had separated church and state a century before it became fashionable in the United States.

Whatever its organization and function, the school system of Indian Territory was commonly acknowledged as superior to that of neighboring states. Certainly a larger percentage of national funds was invested in education; literacy levels may even have been higher.

International Relations

The Five Tribes did not reestablish and develop their national institutions in a vacuum. They constantly interacted with each other, with tribes situated farther west, and with the United States government. In the 1830s and 1840s they met together in International councils, which also were attended by representatives of western tribes, to discuss common problems. Among the more vexing difficulties they faced were efforts by both governments' officials to draw them into the dispute between Mexico and the

Republic of Texas. The agents of both sides had pushed the western tribes to bloody warfare. Open discussion of the problems helped ease some of the tension, but so too did the establishment of new United States military posts: Fort Coffee on the Arkansas River (1834–38), Fort Wayne near the Missouri border (1838–42), and Fort Washita (1834–61) near present Durant.

The western borders of the Five Tribes remained in turmoil through the 1850s. To try to contain and check the turbulence, the United States constructed Fort Arbuckle near present Davis, in Garvin County, and Fort Cobb in Caddo County. Officials also established the Wichita Agency near present Anadarko and undertook to resettle the Wichitas, the Comanches, the Kiowas, and other tribes there to keep them out of Texas and to keep Texans away from them. Had not the Civil War intervened, these arrangements, strongly encouraged by the leadership of the Five Tribes, might very well have brought order to the border.

What Is the Meaning?

Historians have referred to the period before the American Civil War as the golden years of the Five Tribes. The amount and speed of acculturation was truly remarkable. Oklahomans rightly take pride in the accomplishments of the Five Tribes during those years, but we should also understand that the tribes' accomplishments often had little to do with the majority of the tribespeople. Recent studies have demonstrated that the total population of the Southeastern Indians decreased by about 35 percent between the time of removal and the Civil War. Since populations decrease only when they are under great stress, the golden years apparently were golden for only a few.

See History for Yourself

You can best appreciate the sophistication of constitutional government among the Five Tribes by visiting some of the buildings constructed during the postremoval era. Among them are the old Cherokee Supreme Court building at Tahlequah (Cherokee County) and the Chickasaw Council House at Tishomingo (Johnston County). No buildings survive, but the High Springs Council Ground of the Creeks, north of Hichita in McIntosh County, is a great place for a picnic (with the owner's permission).

It will help you to appreciate the missionary activity among the Five Tribes to visit the Old Baptist Mission site north of Westville (Adair County), Dwight Mission northwest of Sallisaw (Sequoyah County), and the Wheelock Church east of Valliant (McCurtain County). Helpful too is a walk over the grounds of the abandoned mission stations, looking particularly at cemetery stones, at New Springplace, south of Oaks (Cherokee County); Park Hill, southwest of Tahlequah (Cherokee County); Koweta Mission, at Coweta (Wagoner County); the first Spencer Academy, at Spencerville (Choctaw County); and Bloomfield Academy, southeast of Achille (Bryan County).

To get a sense of an early Indian Territory town, visit the Cherokee National Museum/Adams Center southwest of Tahlequah (Cherokee County). Also, get a map of the route of the Butterfield Overland Stage across the Choctaw Nation, and see if you can find any traces of the roadbed. You will want to visit Edwards Store, northeast of Red Oak, in Latimer County, for it is the only Butterfield station that survives.

Take a field trip to Fort Washita, northwest of Durant.

Suggestions for Further Reading

Reference

Baird, W. David. *Peter Pitchlynn, Chief of the Choctaws.* Norman: University of Oklahoma Press, 1972.

Bass, Althea. *Cherokee Messenger: A Life of Samuel Austin Worcester.* Norman: University of Oklahoma Press, 1936.

Debo, Angie. *Rise and Fall of the Choctaw Republic.* Norman: University of Oklahoma Press, 1934.

——. *The Road to Disappearance: A History of the Creek Indians.* Norman: University of Oklahoma Press, 1941.

Foreman, Carolyn T. *Park Hill.* Muskogee, Okla.: Press of the Star Printery, 1948.

Foreman, Grant. *Advancing the Frontier, 1830–1860.* Norman: University of Oklahoma Press, 1933, 1968.

————. *The Five Civilized Tribes.* Norman: University of Oklahoma Press, 1934, 1966.

Gibson, Arrell Morgan. *The Chickasaws.* Norman: University of Oklahoma Press, 1971.

Littlefield, Daniel F., Jr. *Africans and Creeks, from the Colonial Period to the Civil War.* Westport, Conn: Greenwood Press, 1979.

McReynolds, Edwin C. *The Seminoles.* Norman: University of Oklahoma Press, 1957.

Morrison, James D. *Seven Constitutions: Government of the Choctaw Republic, 1826–1906.* Durant: Choctaw Bilingual Education Program, Southeastern Oklahoma State University, 1977.

————. *Schools for the Choctaws.* Durant: Choctaw Bilingual Education Program, Southeastern Oklahoma State University, 1978.

Moulton, Gary E. *John Ross, Cherokee Chief.* Athens: University of Georgia Press, 1978.

Perdue, Theda. *Slavery and the Evolution of Cherokee Society, 1540–1866.* Knoxville: University of Tennessee Press, 1979.

Strickland, Rennard. *Fire and the Spirits: Cherokee Law from Clan to Court.* Norman: University of Oklahoma Press, 1975.

Thornton, Russell. *The Cherokees: A Population History.* Lincoln: University of Nebraska Press, 1990.

Tomer, John S., and Michael J. Brodhead. *A Naturalist in Indian Territory: The Journals of S. W. Woodhouse, 1849–50.* Norman: University of Oklahoma Press, 1992.

Utley, Robert M. *Frontiersmen in Blue: The United States Army and the Indian, 1848–1864.* Lincoln: University of Nebraska Press, 1981.

Wardell, Morris L. *A Political History of the Cherokee Nation, 1838–1907.* Norman: University of Oklahoma Press, 1938, 1977.

Woodward, Grace Steele. *The Cherokees.* Norman: University of Oklahoma Press, 1963.

Related Reading

Lafferty, R. A. *Okla Hannali.* 1972. Norman: University of Oklahoma Press, 1991.

Chapter 10: **Indian Territory at War**

United States Army Second Lieutenant William W. Averall had just returned to duty after being on extended sick leave when his commanding officer in Washington, D.C., handed him secret dispatches to deliver to Indian Territory. Dressed in citizens' clothes, he caught a train headed for Missouri on April 17, 1861. From Rolla he continued on by stagecoach to Fort Smith, Arkansas, where he bought an untamed horse to make the 260-mile journey to Fort Washita. Dodging "mounted desperadoes" who sought to ambush him, Averall worked his way west until he finally encountered the United States troops commanded by Major William H. Emory. On May 2 he handed Emory the orders he had brought from Washington. They read: Evacuate all troops under your command in Indian Territory north to Kansas.

Emory had anticipated those orders and was even then in full retreat from Forts Arbuckle, Washita, and Cobb. The dispatches handed him by the courageous Averall merely confirmed his judgment that the Civil War raging in the East would soon disturb the peace and tranquility of Indian Territory. And it did, plunging the Five Tribes into a devastating war that renewed old hostilities and created new ones.

Becoming Confederate Allies

The national debate that raged in the United States in the 1850s touched Indian Territory only slightly. The issues associated with states rights and the tariff had little meaning to the Five Tribes, but their citizens could and did relate to the debate over slavery. The Cherokees, for example, were deeply divided over the question. And all tribal leaders were disturbed by Republican proposals, during Abraham Lincoln's campaign for the presidency in 1860, that Indian lands should be used for white settlement. Understandably, they expected the worst when Lincoln was elected.

Trusted advisors and friends confirmed the fears of the tribespeople. Their long-time agents, all of whom were from southern states, told them that they could no longer trust the United States government. Delegations from Arkansas and Texas came to make the same point. Letters and visits from southern relatives reminded mixed-blood families especially of strong ties with the South.

The Work of Albert Pike

Many leaders of the Five Tribes therefore welcomed the formation of the Confederate States of America in February 1861. The Confederate government moved quickly to take advantage of this sentiment. President Jefferson Davis appointed Albert Pike, a prominent Arkansas attorney, editor, and Freemason, to negotiate treaties with the tribes. Pike set out for Indian Territory in late May.

With good reason Pike expected a warm and friendly welcome. Lieutenant Averall had delivered his secret dispatches and the United States Army had withdrawn from the region. The abandoned forts—Washita, Arbuckle, and Cobb—were safely in the hands of Confederate troops from Texas. Pike also heard that Five Tribes leaders such as the Cherokee Stand Watie were volunteering to raise regiments to fight for the Confederacy. He may have learned as well that pro-Southern Indians had forced antislavery missionaries like John Edwards, who worked among the Choctaws, to flee for their lives.

An Arkansas attorney and Freemason, Albert Pike negotiated the Confederate treaty of alliances with the Five Tribes. Early in the war in Indian Territory he also commanded Confederate Indian troops.

In early June, Pike stopped first at Park Hill in the Cherokee Nation. There he found the tribe was divided in its support of the South, and Chief John Ross was intent on remaining neutral in the American Civil War. Although disappointed, Pike respected the chief's position and moved on to other negotiations at North Fork Town in the Creek Nation, near present Eufaula. There on July 10 he signed a treaty

AN ESCAPE FROM THE SOUTH

A native of New York, John Edwards graduated from Princeton Theological Seminary in 1851. Shortly thereafter he was appointed as a missionary teacher at Spencer Academy in the Choctaw Nation by the Presbyterian Church. In 1853 he became superintendent of Wheelock Seminary for Choctaw girls. Edwards helped translate part of the Bible into the Choctaw language. Although he did not consider slavery a sin, he believed the institution was greatly abused. Those beliefs caused his neighbors to conclude that he was an abolitionist. In May 1861, as the Choctaws were deciding whether they would join the Confederacy or not, Edwards was questioned, and his house searched for weapons by a vigilante committee of Texans and Choctaws. Believing his life was in danger, he made a dramatic escape from the Choctaw Nation in the following month . He recalled his experience forty years later:

Finally, the question was put to me whether I would pledge myself, in case the War came into that region of the country, to take up arms for the South. "Gentlemen," said I, "You might as well ask me to strike my Mother. I was born in the North; my friends and kindred are still living there; I do not believe the Southern states have a right to secede, nor that the Government has given them any cause to rebel. What I wish to do is to stay here quietly and go on with my work for the Choctaws, not taking part in the War on either side. I am willing to give you my pledge to do nothing against you, and to abide by that to the death. Beyond that my conscience will not let me do."

The crisis was reached. They went out and consulted. Returning, [they] asked me how long a time I wanted to get ready to leave. I replied that in the feeble state of my wife's health, I thought I ought to have at least a month. He answered, "It would be a cruelty to compel a feeble lady to travel in this hot weather; but get ready and leave as soon as you can." . . .

[Three weeks later after a public meeting had been held at Doaksville,] I was in my study . . . when Mrs. E[dwards] came in and said, "Mrs Dukes is here and says the committee are to be here today to hang you, and you must get out of the way as soon as possible." I took my keys out of my pocket, handed them to Mr. Libby who was sitting there, and said, "Mr. Libby will you saddle Jerry for me?" Then I went into the house, put on a warmer suit of clothes which had come from my mother a few days before, put some clothes and some snack in my saddle bags, had a prayer with Mrs. E[dwards], took all the money there was in the house, and mounted and started, probably within 15 minutes of the time the word came.

Mrs. E[dwards] wished to know my plans. I told her I would go to Lenox, Dr. Hobbs' station, and wait there for her and the children, if I could. If not I would make the best of my way northward. "What shall I do?" said she. "Get a team and follow me as soon as you can," said I. . . . So I bade her farewell and started. (John Edwards, "An Account of My Escape from the South in 1861," *Chronicles of Oklahoma* 43 (1965): 58–89).

with the Creeks, despite considerable opposition among the full-bloods. Unanimous in their support of the South, the Choctaws and the Chickasaws signed another treaty two days later. A very divided Seminole Nation signed with Pike on August 1, 1862.

From North Fork Town, Pike went west to negotiate with the tribes of the Wichita Agency near present Anadarko. On August 12 he signed two treaties: one with the Wichitas, Caddos, and affiliated tribes; another with the nonreservation Plains Comanches. While he was in the West, he received word that the Cherokees were now anxious to negotiate with the Confederacy. Desiring to preserve the unity of his people, Chief Ross had abandoned all hope of neutrality.

Pike hurried back to Tahlequah, where in early October he quickly negotiated a treaty with the Cherokees. He took the opportunity also to conclude three other treaties with their neighbors, that is, with the Quapaws, with the Senecas and Shawnees, and with the Osages. It had taken nearly five months, but Pike had completed his work successfully. Indian Territory belonged to the Confederacy.

The treaties proved a disaster for the Indian nations, but in October 1861 few would have predicted it. For the moment, they seemed quite generous. The Confederate government assumed all the financial obligations of the old treaties with the United States, promised to protect the tribes from invasion, and guaranteed the right of self-government. It also agreed to protect slavery and to grant procedural rights in Confederate courts. The Five Tribes were given the right to send representatives to the Confederate congress. In return, the Indians agreed to an offensive and defensive alliance with the South and to provide troops at the request of President Jefferson Davis.

George W. Stidham, noted Creek planter and merchant, represented the Creeks in the Confederate Congress in Richmond during the Civil War.

War Comes to Indian Territory

Before the ink was dry on the treaties, the Indians established fighting units under officers of their own choosing. The first was the Choctaw and Chickasaw Mounted Rifles commanded by Douglas H. Cooper, a former Indian agent. In succession the Creeks and the Seminoles formed units led by Daniel N. McIntosh and John Jumper. The Cherokees organized two units, one led by John Drew and the other by Stand Watie. All groups looked forward to winning glory on the battlefield.

Opothleyahola and the Loyalists

Not all Indian Territory people supported a Confederate alliance. Among the opponents was the Creek elder statesman and slaveholder Opothleyahola. He and some 7,000 of his Creek and Seminole followers

Opothleyaholo (*left*), a revered leader of the Creek Upper Towns, led those members of the Five Tribes who opposed the Confederate treaties. Douglas Cooper (*right*), a long-time agent of the Choctaws, commanded the Confederate troops that forced the neutrals to seek refuge in Kansas in 1861.

gathered along the Little River south and west of Holdenville and declared their loyalty to the "old treaties" with the United States. To quiet the dissidents, 1,400 Indian and Texas troops, commanded by Douglas Cooper, marched toward their camp. Opothleyahola heard of the impending attack and retreated north toward Kansas. At Round Mountain, just east of Stillwater in Payne County, the Confederates caught up with the Loyalists and engaged them on November 19 in Oklahoma's first Civil War battle. By withstanding two more bloody encounters the following month, at Chusto-Talasah (north of Tulsa) and Chustenahlah (west of Skiatook), Opothleyahola's people were able to escape into Kansas—only to suffer extreme deprivations there.

Battle of Pea Ridge

By early 1862, Confederate Indian troops had control of Indian Territory. That position of strength soon deteriorated, however, especially after the defeat on March 6–8, 1862, of the Southern army at Pea Ridge, Arkansas, where Indian troops fought bravely and well. The evidence was entirely circumstantial, but Cherokee units at the battle were accused of scalping the Union dead. The Confederate high command tended to accept the charges, and demoralized by that lack of confidence, General Albert Pike retreated with much of his Indian Territory army deep into the Choctaw Nation. Near Nail's Crossing on Blue River, in northwest Bryan County, he constructed Fort McCulloch, primarily with slave labor, and dared the Yankees to attack it.

Weer Expedition

Pike hardly intimidated the Union army. Emboldened by its victory at Pea Ridge, the army planned a June invasion of Indian Territory with regular white units as well as those recruited from among Opothleyahola's followers. The families of the Loyal Indians would follow behind, reoccupying their old homes when it became safe. Colonel William Weer was in command of the "Indian Expedition," which eventually pushed, with only minimal opposition, 100 miles south to Fort Gibson.

At Tahlequah, Cherokee Chief John Ross welcomed the Union troops as liberators. Despite this reception, a failure of leadership and rumors of a counterattack caused the Union troops to withdraw back to Kansas, taking Chief Ross and as many as 2,000 additional Cherokee refugees with them. Ross spent the remainder of the war in Philadelphia.

Confederate forces were unable to capitalize on the collapse of the Indian Expedition. The Cherokees had split into two rival factions: one recognized John Ross as chief—and in his absence, Thomas Pegg—and supported the Union; the other elected Stand Watie as chief and remained supportive of the South. General Albert Pike, believing that the Confederate army discriminated against his troops, resigned his commission, only to be arrested by his subordinate and successor, General Douglas H. Cooper. The resulting chaos reduced Confederate military activity in Indian Territory to guerillalike raids led primarily by Stand Watie. These "scouts" inspired a lot of terror and property damage but had little military value.

Battle of Honey Springs

Southern forces were in no position to challenge seriously the second Union invasion, which began in April 1863. The Indian Brigade, led by Colonel William A. Phillips, marched from Baxter Springs, Kansas, almost unopposed, to occupy Fort Gibson, which was renamed Fort Blunt. When efforts to cut the federal supply line were rebuffed, General Cooper gathered 5,000 troops at Honey Springs on the Texas Road (north of Checotah) in anticipation of a full-scale attack on the fort. Union Major General James G. Blunt, who had just arrived from Kansas, spoiled Cooper's plans. With 3,000 men, he

THE WARTIME CONCERNS OF A MOTHER

Sarah Watie had a husband and son serving in the Confederate army. Her husband, of course, was General Stand Watie, while her son Saladin served on her

husband's staff. Sarah Watie spent most of the war as a refugee in northern Texas. While she was there she sent her husband letters of encouragement and concern. One of those, written on June 8, 1863, addresses the fears she had for her son and for her nephew, Charles Webber:

My dear half
. . . I have not had a chance to write you a long letter since you left. Grady tells me that Charles and Saladin have killed a prisiner   write

and tell me who it was and how it was, tell my boys to always show mercy as they expect to find God merciful to them. I do hate to hear such things   it almost runs me crazy to hear such things I find myself almost dead sometimes thinking about it. I am afraid that Saladin never will value human life as he ought. If you should

ever catch William Ross dont have him killed I know how bad his mother would feel but keep him till the war is over. I know that they all deserve death but I do feel

Cherokee General Stand Watie commanded Confederate troops in Indian Territory during the later years of the war. His wife, Sarah Watie, spent most of the war years as a refugee in North Texas.

for his old mother and then I want them to know that you do not want to kill them just to get them out of your way. I want them to know you are not afraid of there (sic) influence. Always do as near right as you can. . . . (Edward E. Dale, ed., "Some Letters of General Stand Watie," *Chronicles of Oklahoma* 1 (1921–23): 41)

This romanticized sketch of the battle of Honey Springs, July 17, 1863, appeared in *Frank Leslie's Illustrated Newspaper*, August 29, 1863.

marched out of the fort, crossed the Arkansas River, and confronted the Confederates at their camp on July 17.

The battle of Honey Springs was the most important battle of the Civil War in Indian Territory. The Confederate forces were in trouble from the beginning. Their artillery was quickly silenced by Union cannon, and their gunpowder, imported from Mexico, proved useless when it was turned into paste by early morning rains. A charge by Texas troops was quickly turned back by a sharp-shooting Union regiment of African Americans. In less than two hours the battle was over, and the Confederate army was fleeing from the field toward the Red River. Ironically, 3,000 reinforcements arrived that afternoon.

General Blunt followed up his victory with others at Perryville on August 26 and Fort Smith on September 1. His successes meant that Union arms controlled the northern two-thirds of Oklahoma. Many of the several thousand supporters of Opothleyahola and John Ross, who had lived as refugees in Kansas for two years, returned to the Indian Territory. Sadly, most of the Loyalist Indians did not feel safe in their own homes and gathered around Forts Smith and Gibson for protection.

For the Confederate Indians the defeat at Honey Springs brought great suffering. The army ultimately found safety in camps along Red River. There and in Texas they were soon joined by some 15,000 family members, who abandoned their homes in the northern two-thirds of Indian Territory rather than suffer the wrath of Union troops and roving bands of thieves and killers like the notorious William Quantrill and his followers. As it had been for their northern brethren in Kansas, life for the civilian refugees was hard. Food and medical supplies were in very short supply.

D. N. McIntosh commanded the First Creek Regiment of Confederate troops at the battle of Honey Springs.

Guerilla Warfare

Military operations in Indian Territory after September 1863 were primarily guerilla operations designed by the Confederates to interrupt Union supply lines to Fort Gibson. General Stand Watie and his First Indian Brigade were especially effective on such scouts. On June 15, 1864, they captured the steamer *J. R. Williams* near present Tamaha, and on September 19, 1864, with the help of some

Texas troops, they took a supply train of 300 wagons at Cabin Creek just south of Vinita. Colonel Tandy Walker's Second Indian Brigade also contributed to the Confederate victory at Poison Springs, Arkansas, on April 18, 1864.

On one of his guerilla raids in October 1863, Confederate General Stand Watie burned Rose Cottage, the stately home of his old adversary, Cherokee Chief John Ross.

THE ENGAGEMENT AT FLAT ROCK CREEK

G. W. Grayson was one of hundreds of young Creek Indian men who volunteered for service in the Confederate army. His autobiography, written forty years after the Civil War, is one of the best eyewitness descriptions we have of the conflict in Indian Territory. Below is his account of action that took place at Flat Rock Creek on September 16, 1864:

After several days of preparation, some two thousand men, as I believe, consisting of Creeks, Seminoles, Cherokees and Texans with a battery of four pieces of artillery were gotten in readiness for the expedition. I joined this expedition, it having become my rule and purpose to take part in all proposed raids against the enemy when I had a horse in condition to withstand the hardships incident to such expeditions. . . .

We crossed the Canadian, the Arkansas and the Verdigris rivers after two days march and reached an encampment of negro hay makers about two miles beyond the present town of Wagoner, who were cutting and putting up hay for the use of the army at Fort Gibson. There appeared to have been a small escort of negro soldiers, as nearly all the dead and prisoners were negroes, who for a few minutes after our attack returned our fire. One or two cannon shots of grape from our guns, however, caused a stampede, when we charged the encampment. The defenders disappeared among the thickets and very high weeds that covered the banks of the creek and for a few minutes after reaching the deserted camps it did not appear that there was anything for us to do more than burning the camps and the great ricks of hay that stood about the field.

Presently, however, some of our men discovered a negro hiding in the high weeds near the creek and shot and killed him. At another point another one was found and shot, and it now appearing that these were to be found hid in the weeds, the men proceeded to hunt them out much as sportsmen do quails. Some of the negroes finding they were about to be discovered, would spring up from the brush and cry out, O! master spare me. But the men were in no spirit to spare the wretched unfortunates and shot them down without mercy. . . . Some of them were found lying in hiding in the creek with barely their noses out of the water and were shot and dragged and thrown out on the bank. I confess this was sickening to me, but the men were like wild beasts and I was powerless to stop them from this unnecessary butchery. (G. W. Grayson, *A Creek Warrior for the Confederacy: The Autobiography of Chief G. W. Grayson,* 94–96)

Confederate Surrender

Although successful, these operations could not change the outcome of the Civil War. That was determined back east in Virginia. On April 9, 1865, Robert E. Lee surrendered his army to Ulysses S. Grant at Appomattox Courthouse. His action made further resistance by Confederate troops in Indian Territory futile. On May 26, 1865, Edmund Kirby Smith surrendered the white Confederate command; the three tribes most tenacious in their commitment to the South surrendered through their chiefs in June and July. Stand Watie, who acted on behalf of the Cherokees, was the last of the Confederate generals to surrender.

The Price of War

It is hard for historians to know exactly how many members of the Indian Territory tribes fought in the Civil War. Some 3,530 men enlisted in the Union army during the course of the war; there were 3,260 men in the Confederate service late in 1864. Surely as many as 8,000 saw some duty in either the Northern or the Southern army.

Whatever their numbers or their side, the troops in Indian Territory had only a marginal impact on the war effort. The Confederate high command never allocated sufficient resources to the units operating there. In December 1863, for example, at least 1,000 of the Five Tribes enlistees were without guns of any kind, and most of those that had guns were on furlough. Union Indian troops were better armed, but some units had a reputation for "going buffalo hunting" just as campaigns began.

The civilian population of Indian Territory, especially women and children, paid a heavy price for participating in the Civil War. Most Northern sympathizers spent two to four cruel years as refugees in Kansas or huddled around Fort Gibson or Fort Smith; Southern sympathizers spent at least two years on the banks of the Red River. Refugee camps were scenes of deprivation, despair, and death. Most of the estimated 10,000 deaths that are attributable to the war among the Five Tribes occurred in them. Homes abandoned by the refugees were burned, grain was confiscated, livestock was driven off (300,000 head of cattle alone). Schools and churches closed.

Lieutenant Pleasant Porter (*left*) served with the Creek Mounted Volunteers at the second battle of Cabin Creek in September 1864. Colonel Lewis Downing, a former Baptist minister, commanded the Third Kansas Indian Home Guard Regiment of the Union Army. After the Civil War each served as chief of his respective tribe.

In sum, the Civil War devastated almost all that the five Southeastern tribes had built and developed in Indian Territory during their "golden years." Even though the different tribal leaderships could accurately say that they had joined the Confederacy because the Union had abandoned them, the war left the Five Tribes in the position of a conquered foe, and that made the negotiation of a permanent peace much more difficult.

See History for Yourself

Visit battlefield sites at Round Mountain (east of Stillwater), Chustenahlah (west of Skiatook), Cabin

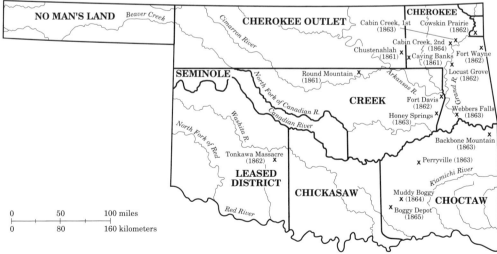

Civil War Battle Sites

Creek (south of Vinita), Honey Springs (north of Checotah), Perryville (south of McAlester), Muddy Boggy (north of Atoka), and Boggy Depot (west of Atoka). Also visit the Pea Ridge battlefield site in northwest Arkansas.

Organize an excursion to the Union and Confederate rooms of the Oklahoma State Historical Museum in Oklahoma City at the State Historical Society.

Suggestions for Further Reading

Reference

Abel, Annie H. *The American Indian as a Participant in the Civil War.* Cleveland: Arthur H. Clark, 1919.

Bearss, Edwin C., and Arrell M. Gibson. *Fort Smith, Little Gibraltar on the Arkansas.* 2d ed. Norman: University of Oklahoma Press, 1979.

Britton, Wiley. *The Union Indian Brigade in the Civil War.* Kansas City: Franklin Hudson Publishing Company, 1922.

Franks, Kenny A. *Stand Watie and the Agony of the Cherokee Nation.* Memphis: Memphis State University Press, 1979.

Gaines, W. Craig. *The Confederate Cherokees: John Drew's Regiment of Mounted Rifles.* Baton Rouge: Louisiana State University Press, 1989.

Grayson, G. W. *A Creek Warrior for the Confederacy: The Autobiography of Chief G.W. Grayson.* Edited by W. David Baird. Norman: University of Oklahoma Press, 1988.

Hale, Douglas. *The Third Texas Cavalry in the Civil War.* Norman: University of Oklahoma Press, 1992.

Rampp, Larry C., and Donald L. Rampp. *The Civil War in Indian Territory.* Austin: Presidial Press, 1975.

Wright, Muriel H., and Le Roy H. Fischer. *Civil War Sites in Oklahoma.* Oklahoma City: Oklahoma Historical Society, 1967.

Related Reading

Dale, Edward E., and Gaston Litton, eds. *Cherokee Cavaliers: Forty Years of Cherokee History as Told in the Correspondence of the Ridge-Watie-Boudinot Family.* Norman: University of Oklahoma Press, 1939.

Josephy, Alvin M., Jr. *The Civil War in the American West.* New York: Alfred A. Knopf, Inc., 1991.

Knight, Wilfred. *Red Fox: Stand Watie's Civil War Years in Indian Territory.* Glendale: Arthur Clark Company, 1988.

McPherson, James M. *Battle Cry of Freedom: The Civil War Era.* New York: Oxford University Press, 1988.

Chapter 11: **Rejuvenation and Reconstruction**

In September 1871 the Creek Indians anticipated electing their first chief according to the terms of a new constitution. How they were to cast their votes divided the tribe into two factions. One side expected to use "paper and count the votes," while the other side would follow the only way that was "right in the sight of God," that is, to line up behind candidates at the Council House in Okmulgee. The two sides—one progressive, the other traditional—finally reconciled their differences, but only after two bitter wars.

The disputes that divided the Creeks suggested something of the dramatic changes that swept our state after the Civil War. Not only did the Confederate-allied tribes have to seek a new relationship with the United States, but they had to reconstruct and rehabilitate their war-torn societies. That proved a difficult task, given the forces arrayed against them.

Allen Wright, an ordained Presbyterian minister, was a member of the Choctaw delegation that negotiated the Reconstruction treaty of 1866. It was he who suggested that the proposed Indian Territory be called Oklahoma.

Reconstruction Treaties of 1866

Initially, the federal government was an obstacle to recovery. In September 1865, Washington officials summoned the tribes of Indian Territory to a peace conference at Fort Smith. There they were told that they had made unprovoked war on the United States between 1861 and 1865 and that they had "rightfully forfeited" all of their annuities and lands. John Ross was accused of leading the Cherokees into rebellion. But happily, they learned, the president was willing to forgive them "of their great crime" and make new treaties.

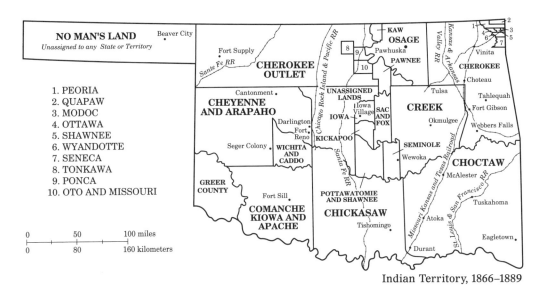

Indian Territory, 1866–1889

NO MAN'S LAND
Unassigned to any State or Territory

1. PEORIA
2. QUAPAW
3. MODOC
4. OTTAWA
5. SHAWNEE
6. WYANDOTTE
7. SENECA
8. TONKAWA
9. PONCA
10. OTO AND MISSOURI

The Indian delegates were stunned but not intimidated. They reminded their federal government counterparts that many of their kinsmen had fought for the Union, that the United States Army had abandoned them in 1861, and that as sovereign states they had been free to negotiate with the Confederacy. Their attitude caused the conference to adjourn without negotiating permanent treaties. Those were deferred until the following year.

The definitive treaties of 1866 were negotiated in Washington. On the whole, the Indians obtained better terms than those that had been threatened at Fort Smith. The tribes were to abolish slavery and give their freed slaves citizenship and property rights. They agreed to the construction of one north-south and one east-west railroad across their countries. They avoided the dreaded territorial government for what was now called Oklahoma, but did consent to an intertribal council. Their annuities were also restored.

The most damaging feature of these treaties was the loss of land. The Five Tribes were required to cede the western half of Oklahoma as a home for other Indians. The Cherokees also ceded lands in Kansas and control of their Outlet to the Plains to the federal government. Hardest hit were the Seminoles. They had to sell their old domain for fifteen cents an acre and then pay the government fifty cents an acre for lands that it had purchased from the Creeks for thirty cents an acre.

ESTABLISHING THE "INITIAL POINT"

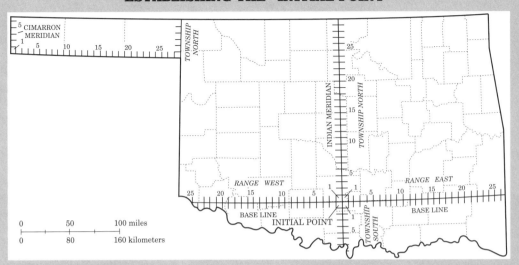

Townships and Ranges

In 1785 the United States Congress established the system by which public lands are surveyed. Essentially it provided for a rectangular survey, the base unit of which was a six-square-mile township made up of thirty-six sections, each one mile square (640 acres). The states formed from the Louisiana Purchase were surveyed according to this system as well.

Long before the Civil War, federal officials pressured the Five Tribes to follow the same pattern. The Indians stoutly resisted "sectionizing" because they feared that it would lead to loss of their land. The Reconstruction treaties of 1866, however, required the Chickasaws and Choctaws to survey and subdivide their domain. The United States commissioner of the General Land Office gave the contract to start that work to Ehud N. Darling, a professional surveyor with extensive experience in the West.

To begin the survey, Darling had to establish the "initial point" at which the east-west "base line" and the north-south "Indian meridian" would intersect. From there Darling proceeded to survey the thirty-six square-mile townships, which were identified as being north or south of the base line and east or west of the Indian meridian. For example, Lindsay in Garvin County is located four townships north of the base line and four townships west of the Indian meridian (T4N and R4W). Ardmore in Carter County, on the other hand, is located four townships south of the base line and two townships east of the Indian meridian (T4S and R2E).

Each community also is located in one of the thirty-six sections. Since Ardmore is in section 32, its location, according to the rectangular-survey system, is in Section 32, Township 4 South, Range 2 East of the Indian Meridian. Such designations enable owners to identify their property precisely—yesterday, today, and tomorrow. But before that could happen, there had to be a survey, and that survey had to begin from an "initial point."

According to his instructions, Darling established the initial point south of Fort Arbuckle in present Murray County in 1870. He marked it with a pile of rocks and a vertically placed stone, upon which he carved "IP." All land in Oklahoma, with the exception of the Panhandle, is surveyed from that spot, as insubstantial as it may appear. The map shows Darling's initial point with its intersecting base line and meridian. The initial point in the Panhandle is its southwest corner.

The treaties of 1866 were harsh but not devastating. Although diminished, the Indians' basic institutions were still intact. Upon them they could reconstruct their nations and recover their societies. Yet things could never be the same. The Indians no longer controlled their own destiny because their sovereignty was limited by the federal government and their resources were open to non-Indian exploitation.

Cherokees Achieve Stable Government

The first task was to rejuvenate tribal governments. The Civil War had rekindled old hatreds and created new ones, leaving most of the Indian Territory tribes divided by factionalism. In the Cherokee Nation those who had favored the removal Treaty of New Echota and had supported the Confederacy were arrayed against those who had opposed the treaty and favored the Union. Delegations from each side represented the tribe in Washington. Tired of the fighting, the conservative full-bloods who had once supported John Ross joined with mixed-bloods who had stood with Stand Watie, to elect Lewis Downing, a former Union officer, as chief in 1867. Downing's Union party controlled Cherokee politics for the next forty years.

The Union party gave stability to the Cherokee government. The constitution of 1839 functioned surprisingly well, both at the national level and in the nine Cherokee counties. Constructed in 1869, the attractive capitol in Tahlequah stands as a memorial to that efficiency. It reflects too how well tribal officials managed the revenues that they received as a treaty annuity from the federal government or as fees from cattlemen pasturing their herds in the Cherokee Outlet. The tribe derived $200,000 annually from the fees after 1880.

Tension over Creek Government

Like the Cherokees, the Creeks were also divided by removal and the Civil War. The two factions put aside their differences to write a new constitution in 1867 that established three branches of government. It provided for an elected principal chief and a second chief. It established a council with two legislative bodies—a house of warriors and a house of kings—to which each of the forty-seven Creek towns sent elected representatives. The constitution also created a sophisticated judicial system, dividing the nation into six districts. Each of the districts had a courthouse, a judge, a prosecuting attorney, and elected enforcement officers (known as light-horse).

Although it was the product of tribal unity, the implementation of the constitution, especially its balloting features, produced major new tensions. Between 1870 and 1872 traditional Creeks and their former slaves, led by Oktarharsars Harjo (Sands) denied the authority of Samuel Checote, who was elected chief by "paper votes." In the so-called Sands Rebellion, he and his supporters occupied the council house at Okmulgee. It required troops from Fort Gibson to establish peace, as it did in 1881 when Isparhecher continued the struggle in the Green Peach War.

Thereafter the Creeks lived in harmony. The construction of their magnificent new sandstone capitol in 1878 at Okmulgee proudly declared that they were adjusting to the demands of constitutional government. It confirmed as well that the tribal treasury, derived from treaty annuities and five-cents-per-acre grazing fees, was adequate for significant public works.

Seminole Factionalism

Factionalism plagued the Seminoles even more than the Creeks. The treaty of 1866 had required them to remove to lands east of their old settlements. After they had begun to rebuild, the Seminoles learned they had not settled on their own reserve. To prevent having to move again, in 1881 they bought additional land from the Creeks. This confusion only intensified factionalism.

The Seminoles divided according to U.S. Civil War and religious loyalties. One group, led by John Chupco, had remained loyal to the Union and was predominately Presbyterian; the other, led by John Jumper, had supported the Confederacy and was primarily Baptist. With no written constitution, the Seminoles organized their government around a national council made up of delegations from the fourteen towns and the principal chief or governor. Since the partisans of Chupco and Jumper acted independently of

each other, the tribe actually had two governments. In 1877, however, Governor John F. Brown was able to unify the two groups, begin cataloging laws, and build a log national capitol building at Wewoka.

Choctaws and Chickasaws

The Choctaws and the Chickasaws were also troubled by factional disputes, but not so severely. They had been more unanimous in their support of the Confederacy, and they had suffered less from the destruction of the war. The Choctaw government functioned effectively according to the provisions of the 1860 constitution; the Chickasaws organized a similar government on the basis of a new constitution adopted in 1867. Local officials operated vital district and county governments, some of which occupied impressive public buildings.

Determining who would control the government accounted for most of the factional disturbances. Campaigns for office were hotly contested by organized political parties—Progressives and Nationals among the Choctaws; Progressives and Pullbacks among the Chickasaws. Sometimes the quest for power produced bloodshed, as it did among the Choctaws in the so-called Locke War at Antlers in Pushmataha County in 1893, when the U.S. Army had to

In 1898 elections the Seminoles vote for their preferred candidates by lining up behind them at Wewoka. When the Creeks abandoned such a practice and cast paper ballots instead, traditionalists resisted the change in two armed rebellions.

restore order. But on the whole, tribal government achieved remarkable stability, as shown by the impressive capitol buildings at Tuskahoma, built by the Choctaws in 1884, and at Tishomingo, built in 1896 by the Chickasaws. The substantial revenues that both governments enjoyed from coal royalties and grazing and other fees (totaling more than $150,000 for the Choctaws in 1890) contributed to stability as well.

Social Rejuvenation

Just as they were anxious to reestablish their own national governments, the Five Tribes of Indian Territory were at pains to repair the social fabrics of their communities. Given highest priority were their educational systems, all of which had been closed during the Civil War. The Choctaws reestablished

Bloomfield Academy (*above*), south of Achille in Bryan County, reopened in 1876 as a "higher school" for Chickasaw young women. The Cherokee Orphan Asylum at Salina (*below*) reflects the social commitment of the Cherokee government.

their neighborhood school system in early 1867; twenty years later they had 160 schools that enrolled 3,427 students. With the help of mission boards, in 1871 they were able to reopen two of their boarding schools (Spencer and New Hope); over the next several years five more were opened, including one for the children of former slaves.

The other four tribes worked just as diligently to resume educational activities. In addition to neighborhood schools, the Chickasaws opened four major boarding schools. The Cherokees reestablished large male and female seminaries at Tahlequah, three schools for children of former slaves, and special institutions for orphans, the blind and the deaf, and the insane. The Creeks rebuilt Tullahassee and Asbury, and over time they constructed six more boarding schools, an orphans' home, and a school and orphans' home for freed citizens. With fewer resources, the Seminoles had no boarding schools until they opened Emahaka and Mekasukey in the 1890s.

As they rebuilt their schools, the Indians also reestablished their churches. If they had left during the war, Presbyterian, Baptist, Methodist, and Moravian missionaries returned to their congregations to help with the reconstruction and to establish schools and orphanages. And new missionaries arrived, representing such denominations as the Church of Christ and the Roman Catholic Church. How many of the tribespeople were practicing Christians is difficult to determine (estimates range from 15 to 75 percent), but one thing is certain: Christianity had a stronger following among the Choctaws, the Creeks and the Seminoles than it did among the Cherokees and the Chickasaws. The Chickasaws had only 10 churches with 500 members in 1876.

The publication of tribal newspapers reflected the mending of the social fabric. The *Cherokee Advocate* resumed publication in Tahlequah. The *Indian Journal,* a periodical that was chartered by the Creek Nation but circulated throughout Indian Territory, began publication in Eufaula. The *Indian Citizen* at Atoka published Choctaw news, although it was independent of the tribal government. Much of the history of our state in the post–Civil War era can be found in these and other such publications.

Economic Rejuvenation

The Five Tribes reconstructed their tribal governments and repaired their social institutions as they were rejuvenating their tribal economies. With slave labor no longer available to them, many mixed-blood tribespeople recruited white and black tenants to break the soil and work the farms that they claimed. Under this arrangement, thousands of new acres came under cultivation. The Washita valley, for example, became a "solid farm for fifty miles."

Others of the tribal elites, like Wilson N. Jones of the Choctaws and George W. Stidham of the Creeks, marked off large ranges for themselves and ran large herds of livestock. Chickasaw ranchers alone in 1882 grazed at least 140,000 head of cattle. A surprisingly large number of these Indian cattlemen built big houses and filled them with expensive furniture.

Full-bloods engaged in subsistence agriculture, and except in a bad crop year lived in relative comfort. The average Creek full-blood owned a wagon and a plow or two; cultivated six to twenty acres of land, growing corn, cotton, and some wheat; and owned six to twenty horses, eight to fifty cattle, ten to twenty hogs, and a few chickens and turkeys. His family lived in a log cabin furnished with bedsteads, tables, and benches made of rough lumber, and wore clothes manufactured from home-grown cotton. Each had a garden plot and an extensive

Making sofke, a corn dish that was a dietary staple of the Five Tribes, was a frequent task for these Creek women.

orchard. Cherokee farmers alone produced an estimated 3 million bushels of corn in 1872.

Once a year many Five Tribes farmers and ranchers gathered in Muskogee to exhibit their produce and stock at the Indian International Fair. From these displays it was clear that the agriculture undertaken in our state matched that of other regions. Beef cattle, prospering on the bluestem grass, were just as fat, if not fatter, and horses were just as fast, if not faster. Above all else, the fair demonstrated the agricultural potential of Oklahoma.

The Railroad: A Mixed Blessing

Nothing contributed so much to the general economic revival of our state after the Civil War as did the railroad. Transportation before and immediately after the war had been limited to horse-drawn wagons and coaches and stern wheeler steamboats. The Reconstruction treaties of 1866, however, gave railroads the right to lay tracks across Indian Territory. This provision had been inserted by Kansas railroad men who saw major economic potential in the domain of the Five Tribes, especially if the Indian Territory were settled by thousands of white farmers.

The MK & T Railroad (the "Katy") was the first company to build across Indian Territory from north to south. It surveyed a roadbed along the old Texas Road in 1870, and in February 1871 trains were running to Muskogee. By early 1872 tracks had been laid through McAlester and Durant to the Red River, crossing into Texas at Colbert's Ferry.

The Atlantic and Pacific Railway Company (later the St. Louis and San Francisco, or "Frisco") built from east to west. It entered Indian Territory through the Quapaw reservation in May 1871, building first to Vinita, then to Tulsa, and ultimately to Oklahoma City. In the mid-1880s the Frisco constructed a southern branch from Fort Smith southwest across the Choctaw Nation to Paris, Texas.

Other major railroad lines—the Atchison, Topeka, and Santa Fe (or "Santa Fe") and the Chicago, Rock Island, and Pacific (or "Rock Island")—penetrated Indian Territory farther west. Many smaller, but equally colorful lines constructed railroads as well. Indeed, construction was so widespread that by 1905, Oklahoma had 5,231 miles of track.

AN EYEWITNESS ACCOUNT:
THE RAILROAD COMES TO MUSKOGEE

A reporter for the *Cincinnati Commercial*, J. H. Beadle was one of the first journalists to travel the new MK & T railroad tracks through Indian Territory in 1872. He was an astute observer and left a vivid account in his book, *Western Wilds and the Men Who Redeem Them* (Cincinnati, 1881), contrasting Muskogee as a boisterous railroad town with the normal routines of life at the Creek Agency and Tullahassee mission school. Is it any wonder that the Five Tribes were suspicious of the benefits of the railroad?

The records of Muscogee are bloody. During the five weeks the [railroad] terminus business and stage offices were there and at Gibson, sixteen murders were committed at these two places, and in a very short time five men were killed at the next terminus. One man was shot all to pieces just in front of the dining-car at Muscogee, and another had his throat cut at night, almost in the middle of the town. It is true, strangers, travelers, and outsiders are rarely if ever troubled. These murders are upon their own class, and new-comers who are weak enough to mix in, drink and gamble with them. . . .

After two days in this lively town, we concluded we had better see the Creeks at home, and started afoot for the Agency, traveling over a beautiful, rich prairie. . . . Eight or ten miles west of Muscogee, we entered a region of rude log-cabins and gaunt farm stock, where black faces peered at us through the cracks of "worm fences." . . . The place is overrun by freedmen. A continuous line of settlements, with "patches" rather than farms, extends for ten miles along the Arkansas, with a population of perhaps a thousand freedmen and a hundred Creeks. . . .

[At nearby Tullahassee Mission] we spent a most delightful Sabbath. . . . This mission has been thirty years in existence, and has educated all the leading men of the Creek Nation. . . . Supper was called soon after our arrival; we took "visitors' chairs," and watched with much interest the orderly incoming of some seventy young Creeks, of every age from eight to twenty-two. Nearly all were purebloods, and the whole scene was a revelation to me. I had seen [the] savage-painted Indian, and the miserable vagabond on the white frontier, but the civilized, scholarly Indian boy and girl presented a new sight. Supper over, a chapter was read, and the school united in prayers and a devotional hymn. Then we were invited to hear classes, who volunteered an evening recitation for our benefit. (Anne Hodges Morgan and Rennard Strickland, eds., *Oklahoma Memories* [Norman: University of Oklahoma Press, 1981], 43, 44, 46)

Benefits of the Railroad

The railroads facilitated the economic recovery of Indian Territory. Surplus grain and beef moved with ease to markets in St. Louis, Kansas City, and elsewhere in "the States," stimulating even greater production. To take advantage of its benefits, many tribespeople abandoned isolated homesteads and relocated nearer the railroad. Yet only the most courageous actually settled in one of the new towns established along the line.

The railroads also made possible the development of a commercial lumber industry. Operators situated

When the MK and T railroad bypassed North Fork Town, the community's merchants removed to locations nearer the tracks and organized the town of Eufaula with a real Main Street. The railroad also brought new consumer goods, which were offered for sale by stores like Grayson Brothers.

steam-powered sawmills along the MK & T tracks at Stringtown and Atoka in Atoka County and processed Oklahoma's virgin forests into railroad ties, telegraph poles, bridge and mining timber, and lumber for other construction. Millions of board feet were shipped out of the state annually.

Railroad Disadvantages

The economic recovery, expansion, and exploitation improved individual standards of living and provided additional revenue for tribal governments, but those blessings had a down side. The opening of Indian Territory, so long feared by tribal leaders, reduced the Indians to a minority in their own land, aggravated lawlessness, and threatened their sovereignty.

Overrun by Intruders

The Native American population of Indian Territory at the close of the Civil War was approximately 50,000. That figure did not include some 8,000 former slaves and 2,500 whites. In 1900 the Indian population remained essentially the same, but the alien population had increased 125 times: whites numbered 109,400, and there were 18,600 blacks. Who were the newcomers? Primarily tenant farmers, coal miners, railroad workers, cowboys, and merchants, only a few of whom were in the territory legally. Outnumbered two to one, the Indians

soon found it difficult to retain political and cultural control of their own country.

In the immediate aftermath of warfare there had
been a virtual absence of local government among
the Five Tribes. Personal survival was more important than law and order. The U.S. Army did occupy
Fort Gibson, but the garrison was not large enough
to undertake extensive policing activity. The U.S.
government's agents to the Five Tribes, who initially were army officers, were little more than administrative officials. And after 1874 there was only
the Union agent, with offices at Muskogee. Put differently, Indian Territory was defenseless against
general lawlessness as well as organized criminal
activity.

The Sources of Lawlessness

Tribal officials perceived their former slaves as one
source of difficulty. Among the Five Tribes only the
Chickasaws had or would grant them citizenship,
and the former slaves had few resources with which
to begin a new life. Most probably practiced subsistence agriculture as did the full-blood Indians, but
a few turned to stealing as a means of livelihood.
Tribal residents responded by organizing night-
ing vigilante patrols who executed or whipped offenders. To protect themselves, the blacks settled
near one another, which led to the development of
several all-black communities like Red Bird in Wagoner County and Boley in Okfuskee County.

A greater source of trouble were the white outlaw
bands who operated in the territory after the Civil
War. These included the James Brothers, the Younger Gang, and the Dalton Brothers, all of whom considered the territory a good hideout and a fertile
field for robbery. The territory attracted so many
desperados that it became known as the Robber's
Roost.

The coming of the railroad only made matters
worse. With the construction crews came prostitutes, whiskey sellers, gamblers, thieves, and other
hoodlums. The camps out of which they worked
were called "Hells on Wheels," and in them street
shootings were routine. The permanent towns they
left in their wake, such as Caddo and Wagoner, were
only slightly less rowdy.

These Choctaw lighthorse-men, or peace officers, found it difficult to maintain law and order in the Choctaw Nation after the Civil War because of the large number of white and black intruders.

Judge Isaac C. Parker

Unable to cope with this crisis of crime, tribal leaders asked the United States to help. In response, the federal government in 1871 located the court for the Western District of Arkansas, whose jurisdiction included the Indian Territory, in Fort Smith. The court was never really effective until 1875 when Isaac C. Parker of Missouri was appointed to the bench.

Parker made a difference. In twenty-one years he tried nearly 9,000 cases, and most of them involved prisoners arrested in Indian Territory. One was the celebrated bandit queen Belle Starr. Of the number tried, 160 were sentenced to death by hanging, and 70 were actually executed, as many as 6 at one time. Known as the "law west of Fort Smith," Parker relied on a corps of deputy U.S. marshals to arrest fugitives and transport them to court, including Bill Tilghman, a white man, and Bass Reeves, a black. The officers worked for fees only, which they lost if their prisoner died on the way to court.

A Vanishing Sovereignty

Parker's court helped institute a measure of law and order in Indian Territory, but it was at the cost of tribal sovereignty. The Indian nations' courts insisted that they had jurisdiction in disputes involving their own citizens in their own countries. Parker insisted that he had authority when whites

THE CHEROKEE TOBACCO CASE

Elias C. Boudinot was the son of Elias Boudinot, the assassinated editor of the *Cherokee Phoenix*. The younger Boudinot had served as the Cherokee delegate to the Confederate congress in Richmond during most of the Civil War. While in Virginia, he became well acquainted with the different dimensions of the tobacco industry, and especially with the manufacture of the popular tobacco plug. Boudinot saw the industry as a means of recouping his personal fortune once the war was over. That was probably in his mind in 1866 when he went to Washington to help negotiate the treaty that restored relations with the United States.

The Cherokee Reconstruction treaty of 1866 contained a provision that exempted tobacco manufactured in the Cherokee Nation from the federal revenue tax on tobacco. Whether Boudinot was responsible for that clause is in dispute, but it is clear that he moved quickly to take advantage of it. Once back in Oklahoma he announced plans to establish a tobacco-plug factory at Boudiville, Cherokee Nation, just across the line from Maysville, Arkansas.

With his uncle, General Stand Watie, Boudinot purchased essential supplies. These included machinery (a hydraulic press, pumps, scales, and moulds) from Missouri, a supply of Burly leaf tobacco, and stocks of sugar, licorice, and grape juice as sweeteners. Once all of that was deposited at the new factory building and warehouse, Boudinot began production of the tobacco plugs, which he sold under the brand name "Boudinot and Watie." Demand for the product was strong since the tobacco, not subject to the federal tax, sold for two-thirds of the price of plugs manufactured in the States. By the summer of 1869 the Boudiville factory was in "a prosperous condition."

Boudinot and Watie were not the only tobacco manufacturers in the Cherokee Nation. There were three other plants: one near present Stilwell, another close to Westville, and a third near Boudiville. The total capacity of the plants is uncertain, but certainly

were involved, regardless of where they were. Among the first whom he hung was a Cherokee man, and in 1892 he sent marshals to blast Ned Christie, a notable Cherokee outlaw, from his hideout. Parker's court showed little respect for the Indian judicial system or for Indians themselves.

The lack of respect extended beyond just the legal system of the United States. Business corporations operating in Indian Territory, especially railroads, ignored tribal laws and bribed tribal officials. White and black farmers planted fields, and ranchers grazed cattle, without paying permit fees; townsmen operated businesses and refused to pay taxes on merchandise. Meanwhile, the U.S. Congress and president demonstrated the least respect of all.

the actual production was enough to impact the marketplace. Manufacturers in Missouri, Arkansas, and Texas chafed under what they considered unfair competition. The federal government was not happy either, for tobacco taxes provided much of its revenue. Declaring that the Cherokee manufacturers were in violation of the federal revenue law of 1868, the United States treasurer ordered the U.S. marshal for the Western District of Arkansas to seize all four factories late in 1869.

Boudinot and others sought relief in the federal courts. When lower courts ruled against them, the case was quickly appealed to the United States Supreme Court. At that level the issue was no longer a matter of property. Instead, the question was whether laws of the United States Congress—in this case the tobacco revenue law—overrode clear stipulations in Indian treaties. The decision was not unanimous, but the high court ruled in 1870 that federal law was supreme.

The decision was a personal blow for Boudinot, Watie, and the other tobacco manufacturers among the Cherokees. But more than that, the decision was a major blow to the sovereignty of all Indian nations, and not just the Five Tribes in our state. Thereafter the treaties solemnly negotiated with the Indians over the years were binding on the federal government only if the United States Congress said they were.

Further reading: Robert K. Heimann, "The Cherokee Tobacco Case," *Chronicles of Oklahoma* 61 (1963).

Cherokee Elias C. Boudinot was a shrewd businessman and politician before and after he invested in the manufacture of tobacco.

Okmulgee Councils and Constitution

At issue was the sovereignty, or ability to act independently, of the Indian nations. Assuming that the tribes had more land than they needed and that their

Delegates to the International Council assembled at the Creek Capitol Building in Okmulgee, 1875. Thirty-four tribes were represented.

lands lacked productive farms and businesses, federal officials had urged them in the Reconstruction treaties of 1866 to form a single territorial government to be called Oklahoma. This new government, Washington officials expected, could help open up Indian Territory to white exploitation despite treaty provisions to the contrary.

Under strong federal pressure, intertribal councils met at Okmulgee after 1868. In 1870 delegates wrote a constitution that included a bill of rights for the future Indian state. But the document was not satisfactory to Washington officials: the tribes retained too much of their independence. The federal government soon pursued new measures expressive of disrespect, including land allotment to tribe members, in an attempt to exploit the resources of Indian Territory. How different Oklahoma might have been had Congress adopted the Okmulgee Constitution!

Summary

The Five Tribes were at pains to reestablish their governments and social institutions in the postwar era. They had hoped to do so without undue external pressure, but the desire to open Oklahoma to exploitation by non-Indians was too strong. The railroad was the engine of "progress," bringing some benefits but far greater liabilities to the citizens of the Five Nations. In the end they lost not only their sovereignty as independent peoples, but their land as well.

Visit the magnificent tribal capitol buildings of the Cherokees, at Tahlequah; the Creeks, at Okmulgee; the Choctaws, at Tuskahoma; and the Chickasaws, at Tishomingo. Visit also some of the county or district courthouses of the Five Tribes: Saline (Cherokee), east of Locust Grove; Tobucksy (Choctaw), in North McAlester; Blue (Choctaw), at Caddo. Visit the Cherokee National Prison in Tahlequah and the Choctaw Nation county jails, of which one is on the capitol grounds at Tuskahoma and the other just west of Panama.

Also make field trips to the sites of the second Cherokee Female Seminary, on the grounds of Northeastern Oklahoma State University in Tahlequah; the Creek Nation's Nuyaka Academy, east of Okmulgee; the Choctaw Nation's Wheelock Academy, west of Valliant, and Goodland Indian Orphanage, southwest of Hugo; and the Chickasaw Nation's Carter Academy in Ardmore.

Visit Judge Parker's courtroom at Fort Smith and the Union Agency building at Muskogee.

Walk through an Indian Territory cemetery, for example, Boggy Depot, in Atoka County; Doaksville, in Choctaw County; Old Stonewall, in Pontotoc County; Park Hill, in Cherokee County; Polson Cemetery, in Delaware County; and the Cherokee National Cemetery, at Fort Gibson.

With permission, visit one of the many rural Indian Christian churches, or visit a campground where traditional religious services are conducted.

Suggestions for Further Reading

Reference

Bailey, M. Thomas. *Reconstruction in Indian Territory: A Story of Avarice, Discrimination, and Opportunism.* Port Washington, N.Y.: Kennikat Press, 1972.

Johnson, Neil R. *The Chickasaw Rancher.* Stillwater, Okla.: Redlands Press, 1961.

Littlefield, Daniel F., Jr. *The Chickasaw Freedmen: A People Without a Country.* Westport, Conn.: Greenwood Press, 1980.

McLoughlin, William G. *After the Trail of Tears: The Cherokees' Struggle for Sovereignty, 1839–1880.* Chapel Hill: University of North Carolina Press, 1993.

Masterson, V. V. *The Katy Railroad and the Last Frontier.* Norman: University of Oklahoma Press, 1952.

Miner, H. Craig. *The Corporation and the Indian: Tribal Sovereignty and Industrial Civilization in Indian Territory, 1865–1907.* 1976. Norman: University of Oklahoma Press, 1989.

Perdue, Theda. *Nations Remembered: An Oral History of the Cherokees, Chickasaws, Choctaws, Creeks, and Seminoles in Oklahoma, 1865–1907.* 1980. Norman: University of Oklahoma Press, 1993.

Wardell, Morris L. *A Political History of the Cherokee Nation, 1838–1907.* Norman: University of Oklahoma Press, 1938.

Related Reading

Littlefield, Daniel F., Jr. *Alex Posey: Creek Poet, Journalist, and Humorist.* Lincoln: University of Nebraska Press, 1992.

Shirley, Glenn. *Law West of Fort Smith.* 1957. Lincoln: University of Nebraska Press, 1968.

Chapter 12: **New Exiles in Oklahoma**

Satank, one of the great war chiefs and orators of the Kiowas, refused to become a farmer. In May 1871 he and others attacked a wagon train near Jacksboro, Texas, killing seven teamsters. Later, at Fort Sill, he defiantly informed General William T. Sherman, "If any other Indian comes and claims the honor of leading the party he will be lying to you for I did it myself!" Sherman believed him and had him arrested.

The next week Sherman sent Satank, along with Big Tree and Satanta, to Texas for trial in a civilian court. Still within sight of the fort, Satank sang his death song: "O sun, you remain forever, but we Ko-eet-senko must die; O earth, you remain forever, but we Ko-eet-senko must die." Then pointing to a nearby pecan tree he said calmly: "When I reach [there] I will be dead." And he was. Ripping the cuffs from his hands, Satank grabbed a concealed knife and stabbed a soldier in the leg. Seven bullets from other soldiers ended his life. His bleeding body was left by the side of the trail.

Establishing New Reservations

The tragedy of Satank illustrates some of the dramatic changes that were taking place in the western part of Oklahoma in the years after the Civil War. The Reconstruction treaties of 1866 with the Five Tribes had required them to give up almost one-half of their lands for the resettlement of other Indian tribes. Pressured by white leaders in Kansas, who did not want Indians living in their state, the federal government began almost immediately to re-move tribal peoples living there and elsewhere on the Southern Plains to the ceded areas. Within twenty years, 12,000 to 15,000 exiles had established homes in Indian Territory, many with cultures and histo-ries far different from those of the Five Tribes. With that migration, sometimes known as the Sec-ond Trail of Tears, the land truly became one of *okla-homma*, or red people.

Each migrating group had a dramatic story of displacement and dispossession that deserves to be remembered. Here, unfortunately, we can only men-tion the broad outlines of the concentrations of tribes in Oklahoma between 1867 and 1884, and our discus-sion is organized geographically rather than chro-nologically.

Kansas-Nebraska Tribes Relocate to Oklahoma

In the northeast corner of Indian Territory (now Ottawa County), the Wyandots, the Peorias, the Ot-tawas, and the Miamis—all exiles from Kansas—settled on small reservations near the Quapaws, the Shawnees, and the Senecas. They were subse-quently joined by a small band of Modocs, who had just lost a war in northern California.

Two large communities of Delawares and Shaw-nees, also forced from Kansas, bought land from the Cherokees. Made citizens of the Cherokee Nation,

The boarding school of the Sac and Fox Agency was located near Stroud. It opened in 1872 soon after the Sac and Fox people relocated in Oklahoma from Kansas.

the Delawares settled in southern Nowata County, and the Shawnees in northern Craig County.

After relinquishing title to their Kansas reservation, 1,500 Osages relocated to lands that had recently belonged to the Cherokees. Now Osage County, the new reservation was not suitable for farming, but in the twentieth century became a virtual fountain of "black gold," making the Osages among the richest people in the world. The Kaws (Kansas) later joined their near kinsmen on lands carved out of the western part of the Osage reservation, now eastern Kay County. A senator from Kansas and vice president of the United States, Charles Curtis (1860–1936) was a member of the Kaw tribe.

West of the Arkansas River in the Cherokee Outlet four other tribes found new homes. Some 2,000 strong, the Pawnees lost their Nebraska lands and were assigned lands in what is now Pawnee County. The Otoes and Missouris moved from a reserve on the Nebraska-Kansas border to a new reservation in what is now Noble County. The Poncas were forced to take up lands in southern Kay County. They won national attention when Chief Standing Bear "fled" the reservation to take the body of his dead son back to Dakota Territory for burial.

The Nez Perce, a Pacific Northwest people, lived as exiles on their reservation in southwestern Kay County for six years before they returned to their Washington state homeland. The Tonkawas, a much abused and maligned tribe from Texas, then took possession of the abandoned reservation.

Five more dispossessed tribes found homes along the western border of the Creek and Seminole nations. The Sac and Fox, the tribe of "America's Greatest Athlete," Jim Thorpe, removed from Kansas to lands that are primarily in eastern Lincoln County. To the northwestern part of that county came the Iowas from a reservation along the Nebraska-Kansas border. The Mexican Kickapoos were tricked into taking up homes just south of the Iowas. The Potawatomi Indians of Kansas relocated their community in what is now Pottawatomie County, ultimately sharing their new domain with the Absentee, or Western, Shawnees.

Southern Plains Tribes Get New Reservations

The federal government was able to relocate the Kansas tribes to Indian Territory without serious resistance. That was not true of the nomadic tribes who hunted buffalo on the Southern Plains. As early as 1865, American officials had met with them in council on the Little Arkansas River in Kansas. There the Cheyennes and the Arapahoes, the Plains Apaches, the Comanches, and the Kiowas all agreed to homelands with definite borders. Because the reservations extended into Kansas and Texas, white homesteaders in those areas demanded new treaties with the Plains tribes that would limit their reservations to Indian Territory.

A second peace council was convened in October 1867 on Medicine Lodge Creek in southwestern Kan-

This Arapaho camp, photographed about 1868 by William S. Soule, was typical of those on the reservations throughout western Oklahoma.

sas. It was one of the most remarkable gatherings of Native Americans ever. Seven thousand were there, including major leaders of all the tribes. Satanta of the Kiowas, a tall, powerful man with a commanding presence, expressed the sentiment of all Indians: "I love the land and the buffalo and I will not part with any. . . . I love to roam over the wide prairie, and when I do it, I feel free and happy." On a reservation, he said, "we grow pale and die," and "my heart feels like bursting with sorrow."

But the government commissioners at the council were not persuaded by the oratory. The Comanches and the Kiowas, with the Plains Apaches, were assigned a tract between the western border of the Chickasaw Nation and the North Fork of the Red River. Assigned first to the Cherokee Outlet, the Cheyennes and the Arapahoes ultimately received a large reservation north of the Comanches and Kiowas. The tribes of the old Wichita Agency—the Wichitas and Affiliated Tribes (including the Keechies, the Anadarkos, the Ionis, and the Wacos), as well as the Caddos and the Absentee Delawares—were assigned a single reserve in what is now northern Caddo County.

Battle of the Washita

Unlike the Kansas tribes who were exiled to Indian Territory, the Plains tribes did not go quietly to their reservations. They continued their old habits of following the buffalo and raiding isolated white settlements in Kansas and Texas. To force them to lead more settled lives, Major General Philip Sheridan mounted a major military campaign in the winter of 1868. His principal target was the Cheyenne band led by Chief Black Kettle, who had narrowly escaped death in the infamous Sand Creek, Colorado, massacre four years earlier.

Operating out of a new post later named Fort Supply in present Woodward County, troops of the Seventh Cavalry led by Lieutenant Colonel George A. Custer found and attacked the Cheyenne camp on November 27. The battle of the Washita (in central Roger Mills County) was a complete victory for the U.S. Army. The Seventh Cavalry killed 100 Cheyennes, including Black Kettle, other men, women, and children, and 800 ponies. Custer lost thirty of his own soldiers, among them the grandson of Alexander Hamilton, Captain Louis McLane Hamilton.

The Winter War worked. Although most Comanches continued to roam the Texas plains, some Cheyennes, Arapahos and Kiowas moved onto their reservations. To see that they stayed there, the army's high command ordered the construction of two major forts and one smaller encampment: Fort Sill, in Comanche County, in 1869 (replacing Forts Arbuckle and Cobb); Fort Reno, in 1874, in present Canadian County; and Cantonment, in 1879, near Canton in Blaine County.

TWO REMARKABLE REGIMENTS: THE BUFFALO SOLDIERS

A company of black infantry, better known as Buffalo Soldiers, at Fort Sill about 1880.

In July 1866, Congress authorized the organization of two regiments of United States cavalry to be "composed of colored men." General of the Army William T. Sherman designated the two units as the Ninth and the Tenth Cavalry and appointed as commanding officers Colonel Edward Hatch of Iowa (Ninth) and Colonel Benjamin Grierson of Illinois (Tenth). Both officers were white, and both had distinguished records of service in the Union Army during the Civil War.

Within a year the Ninth and Tenth cavalry regiments were recruited, trained, and dispatched to the field. The Ninth first did duty in West Texas and New Mexico. The Tenth Regiment was posted to Kansas and Oklahoma, with four companies assigned to Fort Gibson and Fort Arbuckle. Their principal task was to help implement President Grant's Indian policy of re-

Dissatisfaction with the Reservation

On a map the Plains Indian reservations appeared ample. Less than 8,000 Indians shared 8 million acres of land. But the amount of land was not the point: these people were hunters whose economy and culture depended on the buffalo that moved freely on the Great Plains. In the early 1870s finding buffalo was no longer an easy task because the once great herds had been thinned by professional killers with high-powered rifles who slaughtered the animals for their skin only. Tom Dixon, for example, killed 2,173 bison in thirty-six days. Without a stable food

locating Kansas and Southern Plains tribes on new reservations in the western part of our state.

In 1869 the Tenth Cavalry was ordered to construct and occupy a major new post on the Comanche and Kiowa reservation. Grierson selected an appropriate site on Medicine Bluff Creek just north of modern Lawton. Shortly thereafter the Tenth Regiment was engaged in the construction of Old Fort Sill. The native-stone fort was the headquarters of the Tenth for the next seven years.

In southwestern Oklahoma the Tenth Cavalry participated in the so-called Red River War with the Comanches and the Kiowas. They were such worthy adversaries that the Indians named them "Buffalo Soldiers," presumably because their hair reminded them of the hair of the bison. But given the importance of the buffalo to the lifeways of the Comanches and Kiowas, the designation was also an expression of admiration. In 1876 the Tenth Cavalry was reassigned to New Mexico.

In the meantime companies of the Ninth Cavalry, commanded by Colonel Hatch, had been detailed to Fort Reno near present El Reno. This time their assignment was not to fight Indians but to fight Boomers, that is, the landhungry white farmers, led by C. C. Carpenter and David L. Payne, who were determined to settle in the Unassigned Lands in what is now central Oklahoma. The task became so immense that the entire Ninth Cavalry Regiment was transferred to Oklahoma (to Forts Supply and Sill, as well as Reno). Between 1881 and 1885 *black* cavalry units were trying to expel illegal *white* squatters from lands owned by *red* men. It was a unique and very difficult assignment, but one that the Ninth accomplished without bloodshed.

The Buffalo Soldiers were gone from Oklahoma before the Run of 1889. Yet in two decades of service they had left their mark on the future state, although they had to deal continually with racial prejudice. They built permanent forts, surveyed roads, mapped uncharted country, identified sources of water, and provided escort services. They were both fighters and peacemakers. Few have contributed so much in so short of a time.

Further reading: William H. Leckie, *The Buffalo Soldiers: A Narrative of the Negro Cavalry in the West*. Norman: University of Oklahoma Press, 1967.

source, the Plains tribes left their Indian Territory reservations to find a replacement, usually through raids in Texas.

It was on one such foray in 1871 that Satank, Satanta, Big Tree, and 100 other Kiowas attacked a supply-laden wagon train. Satank, of course, was later killed by his army captors. The other two chiefs were tried in Texas, convicted of murder, and sentenced to be hanged. The state governor first commuted their sentences, and then in 1873 he pardoned the two Kiowas. They returned to the tribe and quickly organized new raids in revenge for their captivity. They also joined forces with the resourceful leader of the Quahada Comanches, Quanah Parker, who had participated in the famous attack on buffalo hunters at Adobe Walls in June 1874.

Red River War

By that time it seemed to government officers that there were more Plains Indians off the reservation than on, and that those that were off had set the frontier aflame. The secretary of war ordered the U.S. Army to bring them in. The result was the Red River War. Five columns of troops, involving 3,000 soldiers, converged on the Texas Panhandle during the winter of 1874–75. Few pitched battles were fought, but the Indians were forced to flee their camps and abandon their ponies so many times that they found themselves on foot with little clothing and even less food. In the late spring they admitted defeat. Satanta surrendered at the Cheyenne-Arapaho Agency; Quanah Parker and his Quahada Comanches laid down their arms at Fort Sill, as did most of the other "belligerents."

Satanta, chief of the Kiowas, refused to live on the reservation until forced to do so by the U.S. Army.

The army was not prepared to forgive and forget. Satanta and Big Tree were shipped quickly back to Texas and returned to prison for parole violations; four years later Satanta committed suicide. Nine Comanche, twenty-six Kiowa, thirty-three Cheyenne, and two Arapaho warrior-leaders were shackled in iron chains and transported to a military prison at Fort Marion in Florida. Some of the younger captives, such as Making Medicine of the Cheyennes, became noted for their "ledger art" and for being among the first students of the famous Indian school at Carlisle, Pennsylvania. The rest were allowed to return to their people in 1878. In 1894 they were joined at Fort Sill by still more military prisoners including Geronimo and other Apache survivors of the wars in Arizona. Quanah Parker was not arrested; he became the principal leader of the Comanches as they adjusted to reservation life (see chapter 14).

President Grant's Reservation Policy

It was ironic that the government had to use military force before the Indians actually settled on their reservations. President U.S. Grant had hoped to avoid that when he came to office early in 1869. He, other public officials, and humanitarians agreed that Indian people must abandon their traditional way of living and thinking, if they were to survive in a modern world. Much like Thomas Jefferson seventy years before, they proposed to "Americanize" the Indians, first by isolating them on reservations for twenty-five to thirty years. During that period of time they would be taught to farm rather than hunt, they could enroll their children in schools, they could be converted to Christianity, and they could learn the advantages of individual (as opposed to communal) property rights.

If pursued humanely, President Grant believed, the goals of the reservation policy could be accomplished without bloodshed. But first, tribal boundaries needed to be clearly defined. In Oklahoma that meant the creation of twenty-one separate reservations for 80,000 Native Americans. The reservations were ultimately organized into eight different agencies.

A member of the Quaker fellowship, John D. Miles was U.S. agent for the Cheyenne-Arapaho reservation and responsible for implementing President U. S. Grant's Peace Policy.

Quaker Agents

To administer each jurisdiction and supervise the Americanization process, President Grant appointed an agent who had been recommended by a Christian denomination. All but one of the agents in Oklahoma were Quakers. Opposed to violence on principle, they supported Grant's Peace Policy completely. Serving most notably as agents were Lawrie Tatum, for the Kiowas and Comanches; John D. Miles, for the Cheyennes and Arapahoes; and Isaac T. Gibson, for the Osages. Gibson's nephew, the future President Herbert Hoover, spent one of his childhood years at the agency in Pawhuska.

Since a goal of the reservations was to make the Indians proficient farmers, each agency employed a person to teach them how to plow and to plant. The agents also hired blacksmiths to shoe horses and to fix machinery. There were doctors and nurses on each agency staff as well.

INDIAN AGENCIES IN OKLAHOMA

Listed below are the eight Indian agencies organized in Oklahoma after the Civil War. The asterisk (*) indicates a single reservation. There is no need to memorize the table, but you will understand Oklahoma history better if you have a strong sense of where the agencies were located and the different tribes associated with each.

Agency	Tribes	Area Removed From	Date Arrived
Quapaw Agency (formerly Seneca), at Miami	*Quapaws	Arkansas	1834
	*Senecas of Sandusky	Ohio	1832
	*Eastern Shawnees	Ohio	1832
	*Wyandots	Ohio/Kansas	1867
	*Confederate Peoria	Illinois/Kansas	1867
	Miami	Ohio/Kansas	1867
	*Ottawas	Canada/Kansas	1867
	*Modocs	California	1873
Osage Agency, Pawhuska	*Osages	Missouri/Kansas	1871
	*Kaws	Kansas	1872
Pawnee Agency (formerly Ponca), Pawnee	*Poncas	Dakota/Nebraska	1877
	*Pawnees	Nebraska	1873
	*Otoes and Missouris	Nebraska/Kansas	1882
	*Nez Perce	Oregon/Idaho	1877
	Tonkawas (took reservation of Nez Perces)	Texas	1885
Sac and Fox Agency, near Stroud	*Sac and Fox	Kansas	1869
	*Citizen Pottawatomis	Kansas	1869
	Absentee Shawnees	Missouri/Texas	1868
	*Iowas	Nebraska/Kansas	1876
	*Kickapoos	Texas/Mexico	1874
*Cheyenne-Arapaho Agency, Darlington (northeast of El Reno)	Cheyennes	Colorado	1869
	Arapahos	Colorado	1869
*Wichita Agency, near Anadarko (combined with the Kiowa-Comanche Agency in 1879)	Wichita and Affiliated Tribes	Native/Texas	1700s
	Caddos	Texas/Arkansas	1830s
*Kiowa-Comanche Agency, Lawton (joined with the Wichita Agency in 1878 at Anadarko)	Comanches	Texas	1850s
	Kiowas	Wyoming	1850s
	Kiowa Apaches	Texas	1850s
	Apaches	Arizona	1894
Union Agency, Muskogee	*Choctaws	Mississippi	1820
	*Chickasaws	Tennessee	1837
	*Creeks	Georgia/Alabama	1825
	*Seminoles	Florida	1836
	*Cherokees	Georgia/Tennessee	1829
	Delawares	Kansas	1876
	Shawnees	Kansas	1867

No one expected the Indians to become proficient farmers immediately. Until they learned the necessary skills, and because they were no longer permitted to hunt buffalo, the government provided rations of beef, flour, sugar, and other staples. On designated days members of the exiled hunting tribes would stand in long lines waiting for food handouts. If he had not been so hungry, it would have been more than a proud warrior could stand.

FOOD RATIONS ON THE RESERVATION

Cheyenne and Arapaho Indians wait near Cantonment for their issue of beef.

Lawrie Tatum served as government agent on the Comanche-Kiowa reservation near Fort Sill between 1869 and 1873. He has left a vivid account of how life was sustained during the reservation ordeal of the exiled tribes. Food rations, he wrote

included beef, bacon, flour, coffee, sugar, soap, tobacco and soda, which were "issued" every two weeks to the chiefs, who divided them by having a woman of each family sit on the ground in a circle around him with her sacks, and he would divide it among them, except the beef, which was issued alive, one or more head of cattle to a chief or his representative, who had "beef paper," according to the number of families in his band. The last four weeks' issue that I made, in March, 1873, was to three thousand seven hundred and sixty Indians. To these were issued beef, gross 293,600 lbs.; bacon, 5,040 lbs.; flour, 51,800 lbs.; coffee, 4,146 lbs.; sugar, 8,290 lbs.; soda, 130 lbs., soap, 1,021 lbs.; tobacco, 580 lbs. (Tatum, *Our Red Brothers and the Peace Policy of President Ulysses S. Grant,* 72–73).

Emphasis on Schools and Churches

Government officials believed that education was the most critical aspect of Americanization. Associated with every agency, therefore, was a government-funded school with a curriculum similar to those found in Arkansas or Kansas schools. Some of these became large and influential boarding schools,

Doing the school washing was part of the curriculum for young men and women students enrolled at Riverside Indian School at Anadarko.

AN EYEWITNESS ACCOUNT: PROBLEMS AT A RESERVATION SCHOOL

The government established a school for Arapaho children at the Cheyenne-Arapaho Agency at Darlington, northwest of El Reno, in 1871. John H. Seger began to teach at the school about 1874, learning quickly that "education" meant different things to the tribespeople. Seger spent the rest of his life among the Indians, ultimately opening a manual-labor school for Cheyenne youngsters at Colony.

I . . . could see no progress or advancement among the pupils. The outside Indians were very troublesome. They came into the school-house, into the dining room—in fact any part of the house where work was carried on, and sat around and even lay down on the floor. . . .

[The problem was particular acute at dinner time. With the permission of Agent Miles, one day] I locked the outside dining room door. . . . Looking out a little later I saw five Indians coming out of their lodge near by. They had started promptly at the ringing of the bell, intending, no doubt, to sit down at the first table and enjoy a good square meal, but when they reached the dining room door, which they usually entered, they found it locked. They kicked and hammered a while, being very indignant at my trick.

After the children were seated I unlocked the door, and the Indians who were standing on the door-step undertook to push in. I grabbed the first one . . . by the arm and the back of the neck and gave him a whirl which sent him sprawling on the ground. . . . He jumped up and gathered his blanket around him, taking the edge between his teeth [and putting] . . . his hand on the knife in his belt. He marched up in front of me, straightened up and said in a very dignified way, and rather vehemently, "I am a chief."

I had no knife to take hold of, so I doubled up my fist and shook it in his face and said, "I am a chief, too. You are a chief in camp and I am a chief in school."

He said, "I and all the Arapahoes are friends of the school. We were just coming over to get our dinner. I do not know why you treat me so."

"You know that the rations for the grown Indians are issued from the Commissary," I replied. "But the rations for the children are sent to the school. It is my duty to see that the children get what belongs to them and plenty to eat." . . . White Crow commenced to look less stern and his hand dropped from the handle of his knife. . . . (Seger, *Early Days among the Cheyenne and Arapahoe Indians*, 43–47).

teaching students not only to read and write English but also to change their patterns of behavior to ones deemed acceptable by their white teachers. Graduates often went on to national boarding schools like Carlisle Indian School in Pennsylvania and Haskell Institute in Lawrence, Kansas.

Almost as important as education was Christianization. The federal government promoted Christianity on the reservation in many ways: by selecting officials (agents and teachers) who were Christian, by making religion a part of the school curriculum, and by encouraging Christian missionaries to work among the tribespeople. The policy had an impact. Missionaries not only came, but they preached, made converts, organized churches, and established dozens of schools. Particularly effective were the Methodists (J. J. Methvin), American Baptists (Isabel Crawford and John McIntosh), Mennonites (A. J. Becker), Dutch Reformed (Frank Hall Wright), Episcopalians (Making Medicine), Presbyterians, and Catholics (William H. Ketcham).

Reservation Indians listened respectfully, although at times reluctantly, to the teachers and the preachers. Many changed the way they *did* things (their clothing and housing, and even their work), but only a few altered the way they *thought* about things (that is, their religion). The requirement that they think of land as privately owned illustrates the problem. For Native Americans the surface of the earth was more a spiritual than an economic resource.

Presbyterian missionary women make a call on a Kiowa camp near Anadarko about 1895.

They were offended deeply by the notion of individual ownership, yet it was just such a view that agents, educators, and missionaries promoted.

If Indians were to be real Americans, they were told, they individually had to live on and cultivate small tracts of land to which they alone held title. In other words, they had to abandon those values, or ways of thinking, that kept them Indian.

AN EYEWITNESS ACCOUNT: THE STRANGE WAYS OF THE WHITES

Young Carl Sweezy, an Arapaho of keen intelligence, was very interested in learnng the ways of the whites. His teacher, John Seger, at the Cheyenne-Arapaho school at Darlington nurtured and encouraged that interest. It was a good investment of his time, for Sweezy became a noted painter and author. In his gentle memoir, the Arapaho wrote of his early education:

What astonished us more than anything else was learning that the white man cut and stored ice in winter, for use in summer. . . . At the Agency they built a thick-walled storage house, and when the ponds and streams were frozen solid they sawed the ice into blocks, hauled it in, and packed it in sawdust from the Agency sawmill. We never heard of ice in summer before. It would have seemed like strong medi-

cine, if we had not seen for ourselves how it was done. But when the next summer came, and some of the Indians drank the white man's iced lemonade, and when we tasted his ice cream, we knew that the white man had more schemes for comfort and good living than we had ever dreamed of. (Althea Bass, *The Arapaho Way: A Memoir of an Indian Boyhood*, 39)

Coping with the Reservation Experience

In the late 1860s and early 1870s the exiles had evaded the pressure and the confusion by ignoring the reality of the reservation. After the Red River War that was no longer possible. Instead, many sought to cope with the reservation ordeal by holding onto old traditions, especially rites, rituals, and festivals of native religion. The Kiowas, for example, made efforts to hold an annual Sun Dance until 1890, when they could no longer find the required buffalo head and hide.

The Cheyennes turned the periodic beef ration into a simulated buffalo hunt, while other tribespeople relived their raiding days by performing in Wild West shows like that of Gordon ("Pawnee Bill") Lillie. Still others evaded the disorientation of the reservation by walking away from it: Dull Knife's Northern Cheyennes traveled back to Montana in 1878, and some Kickapoos and Seminoles escaped to Mexico at about the same time.

Another response of those who found it difficult to adjust to reservation life was to seek strength in the messages of Indian prophets. One of those was Wovoka, a Nevada Paiute religious leader who preached that the Indians, if they danced and prayed properly, would one day regain control of their lands and see the buffalo return. In the 1890s, Wovoka's Ghost Dance appealed to the Arapahos led by Chief Left Hand in the Geary area and to the Caddos near Anadarko.

There were far more adherents to "Father Peyote," however. Peyote is the top of a spineless cactus which, when chewed or made into tea, produces a feeling of goodwill toward all humanity. It was and is used sacramentally to cleanse the body internally and to enable worshippers to follow better the "Peyote Road" that leads to the "Suffering Savior." Encouraged by Quanah Parker, many Comanches near Lawton embraced the peyote cult; John ("Moonhead") Wilson,

A Peyote ceremony, sheltered by a tipi, occurs on the Kiowa reservation in 1892. Note the half-moon altar on the floor of the tipi.

a Caddo-Delaware Indian, spread the message to the Quapaws and the Osages in northeastern Oklahoma. After first trying to suppress it, the state of Oklahoma legalized the use of peyote as a religious sacrament in 1918 when the Native American Church was incorporated.

Significance

The story of the Second Trail of Tears is a tragic story of uprooting, relocation, readjustment, military conflict, deprivation, and despair. But it is also a story of survival, determination, and perseverance. There are few chapters in Oklahoma's history that have made such a permanent imprint on the state. Among other things the Second Trail of Tears helps account for the rich variety of people in Oklahoma. It also helps explain why Oklahoma Indians have always provided unusual amounts of leadership in the Native American community both within and without state. Over the years they learned to accommodate change without abandoning their Indianness. The son and granddaughter of Satank illustrate the point: he became an Episcopal minister, and she became a college-educated public-school teacher, yet they never thought of themselves as anything other than Kiowa.

See History for Yourself

Visit the site of one of the agencies established for the benefit of an exiled tribe, particularly the Osage Agency, at Pawhuska; the Pawnee Agency, at Pawnee; or the Cheyenne-Arapaho Agency, at Darlington (northwest of El Reno).

Visit the site and remaining buildings of Old Fort Sill (especially the corral), at Lawton; Fort Reno, at El Reno, Fort Supply (particularly the commissary), on the grounds of Western State Hospital, at Fort Supply; and Cantonment, at Canton. Those in western Oklahoma should make a field trip to the site of the battle of the Washita and to the Black Kettle Museum at Cheyenne.

Visit also sites of government boarding schools for Indians: Fort Sill, at Lawton; Riverside, in Anadarko; Seger, at Colony; Concho, north of El Reno; Chilocco, north of Newkirk; and Pawnee, at Pawnee.

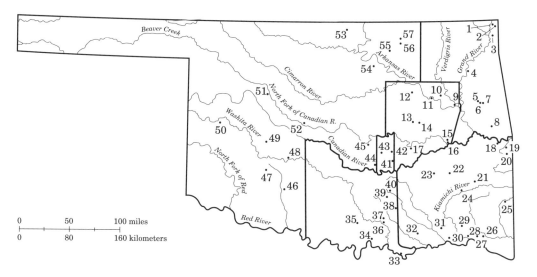

1. Quapaw Industrial Boarding School
2. St. Mary's Boarding School
3. Wyandotte Boarding School
4. Cherokee Orphan Asylum
5. Cherokee Male Seminary
6. Cherokee Female Seminary
7. Park Hill Mission School
8. Dwight Mission School
9. Tullahassee Mission School
10. Koweta Mission School
11. Wealaka Mission School
12. Euchee Boarding School
13. Nuyaka Mission School
14. Creek Orphan School
15. Asbury Manual Labor School
16. Eufaula Boarding School
17. Levering Manual Labor School
18. Fort Coffee Academy
19. New Hope Seminary
20. Cameron Institute
21. Tuskalusa Academy
22. Jones Academy
23. Colbert Institute
24. Tuskahoma Academy
25. Folsom Training School
26. Wheelock Academy
27. Elliott Academy
28. Pine Ridge Mission School
29. Old Spencer Academy

30. Goodland School & Orphanage
31. New Spencer Academy
32. Armstrong Academy
33. Bloomfield Academy
34. Burney Institute
35. Carter Seminary
36. Chickasaw Manual Labor School
37. Harley Institute
38. Wapanucka Academy
39. Collins Institute
40. Chickasaw National Academy
41. Emahaka Academy
42. Ramsey Mission School
43. Mekasukey Academy
44. Sacred Heart Academy
45. Shawnee Boarding School
46. Ft. Sill Indian School
47. Rainy Mountain Indian School
48. Riverside Indian School
49. Seger School
50. Red Moon Indian School
51. Cantonment Mission School
52. Concho Indian School
53. Chilocco Indian School
54. Pawnee Boarding School
55. St. John's School
56. St. Louis Industrial School
57. Osage Boarding School

Indian Academies, 1866–1906

Obtain permission and visit some Indian churches, both Christian and Peyote. Walk quietly through the cemeteries that are generally associated with the churches and read the tombstones. Above all visit the cemetery at Fort Sill where Geronimo is buried.

Visit the Quanah Parker Star House in Eagle Park in Cache (noting the separate rooms he had for each wife) and the Kiowa Tribal Museum at Carnegie.

Finally, visit the Pawnee Bill ranch and museum near Pawnee to get a feel for the Wild West shows in which Oklahoma Indians participated.

Suggestions For Further Reading

Reference

Baird, W. David. *The Quapaw Indians: A History of the Downstream People*. Norman: University of Oklahoma Press, 1980.

Berthrong, Donald J. *The Cheyenne and Arapaho Ordeal: Reservation and Agency Life in the Indian Territory, 1875–1907*. Norman: University of Oklahoma Press, 1976.

———. *The Southern Cheyennes*. Norman: University of Oklahoma Press, 1963.

Blaine, Martha Royce. *Pawnee Passage, 1870–1875*. Norman: University of Oklahoma Press, 1990.

Carriker, Robert C. *Fort Supply, Indian Territory: Frontier Outpost on the Plains*. Norman: University of Oklahoma Press, 1970.

Debo, Angie. *Geronimo: The Man, His Time, His Place*. Norman: University of Oklahoma Press, 1976.

Gibson, Arrell M. *The Kickapoos, Lords of the Middle Border*. Norman, 1963.

Hagan, William T. *The Sac and Fox Indians*. Norman: University of Oklahoma Press, 1980.

———. *United States–Comanche Relations: The Reservation Years*. 1976. Norman: University of Oklahoma Press, 1990.

Hoig, Stan. *Tribal Wars of the Southern Plains*. Norman: University of Oklahoma Press, 1992.

Mayhall, Mildred P. *The Kiowas*. 2d ed. Norman: University of Oklahoma Press, 1971.

Nye, Wilbur Sturtevant. *Carbine and Lance: The Story of Old Fort Sill*. Norman: University of Oklahoma Press, 1937, 1942, 1969.

Prucha, Francis Paul. *American Indian Policy in Crisis: Christian Reformers and the Indian, 1865–1900*. Norman: University of Oklahoma Press, 1976.

Trenholm, Virginia Cole. *The Arapahoes, Our People.* Norman: University of Oklahoma Press, 1970.

Stewart, Omer C. *Peyote Religion: A History.* Norman: University of Oklahoma Press, 1987.

Related Reading

Bass, Althea. *The Arapaho Way: A Memoir of an Indian Boyhood.* New York: Clarkson N. Potter, 1966.

Methvin, J. J. *In the Limelight.* Anadarko, Okla.: J. J. Methvin, 1925.

Momaday, N. Scott. *The Way to Rainy Mountain.* Albuquerque: University of New Mexico Press, 1969.

Seger, John H. *Early Days among the Cheyenne and Arapaho Indians.* Edited by Stanley Vestal. Norman: University of Oklahoma Press, 1934, 1956, 1979.

Tatum, Lawrie. *Our Red Brothers and the Peace Policy of President Ulysses S. Grant.* 1899. Lincoln: University of Nebraska Press, 1970.

Chapter 13: Lifestyles in Indian Territory— Eyewitness Accounts

The lifestyle of those who lived in Indian Territory before and just after the Civil War contrasts dramatically with ours. We can get some idea of the difference by examining what historians call *primary sources*. These are accounts by eyewitnesses who recorded their observations of life in Indian Territory in letters, journals, published articles, autobiographies, and oral interviews. In this chapter you will find brief excerpts from some of those accounts, relating first to Indian people and then to their slaves.

Many of the quotations come from the Indian-Pioneer Papers. In the 1930s interviewers for the Oklahoma Historical Society visited with hundreds of the older residents of our state about what it was like to grow up and live in the Indian and Oklahoma territories. Eventually those interviews were typed and bound into 113 volumes. That massive collection, now available on microfilm from the Oklahoma Historical Society, constitutes a treasure trove of primary source materials for historians interested in Indian Territory lifestyles. Theda Perdue, for example, has used it especially well in her *Nations Remembered: An Oral History of the Cherokees, Chickasaws, Choctaws, Creeks, and Seminoles, 1865–1907* (see "Suggestions for Further Reading" for the full bibliographic citation).

Other selections come from what scholars call the "Slave Narratives." Also gathered in the 1930s, these are transcribed accounts of interviews with African Americans who had the misfortune of being born into slavery. George P. Rawick has published

Above: Built about 1828 by Sequoyah himself, this log house is located in Sequoyah County. It is called a "single pen" cabin because it has only one room. Note that the logs have been flattened by the skillful use of an axe.

Above, right: This one-and-one-half-story Choctaw chief's house in Choctaw County was probably built in the 1830s. Now restored, its two log rooms are separated by a central passageway known as a dogtrot, from which the upper story is entered by a stairway. Note the four doorways.

Right, center: This two-story log house was built in the Creek Nation. It began originally as a single-pen cabin. Note the windows and doors, and how the two pens are joined together.

Right, bottom: Governor William L. Byrd of the Chickasaws added a second story to his home at Stonewall in Pontotoc County in the 1870s. Originally it was a one-story frame house with a large central hallway. Note the window shutters and the columns that support the portico.

many of them in *The American Slave: A Composite Autobiograpy* (see "Suggestions for Further Reading"). Two of the volumes relate to Indian Territory. In this chapter all quotations attributed to former slaves have been taken from one or the other of those volumes (after translation from dialect into modern English).

As you read these primary sources, compare your own lifestyle with those who lived in the domains of the Five Tribes 150 years ago.

Home

Master had a good log house and a brush shelter out in front like all the houses had. It was like a gallery, only it had dirt for the floor and brush for the roof. (Lucinda Davis, former Creek slave, in Rawick, *The American Slave,* vol. 7)

[Isaac Love's] Big House set way back from the road about a quarter of a mile. It was a two-story log house, and the rooms [were] big and [filled with] pretty furniture. The house was made of square logs and the cracks were filled out even with the edges of the logs. It was white washed. . . . There was a long gallery across the front of the house and big posts to support the roof. Back away from the house was the kitchen and nearby was the smokehouse. (Matilda Poe, former Chickasaw slave, in Rawick, *The American Slave,* vol. 7)

Rose Hill [the home of Choctaw planter Robert M. Jones] . . . was a large two-story frame house with tall, ridged columns supporting the porch, which extended all along the front of the house. . . . A wide hall, a room within itself, divided the two large front rooms. At each end of the house were large chimneys of native stone. Immediately back of the hall extended to the north [were] two rooms. A stack chimney of native stone afforded fireplaces for both rooms above and below stairs, as did also the chimneys at either end of the house. (Frank B. Tucker, Choctaw Indian, in Indian-Pioneer Papers, vol. 11)

Food

The [Creeks] cooked everything out in the yard in big pots, and they ate out in the yard too. (Lucinda Davis, former Creek slave, in Rawick, *The American Slave,* vol. 7)

At [B. F. Colbert's] table I saw sugar, butter and pastry—the first two of which have been exceedingly rare articles since I left Fort Smith. . . . (Waterman L. Ormsby, a passenger on the first westbound Overland Mail stage to reach Colbert's Ferry on Red River in 1858, in "Committee Report on Butterfield Overland Mail," *Chronicles of Oklahoma* 36 [Winter 1958–59]: 470)

More affluent members of
the Five Tribes, often intermarried white men, lived in
elegant houses. The two-story
frame Murrell Home in Cherokee County (*above*) was
constructed in 1845 with a
balcony and a full-height
porch. The Murray-Lindsay
Mansion in Garvin County
(*below*) was constructed of
stone blocks in 1879. The
third story and the massively
columned portico were added
in 1902.

Indians cooked just like the negroes and white folks.
. . . Lots of them boiled their food in clay pots that
they would make. (Jim Tomm, former Creek slave, in
L. M. S. Wilson, ed., "Reminiscences of Jim Tomm,"
Chronicles of Oklahoma 44 [Autumn 1966]: 304)

[To prepare Ta-fula, a favorite food of the Choctaws]
soak the corn for a short time or until the hull is
loosened, and then beat it in a mortar until the hull
has slipped off [and] the grains of corn are broken
into three or four pieces. Then take the corn out and
fan it in a basket to separate the hulls from the grains.
It can then be cooked with beans, with wood ashes or
in any other way you wish. Meat is not cooked with
Ta-fula. Use plenty of water and boil it down until
there is a lot of juice. (Peter J. Hudson, Choctaw edu-
cator, in "Choctaw Indian Dishes," *Chronicles of
Oklahoma* 17 [September 1939]: 333)

There were lots of wild game, such as wild pigeons, turkeys, quail, prairie chickens, deer, opossum, raccoon, fox, coyotes, mink, muskrat, squirrel, rabbits, etc. All the streams were full of fish. (Cook McCracken, Cherokee Indian, in Indian-Pioneer Papers, vol. 6)

Clothing

[The] great chief was no painted and plumed warrior. He wore a cotton hunting shirt of rather fantastic cut, a brown low-crowned hat shaded his copper-coloured physiognomy, he looked dusty, as if from a long ride. (Heinrich Baldwin Möllhausen, German artist, in Muriel H. Wright and George H. Shirk, eds., "Artist Möllhausen in Oklahoma—1853," *Chronicles of Oklahoma* 31 [Winter 1953–54]: 404)

The men were dressed with trousers made of common striped bed-ticking and hunting shirts made of factory gingham in [the] form of short, long gowns. They were generally without covering for the head, though some wore handkerchiefs in the form of turbans. (Cassandra Sawyer Lockwood, Presbyterian missionary, in Joseph B. Thoburn, ed., "Letters of Cassandra Sawyer Lockwood: Dwight Mission, 1834," *Chronicles of Oklahoma* 33 [Summer 1955]: 214)

We boys never wore pants until we were about eleven or twelve years old, they were just long shirts. Our clothing was made with a spinning wheel, reel, and loom. (Bird Doublehead, Cherokee Indian, in Indian-Pioneer Papers, vol. 3)

Many wear beads about their necks. . . Rings in the ears are very common, and I have seen one or two instances of a ring in the nose. The face of many in former days was ornamented with black inserted under the skin in zigzag lines from the corners of the mouth to the ears and to each side of the throat. (John Edwards, Presbyterian missionary, in "The Choctaw Indians in the Middle of the Nineteenth Century," *Chronicles of Oklahoma* 10 [September 1932]: 409)

Men's Work

My father and other Indians would go camp hunting back in the mountains. . . . When they would come back they would bring deer meat, turkeys, and some fish. . . . We would barbecue the deer meat and put it away in boxes or hang it up. It would keep for several weeks at a time. (Susan Frazier, Choctaw Indian, in Indian-Pioneer Papers, vol. 25)

I noticed . . . but little farming going on. The fact is, but little land is worked. Though the soil is well adapted for producing corn, tobacco, hemp, etc., they generally prefer to raise stock. They brand their cattle and let them run on the plains. . . . Many of the Choctaws own large herds of cattle, and live well on the increase. (Waterman L. Ormsby, a passenger on the first westbound Overland Mail stage in 1858, in Grant Foreman, ed., "The California Overland Mail Route Through Oklahoma," *Chronicles of Oklahoma* 36 [1958–59] 306)

They take great pride in being *men,* not *women.* The man is the superior, the woman the inferior. If they have but one horse, the man rides; the woman walks and carries the child or bundle. (John Edwards, Presbyterian missionary, in "The Choctaw Indians in the Middle of the Nineteenth Century," 410)

Women's Work

My mother did not own a spinning wheel. She would borrow one from our neighbor and spin cotton and wool into thread, which she would knit into socks and mittens. Mother would pull the seed out of cotton by hand until she got enough to spin and make socks and mittens which were heavy and warm. (Grant Foreman, ed., "Pioneer Recollections," *Chronicles of Oklahoma* 18 [December 1940]: 393)

Indigo, sycamore bark, walnut hulls and pokeberries were used to make different colors . . . blue, brown, tan, and red. . . . They made all kinds of baskets. [They made big] baskets to pick cotton in . . . out of split hickory and little baskets out of cane strippings. They made bowls and little statues of animals out of clay. (Jim Tomm, former Creek slave, in Wilson, ed., "Reminiscences of Jim Tomm," 304)

I was never employed, never drew any salary; but averaged eighteen hours a day doing many things for which there was no money to hire. Curing the meat and rendering the lard from twenty-five or thirty hogs each year, and raising the chickens were two jobs for which I assumed entire responsibility. (Anna R. Fait, Presbyterian missionary, in "An Autobiography," *Chronicles of Oklahoma* 32 [Summer 1954]: 189.

My life has been one of *toil* and *care,* since I have dwelt in this land, but it is *well* to *wear out* in a *good cause.* (Sophia Byington, Presbyterian missionary, in her letter to her brother, May 8, 1851, Cyrus Byington Papers, Gilcrease Museum, Tulsa)

Children's Work

We Choctaw half bloods don't raise up our children aright—we show them too much indulgences—if we would make them work in the corn field from the time they are able to do any thing and at the same time give them the hickory [switch] every time they transgressed they would be some account when they grow up—but as it is in the Nation if a parent has two or three Negroes—they depend on the Negroes doing every thing. (George W. Harkins, Choctaw district chief, in his letter to Peter Pitchlynn, August 12, 1856, box 2, Peter Pitchlynn Papers, Western History Collections, University of Oklahoma)

Cotton was picked into baskets and the seed was pulled out with our fingers: later we put wooden pegs in a board and pulled the cotton through the pegs and the seed would not come through. Every child had to seed so much cotton before they were allowed to go to bed. (Foreman, ed., "Pioneer Recollections," 392)

There were no fences, everyone's cattle and hogs ran wild. . . . I used to help in chasing hogs out of the yard and corn fields. (Samuel Worcester Robertson, son of Presbyterian missionary to the Creeks, in Martin Wenger, ed., "Samuel Worcester Robertson," *Chronicles of Oklahoma* 37 [Spring 1959]: 48–50)

Going to School

[At Kowetah Mission in 1846] the regular study hours are from nine to twelve, and from one to four; and often parts of the evening are employed in giving additional instruction to some of the advanced classes. . . . Before and after school hours, the pupils separate into different companies for work. Some of the boys with their axes repair to the wood pile, others with hoes are put to work in the field. . . .

The girls . . . assist in cooking, others in preparing the tables; some are at the milkroom; others in the clothes room, some making or mending clothes, others ironing, folding and laying them away. . . ; some are pounding corn in great wooden mortars, and others are cleaning it with such fans as the ancients in eastern countries used for winnowing grain; this corn is for *sofky*, and "large hominy." If it is Monday forenoon many of the girls are earnestly and cheerfully at work in the washroom. (Augustus W. Loomis, Presbyterian church official visiting Creek missions in 1846, in "Scenes in the Indian Territory Kowetah Mission," *Chronicles of Oklahoma* 46 [Spring 1968]: 68–70)

[At Dwight Mission in 1834] the little Indian girls sleep with no other accommodation than a blanket in which to wrap themselves as they lie down upon the floor. This [is] their accustomed mode of sleeping at home. . . . The boys play in one grove and the girls in another. They are never permitted to play together. (Thoburn, ed., "Letters of Cassandra Sawyer Lockwood: Dwight Mission, 1834," 218)

[O]ur little log school house . . . was 16 x 20 feet; one door to the east, one window (that is an opening, but no glass) to the west and one to the south. We had puncheon seats, that is what they called benches made out of a log split in the middle and smoothed off with an axe or a plane. . . . My studies were a reader and the old blue back spelling book. . . . (Emma Irvin Christian, Choctaw Indian, in "Memories of My Childhood Days in the Choctaw Nation," *Chronicles of Oklahoma* 9 [June 1931]: 159)

Practicing Religion

There is the ceremony often called the Green Corn Dance that is held every summer in the tribal towns of the Muskogee-Creek Nation. . . . The purpose of this ceremony is to take medicine and cleanse the whole body, internally and externally. (Sampson Tiger, Creek Indian, in Indian-Pioneer Papers, vol. 47)

There is a big wash pot of hot medicine of mixed herbs and a ten gallon jar of cold medicine made of red root. The men take partners, and when one takes medicine the other does, too. First, they drink from the hot pot, then from the cold jar and go out to vomit, as it cleans out the system thoroughly. . . . I believe the stomp way is better than the church. . . . (Nancy Grayson Barnett, Creek Indian, in Indian-Pioneer Papers, vol. 13)

Cherokee families from far and near would come in wagons, on horseback, and on foot to be at and take part in the annual camp meeting. Usually the whole family went, taking with them camping equipment and food. They also hunted during the stay at the camp. The time of the meeting was usually in August and September because the farming was over, the weather was fine, and grass was plentiful for the stock. (Sam H. Adair, Cherokee Indian, in Indian-Pioneer Papers, vol. 1)

Social Life

[The Creeks] . . . always had a pot full of sofky setting right inside the house, and anybody could eat when they felt hungry. If anybody came on a visit, they were always given some of the sofky. If they didn't take any, the old man always got mad! (Lucinda Davis, former Creek slave, in Rawick, *The American Slave,* vol. 7)

[Among the Chickasaws] one custom was to send messengers to the houses of friends where a small amount of cotton would be left with the request that it be spun and reeled. They were then invited to a 'hanking' when they were expected to bring the spun cotton. Usually the guests would find a quilt or two stretched on quilting frames and they would spend the day quilting. As many as twenty-five or thirty women would work. At noon a big dinner was served on long tables set in the yard. Turkey, chicken, pork, vegetables, pies and preserves were set before the guests. When the work was over late in the afternoon, the quilts would be rolled up and fastened to the ceiling beams by means of rings and ropes. Then the house was cleared of furniture, and the husbands and sweethearts having arrived, dancing would be indulged in until a late hour. (Ella Coodey Robinson, Cherokee Indian, in Carolyn Thomas Foreman, "Ella Flora Coodey Robinson, A Cherokee Pioneer," *Chronicles of Oklahoma* 9 [December 1929]: 371–72)

Amusements

We had the very most fun playing horse. We would bend down a sapling and get on it and ride up and down. Sometime we would try and ride one that would take two or three to pull down and would we get thrown when the tree sprang upright if we were not heavy enough to hold it down. (Foreman, ed., "Pioneer Recollections," 393)

Horse racing was one of the greatest attractions of the [Muskogee] fair. Probably the greatest horses in the United States were brought here to [compete] in what we called short races [of] one-quarter mile. (Will P. Robinson, Chickasaw/Creek Indian, in Indian-Pioneer Papers, vol. 8)

But the great game of all games with the Indian is the ball-play. The two sides are sometimes contiguous neighbourhoods, sometimes counties, or even whole districts. They meet on the ground the night previous to the play, and encamp. While on their way, the ball-play call is sounded in concert. A smooth piece of prairie, or open timber-land is selected. It is about 40 rods long. Near each end a couple of posts about 15 feet high are set up close together, one pair as a target for each party. The aim is to hit these posts with the ball the greater number of times. But one ball is used. It is

small, and of sufficient weight to throw well. It is
never touched with the hands. Each player has two
ball sticks, with a loop at the end of each, with which
he seizes and throws, and catches the ball. A skilful
player will throw it a great distance and with great
accuracy. The number on a side is from 30 to 50. They
prepare for the play by taking off most of their clothing, painting their faces, and adorning themselves in
various ways. Each side employs a ball-play conjurer,
whose business it is to direct the ball in its flight; and
greatly does it add to their confidence to have a skillful one engaged. Wherever the ball falls, the players
of both sides rush to take it. He who first gets it,
throws it towards the posts of his party, and hits
them, if possible. Thus it passes back and forth, till
one party wins. Sometimes as many ballsticks as can
be crowded together are reaching for the ball at
once, and most earnest is the strife, till one gets it.
Then others strike it away from him, if possible.
Thus in the highest excitement, and with the utmost
stretch of their physical powers, they spend the day. I
have never seen any game to equal it in intense interest. (John Edwards, Presbyterian missionary, in "The
Choctaw Indians in the Middle of the Nineteenth
Century," 412)

Another sport they enjoyed in warm weather was a
big fish fry. [They damned a creek] with logs and
brush, then they poisoned the water with the roots of
a weed called devil's shoe string. Every man brought
a bunch of roots, which they pounded with hammer
or mallets [onto logs] which were then floated up and
down the creek [to poison the water]. They commenced
pounding the roots early in the morning and by ten
o'clock the fish were coming to the top of the water,
then they began to throw them out, onto the creek
banks, catching them with gigs, spears, pitchforks,
or anything else that they could hold them with. (Emma
Ervin Christian, Choctaw Indian, in "Memories of
My Childhood Days in the Choctaw Nation," *Chronicles of Oklahoma* 11 [Dec. 1933]: 1036.

Customs

When an Indian boy and girl decided to marry they
didn't get a license. They went to the father of each
and their fathers would agree that their children
should marry and they would set the date, and invite
all the relatives and neighbors to the wedding. They
would have a big feast at noon and at supper, then
that night they would have a stomp dance. That was
their wedding ceremony. There was no preacher to

marry them. (Mack McDonald, Mississippi Choctaw, in Indian-Pioneer Papers, vol. 71)

We were married when I was fourteen years old and he was eighteen. (Laura James Gardner, Choctaw Indian, in Indian-Pioneer Papers, vol. 25)

A man and woman belonging to the same clan were strictly forbidden to marry as they were considered to be brothers and sisters within the clan. . . . [If they]. . . were found or known to have had illicit relations with one another, they would be stripped of all their clothes and a strict lecture was given to them before a large crowd. (Lumpsey Harjo, Creek Indian, in Indian-Pioneer Papers, vol. 27)

Some of the Creek Indians had two wives when I first realized things, that is, I remember seeing and knowing that two women were the wives of certain men when I was a child. (Linda Collins, Creek Indian, in Indian-Pioneer Papers, vol. 65)

The Choctaws had no regular cemetery then. When an Indian died, they would bury him near the house where they lived." (Susan Frazier, Choctaw Indian, in Indian-Pioneer Papers, vol. 25)

After [Winchester Jones] had been sentenced to be shot, he asked five days to arrange his business and it was granted him. He stayed drunk for three days, went to church one day, and returned the fifth day to be shot. They set him down by a big tree, painted a spot over his heart, and let the best friend he had shoot him. (Thomas M. Frazier, Choctaw Indian, in Indian-Pioneer Papers, vol. 25)

Smoking is almost universal among the people; and when they light a pipe, they are not selfish with it. (John Edwards, Presbyterian missionary, in "The Choctaw Indians in the Middle of the Nineteenth Century," 409)

Getting Medical Assistance

My oldest sister had a bad sick spell, and Mother sent for an Indian doctor. She came, examined Sister, [and] steamed her several times a day for three days in succession, and gave her teas to drink. After the time of steaming was over she showed Mother a little ball, presumably made of hair and a clot of something like blood on it. She pretended that she drew this out of Sister's side by the steaming process. She said that Sister had been shot by an enemy with a poisoned ball; well she got well and lived to be seventy-seven years of age. (Emma Irvin Christian, Choctaw Indian, in "Memories of My Childhood Days," 161)

Medicine is taken internally as a purgative and is also taken by "scratching." Long scratches are made on the arms, legs and body to let blood out for if you have too much blood in you, you will get sick. It is like taking a blood test. After these scratches are made the patient is bathed in some medicine prepared for that purpose. (Linda Collins, Creek Indian, in Indian-Pioneer Papers, vol. 65)

Traveling

Before the Civil War roads in the Choctaw Nation were marked by notches on trees. Through roads were marked with four notches; roads leading into other roads were marked by three notches; roads leading to settlements were marked with two notches and roads leading to good fishing, hunting, or camping places were marked with stones or by blazes on trees. (Foreman, ed., "Pioneer Recollections," 393)

What was called a "tavern" in those days was a yard fenced in with rails and several log cabins within— one a kitchen, one a dining room, the other bed rooms. (C. W. Turner, long-time resident among the Creeks, in "Events Among the Muskogees during Sixty Years," *Chronicles of Oklahoma* 10 [March 1932]: 22)

Slave Life

Home

All the slaves lived in a log house. The married folks lived in little houses and there was big long houses for all the single men. The young, single girls lived with the old folks in another big long house. (Lucinda Vann, former Cherokee slave, in Rawick, *The American Slave*, ser. 1, vol. 12)

Mostly the slave houses had just one big room with a stick-and-mud chimney, just like the poor people among the Creeks had. Then they had a brush shelter built out of four poles with a roof made out of brush, set out to one side of the house where they do the cooking and eating, and sometimes the sleeping too. . . . [They] never did use the log house much, only in cold and rainy weather. (Nellie Johnson, former Creek slave, in Rawick, *The American Slave*, vol. 7)

Food

We cooked all sorts of Indian dishes: Tom-fuller, pash-ofa, hickory-nut grot, Tom-budha, ash-cakes, and pound cakes besides vegetable and meat dishes. . . .

Although the images date only from the 1890s, these cabins are typical of those occupied by Five Tribes slaves. Note that the chimney of one of the cabins is made of a mixture of mud and sticks.

There was lots of possums and coons and squirrels and we nearly always had some one of these to eat. We'd . . . put [the possum] in a pan and baked him with potatoes. . . . We used the broth to baste him and for gravy. It sure was fine eating in those days. (Polly Colbert, former Chickasaw slave, in Rawick, *The American Slave*, vol. 7)

Our bread was baked most of the time in the ashes and our meat hung over the fire to roast. . . . (Ed Butler, former Cherokee slave, in Rawick, *The American Slave*, ser. 1, vol. 12)

We had [to eat] corn bread, pumpkin bread, bean bread, all kinds of game and fowls, soups, wild berries and fruits and wild honey. (Jim Tomm, former Creek slave, in Wilson, ed., "Reminiscences of Jim Tomm," 304)

Clothes

Our clothes was all made of homespun. The women done all the spinning and the weaving but Miss Betsy cut out all the clothes and helped with the sewing. She learned to sew when she was away to school and she learned all her women [slaves] to sew. (Polly Colbert, former Chickasaw slave, in Rawick, *The American Slave*, vol. 7)

The boys didn't wear no britches in the summer time. They just wore long shirts. The girls wore homespun dresses, either blue or gray. (Matilda Poe, former Chickasaw slave, in Rawick, *The American Slave*, vol. 7)

We never put on shoes until about late November when the frost began to hit regular and split our feet up. (Morris Sheppard, former Cherokee slave, in Rawick, *The American Slave*, vol. 7)

Man's Work

We did not raise much cotton, but we raised corn, grain and vegetables. We had plenty of hogs and horses. . . . The slaves did all the work, and the Indians hunted, and fished, attended councils and guided the work done by the slaves. (Ed Butler, former Cherokee slave, in Rawick, *The American Slave*, ser. 1, vol. 12)

They operated salt wells in the winter time. . . . It took a lot of wood to keep the pots boiling and some of the slaves were kept busy cutting wood, while others were boiling the salt water down, until nothing but pure salt was left in the pots. (Moses Lonian, former Cherokee slave, in Rawick, *The American Slave*, ser. 1, vol. 12)

The slave men work in the fields, chopping cotton, raising corn, cutting rails for the fences, building log cabins and fireplaces. (Phoebe Banks, former Creek slave, in Rawick, *The American Slave*, vol. 7)

Old Master's land wasn't all in one big field, but a lot of little fields scattered all over the place. . . . We all lived around on those little farms, and we didn't have to be under any overseer like the Cherokee Negroes had lots of times. . . . Everybody could have a little patch of his own, too, and work it between times, on Saturdays and Sundays if he wanted to. (Nellie Johnson, former Creek slave, in Rawick, *The American Slave*, vol. 7)

In those days Negroes hired for a mere pittance. I hired mine out, and got five dollars a month for each grown Negro. (Sarah Ann Harland, Choctaw slave owner, in Muriel H. Wright, ed, "Sarah Ann Harland: From Her Memoirs of Life in the Indian Territory," *Chronicles of Oklahoma* 39 [Autumn 1961]: 307)

Women's Work

Washing was done on the creeks by beating the clothes with the hands. (Ed Butler, former Cherokee slave, in Rawick, *The American Slave,* ser. 1, vol. 12)

The slaves were made to card the wool and cotton and would spin it on the spinning wheel into thread and then reel it and run it through the loom and make their own cloth. The thread was usually dyed before it was woven. (John Harrison, former Cherokee slave, in Rawick, *The American Slave,* ser. 1, vol. 12)

We didn't have to work if there wasn't no work to do that day. (Nellie Johnson, former Creek slave, in Rawick, *The American Slave,* vol. 7)

Children's Work

The [slave] children appear almost universally more healthy, robust and happy than young Indians. From them no work is required until they arrive at the age of ten or twelve years and then their duties are very light. (A. W. Whipple, U. S. Army surveyor in Oklahoma, 1853, in Muriel H. Wright and George H. Shirk, eds., "The Journal of Lieutenant A. W. Whipple," *Chronicles of Oklahoma* 28 [Autumn 1950]: 255)

Mammy worked at the Big House and took me along every day. . . . I would help hold the hank when she done the spinning. . . . I helped the cook and carried water and milked. I carried the water in a home-made pegging [that sat] on my head. (Chaney Richardson, former Cherokee slave, in Rawick, *The American Slave,* vol. 7)

I picked cotton in my apron and carried it to a basket and when the basket was full it was taken to the wagon and weighed. . . . We picked the seed from our cotton by hand. That was the way I spent my evenings each fall. (Delilah Franklin, former Choctaw slave, remembering the era after the Civil War, in the Indian-Pioneer Papers, vol. 25)

Going to Church

I went to the missionary Baptist church where Master and Mrs. went. There was a big church. The white folks go first and after they come out, the colored folks go in. . . . We went down to the river for baptizings. The women dressed in white, if they had a white dress to wear. The preacher took his candidate into the water. Pretty soon everybody commenced singing and praying. Then the preacher put you under water three times. . . . (Lucinda Vann, former Cherokee slave, in Rawick, *The American Slave*, ser. 1, vol. 12)

Master wasn't a believer in church but he let us have church. My we'd have happy times singing and shouting. They'd have church when they had a preacher and prayer meeting when they didn't. (Matilda Poe, former Chickasaw slave, in Rawick, *The American Slave*, vol. 7)

Reading and Writing

I didn't get to go to school. Father made me stay at home and work in the field. (Delilah Franklin, former Choctaw slave, remembering the era after the Civil War, in the Indian-Pioneer Papers, vol. 25)

Social Life

We curled our hair on corn shucks. First we greased it thoroughly with lard, and then braided it up with corn shucks, all over our heads. When we got ready to go to these dances we unbraided it and combed it into curls. We used flour for face powder. (Delilah Franklin, former Choctaw slave, in Indian-Pioneers Papers, vol. 25)

Everybody had a good time on old Jim Vann's plantation. After supper the colored folks would get together and talk, and sing, and dance. Someone maybe would be playing a fiddle or a banjo. Everybody was happy. Master never whipped no one. No fusses, no bad words, no nothing like that. The slaves who worked in the big house was the first class. Next, came the carpenters, yard men, blacksmiths, race-horse men, steamboat men and like that. The low[est] class [of slaves] worked in the fields. (Lucinda Vann, former Cherokee slave, in Rawick, *The American Slave*, ser. 1, vol. 12)

Customs

I carry scars on my legs to this day where Old Master whipped me for lying, with a rawhide quirt he carried all the time for his horse. (Former Cherokee slave quoted in Monroe Billington, "Black Slavery in Indian Territory: The Ex Slave Narratives," *Chronicles of Oklahoma* 60 [Spring 1982]: 63)

Life on the plantation as I remember it was happy and useful. Our masters were kind to us but we had to do as they said to do. Once in a while a slave was whipped, but always in moderation. (Ed Butler, former Cherokee slave, in Rawick, *The American Slave,* ser 1, vol. 12)

[T]hese slaves receive from their Indian masters more Christian treatment than among the Christian whites. [T]he Negro is regarded as a companion and helper, to whom thanks and kindness are due when he exerts himself for the welfare of the household. (Heinrich Baldwin Möllhausen, German artist, in Wright and Shirk, eds., "Artist Möllhausen in Oklahoma—1853," 400)

Slaves didn't leave the plantation much on account of the Patrollers. The patroller was low white trash that just wanted an excuse to shoot Negroes. I don't think I ever saw one but I heard lots about them. (Matilda Poe, former Chickasaw slave, in Rawick, *The American Slave,* vol. 7)

See History for Yourself

In northeastern Oklahoma near Tahlequah, in Cherokee County, visit the Adams Corner Rural Village at the Cherokee National Museum, which contains exhibits and buildings of early farm life, as does Har-Ber Village near Grove in Delaware County. Pre–Civil War log houses open to the public include Sequoyah's Home Site and the Judge Franklin Faulkner Cabin near Sallisaw, in Sequoyah County; the Adair House at Fort Gibson, in Muskogee County; and cabin replicas at the Cherokee Courthouse complex near Gore and the Dwight Mission northeast of Sallisaw, both in Sequoyah County. There is only one remaining example of a plantation home in Oklahoma: the Murrell Home at Park Hill near Tahlequah in Cherokee County. It is owned by the Oklahoma Historical Society and open to the public. Constructed in the 1870s and 1880s, homes of other prosperous landowners and merchants can be found in Fort Gibson, Tahlequah, Vinita, and Henryetta. Most of these houses belong to private owners.

In southeastern Oklahoma visit the Choctaw Chief's House northeast of Swink, in Choctaw County, to see a good example of a one and one-half story log house with a dogtrot. Houses constructed after the Civil War and open to the public include the Jefferson Gardner Mansion near Eagletown, in McCurtain County; the Green McCurtain House near Kinta, in Haskell County; the T. G. Overstreet House north of Poteau, and the Peter Conser Historic House south of Poteau, in Le Flore County; and the Murray/Lindsay House at Erin Springs, in Garvin County.

Few buildings relating to slavery remain in Oklahoma. If you live in the eastern part of our state, perhaps you may be able to locate near your home buildings constructed by slaves, sites where slave cabins once stood, places where slaves worshiped, and cemeteries where slaves were buried. Visit Rentiesville in northeastern McIntosh County, the birthplace of John Hope Franklin, a descendent of slaves and one of America's most distinguished historians.

Suggestions for Further Reading

Reference

Ballenger, T. L. *Around Tahlequah Council Fires.* Oklahoma City: Cherokee Publishing Company, 1945.

Benson, Henry C. *Life among the Choctaw Indians.* Cincinnati, Ohio: L. Swormstedt and A. Poe, 1860.

Culin, Stewart. *Games of North American Indians.* New York: Dover, 1975.

Dale, Edward Everett, and Gaston Litton. *Cherokee Cavaliers: Forty Years of Cherokee History as Told in the Correspondence of the Ridge-Watie-Boudinot Family.* Norman: University of Oklahoma Press, 1939.

Goins, Charles R., and John W. Morris. *Oklahoma Homes, Past and Present.* Norman: University of Oklahoma Press, 1980.

Goode, William H. *Outposts of Zion with Limnings of Mission Life.* Cincinnati, Ohio: Poe and Hitchcock, 1863.

Hitchcock, Ethan Allen. *A Traveler in Indian Territory.* Edited by Grant Foreman. Cedar Rapids, Iowa: Torch Press, 1930.

Howard, James H., in collaboration with Willie Lena. *Oklahoma Seminoles: Medicines, Magic, and Religion.* Norman: University of Oklahoma Press, 1984.

Indian-Pioneer Papers. 113 vols. Oklahoma Historical Society, Oklahoma City.

James, John. *My Experiences with Indians.* Austin, Texas: Gammel's Book Store, 1925.

Kimball, Yeffe, and Jean Anderson. *The Art of American Indian Cooking.* Foreword by Will Rogers, Jr. Garden City, N.Y.: Doubleday, 1964.

Ormsby, Waterman L. *The Butterfield Overland Mail.* San Marino Calif.: Huntington Library, 1942.

Perdue, Theda. *Nations Remembered: An Oral History of the Cherokees, Chickasaws, Choctaws, Creeks, and*

Seminoles, 1865–1907. 1980. Norman: University of Oklahoma Press, 1993.

Rawick, George P., ed. *The American Slave: A Composite Autobiography: Oklahoma Narratives.* Ser. 1, vol. 12, supplement. Westport, Conn.: Greenwood Press, 1977.

———, ed. *The American Slave: A Composite Autobiography: Oklahoma and Mississippi Narratives.* Vol. 7. 1941. Westport, Conn.: Greenwood Press, 1972.

Ruth, Kent, and Jim Argo. *Window on the Past: Historic Places in Oklahoma.* Oklahoma City: Oklahoma Historical Society, 1984.

Vogel, Virgil J. *American Indian Medicine.* Norman: University of Oklahoma Press, 1970.

West, C. W. ("Dub"). *Tahlequah and the Cherokee Nation.* Muskogee: Muskogee Publishing Company, 1978.

Chapter 14: **Eight Notable Oklahomans**

The noted English writer G. K. Chesterton once observed, "History is only a confused heap of facts." He saw the past as a series of unrelated events and dates. It is to be hoped that by now you have discovered that the story of Oklahoma is not such a confused heap of facts. Instead, it is an account of an unending chain of experiences shared by many different people in the space that is now our state.

Yet as we recount those common experiences it is easy to overlook the uncommon people who shared and shaped them. What moves history or society along, the historian Thomas Carlyle once suggested, is the work of exceptional men and women. This chapter contains brief accounts of eight exceptional Oklahomans whose lives changed the world around them. They are a group diverse in gender (three women and five men), in ethnicity (four Indians, two Africans, and two European Americans) and in vocation (education, law enforcement, politics, linguistics, exploration, and Christian ministry).

All of those featured in this chapter were born before the American Civil War. Only one was a native Oklahoman, but it was while residing in the state that all eight made or enhanced their principal contribution to the progress of humankind.

As you read, associate the subject of each sketch with events we have already studied. Who participated in the voluntary Indian removal program proposed by President Monroe? Which two were involved in Christian missionary work among the Indians? Who attended schools established by missionary agencies? Who tried to escape some of the pressures of the reservations by use of peyote? When you associate specific individuals with particular events, history takes on life and meaning.

To help you follow the progress of history, these eight are listed in order of their birth.

Sequoyah, 1770s–1843

The Cherokees thought it was witches' work; the Great Spirit had not meant for the Indian to learn to write. In the beginning the first whites had chosen the Great Book, while the Indians had chosen the bow and arrow. Yet here was Sequoyah spending all of his time trying to give the Cherokees "talking leaves" of their own. Even his wife, Sally, thought he was possessed.

For nearly twelve years Sequoyah worked on his project. During those fateful years he did not provide well for his family as a silversmith, blacksmith, storekeeper, hunter, or farmer. Sequoyah, however, had a more noble calling: he wanted to prove that a Cherokee could do anything a white person could do. He realized that Indians had remarkable wisdom in the ways of the world, but that "this knowledge escaped and was lost for want of some way to preserve it." If the Cherokees could write down their discoveries, they could preserve their knowledge and compete with white Americans on the same basis that other nations did.

Sequoyah holds his eighty-six character syllabary and wears his prized silver medal in this 1836 painting by Charles Bird King.

When Sequoyah was born, and who his father was, is shrouded in mystery, as is much of his life. All we know for certain is that his father was a white man who had left his mother's house even before Sequoyah was born. Sequoyah grew up in full-blood communities, spoke only Cherokee, and answered to the name of George Guess, or Gess (or Gist, or Guist, or Guyst). In 1813 he fought in the Creek War against the Red Sticks, participating in the battle of Horseshoe Bend. Afterwards he married and established a home in what is now northern Alabama, and continued to participate in the public affairs of the nation.

Even before he participated in the Creek War, Sequoyah had launched his attempt to reduce the Cherokee language to written form. He first tried to give a distinct symbol to each word, but soon discovered that there were too many words and the number of symbols was unmanageable. Eventually, he decided to give characters to syllables only. He identified eighty-six such characters (compared to twenty-six in our alphabet), adapting them from capital script letters. To read the Cherokee language, all one had to do was to say the names of Sequoyah's characters, much as we would name the letters *x p d n c* to pronounce "expediency."

In 1818, Sequoyah joined the Western Cherokees in Arkansas. There he apparently perfected his syllabary and gained confidence in its usefulness. Three years later he took his invention back to the Eastern Cherokees and with the help of his young daughter convinced even hardened skeptics that the Cherokees could have their "talking leaves" too. In just a matter of weeks, messages were being written and read wherever Cherokees lived.

Cherokees properly took pride in Sequoyah's invention. In 1824 the National Council honored him with a large silver medal that he wore until the day he died. Later it also published a tribal newspaper, *Cherokee Phoenix*, with one-half of its columns in Sequoyah's characters. Christian missionaries even translated the Bible into Cherokee using the syllabary, a use that saddened the inventor.

In the meantime Sequoyah had returned to the Western Cherokees in Arkansas. In 1828 he was one of the commissioners who negotiated the treaty by which the Western Cherokees exchanged their Arkansas lands for ones in northeastern Oklahoma. Later that year he moved his family to a new home and new saltworks on Lee's Creek northeast of present Sallisaw. The one-room log cabin he built at the site still stands, presently maintained by the Oklahoma Historical Society.

By the time the Eastern Cherokees had followed their trail of tears to Oklahoma in 1839, Sequoyah was one of the leading men of the Western branch of the tribe. Unlike many of his fellow westerners, he worked diligently to find common ground on which the "Old Settlers" and the "New Settlers" could live and work together. Yet all the bickering between the two groups saddened him. Perhaps to escape it, in 1843 he organized an expedition to Mexico to find and encourage a band of wandering Cherokees to rejoin the tribe in Oklahoma. He found the group, but before he could persuade its members to return with him, the aged Sequoyah died.

Few have accomplished in one lifetime as much as Sequoyah did. His work alone made an entire nation literate in just a few short years, revitalizing and perpetuating an ancient culture that was on the verge of death. Oklahoma has placed Sequoyah's statue in the United States Capitol. No one deserves the honor more.

Further Reading: Grant Foreman, *Sequoyah* (Norman: University of Oklahoma Press, 1938).

Sophia Nye Byington, 1800–1880

One evening Sophia Byington finished her chores at the barn and returned to her one-and-one-half-story double-pen log house to prepare dinner for her two sons, Cyrus and Horatio. Her husband, American Board missionary to the Choctaws Cyrus Byington, was gone on one of his extended preaching tours. She expected him back to their home near present Eagletown in the next day or two. Her only daughter, Lucy, was away at school in Ohio.

Once inside the house she noticed that thirty-month-old Horatio, born when she was forty-four years old, was feverish. Sophia fed the boy and his older brother and then put the two of them to bed. The fever did not subside during the night, and it got worse through the course of the next day. She was holding Horatio when her husband returned. He administered medicine, but it did not help. Baby Horatio died before the night was over. The next afternoon, August 19, 1846, Sophia and Cyrus buried their son in a small grave adjacent to one where they had earlier buried the baby's older brother.

Sophia's loss was almost more than she could bear. Horatio's "last sigh," she wrote to daughter Lucy, "dissolved earth's charms for me." For nearly nineteen years she had labored with her husband in the Choctaw mission field doing everything from cooking and washing to tending cattle and hoeing corn, to teaching school and nursing the sick, to copying and proofing her husband's manuscripts, to having babies and changing diapers, to being "a lady and every-

Sophia Nye Byington at the time of her marriage to Cyrus Byington in 1827.

body's humble servant." On two different occasions she had nearly died herself from serious illness. And now her baby was dead! How was she to go on? There was no answer other than—"with courage."

In a way "courage" was Sophia's middle name. She had grown up in a prosperous household in Marietta, Ohio, and had the benefit of some kind of education. In October 1827 she met a scholarly but older gentleman who had been working in the mission field for seven years. After less than a week's acquaintance, Cyrus Byington proposed marriage . . . and then left for a preaching tour. He thereafter wrote fervent letters urging her to marry him and to accompany him back to the Choctaws. Sophia was impressed if not smitten, and she *was* twenty-seven. They were married in December. For the next forty-one years they were more than husband and wife: they were coworkers, friends, and mutual admirers.

Sophia courageously said goodbye to her parents and accompanied her husband to his mission post in Mississippi. His duties there included teaching and preaching, but his passion was to learn the Choctaw language and reduce it to written form. Meanwhile, in her "home in the woods," Sophia set up housekeeping, nursed and mothered Choctaw students, copied her husband's manuscripts, worked in the garden, and began her own family. She had given birth to three children by 1835.

When the Choctaws subsequently removed to Oklahoma, the missionaries followed. In 1835, Sophia bundled up her newborn baby and, with her two older children and Cyrus, set out fearlessly on the long trek to the new nation. They established their mission near Eagletown in McCurtain County, naming it Stockbridge. Sophia's first home in our state was a log cabin with plank wood floors. Nearby were a small cabin, which provided a study for her husband, and another which served as a schoolroom. The family lived in those quarters for the next nine years. Then they moved to the larger log house where Horatio died, which was closer to Iyanubbi, the boarding school that her husband superintended after 1844.

Sophia Byington and her husband served the Choctaws until the close of the Civil War. They ministered continually to their spiritual, educational, and physical needs. And always the Byingtons, with the help of some others, worked on giving their "beloved Choctaws" a written language. The best measure of their work was that the Choctaws were widely acclaimed as a literate and Christian people by the time the Byingtons retired in 1867. In that year the couple moved to their daughter's Ohio home. Cyrus died there the next year; Sophia died twelve years later.

Sophia Byington was not the only nineteenth-century Oklahoma woman who suffered intense grief and pain or exhibited fearless courage. Thousands did. Nor was she the only one who committed herself to a life of Christian service. Hundreds did. But few saw their duty so clearly and did it so diligently. "It is *well*," she said, "to *wear out* in *a good cause.*" She did just that.

Further reading: Louis Coleman, "Cyrus Byington: Missionary to the Choctaws," *Chronicles of Oklahoma* 52 (Fall 1984): 360–87; and W. David Baird, "Cyrus Byington and the Presbyterian Choctaw Mission," in *Churchmen and the Western Indian, 1820–1920,* ed. Clyde A. Milner and Floyd A. O'Neil (Norman: University of Oklahoma Press, 1985), 5–40.

Black Beaver, 1806–1890

This artist's sketch of Black Beaver shows the great Delaware guide as a Baptist layman.

Black Beaver once was trying to impress on a Comanche friend that the ways of the whites were better than those of the Indians. In signs and in broken Comanche, Black Beaver told him that white people knew that the earth was round. How could that be, his friend asked, when everyone could see that the prairie was flat? What was more, the Comanche's grandfather had actually been to the end of the earth and seen the sun set behind a wall. Black Beaver then described the steam engines that he had seen with his own eyes and how they propelled huge boats up rivers. The Comanche did not believe it, and said that Black Beaver must have been dreaming.

United States Army Captain Randolph B. Marcy observed the entire conversation. He thought that maybe both Indians would be impressed with the wonders of the new telegraph. He explained the invention to Black Beaver and then told him to tell the Comanche. Black Beaver thought about that for a moment and said: "I don't think I tell him that, Captain, for the truth is, I don't believe it myself."

Black Beaver was a member of the Delaware tribe. His people took great pride in having signed the first treaty with William Penn. Since those days of power and prestige, they had been pushed steadily westward. In the early nineteenth century when Black Beaver was born, the Delawares lived in what is now Ohio and Indiana. From there most moved to eastern Kansas, although about one-third of the tribe relocated first in northeast Arkansas and subsequently in northeast Texas, where they were befriended by the Caddos and Wichitas. By the late 1820s some of the latter had also established lodges along the Canadian River in present-day south-central Oklahoma.

The Delawares had always been exceptional guides, and Black Beaver was one of the best. Any geographical landmark he saw once, he always recognized again, even if he saw it from a different direction. He could also ride into any abandoned Indian camp and tell exactly what tribe had camped there and when.

With such skills Black Beaver was in great demand as a guide. As a young man he had accompanied brigades of the American Fur Company on expeditions to the headwaters of the Missouri River. In 1843 he helped escort John James Audubon to the Yellowstone country. Black Beaver also served as a guide for several army units exploring the Great West, including one of those commanded by John Charles Frémont and two led by Randolph B. Marcy. In 1846 he signed on as a scout for Colonel William S. Harney during the Mexican War. According to Black Beaver's own account, by 1853 he had seen the Pacific Ocean seven different times.

In the 1850s, worn out by his journeys, Black Beaver turned his attention to his family and farm. By then he was "a meager-looking man of middle size, and his long black hair framed a face that was clever, but which bore a melancholy expression of sickness and sorrow." He and other Delawares occupied the abandoned buildings of the first Fort Arbuckle in McClain County, where they cleared fields and planted corn. In 1859 they joined the Wichitas and other tribes on a new reservation farther west. There Black Beaver built a four-room log house, put ninety acres under cultivation, and ranged 600 head of cattle and 300 head of hogs.

When the Civil War came to Indian Territory in

1861, the Delaware guide lost all those improvements. He led the outnumbered United States troops to safety in Kansas, where he and his family stayed throughout the war. At the conclusion of the conflict, however, he returned to the Washita River valley, establishing a homestead not far from the Wichita Agency. Shortly thereafter he had 100 acres planted in corn and a new house, the first in what is today Anadarko.

In the last years of his life Black Beaver participated in Indian councils called to promote peace on the Southern Plains. He also embraced Christianity, becoming an active member of the Baptist Church.

Captain Marcy had found Black Beaver reliable, brave, competent, and without vanity. A fellow Baptist described him as "one of God's noblemen, honest and truthful." He was all of that, and much more. He brought international recognition to Oklahoma during the nineteenth century as one of the foremost guides of the American West. Above all he demonstrated that Indian society was not rigid and inflexible, that over time it could adapt to different cultural patterns. Black Beaver, after all, in the course of just one lifetime had been a hunter, a warrior, a guide, a farmer, a peacemaker, and a lay Christian preacher.

Further reading: Carolyn Thomas Foreman, "Black Beaver," *Chronicles of Oklahoma* 24 (1946): 269–92.

John Horse, 1812–1882

Lieutenant E. R. S. Canby of the United States Army was given the responsibility of conducting about 100 Seminole Indians from Florida to the Creek Agency in what is now Oklahoma. In August 1842 he took them by steamboat to New Orleans and then up the Mississippi and Arkansas rivers. At Little Rock low water grounded the steamboat. Canby sought to purchase provisions to continue the trip overland, but he found that he did not have enough money. To his surprise, one of the Seminoles volunteered to make him a loan of $1,500. That was unusual in itself, but what made this offer exceptional was that it was extended by John Horse, and John Horse was a black Seminole slave.

Of Indian, Spanish, and African ancestry, Horse

was born about 1812 in Florida. He was
born a slave, but among the Seminoles
slavery was different from elsewhere.
Slaves had a lot of personal freedom
and generally lived in separate villages
adjacent to the Seminole towns. About
the only thing their masters required
of them was a tribute of agriculture
products and a recognition of subser-
vience.

In the Seminoles' war with the United
States, which began late in 1835, John
Horse served as a representative of
both the war chief, Alligator, and the
head chief, Micanopy. Their war was
John Horse's war because removal to
Oklahoma could very well have meant
that the black Seminoles would be sold
to white or Creek slaveholders. He
fought so bravely over the next two
years that he was recognized by the
traditional leadership of the tribe as a subchief of
the black Seminoles.

This sketch of John Horse,
or Gopher John, is the only
image we have of him.

Ignoring flags of truce, in September 1837 the
United States Army imprisoned John Horse, Wild
Cat, Osceolo, and other chiefs at Fort Marion in St.
Augustine, Florida. They were captives for less than
ninety days. Working an iron bar loose from a gun
slit, Horse, Wild Cat, and twenty other Seminoles
slipped through the opening to freedom. They re-
joined their comrades and continued to fight for
another year, by the end of which Micanopy and
Alligator had tired of the struggle and even consented to remove to Oklahoma.

That decision by his chiefs (and master?) caused
John Horse to change sides in the conflict. Thereafter and until 1842, he and other black Seminoles
worked for the United States Army as scouts and
interpreters in an attempt to round up Seminole
bands who continued to resist removal to Oklahoma.
It was not popular work, but it was lucrative, and
probably it was his army pay that John Horse loaned
to Lieutenant Canby on the trip to Oklahoma.

Once in our state, John Horse joined the emigrant
Seminoles in their camps near Fort Gibson. They
had refused to make permanent settlements far-

ther west among the Creeks because they feared that the larger tribe would kidnap their slaves. Micanopy welcomed Horse to the tribal councils and, in appreciation of his loyalty and his skills as a diplomat, in the following year he had an ordinance passed declaring him a free man. But freedom was a mixed blessing: John Horse now lived in daily fear of being abducted by slave catchers from Arkansas and sold back into bondage. He also faced danger from some Seminoles who resented his support of the United States Army in the recent war. One of those had shot a horse out from under him. He did not know which was worse: angry Indians or thieving slave catchers.

By the 1840s, Chief John Horse had become one of the principal spokesmen for the Seminoles. He was an interpreter for a tribal delegation that went to Washington. He also helped negotiate an agreement with the Creeks whereby the Seminoles and their slaves were permitted to settle in the western part of the Creek Nation. The chief then helped his band of black Seminoles establish the community that they called Wewoka, the capital of the Seminole Nation and now the county seat of Seminole County.

John Horse had hoped that the black Seminoles could live peacefully in their separate towns. Sadly, whites and Indians constantly sought to take them captive and sell them into traditional slavery. By 1849, Chief Horse had had enough. He and his friend Wild Cat gathered both red and black Seminoles and fled south to find refuge in Mexico. You can find descendants of those people along the Rio Grande today. John Horse served as their chief until his death in 1882.

Horse was in Oklahoma for only seven years. His importance lies not in the length of his stay or even in what he did when he was here. It is that he reminds us that among the early pioneers of this state were several thousand black men and women who lived and worked in obscurity but nonetheless helped knit the social fabric that is Oklahoma today.

Further reading: Kenneth W. Porter, "Seminoles in Mexico," *Chronicles of Oklahoma* 29 (1951): 163–64; and Kevin Mulroy, *Freedom on the Border: The Seminole Maroons in Florida, the Indian Territory, Coahuila, and Texas* (Lubbock: Texas Tech University Press, 1993).

Ann Eliza Worcester Robertson, 1826–1905

A letter came to Ann Eliza Robertson in June 1892 at her Muskogee address. The board of trustees of the University of Wooster in Wooster, Ohio, had awarded her an honorary doctorate in recognition of her linguistic studies. The news, that she was the first woman in the United States to receive an honorary Ph.D., was unexpected but also very welcome. Finally she had received proper recognition of her lifework.

Robertson was born into a family where language was a matter of considerable importance. Her father, Samuel A. Worcester, was one of the earliest Christian missionaries to work among the Cherokees. At his post at Brainerd, in present Tennessee, he began a careful study of the Cherokee language, became fluent in it, and learned to write it using Sequoyah's syllabary. Subsequently, Worcester secured a printing press and published Cherokee language materials, many of which were biblical texts he had translated. The Cherokees, Worcester believed, should hear and read the Christian Gospel in their own language.

Ann Eliza Worcester Robertson received her honorary Ph.D. in 1892, not long before this photograph was made.

One of four Worcester children, Ann Eliza came with the family to Indian Territory to reestablish Samuel's mission and press at Park Hill, near present Tahlequah. At the age of fifteen she journeyed to Vermont to begin her own formal education, during which she showed uncommon aptitude for both Greek and Latin. After five years she returned to Park Hill to help her father as a classroom teacher in the mission school.

She did not stay there long. In 1850, William Robertson, a young Presbyterian minister and preacher, carried her away as his wife to Tullahassee, a mission school for the Creek Indians near present Muskogee. Ann Eliza lived and worked at Tullahassee for the next thirty-five years. Her responsibilities were enormous. She shared both the administrative and the teaching duties at the boarding school, which often enrolled more than 100 students. On one occasion she taught six hours each day in addition to supervising household chores that ranged from dipping candles to washing and ironing for the whole school. She also had four children of her own to care for, and she endured ill health.

Actually, ill health enabled Robertson to devote time to her real interest—translation of the Bible into the Muskogee language. That work alone, she believed, would give the Creeks and the Seminoles, both Muskogee speakers, access to the saving power of the Gospel. Over the next half-century she became a thorough and appreciative scholar of the native language. She spoke it fluently, she contributed to the process of committing it to written form, and she learned its rules of grammar. To her, the Creek language was not "the work of man but the Creator's gift to man."

To translate Scripture into Muskogee, Ann Eliza worked directly from the original Hebrew or Greek text. Others joined her in this labor, including her husband and a corps of talented young Creek men, but she was the leading scholar. She had "an instinctive feeling for the function of language," one historian has written, and "an imaginative comprehension of how to adapt the modes of one language to those of another so that the translation is easily comprehensible." The crowning joy of her life came in 1887 when she received the first edition of the complete Muskogee New Testament.

Not everyone believed that Robertson was using her time to the best advantage. The secretary of the mission board that supported her and her husband's ministry thought that the effort was wasted because the Creeks would soon understand English. Some of her kinfolk wrote that spending money, time, and life on the Indians was of little use. Even members of her immediate family questioned her labor of love. "A mother's first duty is the care of her own offspring," her son later wrote. Her three daughters, however, followed her into a life of service. One of them, Alice, was elected as Oklahoma's first woman member of the United States House of Representatives.

Ann Eliza Worcester Robertson never wavered in her commitment to providing the Creeks and the Seminoles a Bible in their own language. How many embraced Christianity as a consequence of her labor is difficult to say. But one thing is clear: her efforts clearly helped preserve the Muskogee language, and in preserving the language, she helped preserve the Creek and Seminole culture that persists in eastern Oklahoma today.

Further Reading: Hope Holway, "Ann Eliza Worcester Robertson as a Linguist," *Chronicles of Oklahoma* 37 (Spring 1959): 35–44.

Bass Reeves, 1840–1910

On May 10, 1875, Bass Reeves stood before Judge Isaac C. Parker of the United States Court for the Western District of Arkansas and took the oath of office as a deputy United States marshal. Reeves was only one of 200 deputies appointed that day in Fort Smith to help police the vast Indian Territory, but the appointment meant more to him than to the rest. He was black, and he had been a slave.

Reeves grew up on a plantation near Paris, Texas, on the south side of Red River in Lamar County. Like other slaves in Texas and Indian Territory, he had had no opportunity for an education. Yet as a youngster he had become the companion of his master's son and a familiar figure in the "Big House." He and his master often played cards together. Those games were not always for fun, and in the middle of one of them Reeves rose to his feet and laid his master "out cold with his fists."

To hit a white man, much less your master, was for a slave an offense punishable by death. Knowing that, Reeves ran for his life, going north across the Red River into Indian Territory. He did not stop until he got to the Creek and Seminole nations where slavery rested comparatively easier on blacks. Moreover, on the western frontier of those nations one could even escape notice as a runaway slave.

Bass Reeves was the most feared U.S. deputy marshal in Indian Territory after 1875. He took great pride in his personal appearance.

When Reeves first came to Indian Territory, and how long he was there, we do not know. He was in residence long enough to become relatively fluent in the Creek language, to learn some cultural habits of the tribe, and to become well acquainted with the geography of the Indian country. When the Civil War was over, Reeves found his way to Van Buren, Arkansas, where he obtained land and soon became a successful farmer-stockman. By that time he had married and had fathered the first of ten children.

Officials of the Fort Smith court actually recruited Reeves for the deputy marshal position. He stood six feet two inches tall, weighed 200 pounds, and had muscular arms and tremendous fists. He was a neat dresser and was courteous in his manner. He could not read or write, but he did have a remarkable memory. Particularly important was that he was an excellent shot with a rifle and knew the people and places of Indian Territory well. Being ebony-skinned also helped, for among some tribal people white skin created suspicion.

As officers of the court, deputy marshals served subpoenas, delivered warrants, and made arrests, among other things. Those who rode for Judge Parker, the Hanging Judge, did all of that in the 74,000-square-mile Indian Territory. They received no salary, only expenses and the fees paid for each arrest or order that they executed. If they killed a fugitive in the process of making an arrest, the deputies forfeited the fee and even had to pay for the burial.

Reeves served as a deputy marshal for thirty-two years. For the last eighteen years he was attached to the federal court in Muskogee, Oklahoma. His career was often controversial. During the course of it he killed fourteen men and his critics said that many of those killings were unjustified. Yet Reeves always was able to prove that they were in self-defense or, in the case of his own cook, accidental. At any rate, Bass Reeves won a reputation as the "most feared U.S. marshal in the Indian country."

Reeves retired as a deputy marshal of the federal court in 1907 when Oklahoma became a state. Long a resident of Muskogee, he then signed on as an officer in its police department. Until his death his assignment was to patrol Muskogee's large black community.

Bass Reeves was one of those rugged lawman who brought law and order to the American West, and more particularly to nineteenth-century Oklahoma. He is especially important, but not because of his thirty-two years as a marshal or his feats of bravery. He is important because he represents the way Oklahoma really was—the early multiracial Oklahoma, when the men who "wore the star" were not necessarily white but sometimes were black.

Further reading: Nudie E. Williams, "Black Men Who Wore the 'Star'," *Chronicles of Oklahoma* 59 (1981): 83–90; and "Bass Reeves: Black Lawman on Trial," *Chronicles of Oklahoma* 68 (Summer 1990): 154–67.

Jane Austin McCurtain, 1842–1924

In 1858, Jane Austin was sixteen years old and had never been more than fifty miles from her Doaksville home in the Choctaw Nation. Almost a full-blood Indian, she had spent the previous five years as a boarding student at Wheelock Academy, where she had demonstrated a keen intelligence. Jane had been selected to continue her education at a school in the States. Now she was on a steamboat that would take her far away from her Choctaw home. For so young a woman, it was both a frightening and exciting adventure.

Jane enrolled in Edgeworth Seminary at Sewickley, Pennsylvania. She was one of three young Choctaw women at the school; elsewhere in the United States there were fourteen other students from her nation. Giving women educational opportunities was considered important by the Choctaw leadership. "The surest way to civilize and improve the condition of our people is to educate our females," one of them had written. Records are few, but Jane apparently took advantage of the opportunity presented to her. She studied language, literature, mathematics, science, and religion, and she learned how to conduct herself like "a lady."

Jane remained at Edgeworth for two years. In September 1860 she was back in the Choctaw Nation, where she was described as "a neatly dressed and lady-like girl" who expected "to begin teaching shortly." Indeed, Jane did take a position in one of the Choctaw neighborhood schools near her home that fall. Unfortunately, the onset of the Civil War made her first job a short one. All tribal schools closed between 1861 and 1865.

Sometime during the course of war the elegant young schoolteacher met Jackson McCurtain, the dashing captain of the First Choctaw Regiment of the Confederate army. He was a member of a distinguished Choctaw family and a widower. As soon as the war was over, McCurtain proposed marriage to Jane. She kept him guessing for several months, but they were married in November 1865.

For the first few years of their married life, the McCurtains lived in what is now Latimer County. In 1868 they took up residence near present Kent in northern Choctaw County. Jackson ran livestock and

Jane Austin McCurtain, who once served as superintendent of Jones Academy, was a strong advocate of education for young men and women among the Choctaws.

farmed, but primarily he was a politician. Between 1868 and 1880 he served in the Choctaw Senate, and from 1880 to 1884 he was principal chief of the Choctaw Nation. During those years Jane gave birth to five children, managed the house, and was her husband's personal secretary and closest confidant. Indeed, she collaborated with him in preparing his state papers. Jackson McCurtain is remembered as one of the most successful Choctaw chiefs. He wins that distinction primarily because Jane Austin McCurtain was his "secretary of state."

On McCurtain's recommendation, in 1884 the Choctaw Nation constructed a beautiful new capitol at Tuskahoma. Jane, Jackson, and the children moved to a home they had constructed for the family near the capitol. Jackson enjoyed the house for only a short time, dying unexpectedly late in 1885.

Jane proceeded to make the best of *her* world. Her home next to the capitol became a center of activity for the so-called Progressive party in Choctaw politics. Two brothers-in-laws, Edmund and Green, drew on its resources to be elected principal chief of the nation. Jane's continual advice to them and their colleagues was that they must prepare the Choctaws to live in harmony with the whites. "Educate the boys and girls for leadership," she would say.

In part because of her remarkable influence, the Choctaw Nation created two additional boarding schools in 1891. Three years later Jane McCurtain was appointed superintendent of one of them, Jones

At her house adjacent to the capitol at Tuskahoma, Jane Austin McCurtain helped shape Choctaw political affairs. She stands on the balcony at center; her brother-in-law, Green McCurtain, is on the porch to the right of the X.

Academy, near present Hartshorne. She held that position for two years. Thereafter Jane returned to her home at Tuskahoma, where she served as custodian of the capitol building until her death in 1924.

In a time when women in general, and Choctaw women in particular, seldom involved themselves in public affairs, Jane Austin McCurtain did. That made her a woman ahead of her time, but more important, it also meant that the boys *and* girls of the Choctaw Nation were better prepared to cope with a rapidly changing world.

Further reading: Anna Lewis, "Jane McCurtain," *Chronicles of Oklahoma* 11 (September 1933): 1025–33.

Quanah Parker, 1852–1911

After seven years of stiff resistance the Quahada band of the Comanches had decided to give up their hunting and raiding traditions and settle on the reservation in what is now southwestern Oklahoma. Messengers from the band conveying this welcome

Quanah on one of his favorite horses in 1901. Note the pistol on his saddle and the eagle feathers in his hand.

news arrived at Fort Sill on May 13, 1875. One of them took the opportunity to search out Colonel Ranald Mackenzie, commander at Fort Sill, and ask if the cavalryman knew whether the Comanche's mother and sister were still alive. His mother, the Quahada said, was a white woman, whom he had not seen since he was nine years old. Whether Mackenzie knew anything about the family is unclear, but he did take an immediate interest in the proud and handsome young man who told him about it, who introduced himself as Quanah.

Actually the story of Quanah's mother, Cynthia Ann Parker, was well known on the Southern Plains. In 1835, when she was only nine years old, Comanche raiders had taken her captive in a famous attack on Fort Parker in the Republic of Texas. Over time she adapted to the lifestyle of the Quahadas and became the wife of Peta Nocona, a prominent war chief, with whom she had three children. When Texas Rangers overran their camp in 1861, all the family escaped except Cynthia Ann and her daughter, Prairie Flower. Quanah's mother was restored to the Parker family, but she never adjusted to the loss of her Comanche family. Prairie Flower died within three years, while Cynthia Ann died in 1870.

It was too late to see his mother when the Quahadas came to Fort Sill, but Quanah held her memory sacred all of his life. On the reservation he came to think of himself more and more as Cynthia Ann's son and less as Peta Nocona's, even adding the surname of Parker. Being the son of a white woman certainly elevated him in the estimation of agency personnel. They looked to Quanah to help explain the rules and regulations of reservation life to the Comanches. Quanah was more than willing to act in such a capacity, for it raised his status both within the tribe and among white officials. It also gave him a secure financial position. He was soon recognized as one of the "more important" chiefs of the Comanches, and then in time as "the chief" of the Comanches.

Quanah was an effective leader of his people during the reservation era. He negotiated grazing leases with Texas cattlemen that produced hundreds of thousands of dollars in revenue for the tribe. To encourage Comanches to enroll their children in boarding schools, he sent his own youngsters to schools at Fort Sill and at Carlisle, Pennsylvania. As judge of the agency's Court of Indian Offenses, his judicious decisions won respect for new forms of law and order. His perceptive questions also caused the allotment commission, sent to break up the reservation, to deal more fairly with the Comanches. Quanah also modeled a new lifestyle for his people that included "citizen" dress and his wood-frame Star House.

Quanah Parker wished for the Comanches to follow the road of his mother's people. He himself was doing so, and it had made him powerful and wealthy, a celebrity. Yet Quanah would not have the Comaches abandon all of their traditions. He, for example, proudly wore braids. Nor did he give up his plural wives. During his life he had at least eight wives, although the most he ever lived with at one time was five. This much-married condition gave him twenty-five children, but it also created many problems for him among government officials. Quanah was also one of the principal leaders in the peyote cult, a spiritual tradition that uses peyote as a sacrament to encounter the Suffering Savior. He defended the use of peyote before the Oklahoma state legislature in 1908.

In early December 1910, Quanah Parker located his mother's grave and had her few remains reburied in a cemetery near present Cache in Comanche County. He commented then that whites and Indians were "all the same people anyway" and that in time "we will all lie together." In less than two months he himself was dead, and his body lay next to his mother's.

Quanah's Star House, about 1911.

Historian William T. Hagan has written that Quanah was a classic mediator, with one foot on the white man's road and one foot on the Comanche trail. Unlike other middlemen during Oklahoma's reservation era, Quanah managed to retain the respect and admiration of both whites and Indians. It was a testimony to his forceful character, his intelligence, his romantic origins, and his personal credo that we are "all the same people anyway."

Further reading: William T. Hagan, *Quanah Parker, Comanche Chief* (Norman: University of Oklahoma Press, 1993).

A Question

As you reflect on the subjects of these brief sketches, ask yourself, do these men and women share a common quality or characteristic that enabled them to contribute to the betterment of humankind? What was it? Are there people today who possess it?

See History for Yourself

Visit Sequoyah's cabin northeast of Sallisaw and Black Beaver's grave in Anadarko. Visit the Seminole Nation Museum in Wewoka to understand more about John Horse's travails in Oklahoma, and tour Judge Parker's courtroom and jail in Fort Smith to see where Bass Reeves worked. Take a trip to the Choctaw capitol at Tuskahoma and see the building to which Jane McCurtain devoted the last years of her life. Also, visit the Quanah Parker Star House at the Eagle Park Ghost Town near Cache. Finally, visit the library of the Oklahoma Historical Society and look at publications printed in Choctaw and Muskogee, and marvel at the intellectual contributions of Ann Eliza Worcester Robertson and Sophia Nye Byington.

Unit 4: **OKLAHOMA ON GLASS— A PHOTOGRAPHIC ESSAY**

Oklahoma on Glass—
A Photographic Essay

By John R. Lovett

During the late 1800s and early 1900s amateur and professional photographers were very active in Oklahoma and left thousands of images of historical events. Their cameras recorded cowboys, settlers, farmers, American Indians, town builders, and many others who played a part in the early history of the state.

As a result of advances during the American Civil War and in the years following, photography became an important part of American life. Many Oklahoma photographers used glass-plate negatives in their trade. Although very fragile, the glass plates provide superb, highly detailed images when the negatives are printed onto photographic paper. The photographs in this chapter were printed using the original glass-plate negatives of five of Oklahoma's early photographers.

William S. Prettyman

William S. Prettyman was born in Maryland and migrated to Kansas in 1879. While living in Kansas, he photographed several Osage Indians who visited his photography shop. That event sparked a new interest for Prettyman, who then decided to travel into Indian Territory to photograph the tribes who lived there. In September 1883 he loaded his wagon with his camera, chemicals, glass-plate negatives, and other photography supplies and traveled to Indian Territory, where during the next few years

Members of the Sac and Fox tribe in front of their bark house. William S. Prettyman made this image during one of his several trips into Indian Territory.

In this Prettyman image, the farmer and his wife were photographed with their horses and their log cabin home.

Indian students working in the fields at Chilocco Indian School took time from their work to pose for Prettyman.

Prettyman photographed these cowboys as they watched cattle on the Salt Fork of the Arkansas River.

he made several more trips, taking photographs of American Indians and settlers alike.

One of Oklahoma's best amateur photographers was Annette Hume, wife of the Kiowa and Comanche agency physician. The Humes moved to Anadarko in December 1890. Annette Hume usually took her camera during her frequent visits to the agency, and during those visits she would photograph her Kiowa and Comanche friends. Many of her glass-plate negatives have survived and provide visual documentation of the Kiowa and Comanche tribes at the turn of the century.

In 1902, Annette Hume photographed Tso-Tuddle and Red Bone cutting up meat and drying it at the Kiowa-Comanche Agency.

Indian students at the Presbyterian school near Anadarko, as photographed by Annette Hume.

George and Eva Mopope, Kiowa, were photographed by Annette Hume at the Hume House.

A Comanche baby in a cradle-board carried by the mother, photographed by Annette Hume.

Andrew Alexander Forbes

Andrew Alexander Forbes was a traveling photographer in Oklahoma during the late 1800s. Like many other traveling photographers of the period, he took his studio (namely, his wagon) right to the doorstep of his potential customers. Forbes would visit settlers at their homesteads, make a glass-plate nega-

Settlers would put on their best clothes to have their photographs taken by traveling photographers such as Andrew Alexander Forbes.

Forbes photographed these cowboys having dinner at the chuck wagon.

tive of the family, develop the negative, and provide the family with their photograph before he moved on to the next homestead. Forbes also photographed cowboys in western Oklahoma in the same manner as he did settlers, except that he usually made negatives of large groups of cowboys. Thus he could sell more prints from one negative than when he visited single-family homesteads.

Harmon T. Swearingen

Harmon T. Swearingen was an early photographer who came to Guthrie after the land run of 1889. He settled there and opened a photography studio, which he operated until his death in 1931. Swearingen's glass-plate negatives record the early development of Guthrie when it was the territorial capital. He captured images of the town from its beginning as a tent city to the first brick buildings.

Swearingen photographed Captain Arthur MacArthur and three other U.S. Army officers at Guthrie in May 1889.

Top: Harmon T. Swearingen made this image of Guthrie six days after the land run of 1889.
Center: Two settlers posed for Swearingen on their town-lot claim in Guthrie.
Bottom: The owner, employees, and customers of the Palace Hotel and Restaurant were the subjects of this Swearingen photograph.

Photographer J. A. Shuck was born in Ohio, but his family moved west to Kansas, and Shuck eventually settled in El Reno, Oklahoma Territory. Although Shuck owned a photography studio in El Reno, he also traveled around the area making glass-plate negatives of Cheyenne and Arapaho Indians, Fort Reno, and other subjects for profit and for his own interest. Shuck also helped preserve images of western Oklahoma by collecting the glass-plate negatives of other photographers who worked in and around El Reno.

The work of many other photographers provides a look back at Oklahoma's rich heritage and history. Someone once commented that the camera was a "mirror with a memory" that produced silent images of reality. The glass-plate negatives that these Oklahoma photographers made provide us with a vital link to the past.

The Red Barn Livery Sale and Boarding Stable as photographed by J. A. Shuck.

A Cheyenne and Arapaho village photographed by Shuck.

Shuck made this image of Cheyenne councilmen and a young boy at the Darlington Agency.

Soldiers stationed at Fort Reno posed for this Shuck photograph.

An Arapaho camp near Fort Reno, photographed by Shuck.

Unit 5: THE AMERICANIZATION OF OKLAHOMA

Introduction

The generation of Oklahomans that saw the nineteenth century become the twentieth also saw changes that were much more important than the calendar's turn. When people in that generation were born, Oklahoma was Indian country. The Five Tribes lived and ruled in the eastern lands. Plains Indians and other tribes lived on reservations in the western half of the future state.

By the time that generation of Oklahomans had reached middle age, all that had changed. In the east the Indians were a minority in what the mapmakers called Indian Territory. The name was deceptive, since the five Indian republics were no more. In the west the Indian reservations were gone too. In their place was a new territory—Oklahoma Territory. Only seven years into the new century, the people of both territories combined to form the union's newest state.

The process that led them to do that was a process in which the distinctive Indian republics and reservations gave way to something more like the rest of America. The so-called "land of the red man"—the land of the First Americans, both men and women—became America's forty-sixth state: Oklahoma. This section explains why and how that happened.

Chapter 15: Changes in Indian Territory

The railroad system that came to so-called Indian Territory because of the Reconstruction treaties had a tremendous effect on the Five Tribes. Ever since their removal, most Indians had kept as far away from whites as possible. Physically isolated, they were economically isolated as well. Indian families generally grew their own food, built their own homes, spun their own cloth, and sewed their own clothes. Even if they had wanted to trade with white people in the States, that was hard to do. Except by way of a few dangerous rivers and some rough, unpaved roads, it was very difficult for Indians to send their products out of the territory, and just as hard to bring goods into it. Theirs was less a commercial than a *subsistence* economy. Its purpose was to provide what was necessary to support life, not products to be sold for profit. In such circumstances, most Indians were much more interested in living simply than in earning money.

Life in Indian Territory let them do that. None of the Indian governments allowed any individual to own land. Instead, the entire domain of each Indian republic was owned as collective or communal property by the entire nation. An individual tribal citizen could use as much land as he or she needed, and as much as was needed of the nation's other natural resources such as timber, water, and grass. Because of the tribes' small numbers but great resources, hardly anybody got very rich, but nobody was very poor either under such a system.

Railroads and Early Industry

The coming of the railroads changed all of that. The Indian Territory steel rails were connected to a network that spanned the United States. Over those rails, iron locomotives made it easy to ship the territory's products all across America. It was just as easy to bring goods and people into the Indian lands. Very quickly, much of the territory's economy shifted from simple subsistence to commerce—buying and selling to make money. For that reason, access to land and other communal resources become important to individual wealth.

Coal and Its Miners

One example involved coal. The Indians called it "the rock that burns," and they always had known that it was an abundant natural resource. Particularly in the Choctaw Nation, they long had used the outcroppings that brought coal to the land's surface, where they had gathered fuel to heat their small homes and fire their simple forges.

When the railroads came, it became possible to do much more than that. The railroads could pull long trains piled high with coal to eastern factories that were hungry for fuel. The railroads themselves needed tons of coal to run their locomotives. Under those new circumstances, what had been a natural resource became a valuable commercial product.

The first to take advantage of the situation was a former Confederate soldier named James J. McAlester. While living in Arkansas after the war, he learned that coal lay right on the ground near the crossroads of the trails to California and Texas. McAlester came to the Indian nations and built a store—"McAlester's Store"—on the spot. By marrying a Chickasaw he became a citizen of both his wife's nation and of the Choctaw Republic, since the two shared citizenship. That gave him the right to "use" as much coal as he could mine. When the Katy Railroad reached his store in 1872, McAlester began to use quite a lot of it. He used it as something to sell to the railroad, and he used the MK&T to ship more coal to sell to eastern factories.

Although a few other Indian citizens also became coal producers, most of the mining came to involve

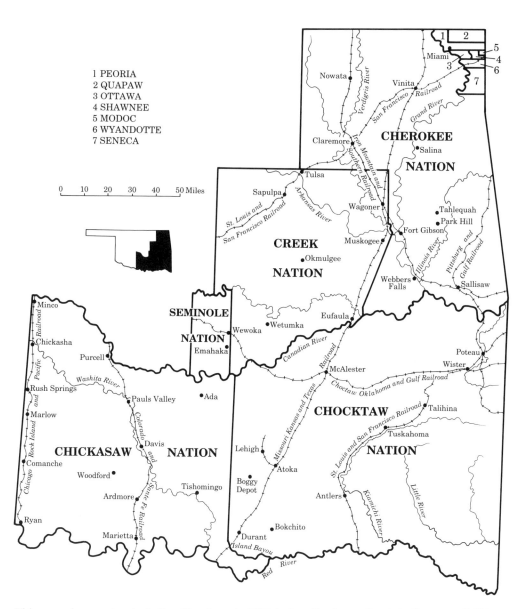

1 PEORIA
2 QUAPAW
3 OTTAWA
4 SHAWNEE
5 MODOC
6 WYANDOTTE
7 SENECA

0   10   20   30   40   50 Miles

CHEROKEE NATION

CREEK NATION

SEMINOLE NATION

CHOCKTAW NATION

CHICKASAW NATION

Nowata
Vinita
Miami
Claremore
Salina
Tulsa
Sapulpa
Wagoner
Tahlequah
Park Hill
Fort Gibson
Muskogee
Okmulgee
Webbers Falls
Sallisaw
Wetumka
Eufaula
Wewoka
Emahaka
Poteau
Wister
McAlester
Talihina
Tuskahoma
Minco
Chickasha
Purcell
Rush Springs
Pauls Valley
Ada
Marlow
Davis
Lehigh
Comanche
Woodford
Tishomingo
Antlers
Ardmore
Ryan
Marietta
Durant
Bokchito
Atoka
Boggy Depot

Verdigris River
San Francisco Railroad
Grand River
Iron Mountain and Southern Railroad
St. Louis and San Francisco Railroad
Arkansas River
Illinois River
Pittsburg and Gulf Railroad
Canadian River
Missouri Kansas and Texas Railroad
Choctaw Oklahoma and Gulf Railroad
St. Louis and San Francisco Railroad
Kiamichi River
Little River
Washita River
Colorado and Santa Fe Railroad
Chicago Rock Island and Pacific Railroad
Island Bayou
Red River

This map shows not only Indian Territory in 1889, before its absorption into the state of Oklahoma, but also its swift penetration by railroad lines after the Civil War. Note that eastern
Oklahoma's largest towns and cities today tend to be those that enjoyed railroad connections
more than a century ago.

INDIAN TERRITORY IN FICTION AND FILM

Western writers and film-makers have long been fascinated with life in the Indian nations. One of those was the novelist Charles Portis, whose novel *True Grit* was a best-seller and the basis of the popular motion picture that earned John Wayne his only Academy Award.

In the story, Mattie Ross and U.S. Marshal Rooster Cogburn (played in the movie by Kim Darby and Wayne) go to Indian Territory to find the man who killed Mattie's father. They learn that the killer has joined the gang of Lucky Ned Pepper. Tracking the gang, they make their way to McAlester's store. The novel's description of the store is probably accurate:

We reached J. J. McAlester's store about 10 o'clock that morning. It must have been a trading day for there were several wagons and horses tied about the store. The railroad tracks ran behind it. There was little more to the place than the store building and a few smaller frame and log structures of poor description.

Mr. McAlester, who kept the store, was a good Arkansas man. . . . His wife served us a good country dinner with fresh buttermilk.

noncitizens. The railroad companies and other corporations, not individual citizens or their tribal governments, took direct advantage of the land's resources. The railroads in particular assured themselves a cheap and steady supply of coal by operating their own mines. They also guaranteed themselves a profit when they shipped coal to eastern buyers. The Katy itself came to own the largest single coal company, the Osage Mining and Coal Company. Other railroads took leases to 43,000 acres of the very best coal lands—roughly half of all the known fields. Although the land still belonged legally to the Indian nations, it was controlled completely by a few corporations. By 1907 it had earned those corporations the annual profit from 3 million tons of "the best steam coal west of Pennsylvania." All that the Indian governments received were small lease fees and token royalties.

Individual Indians hardly were involved in the mining at all. Nearly all of the miners who worked in the coalfields came from outside the territory, most of them recruited and imported by the coal companies. In fact, nearly two-thirds of the 8,000 coal miners in 1907 were foreign-born. The dark mines echoed with Italian, Polish, Russian, German, and other languages. A good number of English, Scottish, and Irish accents added to the noisy clatter.

Most miners brought their entire family with them, and both women and children found jobs around the mines. The coal companies laid out (and controlled) entire new towns to house the miners. Many modern Oklahoma communities, such as Krebs, Hartshorne, Alderson, Lehigh, Coalgate, Wilburton, and Stringtown, had their beginnings in that way. All still have a strong flavor of their immigrant origins.

The coal miners' lives could be short. These Italian miners of the Krebs area also could testify to how dirty it was at best.

Krebs, for example, still hosts an annual Italian festival that attracts thousands, and tiny Hartshorne maintains one of the few Russian Orthodox churches west of the Mississippi River.

MAKING GOOD

Not all of the Italians who came to the coal mines stayed in them. One who did not was Pietro Piegari. Born at San Gregario Magne, Italy, in 1895, he came to America when he was only eight. Because the American immigration officials could not pronounce his name, he took to calling himself Pete Prichard.

When he was eleven years old and had only three years of schooling, Pete went to work in the mines near Krebs. Ten years later a mine accident left his left leg crushed and also left him unable ever to work again in the mines.

Pete then started to support himself by selling home-brewed beer to the miners. After a while he started selling them food too, which he cooked himself and sold out of his house. In the early 1930s his business was so good that he turned the entire house into a restaurant. Its fame spread all over the state and beyond it. In time its customers included politicians, astronauts, movie stars, and foreign ambassadors. All of these came—and they still come—to the tiny town of Krebs, Oklahoma, where they eat great Italian food in a restaurant that used to be a house. Maybe they do not know why its dining rooms are so small, but they know its name: Pete's Place.

THE MOST DANGEROUS MINES IN THE WORLD

Because Indian Territory's coal mines lay outside of the United States, there were no state laws to protect miners in this very dangerous industry. Since neither the federal government nor the Indian governments provided much protection, the territory's coal mines were the most dangerous in the world. On the average, the blood of thirteen dead min-ers stained every million tons of coal mined.

The territory's worst single tragedy has been described by an historian of Oklahoma's Italian people:

With the usual hard labor of the mines came the real danger of mining disasters. . . . On January 7, 1892, an explosion ripped through Osage Coal and Mining Company's Mine No. 11, immediately kill-ing eighty-seven and injuring about 150 more. Several Italians died or were injured in this mine disaster, the worst in Oklahoma's history. . . . One survivor recalled: "All about me there were agonized groans, shouting, and bedlam. Men were tearing at their flaming clothing, dropping in their tracks." (Kenny L. Brown, *The Italians in Oklahoma* [Norman: University of Oklahoma Press, 1981])

Tri-State Mining

Indian Territory's extreme northeastern corner provided other mineral resources for mining. Lead mining companies from southwestern Missouri and southeastern Kansas entered the area in the early 1890s. At the tiny community of Peoria they discovered a rich vein of lead. Almost overnight, 1,500 miners descended upon the spot. Subsequent discoveries of zinc and even more lead deposits brought thousands more into new boomtowns like Commerce, Picher, and Miami. In fact, the Indian lands became the richest single area in the so-called Tri-State District (Missouri, Kansas, and Oklahoma) of hard rock mining.

Black Gold!

Of course, Oklahoma's most important mineral resource has been its petroleum. Again, Indians had known of its existence almost since their arrival. Oily seepage often fouled their drinking water and ruined their wells. It seemed that oil had only one good use: blankets soaked in it yielded a medicine to cure rheumatism and other diseases. White people used it the same way at the time, but they soon discovered other, more profitable uses. Most important was that it could be turned into illuminating oil for their lanterns.

Early wells dug in Pennsylvania and Texas brought

oil to the surface, light to the night, jobs to thousands, and fortunes to a few. Soon wells drilled in Indian Territory began to do the same. This was especially true after the discovery of a large underground lake of oil just south of modern Tulsa, beneath the farm of Ida Glenn. The opening of the Glenn Pool in 1905 ignited another rush of businesses and workers to exploit what turned out to be some of the richest oil fields in the world.

The Glenn Pool field, the oil patch that helped transform the Indian Territory.

Entire cities resulted from the new commercial activity. Some came almost from nothing—nothing except the natural resources that lay near them and that made a new city like McAlester possible. Others, like Tulsa, had been sleepy villages of just a few residents until the discovery of nature's nearby wealth drew thousands to them.

Changes in the Countryside

The countryside shared in the changes, too. Communal land tenure let tribal citizens use almost any land that they wanted. The new railroad lines made it possible for any of the land's products to be shipped and sold all over America and the world. The result was that some tribal citizens began to use huge tracts of land—use it not to grow a little food for themselves but to produce valuable products to sell outside the territory.

A few of those who did so were full-blood Indians. More often they were mixed-bloods whose part-Indian ancestry gave them tribal citizenship. Sometimes they were not Indians at all; rather, they were people who had married Indians and thus had become citizens of their spouse's nation. In any case, there were some who turned their tribal citizenship into large personal fortunes.

Meanwhile the great majority of Indians, particularly the full-bloods, continued to cling to their old ways. They still preferred a simple life in which all persons met their own needs with their own hands. They did not consider the making of money to be a very important need at all. These Indians still were not poor, for they had everything that they believed they needed.

Others of their fellow citizens wanted to make money—lots of it. Their citizenship gave them the right to take as much land as they needed in order to do that. There may not have been very many of them, but some did become rich indeed.

Livestock raising was one way to do that. Cheap barbed wire allowed individuals to fence off giant ranches to graze their own cattle and other animals. In the Creek nation, for example, F. B. Severs enclosed enough land to raise and sell 15 to 20 thousand cattle every year and another 300 to 500 horses that he sent east to be sold as polo ponies. In the same nation, George Perryman maintained several ranches and farms that altogether ran to several thousand acres. Severs and Perryman were two of just sixty-one Creek citizens who between them controlled 1,072,215 acres in 1896—almost one-third of their nation's entire land surface.

Much of the land in the Indian nations became giant farms. Of course, no one individual could farm very much land in those days before tractors and other machine-powered farm tools. They had to

A CONTEMPORARY REPORT

Every year the agent to the Five Tribes filed an official report with the Bureau of Indian Affairs on life in Indian Territory. In 1886 the agent was a Cherokee mixed-blood named Robert L. Owen. His report registered some of the changes that were sweeping the territory by declaring that the area of farming lands has probably doubled in five years, and is increasing in geometric ratio. The Washita Valley, in the Chickasaw Nation, is almost a solid farm for 50 miles. It is cultivated by white labor largely, with Chickasaw landlords. (I saw one farm there said to contain 8,000 acres, another 4,000 acres, and many other very large and handsome places.)

The number who so enriched themselves, was not very large. Ten years after Owen's report, it was estimated that a mere twenty families controlled 90 percent of all of the land in the Chickasaw Nation.

rely on human labor, not machinery. Many did that. They became landlords who rented land to some of the tens of thousands of non-Indian farmers who came into the territory looking for land to work.

Many people were available to work farms in the Indian Territory because most of the West's free land was gone by the 1890s. On top of that, the whole country suffered from a severe economic depression over most of that decade. Since farmers were among those most hurt, many left their homes in Kansas, Missouri, Arkansas, and Texas and came into Indian Territory to get a new chance.

Tribal laws gave them that chance, but because each tribe owned its land communally, there was no land left for these people, whom the Indians called "intruders." Instead, the usual arrangement was that the newcomer would find a tribal citizen who would set him up on a piece of unused land. The newcomer would clear the trees, erect fences and buildings, and farm the land for five to ten years. During that time he would pay no rent; at its end, however, all of his improvements would go to his tribal landlord. (Remember that many of the tribal citizens were only part-Indian and that some were not Indian at all.) The farmer would either move on to a similar arrangement someplace else or rent the land for cash or as a sharecropper. A sharecropper paid the landlord with a share—usually a quarter or one-third of their crops.

In that way the amount of land used for farms in the territory increased very fast. Every year land that barely had been touched by human beings was cleared, plowed, and planted. In a few years, some tribal citizens were able to build up huge farms composed of many pieces of rented land. Each separate piece was worked by a different family of renters.

An obvious effect of these economic changes was a great social transformation as the nature of the territory's population swiftly shifted. Every year tens of thousands entered the Indian nations to work on farms or ranches, in coal or lead mines, or in the growing cities. The population not only grew but changed in composition. Many spoke of a steady "bleaching" of the population—referring to the great numbers of whites. So great and swift was the addition of that white population that the Indians themselves soon became a small and rapidly declining minority in their own Indian Territory.

CHANGING POPULATION: THE CENSUS RECORD

Unlike Oklahoma Territory, which was later the object of dramatic land runs, the Indian lands on the east fell prey to what contemporaries called a "silent migration." If it was silent, it was nonetheless quite remarkable.

At the Civil War's end in 1865 probably no more than a few thousand non-Indians had lived in the five republics; however, a single generation later, Oklahoma's first federal census recorded just how rapidly the proportions of the races had changed by 1890 and how much change there was in the years thereafter:

Race	1890		1900		1907	
White	110,254	(61.2%)	302,680	(77.2%)	538,512	(79.1%)
Black	18,636	(10.3%)	36,853	(9.4%)	80,649	(11.8%)
Indian full-bloods or mixed-bloods	51,279	(28.5%)	52,500	(13.4%)	61,925	(9.1%)

(United States Bureau of the Census, *Population of Oklahoma and Indian Territories, 1907* [Washington: Government Printing Office, 1907])

Black Newcomers

To speak of "bleaching" was, however, deceptive. White people were not the only ones coming into Indian Territory. Blacks also migrated in from neighboring states. They came for most of the same reasons that whites had, but they had another one. Many of the southern states were beginning to take away most of the rights that African Americans had gained after the Civil War. Many southern states already had ended their most important right—the right to vote—and others were ready to do the same. These states also were requiring that the black citizens be segregated from the whites in different (and almost always inferior) schools, neighborhoods, and the like. Little wonder then that thousands of black people left their home states and came to the Indian nations.

In their new homes these blacks found not just jobs to work or land to farm but also governments that did not single them out for special and demeaning treatment. And they found other black people already living in Indian Territory. These were the Indians' own freed slaves and their descendants. Many of them already lived in all-black communities like Rentiesville or Red Bird, communities that gave both them and the newcomers an independence rare for that day.

Outsiders in Indian Territory

That both white and black Americans kept pouring into the Indian nations was proof that they believed that they could improve their lives there. That is not to say, however, that they experienced only improvements. Living in Indian republics meant that the newcomers faced some unusual problems, too.

Because they were living in *Indian* republics, very few of the newcomers could ever become citizens of those nations. They lived without the political rights that Americans had come to expect. Since they lived in no state, they could not vote in any federal election. In fact, they could not vote in *any* election, since the Indian governments confined the right to vote to their own citizens. Because the newcomers enjoyed representation neither in Washington nor at home, they constantly complained that government ignored their wishes and needs.

In several ways that unquestionably was true. One of the most obvious involved schooling. The Indian governments maintained fine schools for their own citizens but none at all for the white and black children who were entering their lands. Many chil-

Among other things, Indian Territory's new population provided its own musical entertainment.

The Chickasaw Nation maintained Bloomfield Academy near Achille for its more prominent women citizens. Notice, however, the obvious mixed-blood status of these.

dren had no schools at all; those who did went to subscription schools that were financed by the families in their communities. Each family typically paid a dollar or two a month for each child. At best the money might hire one poorly prepared teacher for all grades and provide the pupils a crude building and a few rough benches and desks.

The school year usually lasted only a few months because the children's families needed them to work at home. In fact, many young children worked at what we would consider adult jobs today—mining coal, drilling oil wells, and plowing fields, for example. Most of the territory's children worked hard at home or at jobs, and many worked at both. Most went to school for no more than a few years—just one or two in many cases.

Other than schooling, the Indian governments provided few services to their own citizens and none at all to the newcomers. If the new people wanted roads, they had to build them. If they wanted water or sewer lines, they had to lay them. If they wanted fire protection, they had to protect themselves.

In a sense, the Indian nations could not provide for law enforcement even for their citizens. The Indian police could not arrest noncitizens, and Indian courts could not try them. Noncitizens were subject only to the federal authority represented by a few distant federal courts (of which the closest and most important was in Fort Smith, Arkansas) and a handful of federal marshals.

Under those circumstances it is surprising that the movie and television image of the "Wild West" was not more accurate. Few residents ever saw a gunslinger. Few ever witnessed a shootout on Main Street. Few, in fact, ever heard a pistol or a rifle shot except for those they fired themselves at coyotes or tin cans. Work and family took too much energy for such nonsense. In addition, most residents cherished order, respected their neighbors, and feared their God.

Of course, there were those who cherished only easy money, respected no person, and feared nothing. Indian Territory had its authentic bad men who used the nations to plunder honest folk while escaping the law's reach.

Most of those outlaws did not escape permanently. Quite a few wound up in Fort Smith at the end of Judge Parker's rope. "Hanging Judge" Parker dispatched many an evildoer whom his marshals brought before his court. Other outlaws never made it that far, since they were killed by marshals—often in real shootouts, but rarely on Main Street. Some also met their end at the hands of outraged citizens who defended their lives and property as best they could.

Problems Without Solutions

The rare occasions when violence erupted were quite dramatic. Less dramatic, but much less rare were the simpler legal problems that had no easy solution. Indian courts lacked not only criminal but also civil jurisdiction over nontribal citizens. That meant that white and black newcomers had no local authority to settle their business or other disputes. If one man sold another a horse, for example, and the horse turned out to be blind, did he have to give the money back? There was no judge to answer the question either way.

LUCKY NED

Novels and movies can have some basis in real fact. Consider the case of the outlaw Ned Christie.

People called him Lucky Ned because he always managed to evade Judge Parker's marshals and deputies. On one occasion the lawmen had him cornered in a log cabin. Although they poured steady gunfire into it for two days, Christie nonetheless escaped after bursting from the cabin and shooting his way out.

Christie apparently did not trust entirely to his luck. He subsequently built a well-stocked fort outside of Tahlequah, in the Cherokee Nation. Marshals trapped him in it, but the fort withstood their pistol and rifle fire. It even withstood the thirty cannonballs that they shot into it. Only after their dynamite had leveled one of its walls could they break into the fort. That was when Lucky Ned's luck ran out—the marshals shot and killed him on the spot.

Lucky Ned Cristie was largely forgotten after that. Maybe students who read Charles Portis's *True Grit* or see John Wayne kill Lucky Ned Pepper in the movie will remember him.

Lucky Ned Christie, after his luck ran out.

There were always such problems, and the faster the non-Indian population grew, and the more complex their lives became, the bigger such problems became. Always, too, there were economic problems that were unavoidable under the Indian governments. The tribal governments required that the newcomers pay annual fees for permits to live in their nations. The money was, in effect, a tax on the newcomers. The fees were not all that high, but they were a burden. They also meant that the newcomers were the only ones who paid taxes, since tribal citizens paid none at all. Moreover, the tribes had the right to evict any non-citizen at any time, and they sometimes did evict the "intruders" who made trouble for them.

They did not often do that because they needed the noncitizens. They needed them to clear more land, to work new farms, and to toil in the mines and oil fields. But because none of them could own land, the newcomers worked on farms they could not own. If they worked in the mines or the oil fields, they could put up houses and even business buildings, but they could not own the lots where they lived and worked. With no right to vote, with little government, with few laws but many problems, they were Americans living under circumstances unique in America.

It is true that they had put themselves willingly in those circumstances. But it also is true that the growing number of newcomers had cause to resent the tribal governments and their way of holding land. Indian Territory's population was becoming more like the rest of America's. It was inevitable that the new people would demand that their new homeland become more like the rest of America, too.

See History for Yourself

Many of Oklahoma's major highways follow the paths blazed by the early railroads. This is particularly true of U.S. Highway 69, which generally follows the route of the old Missouri, Kansas, and Texas ("Katy") Railroad. The stretch of highway between McAlester and Atoka generally parallels the old railroad line as it passes through small communities that early developed as coal-mining towns. In McAlester itself the McAlester Building Foundation maintains an exhibit that illustrates life during the last days of the Choctaw Nation, including materials used in the early coal mines. In Coalgate the Coal County Historical Society maintains a similar Historical and Mining Museum with working models of two early coal mines.

In Bartlesville the Nellie Johnstone No. 1, the state's original oil well, has been fully restored and is maintained in Johnstone Park. Visitors can also learn much about the early oil industry in that part of Oklahoma in the Exhibit Hall that is maintained by the Phillips Petroleum Company. The Picher Mining Field Museum in Picher is a similar resource for understanding the hard rock mining that transformed the historic Tri-State District. Not to be overlooked as one of Oklahoma's prime natural resources is its timber. Beavers Bend State Park, located just north of Broken Bow, reveals that story to visitors in the Forest Heritage Center.

Many Oklahoma communities recently have restored their old train depots and turned them into impressive local museums. The Katy Depot Center in Checotah and the Frisco Depot Museum in Hugo are good examples appropriate to this chapter. The latter, operated by the Choctaw County Historical Society, even offers train rides on most Saturdays.

Outside of Grove, Har-ber Village maintains over 100 exhibits that record life in the last days of Indian Territory. On the grounds visitors can enter very realistic settlers' cabins and examine the farm and household implements that were the stuff of everyday life for most "intruders."

Suggestions for Further Reading

Reference

Brown, Kenny L. "Peaceful Progress: An Account of the Italians of Krebs, Oklahoma." *Chronicles of Oklahoma* 53(1975):332–52.

Clark, J. Stanley. "Immigrants in the Choctaw Coal Industry." *Chronicles of Oklahoma* 33(1955–56):440–55.

Graebner, Norman A. "Cattle Ranching in Eastern Oklahoma." *Chronicles of Oklahoma* 21(1943):300–311.

Kalish, Phillip A. "The Ordeal of the Oklahoma Coal Miner." *Chronicles of Oklahoma* 48(1970):331–40.

Masterson, H. V. *The Katy Railroad and the Last Frontier.* Norman: University of Oklahoma Press, 1952.

Nesbitt, Paul. "J. J. McAlester." *Chronicles of Oklahoma* 11(1933):758–64.

Nieberding, Velma. "Old Peoria." *Chronicles of Oklahoma* 50(1972):142–55.

Related Reading

Croy, Homer. *He Hanged Them High: An Authentic Account of the Fanatical Judge Who Hanged Eighty-eight Men.* New York: Duell, Sloan, and Pearce, 1952.

Giles, Janice Holt. *The Kinta Years: An Oklahoma Childhood.* Boston: Houghton Mifflin, 1973.

Harman, S. W. *Hell on the Border: He Hanged Eighty-eight Men.* 1898. Muskogee: Indian Heritage Publications, 1971.

Harrington, Fred Harvey. *Hanging Judge.* Caldwell, Idaho: Caxton Printers, 1951.

Shirley, Glenn. *Henry Starr.* New York: David McKay Company, 1965.

Portis, Charles. *True Grit.* New York: Simon and Schuster, 1968.

Chapter 16: The Promised Land— Oklahoma Territory

You will recall that the land that the federal government took from the Five Tribes after the Civil War eventually went to create reservations for Plains Indians and other tribes. The one important exception was a piece of what had been Creek and Seminole lands. Taken from those tribes for the purpose of relocating other groups there, this area was never turned over to any others. For that reason, it was known as the Unassigned Lands.

The Unassigned Lands

Not only were the Unassigned Lands not used by Indians, they were nearly unused by anyone at all. A few people worked for the Atchison, Topeka, and Sante Fe Railroad, which ran over the open spaces. A few others used the free grass to feed small cattle herds that roamed over parts of the area. Otherwise, it was unsettled, a vacuum of unused land— possibly the best unoccupied land left in America in the late 1800s.

That is why the Unassigned Lands drew first the attention, then pressure, and finally demands from non-Indians to settle what would become Oklahoma Territory. In particular, one federal law made the empty real estate something of a "Promised Land."

That law was known as the Homestead Act. Congress had passed it during the Civil War. It allowed any American citizen to claim up to 160 acres, one-quarter of a square mile section, of the publicly owned lands. Those who lived on their "claims" for five years then owned them outright. In that way the Homestead Act already had provided free homes and free farms across the West.

The Homestead Act made the Unassigned Lands especially attractive. If federal authorities would only declare that the lands taken from the Creeks and the Seminoles to relocate others were part of the public lands of the United States, then settlers could enter them, make their claims, and divide them up into tens of thousands of 160-acre farms.

The Boomers

Many Americans were convinced that the Unassigned Lands (which they also called the Oklahoma District) already were eligible for immediate homestead settlement. Many black Americans thought so. When the federal government had first taken the lands from the Indians, one plan had been that they might provide homes for "freedmen"—the newly freed slaves, particularly those who had been held in bondage by Indian masters. That accounted for many blacks' insistence that they be allowed to homestead the lands immediately. The federal government, however, ignored their demands. Instead, it maintained that the Unassigned Lands were not covered by the Homestead Act at all. Because they had been taken from the Creeks and the Seminoles for an explicit purpose, Washington reasoned that they were not part of the public lands, even if the purpose had never been effected.

For the same reason, the government also ignored similar demands made by whites and others. One of the first of those came from Elias C. Boudinot, the part-white and part-Cherokee descendent of the famous family. In 1879, Boudinot published an article in the *Chicago Tribune* which claimed that all of the Unassigned Lands (and much else of Oklahoma) was, in fact, eligible and ready for immediate homestead settlement. While federal authorities continued to reject that view, other Americans did not; indeed, they prepared to act on it.

One who did so was Charles C. Carpenter. Carpenter was already something of a celebrity along the western frontier, for he had led an 1878 invasion of settlers into South Dakota's Black Hills—land that the government also had insisted was not covered by the Homestead Act. Carpenter and his invaders had gone into them anyway, and unable to dislodge the whites, the government had allowed them to go ahead and make their homes in the Black Hills.

In 1879, Carpenter decided to do the same thing with the Oklahoma District. Merchants in Independence, a small town just across the Kansas border, brought him to their town. Once in Independence, Carpenter gathered many would-be homesteaders, whom he instructed to buy provisions from his local sponsors. Boldly Carpenter announced that he would lead them and their supplies to their "Promised Land."

Again, the federal government emphasized that the "promise" was not for them. This time, it backed its words with force. Cavalry patrols closed the border, and the army informed Carpenter that any repeat of his Black Hills invasion would mean his arrest and imprisonment. Thereupon, Charles C. Carpenter disappeared. But the demands to open the Unassigned Lands diminished not at all.

In fact, the people who continued to call for Oklahoma's homestead settlement soon found a name. They were called Boomers because they incessantly "boomed" Oklahoma's non-Indian settlement. Newspapers across the region and around the nation wrote of them. In doing so, they did more than give them a name; they publicized their demands and added to the attention paid Oklahoma's lands. Their stories also attracted the interest of a man whom the newspapers would come to call the "Prince of Boomers."

That man was David L. Payne. Born in Indiana,

David L. Payne (*seated second from left*) with other Boomer leaders.

Payne was a typical westerner of the day. He had moved to Kansas, had served in the Union army, and had returned to open several businesses—all of which had failed. He also had served briefly in the Kansas legislature before the voters had retired him in 1872. A Kansas congressman then found him a new, but most obscure job—assistant doorkeeper to the United States House of Representatives. It was in that otherwise insignificant capacity that Payne met Elias C. Boudinot, who then was working in Washington for railroads. That also was where Payne learned of Carpenter's failure and where he pored over the newspaper accounts that followed it. Almost immediately, Payne left Washington and returned to Kansas. There he organized what he called Payne's Oklahoma Colony.

The Oklahoma Colony became the most important organization of Boomers. The colony sold thousands of memberships (14,000 in the first five years alone) at $2.50 each. In exchange, it promised members that the colony would find them choice quarter-section farms in Oklahoma. The colony also assembled many of its members in the Boomer camps that soon stretched across the entire southern border of Kansas. Payne and his group published their own newspaper, the *Oklahoma War Chief.* Of course, they also continued to attract considerable publicity from national newspapers.

Invading the Land

That publicity really took off when Payne and his Boomers pursued the strategy that Carpenter had abandoned: direct invasions of the Oklahoma lands. The first came in the spring of 1880, when Payne and 153 other Boomers crossed the Kansas border and made their way to the future site of Oklahoma City. With stakes and ropes, they laid out a city, pitched their tents, and awaited their inevitable expulsion. Soon troops of the Tenth Cavalry stationed at Fort Reno pulled up the stakes, removed the ropes, and escorted the band back to Kansas. In July, however, Payne and twenty of his followers returned, only to be expelled once more. This time, however, the government arrested the princely Mr. Payne.

Taken to Fort Smith, Arkansas, for trial in 1881,

A CREEK'S DESCRIPTION OF PAYNE'S BOOMERS

Not everyone saw the Oklahoma Boomers as honorable American pioneers. Not everyone saw their cause as just. Not all of their publicity was positive. In particular, leaders of Indian Territory's Five Tribes viewed the entire Boomer movement as a deadly threat to the Southeastern Indians' way of life.

For that reason the Indians dispatched a delegation late in 1881 to visit the largest Boomer encampment and report on its activities. The report, written by Creek G. W. Grayson, gives a fascinating (if inescapably biased) contemporary account of David L. Payne's movement and followers.

A real crisis in the affairs of the Indians of our Territory was about to be precipitated upon us, the effect of which would be unmitigated evil to our existing nationalities. Our Chiefs and governors understood well the nature of the spirit which some times moved the people of the bordering states; they fully understood the vague notions of right and justice when Indians formed a party to a controversy, and in the light of this knowledge they could not look upon the movement of D. L. Payne and his coadjutors but with the deepest concern and anxiety. We now speak of Payne's attempted invasion . . . which cast a withering shade over the spirits of many of the truest patriots of our Indian people.

Our first act . . . was that of going and seeing the enemy. To ascertain if possible the number, respectability, and general *morale* of these now famous adventurers. Upon our arrival at Caldwell in southwest Kansas, we drove to their camps and there observed about seventy five hungry, half-clad, back-woods white men, than whom a more worthless horde can hardly be found in all the balance of Christendom. (Report of G. W. Grayson to the National Council of the Muscogee Nation, October 1881, Creek National Papers, Oklahoma Historical Society, Oklahoma City, Oklahoma)

Payne came before Hanging Judge Parker. The otherwise merciless Parker freed Payne by ruling that the only penalty applicable for his actions was a $1,000 fine. The court, he admitted, could not collect even that. Because David L. Payne had no money, owned no property, and could not be jailed for debt, it seemed that there was no applicable penalty for his deeds.

Thus Payne went free. He also went back to Oklahoma, and expelled again, he returned again. A cycle of invasion, expulsion, and reinvasion unfolded. It persisted even after the "Prince's" death in 1884, when William L. Couch took over the colony and continued Payne's tactics. Each invasion added to the attention paid the Boomers and Oklahoma. Each increased the pressure on federal authorities to do something about the Unassigned Lands.

The Commercial Imperative

That pressure came not only from ambitious but impoverished promoters like David L. Payne and his ragged followers but also from more powerful sources. One was railroad companies, then the most powerful businesses in America. The Reconstruction treaties had allowed the companies to build lines across Oklahoma, but they had not assured them of any business. The Indians living in the eastern republics and on the western reservations brought in almost nothing over the rails, and they shipped out even less. The Unassigned Lands shipped nothing at all. One railroad manager captured the business meaning of that when he observed that his company managed to build a railroad through a 300-mile tunnel. Of course, the Indian and Oklahoma territories were not literally a tunnel cut through stone, but economically the area was like a tunnel, built where there was nothing to ship, no business to do, and no money to make.

Fill that land with homesteaders, the railroads knew, and all of that would change. The newcomers would need lumber and supplies—all brought over the shining steel rails. Soon they would produce crops and other goods—all carried out by huffing locomotives. Open Oklahoma to homestead settlement and the railroads finally would open Oklahoma to profitable commerce.

Others too saw profits to be made in Oklahoma's settlement. The supplies that settlers would bring in over rail lines would have to be bought from someone. That someone most likely would be a retail merchant in Independence, Caldwell, Wichita, Arkansas City, or another Kansas town. Wholesalers in Kansas City, Saint Louis, and Chicago also could tap a huge and hungry market. For those retail and wholesale merchants, as for the railroads, Oklahoma's "Promised Land" was the promise of money to be made—money to be made *if* Oklahoma was opened to homestead settlement.

Opening the Territory

The wish to put farmers on free homesteads, the desire to help railroads earn money, the longing to befriend merchants seeking customers—all of those were powerful incentives to open the Unassigned Lands and all of Oklahoma to non-Indian settlement. That was especially true for midwestern congressmen. Their constituents included the very farmers, railroad officers, and merchants who were demanding Oklahoma's homestead settlement. One of the congressmen, Sidney Clarke of Kansas, had introduced a bill to open the lands even before David L. Payne launched his first invasion. Clarke's bill never became law, and he soon left Congress. But other midwestern congressmen took up the cause and regularly presented their own bills, at least one in every subsequent session of Congress. All of them failed, but the pressure mounted by Boomers, railroads, and merchants steadily wore away at the opposition.

Finally, near the end of its 1889 session, Congress added an amendment authored by Indiana's William Springer to the Indian Appropriations Act. Paying the Creeks and Seminoles a small sum to remove any lingering claim of theirs to the Unassigned Lands, the amendment directed President Benjamin Harrison to set a time to allow homesteaders to enter the Oklahoma District. Harrison choose twelve noon, April 22, 1889. Citizens there after that time could claim up to 160 acres for their homesteads. Those unauthorized to be in the district before that moment were ineligible to make claims.

Land Runs and Other Openings

The effect was that tens of thousands lined up on the Oklahoma District's borders, hoping to be among the first to enter the area right at 12:00 P.M. on April 22. When the time came, they spurred their mounts in wild confusion in what they always would remember as "Harrison's Horse Race."

Although novelists, filmmakers, and others later romanticized the hardy '89ers, most probably resembled this family as they awaited the opening of the Oklahoma District.

HOW TO DO IT: STAKING A CLAIM

It seems that nothing that the government does is ever easy on a person. So it was in making a homestead claim.

Well before the land openings, the federal government's surveyors had marked off Oklahoma's lands into a giant checkerboard as explained in chapter eleven. According to legend, the first thing that homesteaders did on finding their claims was to "stake" them—literally to drive wooden stakes into the earth to let late-comers know that the claim already was taken. Many probably did that, but the important thing was not to drive wooden stakes into the land but to find the rocks that already were there. Government surveyors had left them, each carefully inscribed to let the homesteaders know just where they were and what claim was there.

Upon locating the markers and writing down the numbers on them, the homesteaders rushed to the nearest federal land office, such as the one at Guthrie or Kingfisher. After standing in long lines, they would fill out long forms to identify the claim and swear their eligibility to take it under the Homestead Act.

Of course, some—known and detested as Sooners—tried to swear falsely. They were *not* eligible because they had been in the lands *sooner* than the law allowed, often hiding in caves or creek valleys so that they could rush out to make their claims early. Some managed to cheat honest folk of their rightful claims. In most cases, however, settlers were honest. If at least one was not, or if both honestly were confused, lengthy court suits determined who finally would own the land—provided, of course, that the winner managed to live on it for the five years required under the Homestead Act.

The 1889 opening of the Unassigned Lands became for many future Oklahomans the most stirring single event in their state's entire history. At the time its effect was to start a process by which all of the Indian reservations in western Oklahoma soon were opened to homesteaders. In each case the federal government first gave each Indian as much as a 160-acre quarter-section of land. Because the tribes were not very numerous, that left most of their reservations available for homestead settlement.

Some reservations were opened as the Unassigned Lands had been—through land runs that repeated all of the excitement (and all of the confusion) of 1889. Other methods included lotteries in which hopeful claimants entered their names to be drawn from huge barrels. The lucky winners then made their choices as their names were drawn. But by whatever method, the Indian reservations soon passed away. In their place was something altogether different: Oklahoma Territory.

As a political unit, Oklahoma Territory took shape from a congressional statute, the Oklahoma Organic Act of 1890. That law created a simple structure of government for the new territory. It also declared that as each new reservation was opened, it would

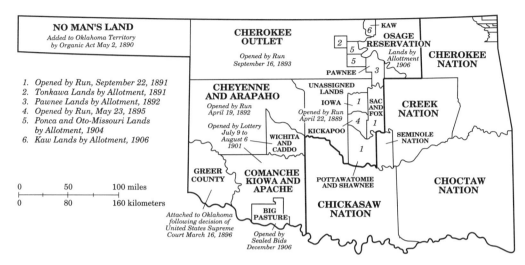

As the map demonstrates, Oklahoma Territory's land openings came in spurts by different means. This map not only dates each opening but indicates the method employed in each case.

become a part of Oklahoma Territory. We will look at its government later.

Life in the Territory

For now we must remember that Oklahoma Territory was not just a government, it was a place where people lived. Their lives will probably sound odd to us, and certainly we will think them difficult. But those people lived in a different time, one with different expectations. Their expectation had been that the territory would be a Promised Land. The lives they made in Oklahoma fulfilled much of what they understood its promise to be.

For many the promise had been a free farm in a new land. The Homestead Act made the original claimants' land free, but no legislative statute could make it productive. That required work and lots of it. Entire families fell to work cutting down trees and removing the stumps with teams hitched to chains or, for especially large stumps, by blasting them loose with dynamite. Never easy, that was all but impossible in the Cross Timbers, which ran up to fifty miles wide all along the eastern edge of the Oklahoma Territory. Everywhere settlers confronted thick native grasses, their roots tightly intertwined and matted. Settlers used heavy iron plows pulled by straining animals to cut through the sod and prepare the soil for planting. Meanwhile they had to build fences to keep roving animals out of their fields, as well as some kind of shelter for themselves, their families, and their livestock.

Many times their first houses came from the sod that they had cut from the prairies. Known as sod houses, or "soddies," these crude structures were built of thick blocks of grass and dirt. Within their walls pioneer families huddled away from the rain and the cold. Often taking shelter with them was a good assortment of snakes and spiders.

This family's 1890 home may be a soddie, but the family already has erected a mechanical windmill and purchased a McCormick reaper for their crops.

The early years generally were the hardest. That was when the land demanded maximum effort. Many openings—like those for the Unassigned Lands in 1889 and the Cherokee Outlet in 1893—came too late in the year for farmers to plant most crops. A series of droughts in the first few years only added to their problems. Until they could grow cash crops, many settlers earned their only money by selling bleached buffalo bones for fertilizer and dried buffalo dung for fuel. Families often lived on wild sand plums that grew along creek banks and a few garden crops. The lowly turnip was the main crop since it was one of the few that could be planted late and still harvested before winter's killing frosts.

The Townspeople's Frontier

Knowing the hard work involved in farming, many early settlers chose to live in towns. The Homestead

TURNIPS!

No one disputed the nutritional value of the turnip, and certainly it was easy to grow. But a steady diet of turnips could get awfully old, even if homemakers tried various ways to cook them. Boiled, baked, mashed, or fried—they still were turnips.

In some form, many homesteaders ate them three times a day. They also fed them to their cows, and they got milk that tasted like turnips. They fed them to their chickens, and they got eggs tasting like turnips. They fed them to their hogs, and

they got pork that seemed to have been cooked with turnips.

More than one child also discovered but a single present under the Christmas tree during the first lean winter. The present? A carefully wrapped turnip.

Act gave them the choice of claiming 160 acres of unbroken land or taking a lot in a townsite. In some cases—Oklahoma City was one—the original townsites were no more than grassy lands that lay immediately around a sleepy railroad depot. In others, ambitious settlers laid out a townsite on the raw prairies. Some never became more than an ambition; ropes and stakes marked off lots, streets, and alleys that never existed, for no one ever came to live there. In others—Stillwater was one of many—the townsite did draw settlers, who first pitched tents, then built simple frame structures, and finally put up homes and businesses of brick, iron, and wood.

If the town grew, it was only partly due to luck. Much more important was work, hard work much like that necessary to make a farm succeed. In one way, the towns may have demanded even harder work. Like farmers building homes and plowing fields, townspeople built their own houses and stores.

Every town needed businesses, and every business needed signs. Guthrie was lacking in neither.

THE GAMES CHILDREN PLAYED

Life for Oklahoma's pioneer children was not just unrelieved toil. Both at their homes and during their school recesses they found ways to play—ways that they often invented themselves and that required little equipment. In the 1930s federal agents interviewed older Oklahomans about the games that they had played as children. Their reports indicate both how different and how similar their lives were from our own.

For example, a popular playground game was Black Man. In that game two leaders took their places in the middle of a field with bases about forty yards apart. The rest of the children stood at one of the bases. The leaders then called, "What are you doing there?" and the other children answered, "Stealing pears." Then the leaders would ask, "What will you do when the black man comes?" To which the other children would reply, "Run right through like we always do." At that point all of the children would attempt to dash past the two leaders to the opposite base while the leaders captured as many as they could. The game would continue until all of the children were caught.

A similar playground game was Red Rover, in which the children would divide into two equal lines, each child tightly grasping the hands of those on each side. In turn, the children on each line would shout, "Red Rover, Red Rover, let ——— cross over." At that, the named child would attempt to break through the opposite line. If unsuccessful, he or she would then join that line. The game continued until all of the children were in the same line.

Perhaps the most common game to play alone was Jacks. The game required a small rubber ball and several small metal pieces, the Jacks. Although the basic object was to bounce the ball and pick up the jacks before catching the ball, there were innumerable forms. In Babies, one could throw and catch the ball with one hand while picking up jacks with the other. Ups were harder: the ball would be tossed up, the jacks collected, and the ball caught, all with the same hand. Downs were harder yet, for the ball would be thrown downward, requiring much more speed and coordination. Fast Downs were hardest of all, for the ball would have to be thrown downward hard. Adding to the options were Onesies, Twosies, Threesies, and so on. In those cases the child would try to pick up exactly the required number of jacks as the ball bounced.

(Oklahoma Writers' Project, Federal Writers' Project Papers, Manuscript Division, Library of Congress, Washington, D.C.)

Schoolchildren's favorite subject: recess.

But each town dweller also had to pitch in to help his or her neighbors, the entire town, to succeed and prosper. They had to provide for themselves things that people living in the country did not need, and things that those living in established eastern towns unthinkingly inherited. They had to plat the town—mark off its streets and alleys and designate its lots. They had to create instant schools, instant churches, instant police and fire service; they had to build everything almost instantly if they hoped to attract late arrivals to their town rather than one of a hundred others.

OKLAHOMA'S ETHNIC TOWNS

As America always has done, Oklahoma attracted some immigrants who hoped to maintain their ethnic identity by gathering in separate communities. For example, some Czechs participated in the land run that opened the Sac and Fox reservation in 1891. Many of them took adjoining homesteads in what became Oklahoma's Lincoln County. Within a few years other Czechs came by way of Nebraska, Kansas, Iowa, and Wisconsin to join them. So dense did the Czech population become that they built a town and named it after their beloved city in Europe: Prague.

Similarly, a group of Poles left their farming community in Marcha, Pulaski County, Arkansas, in 1892. By covered wagon they came as a group to find new homes and to found a new town: Harrah.

Perhaps the territory's most-famous ethnic community lay twelve miles northeast of Guthrie. E. P. McCabe, a Boomer from Kansas, founded it and named it for a personal hero, John Mercer Langston, a Virginia congressman. Like Representative Langston, E. P. McCabe was black, and his town briefly was the largest all-black city in Oklahoma and in America.

Mostly a town's survival required that it win a connection to a railroad so that its residents could bring in supplies like lumber, hardware, and groceries. More importantly, railroads enabled a town's merchants to draw the business of farmers in the countryside who needed their own supplies and needed even more to ship their products out.

The towns that failed to do what was necessary generally failed themselves. Without schools, churches, and railroads they became ghost towns, haunted by unmet promises. Their residents left for other places where the citizens had worked harder or perhaps just had been luckier. Thus Frisco disappeared, but Oklahoma City filled, then overflowed its grassy lands. Cross withered while Stillwater bloomed.

Just when some townspeople began to move into

nice new houses and open fine new stores, the territory's farmers began to produce and sell good crops of wheat and corn. Then, for both kinds of homesteaders, western Oklahoma became not a Promised Land but a home. When that happened, the territory became much like the rest of America. Town folks owned houses and business properties. Farmers owned homesteaded land.

THE DALTONS: GOOD GUYS AND BAD

Movie heroes (like John Wayne's Marshal Rooster Cogburn) and movie villains (like Lucky Ned Pepper) often are based on historical figures, but history is usually more complex than Hollywood's good-guy-versus-bad-guy formula. Real history is filled with real people like the Dalton brothers.

One Dalton—Frank—was one of Judge Parker's lawmen. Trying to arrest some outlaws, he was murdered and buried as a hero. Three of his brothers—Grat, Bob, and Emmett—became law officers, too. Grat started working for Judge Parker, Bob built a police force for the Osage Nation, and Emmett became one of his deputies.

They did not stay long on the right side of the law, however. Grat lost his job after he shot an apple off a boy's head in Tulsa. Bob and Emmett lost theirs for accepting bribes from whiskey peddlers. The three then became horse thieves, and they soon added cattle rustling to their resumés. In time they graduated to becoming professional bank robbers. They did that until October 1892, when they daringly attempted to rob two banks simultaneously in Coffeyville, Kansas. Enraged townspeople killed Bob and Grat in the street, and they captured Emmett.

Bob and Grat Dalton were buried beside their brother, the heroic United States Deputy Marshal Frank Dalton. Emmett? He served his time and went to Hollywood to make movies about good guys and bad guys.

The less fortunate of the Daltons after incurring the wrath of Coffeyville's citizenry.

On the east, however, such promises hit squarely against the walls of tribal governments and communal land ownership. If eastern Oklahoma ever were to meet what many Americans took as its promise, those walls would have to be leveled. When they were, the promise that some saw as fulfilled became the process that others experienced as betrayal.

Oklahomans—particularly in the state's western half—celebrate no period of their state's history more thoroughly than the era of settlement. Literally dozens of local museums proudly display the materials that homesteaders brought with them to the "Promised Land," along with those that illustrate the lives they built there. If your home is in the old Oklahoma Territory, the odds are good that there is at least one such museum—and perhaps there are several—near you. Perhaps the rarest is in the little community of Aline, where the Oklahoma Historical Society lovingly maintains an authentic soddie, the last surviving example of the primitive structures that first sheltered thousands of homesteaders.

Several towns operate museums that document early life in their surrounding regions. Lawton, for example, has the Museum of the Great Plains; Altus, the Museum of the Western Prairie; and Alva, Blackwell, Woodward, and Ponca City all have museums devoted to life in the so-called Cherokee Strip.

Of particular interest is the 1,400-acre Guthrie Historical District. Oklahoma Territory's capital, Guthrie was the state's capital as well until 1910, when Oklahoma City became the seat of government. Thereafter Guthrie went into a long decline that recently has been marvelously reversed by the careful restoration of the entire fourteen-block original downtown. Something of a Williamsburg on the prairie, the site and its beautiful Victorian buildings are now listed on the National Register of Historic Places. Guthrie's downtown is the largest urban area in the nation to be so honored. Among other sites, visitors will enjoy the Blue Belle Saloon, the Pollard Theater, the Victor Building, and the Harrison House. Be sure to see too the State Capital Publishing Company Museum and the Oklahoma Territorial Museum.

Oklahoma City, the winner of the capital war with Guthrie, maintains the Museum of the Unassigned Lands, devoted to the area of the original Eighty-niners' conquest. A wonderful facility—particularly for school groups but also for all ages—is the 1889er Harn Museum and William Fremont Harn Gardens. Situated on ten acres just north of the state capitol, the site includes the restored and refurnished home of the unusually successful early settler along with a working barn, orchard, and restored one-room school.

Suggestions for Further Reading

Reference

Alley, John. *City Beginnings in Oklahoma Territory.* Norman: University of Oklahoma Press, 1939.

Eisele, Fannie L. "We Came to Live in Oklahoma Territory." *Chronicles of Oklahoma* 38(1960): 55–65.

Giezentanner, Veda. "In Dugouts and Sod Houses." *Chronicles of Oklahoma* 39(1961): 140–49.

Harper, Roscoe E. "Homesteading in Northwestern Oklahoma Territory." *Chronicles of Oklahoma* 16(1938): 326–36.

Hastings, James K. "Log Cabin Days in Oklahoma." *Chronicles of Oklahoma* 28(1950): 143–53.

Lemon, G. E. "Reminiscences of Pioneer Days in the Cherokee Strip." *Chronicles of Oklahoma* 22(1944–45): 435–57.

Rister, Carl Coke. *Land Hunger: David L. Payne and the Oklahoma Boomers.* Norman: University of Oklahoma Press, 1942.

Stewart, Roy P. *Born Grown: An Oklahoma History.* Oklahoma City: Fidelity Bank, 1974.

Swartz, Orvoe. "A Pioneer's Sod House Memories." *Chronicles of Oklahoma* 41(1963–64): 408–24.

Related Reading

Bartel, Irene Brown. *No Drums or Thunder.* San Antonio: Naylor Company, 1970.

Cunningham, Robert E. *Stillwater: Where Oklahoma Began.* Stillwater: Arts and Humanities Council of Stillwater, 1969.

Debo, Angie. *Prairie City: The Story of an American Community.* 1944. Reprint. Tulsa: Council Oaks, 1992.

Marquis James. *The Cherokee Strip.* 1945. Reprint. Norman: University of Oklahoma Press, 1993.

Chapter 17: The End of Indian Territory

Through much of the 1800s there was nothing at all unique about Oklahoma's Indian Territory. In fact, it was just one of many areas that the federal government had set apart as Indian lands. Even after the Civil War the five Indian estates in eastern Oklahoma were only a small portion of the lands that the government still maintained for Indians. Some of those were the reservations in western Oklahoma, and many more reservations dotted the entire American West.

By the end of the 1800s, however, most of those other reservations had disappeared. A federal law— the Dawes Act of 1887—directed the division in *severalty* of the reservations. That meant that large bodies of land that had been set aside for entire tribes and that had been owned collectively by the tribes were divided into individual parcels of up to 160 acres each. An individual Indian then received one of the pieces as his or her personal *allotment*. Because the tribes had small populations and big reservations, most of the land subsequently became available to homesteaders under the 1862 Homestead Act. As we have seen, exactly that process occurred in western Oklahoma.

The Five Civilized Tribes

Eastern Oklahoma was different and with each passing year it became more different still. The Five Tribes always had enjoyed a special relationship with the federal government. Most Americans still called them the Five *Civilized* Tribes, unfortunately implying that no other Indians were civilized. That, of course, was not true, but it was true that the civilizations of these particular Indian tribes were quite like that of the whites of that time and place. One sign was that they had officially recognized governments modeled on the United States federal government and American state governments. Their written constitutions contained some provisions almost exactly like sections of white constitutions, to create tribal executives, legislators, and judges. Another expression of their special status was that the Dawes Act specifically exempted Oklahoma's Five Tribes from the forced breakup suffered by other Indians' tribal estates. So while other Indian lands passed to whites annually, Oklahoma's five Indian republics remained a special Indian Territory—more special every year.

Of course, that did not mean that they were immune from change. As we have seen, their economies grew steadily more commercial and their populations both much larger and much less Indian. With each passing year the newcomers living on the tribes' lands grew more and more at odds with the tribal governments that gave them few services and even fewer rights. With each passing year white and black settlers grew more frustrated and angry with Indian ownership of land and resources. To those people, the Indian republics were not just special; they were bizarre, deviant, unsatisfactory, and unacceptable.

As the federal government steadily went about dissolving other Indian reservations, it began to reassess the Five Tribes' special status. If Washington's Indian agents and military commanders were eliminating the authority of Sioux and Comanche chiefs, why did federal power bow before Creek and Cherokee rulers? If the Omahas' and the Chippewas' lands were divided up and parceled out, why not the Choctaws' and the Chickasaws'? The pressures that mounted from Indian Territory's new economic circumstances and new population combined with those questions to create a steady drive to end the Five Tribes' special relationships with Washington.

Washington's New Authority

Preliminary steps toward that end had come even before the Dawes Act. The Reconstruction treaties had required that the tribes create an intertribal council as a step toward unifying the Indian republics into a single territory and government. Correctly sensing that any such change would jeopardize their special status, the Indians at first simply ignored that provision. Only when Congress began to take up bills to destroy their separate governments outright did they take any action at all. Between 1870 and 1876 delegations from each tribe met annually at Okmulgee.

Washington's officials were hardly pleased with those meetings. About all that came out of them was a steady stream of resolutions protesting any change at all in Indian Territory. The meetings' one lasting contribution was important but entirely inadvertent. Resentful that one government should be even considered in place of their beloved five republics, the Indians nonetheless debated what such a territory would be called. Their answer came when Allan Wright, a Choctaw delegate, proposed a name that combined his language's words for "red" and "people." "Oklahoma" was the new word. But the Indians wanted none of it.

Lacking cooperation from the territory's tribes, the federal government gradually but steadily moved to end their special status, using Washington's authority alone. If the Indians refused to unify their governments, Washington still could unite its dealings with the tribes by creating one central Indian agency in place of the five separate ones. This was done in 1874 when the federal government opened the Union Agency at Muskogee. Thereafter the government's business with each of the Five Tribes flowed through that one office and its agents.

Another sign that the Indian republics were losing their special status was Washington's extension of its judicial authority into the territory. Indian courts and Indian police had been among the distinctive institutions of these nations. Those law-enforcement bodies, however, had no authority over the nontribal citizens who might break tribal laws and who also were the growing majority of the territory's population. Moreover, the federal government had no way of prosecuting Indian citizens for violating the laws of the United States except to haul them to Fort Smith, Arkansas, for trial at the nearest federal district court.

In addition to problems of criminal law, there were also severe problems in commercial litigation. As we have seen, every year business in Indian Territory grew bigger and more complex. Every year the inevitable business disputes grew more common and more difficult. Except for the very few such questions that involved no one but tribal citizens, none of the cases could be presented even in the tribal courts, and the territory had no others.

For those reasons Congress in 1889 established the first United States Federal District Court in Indian Territory and located it at Muskogee. Other such courts soon followed at Ardmore and McAlester. Each brought convenient legal authority to nontribal citizens. Each also brought immediate federal jurisdiction to the Indians themselves. With federal judges, federal marshals, and federal deputies, the Indian republics were becoming more like other Indian lands and less like independent nations that had survived as special cases in federal-Indian relations.

Perhaps the most significant change in Washington's dealings with the tribes came in 1871. Since the first Europeans had reached North America, their governments had dealt with Indian tribes through *treaties*, legal devices that bound two presumably sovereign governments to mutual decisions. However often they were violated, treaties did imply that the Indians' governments were equal to the whites' and that any subsequent changes would require the Indians' consent. Moreover, the United States Constitution gives treaties a special status. Under Article 6, treaties are superior to both state and federal laws.

After 1871, however, the federal government refused to negotiate treaties with Indian tribes. Instead, the federal government and the tribes would negotiate *agreements*. The difference was much more than the substitution of one word for another because the agreements neither presumed the equality of the Indians' governments nor implied that they could be altered only with the tribes' consent. Lacking the constitutional status of treaties, agreements could be altered by the mere passage of a federal law, with or without the Indians' assent. It was true that Washington thereafter tried to get the Indians' consent to changes, but everyone knew that, if need be, the white government would have its way with or without Indian approval.

By the late 1800s many were demanding the most sweeping change of all. To divide the tribes' lands and other resources into individual allotments (as was being done elsewhere under the Dawes Act) would end Indian Territory's special economic status. Abolishing the five tribal governments would end the Indians' special place completely.

Obviously, most of those demands came from the people who had moved into Indian Territory from the surrounding states. Tribal land ownership and tribal government meant nothing to them—nothing, that is, except barriers to what they took to be their rights as American citizens. Every year their numbers grew. Every year their frustrations increased. Every year their demands did, too.

Outside the territory, there were those who agreed. Railroad men and merchants believed that allotment would open Indian Territory to new enterprise, new investments, and new industries—as well as create new opportunities for themselves. Many who considered themselves to be friends of the Indians also agreed. They argued that the time had come for the people of the Five Tribes to put aside their traditions, take up private property, and exchange their tribal citizenship for American citizenship. According to their view, the Five Tribes thereby would complete the process of becoming truly civilized.

Responding to such arguments, congressional sessions from 1888 onward considered bills to extend the Dawes Act to Indian Territory. Finally, in 1893, Congress did pass a law that created a special commission to negotiate with the Five Tribes. Hoping to earn the Indians' consent to an "agreement" to divide their lands and destroy their governments, the commission traveled to Indian Territory the next year. Henry L. Dawes, the author of the famous Dawes Act, headed the group, which therefore was known as the Dawes Commission. It even retained that name after Senator Dawes left the commission in favor of Tams Bixby.

Over the next three years the federal commis-

sioners met with tribal leaders for rounds of talks
that amounted to little more than threats and protests. Only one agreement was ever reached, the so-
called Atoka Agreement with the Choctaws and the
Chickasaws. Even that led nowhere. In a required
referendum the Chickasaw voters solidly rejected
what their tribal leaders had negotiated.

At that point Washington demonstrated its determination to proceed even without the Five Tribes'
consent. In 1895, Congress ordered that the tribes'
lands be surveyed, and in the next year it directed
the preparation of citizenship rolls. These were the
necessary first steps toward the certain final end:
the breakup of the nations into individual allotments. In 1898 came the most determined step of all
when Congress approved the Curtis Act. Written by
Charles Curtis, a Kansas representative (and a
mixed-blood Kaw Indian), the law established an extremely harsh process whereby the tribes' lands
would be divided and their governments abolished
without their consent. It left them but one escape:
its terms would not be enforced if the tribes agreed
to other methods to distribute their property and
end their governments.

The Allotment Process

The Curtis Act had its intended effect. Determined
to influence what they could not prevent, the tribes
hurried to negotiate a set of agreements with the
federal government. The details varied from tribe
to tribe, but all provided essentially the same things:
the allotment of the national estates and the abolition of the tribal governments. Federal officials

To guide census takers, federal officials provided model forms such as this to be used in recording the Creek Nation's freedmen.

would enroll all tribal members to complete detailed lists of the citizens of each tribe. Other agents
would survey and appraise the entire land surface
of each nation. Some land (for example, cemeteries)
would be maintained as small pieces of tribal property. Other real estate (like townsites and land known
to have coal and asphalt deposits) would be sold at
auction. The great bulk of the land—an area approximately the size of the state of Indiana—would be divided among the tribal citizens. At that point the
tribal governments would close, and Oklahoma's five
Indian republics would pass into history.

The actual division was a very complicated matter.
In most of the tribes an individual's share depended
on just what kind of citizen he or she was and just
how good the land involved was. Was the person a
full-blood Indian, a mixed-blood, an intermarried
white, or a freed black man holding tribal citizenship? Was the land covered with rocks and brush, or
was it rich bottomland? Such distinctions affected
the size of the final allotment. Was the land the actual site of the person's home? If so, it was a homestead, usually equal to forty acres of average land.
Each individual also received additional land—known

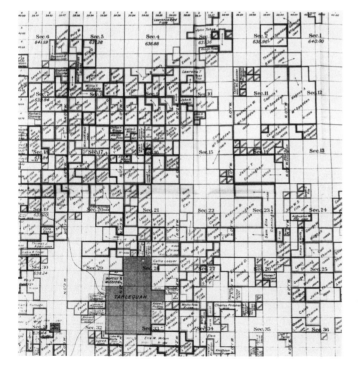

Once allotment was complete,
land officials recorded the
results. In this case, the
townsite of Tahlequah was
reserved, its lots sold at
auction. The immediate
surrounding area, however,
went to individual Cherokee
citizens, their allotments
carefully recorded.

as his or her "surplus"—until all of the tribe's lands had been divided among all of the tribe's citizens.

Another complication was that the agreements provided for various restrictions on these allotments. These were designed to protect the individuals from losing them outright. The restrictions generally governed the sale of the allotments for a period of time. Again, the exact restrictions varied according to the agreement involved, the individual's bloodline, and the form of his or her allotment. Generally, they were tightest on the land that full-bloods used for their homes and farms, their homesteads.

Towering above all those intricate complexities was one simple truth: Oklahoma's Five Tribes were losing the sovereignty that had been promised to them for as long as the grass grew and the waters ran. All of the arguments about the newcomers' "rights," business "opportunity," and economic "progress" meant nothing to those who cherished those old promises. In most cases these were full-blood Indians who had refused to learn the whites' tongue and walk the white road. Living in the hills and valleys far from the new towns and cities, they had been content with a few acres of corn and nearby woods where they could forage their animals, animals as free and as independent as their owners.

Native Resistance

Many who felt that way met the changes by ignoring them. They hid from government census takers, refusing to see their names added to the whites' rolls. They failed to go to the land offices to designate their allotments. When federal officials went ahead, chose allotments for them, and mailed them forms telling them what they owned, they returned the letters unopened.

More organized resistance came from the Four Mothers Society. Active in every tribe except the Seminole, it claimed 24,000 members who refused to let go of the old promises. Among the Creeks, such resistance took violent expression. In 1901 an elderly full-blood named Chitto Harjo organized a shadow government with its own council and its own laws, which forbade Creeks to accept their allotments, rent land to non-Creeks, or employ white

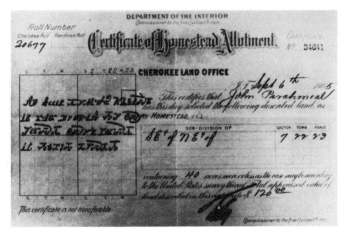

Many Indian full-bloods wanted no part of the forced allotments that both divided their lands and destroyed the material basis of their traditional cultures. In this case a Cherokee full-blood has returned his allotment document with a note inscribed in his native language through Sequoyah's famous alphabet: "I don't want this paper or the land. I return the paper and don't want any more."

labor. On occasion Harjo's government enforced those laws by arresting and whipping those who did such things. Because Chitto Harjo's name could be literally translated into English as "Crazy Snake," white folks called the whole episode the Crazy Snake Rebellion. They meant no humor by the name, for they called for federal force to crush the pitiable insurrection. Federal authorities rounded up ninety-four Creeks, most of them elderly and nearly all of them full-bloods, and sent them to prison.

If the Crazy Snake Rebellion represented one way that Indian Territory confronted change, a much more important way came in the rise of an entire new industry, an industry that swiftly became the largest and most profitable in the territory. Those who observed it, those who were its victims, even those who practiced it, all called it by a single name: *grafting*. Those who did it proudly called themselves *grafters*. Theirs was the business of taking away, by hook or by crook, the Indians' allotments.

Chitto Harjo, or Crazy Snake.

The Business of Grafting

Ironically, grafting was made possible by the very restrictions that had been intended to protect the Indians and their property. What property could be sold? When? By whom? How? The answers to all those questions lay somewhere in the tribe, the degree of Indian blood, and the form of the allotment. Only the most sophisticated could make their way through that maze. Only rarely could Indians do it alone.

It was certain, however, that someone would get through the maze of restrictions. The land was just too valuable to expect otherwise. Newcomers wanted it, and they were willing to pay money to get it. Many Indians needed their money. No longer able to use just any land they wanted to produce everything they needed, they had to have cash to buy what the whites sold.

All of those things made grafting possible. To say that is not to excuse it, for its methods were selfish at best and evil at worst. It does, however, help us understand why some people apparently were willing to set aside the most basic principles of fair dealing where Indian allotments were concerned.

Grafters were involved right from the beginning of the allotment process. Once the federal government had enrolled the Indians on their tribal rolls and surveyed their national lands, there had to be some way for individuals to designate and take legal title to their allotments. Often it was a grafter who found the Indian, took him or her to the land office, and filled out the government's forms. Many times the grafter even indicated what land the Indian would take as his or her individual allotment, both as homestead and as surplus.

Choctaw and Chickasaw citizens registering for their land allotments.

Grafters rarely did such things from a desire to help the unfortunate. Often they designated land for allotment because they wanted it themselves. If the restrictions would not allow them to purchase it, they still could get it in several other ways. Once they had it, they could use it themselves or, more likely, rent it to some of the tens of thousands of newcomers who were streaming into the collapsing Indian republics.

One way the grafters could get the land was through leases. Restricted land could be not be sold, but it could be leased, and grafters were anxious to lease the Indians' allotments. Often the leases were signed as soon as the individuals designated their allotments. The leases might run for as long as ninety-nine years, and for them the grafters might pay no more than ten or fifteen dollars. Of course, grafters could get several leases, even hundreds, in that way. That was how one group in the Creek Nation managed to gain control over more than 80,000 acres of allotted lands. That particular organization was hardly the only one, however. Pleasant Porter, the chief of the Creeks, estimated in 1902 that grafters already controlled over 1 million acres of Creek allotments through such leases.

A specialized form of grafting involved the land given Indian children. As tribal citizens Indian children shared in the division just as the adults did, all receiving their own allotments. For grafters these allotments became something like a natural resource to be mined and exploited. The allotments of full-blood and orphaned children were especially vulnerable, for the law gave control over them to guardians, who often were grafters. Many were so specialized in this particular line of the trade as to be professional guardians, controlling hundreds of children's allotments. These they leased at a handsome profit for themselves while providing little or nothing to the children.

Equally lucrative was the land given elderly Indians. Although it generally could not be sold because of the restrictions, the land could be willed to another who would gain full title at the time of the Indian's death. Grafters knew this, and for that reason they often sought out the very elderly. For a little money the Indians would sign wills that became known as death claims. That is, the grafter would own the land outright as soon as the Indian died. One federal official estimated in 1906 that there were at least 2,300 such death claims in force by 1906.

Even restricted allotments could be sold if an individual asked Congress to pass special legislation allowing him or her to sell the land. Several thousand did so, and Congress obligingly and routinely lifted the individual restrictions. No doubt many were astute financially and profited thereby. Many others, however, probably never knew what was happening. For a few dollars grafters could get Indians to sign papers—often with an X witnessed by the grafters. The papers meant nothing to the Indians, but meant everything to the grafters, for they were petitions asking Congress to end restrictions on the sale of the individuals' land. The grafters would then be able to buy the land directly—sometimes for no more than twenty dollars.

In certain circumstances grafters did not need to be that devious. Under the Creek agreement all of the restrictions on surplus lands (except those allotted to full-bloods) expired at 12:01 A.M. on August 8, 1907. During the previous day and evening grafters brought ignorant mixed-bloods and freed citizens into Muskogee. Many traveled on special trains that the grafters had chartered for the purpose. Buying began promptly at one minute past midnight. One territorial newspaper estimated that half of the 437,790 acres involved were sold in the very first hour—most of it for absurd prices.

No one has been able to calculate how many Indians lost how much land by such means. But this much is certain: the prime beneficiaries of the allotment process were not the people of the Five Tribes; they were the grafters who took advantage of those people. It is hardly the most inspiring story in Oklahoma's history.

Chitto Harjo's Long Road

It was, however, in that way that Indian Territory finally passed out of existence. One who saw it happen was Chitto Harjo, or Crazy Snake. In 1906 he carried a copy of the treaty that Washington had made with his Creek ancestors to the U.S. Capitol. He wanted to ask the president himself, Theodore Roosevelt, if that treaty's promises of a permanent Creek nation in the unique Indian Territory were no more. Chitto Harjo met President Roosevelt, who firmly shook his hand, turned, and quickly walked away.

Chitto Harjo returned not to the Creek nation that had been promised his people but to a territory of growing cities, towns, and farms. He had traveled a hard and strange road, but one no harder or stranger than the one that Indian Territory had taken to become like the rest of America.

See History for Yourself

In marked, if not surprising, contrast to western Oklahoma, the final settlement of the former Indian Territory is less likely to be celebrated. In fact,

VOICES OF INDIAN TERRITORY

The complicated dispersal of the Five Tribes' estates generated wealth for some, poverty for others, and confusion for most. Attempting to penetrate the veil of perplexity, the United States Senate formed the Select Committee to Investigate Affairs in the Indian Territory in 1906. In public hearings in several cities, the senators heard from politicians, bureaucrats, businessmen, newspapermen—and grafters. They also heard from the simple citizens whose lives were most affected by the process.

At the conclusion of the committee's work, the senators filed an official report and went on about their business. That report, two massive volumes of verbatim testimony, can now be found only in a few libraries. The reader who opens their brittle pages can hear even now the cries of the wounded whose pitiable confusion grew out of a sense of the greatest betrayal.

Eufaula Harjo, Creek:

We are pushed out of all that we had. The full-blood Indian people are pushed out today, and they have left their homes and taken what they have, and everything, and are camped out in the woods today. . . . It is going to be cold weather after a while, and there is the women and the little children and the old people, and we don't know what to do with them or where to get a house to put them in. All the property such as cattle and hogs and horses—it is all gone, we have not got anything left. We used to have plenty and more than we wanted and now we haven't got anything.

Redbird Smith, Cherokee (who showed the senators a copy of his tribe's original removal treaty along with the eagle feather that had been given his great-grandfather on its negotiation) said:

I say that I will never change; before our God, I won't. It extends to heaven, and the great treaty that has been made with the Government of the United States. Our treaty wherever it extends is respected by the Creator, God. . . . I can't stand and live and breathe if I take this allotment. Under the allotment rules I would see all around me . . . people who are ready to grab from us my living and my home. If I would accept such a plan I would be going into starvation. To take and put the Indians on the land in severalty would be just the same as burying them, for they could not live.

Willis Toby, Choctaw:

They took all our children from their father and mother and made a guardian for them in the United States court, and we don't want it that way. I am still faithful to the Great Father of the United States, who made this treaty with the Indians, and I am faithful to that treaty, and the Almighty God that rules the world.

Osway Porter, Chickasaw:

I love this country as I love my mother, for it is my mother. I love it as I love my own father. I love its hills and mountains, and its valleys and trees and rivers and everything else that is in this country. I am here before you my father, humbly asking for your help, and humbly asking you to protect me and my people. We are poor and ignorant, but we know that we love our country, and have confidence in our father's protection. I am faithful and my people are faithful, and we trust that our original rights will be restored.

And finally, Chitto Harjo himself:

In the agreement made between me and my government and the Government of the United States there was a misunderstanding, and . . . I think I have the privilege of appealing to the other tribes and notifying them. . . . I do not mean the other four civilized tribes, but I call upon the Spanish Government and the British Government and the French Government—I call on four of the civilized Governments across the mother of waters to come and see that this is right. That is all I have to say.

(*Report of the Select Committee to Investigate Matters Connected with Affairs in the Indian Territory* [*Senate Reports*, 59th Cong. 2d sess., no. 5013.])

the version described here often is deliberately and conveniently forgotten. Thus it is especially difficult to direct students to sites that display the visible record of this story. There are, however, some lingering signs.

One is almost certainly in the legal records of land ownership. If anyone in your family owns land in what once was one of the five Indian republics, its legal history is available in the abstract of that land's title. Ask if you can see it. Its first page will contain the record of that land when it (and the rest of that Indian nation) was owned communally by the tribe. The second page will record that particular piece of land's division into a severalty allotment. It will record the name of the tribal citizen who received it when the tribal domains were broken up and parceled out. In nearly every case, several decades will separate the dates of those first two pages. Quickly, however, more pages will accumulate, one for each time the land changed owners. In the great majority of cases, a very early page will show it passing out of the original allottee's hands. Behind the legal formulas drily maintained is the record of what probably was the "grafting" of valuable property.

Another way to see that process and its effects is to notice how very little land still remains in tribal hands in eastern Oklahoma. In Tulsa, for example, the Perryman family of Creeks once operated a ranch that covered several thousand acres, extending from roughly present Tenth Street as far south as modern Jenks. The allotment of the Creek Nation's lands broke the Perryman ranch into many different plots, each assigned to an individual owner. Nearly all of those individuals lost it, and lost it very quickly. Today one of the few remaining pieces of tribal property in the area is a small plot—about the size of a city lot—on South Utica Avenue at about Thirty-second Street. Surrounded by fine homes, the site often is overgrown with weeds. Should you pass it, though, stop your car and walk through the weeds. The tombstones, many tumbling from decay or vandalism, tell you that this is the Perryman family cemetery. One of the few sites exempted from the allotment process, it is all that remains of the once great Perryman ranch.

Suggestions for Further Reading

Reference

Debo, Angie. *And Still the Waters Run: The Betrayal of the Five Civilized Tribes.* Princeton: Princeton University Press, 1940, 1990.

————. *Tulsa: From Creek Town to Oil Capital.* Norman: University of Oklahoma Press, 1943.

Otis, D. S. *The Dawes Act and the Allotment of Indian Land.* Norman: University of Oklahoma Press, 1973.

Savage, William W., Jr. *The Cherokee Strip Live Stock Association: Federal Regulation and the Cattleman's Last Frontier.* 1970. Norman: University of Oklahoma Press, 1990.

Related Reading

Fall, Thomas. *The Ordeal of Running Standing.* 1970. Norman: University of Oklahoma Press, 1993.

Strickland, Rennard. *The Indians in Oklahoma.* Norman: University of Oklahoma Press, 1980.

Chapter 18: The Twin Territories

All through this book, we have used the term "Oklahoma" as it is currently understood. It is, we all know, the name of a state that is shaped somewhat like a ragged-edged meat cleaver. It covers approximately 70,000 square miles and lies between Texas on the south and west and Kansas on the north. Arkansas extends along its eastern border. Partly a geographical term, "Oklahoma" is even more a political term. It is the name officially given a *state,* which is, after all, a political concept. Before there was any state of Oklahoma, there were two territories—the Oklahoma and Indian territories—which commonly were called the Twin Territories. In some respects their eventual combination into one state was a product of accident. But in another sense, it was no accident at all. The political reality, Oklahoma, grew from circumstances that were both predictable and political themselves.

However closely related, the Twin Territories were hardly identical. Roughly the western half of the modern state was known as Oklahoma Territory. On the east lay the estates of the Five Tribes. Although commonly referred to as Indian Territory, that particular term was much less political than it was geographical in meaning. After all, there was no single, unified government over those lands. Instead they were separated into five independent and quite distinct Indian republics.

As we have noted, political participation in each of those republics was tightly limited to the citizens of the separate tribe. Except for a handful of newcomers who had married into those tribes and thereby had acquired the status of tribal citizens, neither the whites nor the blacks who were flooding into the territory enjoyed any of the benefits of Indian citizenship.

For tribal citizens, however, those governments were quite important. Both the full-bloods and their mixed-blood cousins were proud of their Indian heritage, and intermarried citizens also recognized the significance of tribal traditions. Not the least element of that heritage and those traditions was the set of tribal governments that had begun right after the removals. With a written constitution (except in the tiny Seminole Nation), a bicameral legislature, elected executives, functioning courts, and formal political parties, each of the five republics continued to maintain its separate and independent government right until the eve of Oklahoma's statehood.

The Choctaw council (which served as what whites would have called the senate), photographed at its last official meeting.

Although the forms of these tribal governments (their constitutions, separate branches, political parties, and the like) looked much like those common in most of the United States, the reality behind them was unique to Indian Territory. For example, although each tribe had at least two political parties, in no tribe were these at all related to the Democratic and Republican parties that existed throughout the rest of the nation. Instead the tribal parties continued to reflect distinctly Indian differences, many of which went back to preremoval divisions. Thus the Creek Nation's political parties in the late 1800s still reflected the ancient split between Upper and Lower Creeks. Similarly, the Cherokee parties continued the rivalries between the Ridge and Ross factions that first had arisen back in Georgia.

Beneath their white forms, other political institutions were just as distinctly Indian. The elaborate constitutional provisions for separate executive, judicial, and legislative branches were one thing on paper but quite another in practice. In most cases, the reality was that a tiny natural aristocracy of educated, wealthy, and interrelated families controlled most areas of influence. Typically they did so for generation after generation. Rather than an exercise in mass democracy, tribal elections usually drew few voters. Those who did vote generally did so only to choose among the aristocrats who offered to govern them.

The powers of those office holders were no less special to Indian Territory. For example, because tribal courts had no jurisdiction over non-Indian citizens, the great bulk of the population lived beyond their reach and influence. Although tribal legislatures could pass bills, and tribal executives could sign them into law, such acts had little meaning for the 70 to 90 percent of the population that were not tribal citizens.

In practice, therefore, the Indian governments exercised only the most limited powers. Although they continued to maintain fine schools for their own children and effective police forces for their own citizens, their authority over most questions and over most of their residents was minimal. For example, the federal constitution's "commerce clause" gave ultimate power over the Choctaw Nation's coal industry to the Congress in Washington rather than to the Choctaw legislature in Tuskahoma. Similarly, the Bureau of Indian Affairs agents at Muskogee and the Justice Department's judges, marshals, and deputies there and elsewhere had far greater impact on most residents than did the chiefs, legislators, and lighthorsemen working out of Tahlequah.

In practice, therefore, the Indians' tribal governments were hardly at all like those of American states or territories. As time passed, most of their work was given over to disbursing the annuities that Washington provided, and attempting (with limited success) to collect the licenses, royalties, and other fees that they tried to impose on "intruders" and the new industries. Otherwise, their main activity was to protest any diminution of their authority over their own people or any change at all in their communal ownership of tribal land and resources.

All of this did not mean that the majority of white and black newcomers had no interest in Indian Territory's politics. As far as the tribal governments were concerned, the single interest of most of the newcomers was their abolition. Otherwise, their political energies took other forms.

One immediate focus was on the governments of their municipalities. As the various tribal "agreements" went into practice, the new residents were authorized to incorporate towns and cities, complete with governments that were largely independent of the fading authority of the tribes. In places like Vinita, Muskogee, McAlester, and Ardmore—each a thriving and incorporated city—the newcomers divided into Republicans and Democrats and conducted spirited campaigns to win mayorships and seats on city councils.

Oklahoma's several all-black towns produced all-black town governments such as this one for Boley.

The new residents also organized politically beyond the municipal level. Utterly ignoring the party divisions of the Indian republics, they did as Americans had done since the Civil War—they politicked as Republicans and Democrats. At least once every four years Indian Territory's towns would send aspiring politicians to raucous party conventions. There they passed solemn party platforms, praised the contributions of their own political party to the nation, and damned the misdeeds of their rivals. Only one fact distinguished these assemblies from those being held all over the United States and its territories. In Indian Territory—and only in Indian Territory—the fired-up partisans adjourned after the convention with their work entirely complete. Unlike Republicans and Democrats in Kansas, Arkansas, or even Oklahoma Territory, those in Indian Territory had no immediate objects for their striving. They could not compete for state offices. Neither were there territorial offices to seek. They could not even vote in national elections for the president and Congress.

Why then did they even bother? One answer is that they believed that their current political position was only temporary. After the inevitable abolition of the tribal governments, there would be territorial, state, even national offices to seek, and they wanted to be ready. Something else was involved, too. That was the force of habit, habit deeply ingrained in Americans of their generation.

Theirs was an age of intense political interest, most of it directed toward the two great national political parties. Everywhere—even in Indian Territory—those Americans viewed politics with something of the enthusiasm that members of a later generation would reserve for collegiate or professional sports. In a sense, they were fans, fans not of the Sooners or the Cowboys but of the Republicans or the Democrats. Thus the chief purpose of much of their busy activity was something close to modern cheerleading.

More than anything else, the Civil War and its remembered aftermath explained the intensity of their devotion. Most of those who had lived in the North saw the Republican party as the party that had saved their precious union. Those of southern stock saw it as the despoiler of their independence during the war and, worse, as the perpetrator of the Reconstruction that followed it. For as long as those memories persisted, Americans would continue to vote as they had shot. Those who had worn the Union blue, and their children, passionately supported what they still knew as the GOP, the Grand

Old Party, the Republican party. Those who had
worn Confederate gray and their offspring with
equal intensity allied themselves with the Democratic party. Thus it was that no convention of Indian Territory's Republicans was complete without
resolutions solemnly blessing their party for the
preservation of the union and thanking their Creator for the leadership of Abraham Lincoln. Neither
could any Democratic convention close without solemn tributes to the sacred memory of the gallant
Robert E. Lee and the Lost Cause of the fallen Confederate dead.

One consequence of that persistent pattern was
obvious to every political observer. Bordered as it
was by former Confederate states, Indian Territory
attracted far more Democrats than Republicans.
Should tribal governments disappear and a single
state be made of Indian Territory alone, that state
was almost certain to be Democratic in its politics.
Its elected governor would be a Democrat, its elected
legislators would be Democrats, and its congressmen and two United States senators would be Democrats, too.

Political Parties in Oklahoma Territory

Over on the west, in Oklahoma Territory, the same
patterns prevailed but with considerably less cer-
tainty about their eventual outcome. Oklahoma Territory's lands were bordered both by Union (and
Republican) Kansas and by Confederate (and Democratic) Texas. Thus its original settlers tended to
be roughly balanced in their party preferences, and
generally that division was geographical. Drawing
more of their homesteaders from Kansas and the
rest of the Middle West, the northern portion of the
territory was strongly Republican. Attracting more
settlers from Texas and the rest of the old Confederacy, the southern portion was just as strongly
Democratic. So equal were those divisions that the
balance of power often rested with yet a third
demographic group, a group of southern ancestry
but of a southern stock that shed no tears for
the Lost Cause. These were the territory's black
homesteaders.

As we have noted, blacks came in good numbers
and for good cause to Oklahoma Territory. Once

there they had, as they often did not in their former homes, the same right to vote that every other person had. (Remember that in those days the right to vote usually extended only to adult males, not women or persons under twenty-one.) Roughly one out of every ten of Oklahoma Territory's voters was black, and almost every single one of them represented a dependable vote for the party of Lincoln, the party of emancipation, the Republican party. Of course, the same thing was true over in Indian Territory. The difference was that in Indian Territory there was little voting to do and the number of southern whites living there greatly exceeded the total of northern whites and blacks combined. In Oklahoma Territory there was much voting to do, and the black voters could make all of the difference in the world.

Government in Oklahoma Territory

Another difference separated the political affairs of the Twin Territories. Unlike Indian Territory, where the five Indian republics long maintained their independence, Oklahoma Territory did have a formal territorial government. It was established by the Oklahoma Organic Act of 1890 that created Oklahoma Territory. As each of the western reservations was opened to homestead settlement, its lands and people were added to the territory.

Modeled on similar statutes that had defined the transition from territory to statehood since the birth of the union, the Oklahoma Organic Act provided a simple structure of government. Executive authority was exercised by a governor (who was appointed by the president), assisted by a territorial secretary (another presidential appointee). Legislative authority was charged to a bicameral legislature, with twenty-six members sitting in the lower house and thirteen in the upper. Each member was elected by the voters of his district. Three judges (also selected by the president) maintained separate territorial courts. When meeting together, they comprised the territory's supreme court. Within that overall structure, provision was made for county governments as well as governments for municipalities and rural townships. Most of the latter officeholders were publicly elected, too. Voters of the entire territory also elected one other official: the territory's delegate to Congress. Although ineligible to vote on the floor of the House of Representatives, the delegate was allowed to represent the territory by speaking on the floor and voting in committees, where most legislation was actually created.

That framework of government provided more than adequate tests for the territory's two major parties, and by those tests, the Republican party was generally supreme. In both the congressional and the legislative races, the outcome usually was close, but the Republicans even more usually were favored. Except for a single instance when the Democrats managed to combine with a third party (the Populists) to elect the delegate, every representative that won the seat in Congress in eight successive elections was a Republican. Similarly, the Republican party controlled most assemblies of both houses of the elected legislature.

The most ready explanation for the GOP's advantage was simply that Oklahoma Territory was home to more Republican loyalists than Democrats. Midwestern whites plus southern blacks combined to equal just over half of the total population. But the Republicans had other advantages as well: because Oklahoma Territory's governor, secretary, and judges were all appointed by the president (not to mention hundreds of other officials, such as United States marshals), the party that occupied the White House had many prizes to offer its members as rewards for their political labors. For thirteen of Oklahoma's seventeen years as a territory, Republicans held the presidency. Thus it was that the Republicans benefited from the appointments, known collectively as *patronage*. Little wonder that every territorial governor was a Republican except for one lone figure, William C. Renfrow, who sat during the brief period that Democrat Grover Cleveland was in the White House. Each of the governors had his own patronage to dispense—appointments as territorial officers, designation of official printers, and the like. Understandably, the governors appointed by Republicans in Washington appointed Republicans at home. The grateful holders of federal and territorial appointments then became a sizable and effective army for the GOP's election campaigns.

While the Republican dominance in Oklahoma

Territory was comprehensible, it was also somewhat irrelevant. At Guthrie, the territorial capital, legislators debated, officeholders schemed, and governors pronounced—all with surprisingly little consequence to the average territorial resident. As long as politics turned on lingering memories of the Civil War, the substance of politics—what the government did—was little. After all, slavery, secession, and Reconstruction were hardly burning issues a generation after Appomattox. Fearful of any issue that might divide their followings and doom them to defeat, politicians learned to avoid controversy in favor of beating the familiar drums of party loyalty. They would do it just as long as their followers kept marching to the old familiar beats.

The "Merger Movement"

Only in time did thunderous new issues become unavoidable. Many of these arose from a profound economic change that was transforming the Twin Territories even as it was revolutionizing the nation. That was the rise of massive, integrated, and powerful business corporations.

For most of America's history a typical business company consisted of no more than one or two owners who managed a few hundred dollars of capital and a handful of employees. Beginning in the early 1890s and accelerating with every passing year, all of that changed. Suddenly business meant the International Harvester Corporation, General Electric, American Tobacco Company, or United States Steel Corporation. The last of those new giants alone represented a capital investment of nearly $1.5 billion. It employed tens of thousands in plants and mines scattered across the continent. From its headquarters in Pittsburgh, it daily issued orders that affected the lives and well-being of millions. Such awesome giants became symbols of America's new economic order. At home, they found their shadows in the swift combination of the territory's railroads, utilities, and other companies into massive and powerful corporations. Oklahomans (like many others) greeted such changes with fear and trembling.

Those feelings were due to citizens' sense of powerlessness. In the face of such economic might, how could common consumers be assured of fair prices and decent treatment? How could farmers get their crops to market at a fair rate? How could the lone worker be secure in his or her livelihood? How could families be sure that their young children were not abused by their powerful employers? How could citizens prevent the new economic powers from corrupting the process of democratic politics?

Progressivism

Out of such questions came a new political movement. Known as *progressivism,* it sought to address the expanding powers of business by expanding the powers of government. For that reason, "progressives" wanted to charge their states with regulating powerful corporations in the name of the average consumer. They also called for laws to protect farmers, workers, children, and others from unfair corporate power. Finally, they wanted to change the whole form of politics by creating new devices for the people's power.

In the Twin Territories such progressives saw a magnificent opportunity to achieve all of those things and to achieve them all at once. Statehood would require Oklahomans to write a constitution. Progressive reformers could place every one of their ideas right in the heart of that constitution.

Among the first to see that were a few Democrats over in Indian Territory. The wisest of them—men like William H. Murray and Charles N. Haskell—

Easily Oklahoma's most-famed frontier statesman was William H. Murray. Even before statehood, he was renowned as "Alfalfa Bill." Neither the nickname nor his primitive law office interfered with his relentless drive for political prominence. Yes, Murray is the one to the right. The better-dressed gentleman is his secretary.

turned General Lee's portrait to the wall and began to talk about the new, popular, progressive issues. Uniting with others of like mind, they met in Muskogee in 1905 and gave form and substance to their ideas. Proposing to create a new state of Indian Territory alone, they gave it a name—Sequoyah, in honor of the great Cherokee—and they also wrote a constitution for it. Contained within the proposed constitution was nearly every item on the progressives' wish list.

Of course, Sequoyah never became a state in the union. Progressive or not, any state formed from the Indian Territory was certain to be, as we have seen, Democratic. Republican President Theodore Roosevelt and the Republican majorities of both houses of Congress had no interest in such a prospect. Instead, they insisted on a *joint statehood* of Democratic Indian Territory combined with Republican Oklahoma Territory—a single state—that had some chance of sending Republicans to Washington. To prepare the way for its entry into the union, Congress approved the Oklahoma Enabling Act in 1906.

The Constitutional Convention

The enabling act authorized citizens of both territories to elect a single convention later in 1906. The 112 elected delegates (55 from Oklahoma Territory, 55 from Indian Territory, and 2 from the semi-independent Osage Nation) would then meet in Guthrie to draft a proposed constitution for the new state. Within broad guidelines contained in the enabling act, the convention would be free to write anything its members wanted.

In preparation for those elections, progressives in both territories began to mobilize. Farmers in both territories organized into the Indiahoma Farmers' Union and met at Shawnee with the workers' Twin Territorial Federation of Labor to draw up a list of twenty-four progressive demands and pledge their votes to the party and candidates that would support them. Led by the veterans of the Sequoyah convention, Democrats from both territories met in Tulsa, accepted those demands, and added some others. They reminded any and all of the progressive notions that they already had packed into the earlier constitution for Sequoyah.

Through all of those activities, the territories' Republicans remained strangely silent. Feeling confident and secure, they continued to dispense patronage and remind voters of the GOP's fidelity to the union. In fact, only one thing changed for that party—and that change was fatal.

As we have noted, most southern states already had passed laws requiring the separation of blacks and whites in education, transportation, and other public facilities. Known as *segregation* or *Jim Crow* laws (Jim Crow being the name given a stereotypical black person), these laws were one reason that so many blacks had left their homes for the territories. Now, however, the Democrats in those territories added one more demand to their list of desired changes: the new constitution must bring Jim Crow to Oklahoma, too.

Their common southern ancestry moved the Democrats to that position, and alas, segregation was quite popular with most white people, including those who usually voted Republican. That led the territories' Republicans into an impossible dilemma. If they opposed Jim Crow, many of their white followers might vote Democratic, if they voted at all. If they supported segregation, their black followers surely would not vote Democratic, but they might not vote at all. Calculating that the blacks really had nowhere else to turn, the GOP made its decision. It would remain the party of the Union but not of Lincoln. It too called for Jim Crow provisions in the new constitution.

With all of those developments in mind, we can understand the stunning change that came with the election of Oklahoma's constitutional convention in 1906. The majority of white voters marked their ballots for the party committed to progressive reform. Most black voters did not vote at all. After years of Democratic impotence in Indian Territory and Republican domination in Oklahoma Territory, the Democrats elected no fewer than 100 of the 112 convention delegates.

Meeting at Guthrie through the last weeks of 1906 and early 1907, the Democratic victors proceeded to keep nearly all of their many pledges. One result was that they produced the longest constitution yet written by human hand, in which their convention manifested their beliefs with agonizing detail. An-

WHY IS *THAT* IN THE CONSTITUTION?

The extreme detail of the 1907 Oklahoma constitution has attracted considerable attention. Noting its fierce opposition to undue corporate influence of all kinds, many progressives of its day proclaimed it to be a model state constitution. William Jennings Bryan, the Nebraska reformer who three times ran for the presidency on the national Democratic ticket, proclaimed it superior even to the federal Constitution of 1787.

Later students of government usually have not been so kind. In their view, its exceeding detail often prohibits new responses to new conditions. Moreover, they often point to provisions that seem to be unfitted to fundamental constitutional law. One frequently cited example is the constitution's famed Article 20, "Manufac-ture and Commerce." That article's second section reads: "Until changed by the Legislature, the flash test for all kerosene oil for illuminating purposes shall be 115 degrees Fahrenheit; and the specific gravity test for all such oil shall be 40 degrees Baume." Unlike such basic principles as the right to vote and the composition of the legislature, such a provision, they assert, more properly belongs to the state's statute books than to its constitution.

The background to that admittedly odd provision gives us, however, something of a case study of the origins and nature of Oklahoma's progressivism.

Before the mass production and distribution of automobiles, the main use of refined petroleum was as kerosene, which was used as an illuminating oil. It was a very important product, almost universally used to bring light in those days before widespread use of electric lights. Refining companies discovered that they could reduce the cost of their manufacturing by mixing a bit of gasoline (then a nearly worthless by-product) with the kerosene. Although that allowed them to earn a greater profit, it had one distinct disadvantage. The adulterated mix had a very low "flash point," meaning that it tended to explode when ignited. Some of the companies said to be engaging in the practice were part of John D. Rockefeller's Standard Oil Company. That company, known as the "Oil Trust," was damned around the country for its alleged insensitivity to consumer interests in its unbridled

other result was that Oklahom's constitution was regarded as the most progressive of its day. Strict corporate regulation, safeguards for farmers, protection for workers, rights of children, new instruments of popular rule—all of these and other provisions found their way into the 250,000-word document. There, too, was the mandate of segregated schools in the new state.

With the constitution as their platform, the Twin Territories' Democrats crafted a careful slate for offices in the proposed state. At its head they placed Charles N. Haskell, the Muskogean who had been a leader both at the Guthrie convention and earlier at the Sequoyah assembly. Around him flocked other ambitious Democrats. Even those not part of the Guthrie assembly ran on a platform that amounted to "Me and the Constitution."

pursuit of power and profit. In Oklahoma Territory the charge that Standard Oil adulterated its kerosene added to those beliefs.

Responding to the charges, Territorial Governor Thompson B. Ferguson asked the territorial legislature to require that all kerosene sold to residents first be inspected to eliminate the dangerous mixes. The Republican legislature did pass a bill, but it was a weak one. Each county would have a single inspector for all kerosene sold. Appointed by the governor, the inspectors would add to the army of patronage employees and thereby benefit the party. On the other hand, any public costs were to be as limited as the probable public benefits. The inspectors were to be paid no salary. Instead they were authorized to keep a small fee for each railroad carload of kerosene that they actually inspected.

Under those circumstances it was not surprising that the inspectors performed their assignments with less than rigorous devotion. In fact, some learned that they could collect more in oil-company bribes *not* to inspect the product than they could earn from the legal fees. At least one apparently succumbed to the temptation with certainly fatal results. As a housewife in Orlando lit her family's evening lantern, the deadly and illegal mixture exploded. The woman and two of her children died in the resulting fire, which also destroyed part of the town.

Angry, Governor Ferguson demanded that the next legislature change the law to provide for salaried inspectors who would be independent of the companies. Alas, those same companies began to ply the legislators with money and other gifts. The governor charged that they openly paid several for their votes. Not only did the legislature defeat Governor Ferguson's reform, its final bill eliminated any form of inspection whatsoever.

When Oklahoma's progressives complained about the powers of the new corporate giants, they had episodes like that in mind. When those same progressives wrote our constitution, they drew on the lessons. The concrete result, in this case, is the odd Article 20, Section 2.

Yes, it is odd. And maybe it does not properly belong in a constitution. But it must be said that no town has burned since.

The Republicans had no chance. Repeating many of the errors of the previous year—including renewing their support of Jim Crow—the GOP took another drubbing in the first statehood election. Overwhelmingly, voters ignored the Republicans' counsel to defeat the proposed constitution. They also refused to put it in the hands of its enemies to assassinate. Instead they elected Democrats (including Haskell) to every statewide office in the new government. They also selected massive Democratic majorities for both houses of the First Legislature, and placed Democrats in every congressional seat but one.

On November 16, 1907, just as President Roosevelt was signing the official proclamation of Oklahoma's statehood, an excited crowd gathered before Guthrie's Carnegie Library to watch Governor Haskell

Already twice the Democratic presidential nominee, William Jennings Bryan was the idol of many early Oklahoma Democrats. On their behalf he conducted a speaking tour during the 1907 campaign, everywhere urging his audiences (as here in Woodward) to vote Democratic.

take his oath of office. First, however, there was a mock wedding ceremony. A man dressed as a cowboy "married" a woman made up like an Indian. Symbolically, the event marked the marriage of the Twin Territories to become the union's forty-sixth state. The Twin Territories were no more. Instead, Oklahoma had become much like its neighboring states and the rest of America.

Maybe that is why few people noticed that the Miss Indian Territory was barely Indian at all. Neither did they notice that there were few black faces in the celebrating crowd.

Statehood Day, November 16, 1907: Hardly visible, Charles N. Haskell takes his oath as Oklahoma's first governor.

A LAST LETTER

Not every one of the new state's citizens greeted its elevation to statehood with joy. After all, the birth of the state of Oklahoma required the death of something else—the five republics of Indian Territory. Mary L. Herrod, born a citizen of the Creek Nation, described her feelings about that exchange in a letter to the *Okmulgee Democrat*:

As Friday the 15th of November, will be the last day of the Indian Territory and after that we will no longer be a nation, some of us feel that it is a very solemn and important crisis in the history of the Indians. And we want you to join with other women of your neighborhood and spend this last day in fasting and prayer to Almighty God.

I can remember as a little girl hearing my people tell of the trip from Alabama. I can remember them telling of their wrongs and how the white people induced them to come west and made such great promises. I can remember how some of the wiser ones used to predict that in the end all of our power would be taken from us.

Since I've grown up I've witnessed the sly encroachments, step by step, until now I've lived to see the last step taken and the Indian does not count any more even in his own territory. I tell you, our people would not have come out here if they had not been given great promises. They did not want to come. And we had a good government. Our chiefs governed well, I tell you. Our laws were enforced. We had order. We had none of this battling until the white people came among us. We had honesty in our dealings. Our chiefs and our judges were good men nearly all.

"I shall never write another letter," Mary Herrod added. "I cannot date my letters 'Indian Territory' and I shall not write."

(Okmulgee Historical Society, *History of Okmulgee County, Oklahoma* [Tulsa: Historical Enterprises, 1985], 163)

See History for Yourself

The restoration of Guthrie's historic district has made it possible to see something of what Oklahomans saw on the November day in 1907 when their state entered the union. Of particular interest at this point are three sites. Adjoining the Territorial Building is Guthrie's Carnegie Library, one of hundreds of American libraries built by the famous steelmaker Andrew Carnegie. It was on the steps of this library that Mr. Oklahoma Territory "married" Miss Indian Territory, and Charles N. Haskell took his oath as Oklahoma's first governor.

The building that now serves as the Logan County Courthouse provided the state many of its first offices. Had Guthrie kept the capital, there were plans for a permanent building. The site had been designated as early as 1890. Although Oklahoma City soon took the capital away, the site remains. Today, it is the location of the Scottish Rite Masonic Temple, one of Oklahoma's truly marvelous buildings.

Suggestions for Further Reading

Reference

Debo, Angie. *The Rise and Fall of the Choctaw Republic.* Norman: University of Oklahoma Press, 1934.

———. *The Road to Disappearance.* Norman: University of Oklahoma Press, 1941.

Fisher, Le Roy H., ed. *Territorial Governors of Oklahoma.* Oklahoma City: Oklahoma Historical Society, 1975.

Gittinger, Roy M. *The Formation of the State of Oklahoma, 1803–1906.* Norman: University of Oklahoma Press, 1939.

Goble, Danney. *Progressive Oklahoma: The Making of a New Kind of State.* Norman: University of Oklahoma Press, 1980.

Maxwell, Amos D. *The Sequoyah Constitutional Convention.* Boston: Meador Publishing Company, 1953.

Mellinger, Phillip. "Discrimination and Statehood in Oklahoma." *Chronicles of Oklahoma* 49(1971): 340–78.

Miller, Robert Worth. *Oklahoma Populism: A History of the People's Party in the Oklahoma Territory.* Norman: University of Oklahoma Press, 1987.

Wardell, Morris L. *Political History of the Cherokee Nation, 1838–1907.* Norman: University of Oklahoma Press, 1938.

Wright, James R. "The Assiduous Wedge: Woman Suffrage and the Oklahoma Constitutional Convention." *Chronicles of Oklahoma* 51(1973–74): 421–43.

Related Reading

Beard, Charles A. "The Constitution of Oklahoma." *Political Science Quarterly* 24(1909): 95–114.

Hurst, Irvin. *The Forty-sixth Star: A History of Oklahoma's Constitutional Convention and Early Statehood.* Oklahoma City: Semco Color Press, 1957.

Unit 6: **BRAND NEW STATE**

Introduction

From 1907, when Oklahoma achieved statehood, to the end of the Second World War in 1945, Oklahomans passed through a series of trials. State politics was a series of bruising struggles that featured an odd cast of characters. They included everyone from business-minded civic leaders to determined revolutionaries, with at least one former inmate of an insane asylum thrown in as well. Sometimes the result was tragedy. Sometimes it was comic. Always it was colorful. Such was the process whereby the new state emerged from its frontier style of politics.

The same crosscurrents accompanied the transition from a frontier economy. Some years were good ones, others were very bad, indeed. In fact, those decades saw both the very best years and the very worst years for Oklahoma's economy. Both accompanied national trends. The difference was that Oklahoma exaggerated the national prosperity of the 1920s just as it magnified the nation's collapse in the Great Depression of the 1930s. Through all of this, the people of Oklahoma managed to grow their crops, tend to their businesses, educate their children, and go about the business of living.

Just as this period was ending, *Oklahoma!* opened on New York's Broadway. In the prelude to the musical's main theme—the song that later became the state's official song—the cast sang of a "Brand new state, / Brand new state. / 'Gonna treat you great!" Nearly 1,500 miles from the stage on Broadway, some of those who had just endured the growth of the "brand new state" had been treated great. Others had been less fortunate. This is the story of both and of those in between.

Chapter 19: Politics Through the 1920s

As we have seen, Oklahoma entered the union in 1907 with the Democratic party firmly in control. That party had elected every single state official, the great majority of both houses of the state legislature, and every member of the new state's congressional delegation but one.

No one knew, however, if that Democratic domination would continue. Oklahoma Territory, at least, had been ruled by Republicans right up until statehood, and the recent Democratic victories in the new state had owed something to luck. Democrats had won partly because they had managed to identify themselves with popular progressive reforms while the Republicans had disintegrated at the critical moment. With statehood realized, both parties prepared to renew their battles. These would continue until the Great Depression of the 1930s put a temporary end to effective party competition. Until then the struggle between Oklahoma's Democratic and Republican parties continued without letup. For that reason Oklahoma's ship of state often sailed on stormy seas.

The storms were particularly ferocious in the very first years of statehood. No sooner had the Democrats swept to power in the new state than they began to fall out among themselves.

Democratic Storms

In some ways the quarrels among Democrats were predictable. After all, the party's platform had been fashioned only shortly before the constitutional con-

vention, when Democrats of the Twin Territories
had joined forces and built their coalition by appealing to a diverse group of reformers. Once elected,
those same Democrats had to translate their appeal
into policy. As they did so, their new and fragile
coalition began to fall apart.

Most farmers had voted Democratic because that
party had promised policies to ease their plight.
Most workers had done the same, and they had done
it for the same reason. What both groups discovered was that the politicians they had elected were
often powerless to protect them. The first years
of statehood were accompanied by a national economic depression, which drove farmers' prices and
workers' wages downward across the entire country. No governor and no legislature in any state, or
of either party, was able to reverse those trends. In
fact, those who held office were typically (if un-
fairly) blamed for the situation. In Oklahoma that
blame fell directly on the Democrats.

Moreover, party leaders swiftly discovered that
the policies stoutly favored by one group of their
supporters were just as strongly opposed by others.
For example, workers who felt that their wages suffered from the competition of poorly paid children
pressured the legislature and the governor for statutes forbidding the employment of children in the
state. Although many Democratic officials agreed,
other Democrats were beholden to farmers (many
were, themselves, farmers), and they argued that
such a law would eliminate a necessary source of
farm labor. The result was no legislation at all, yet
considerable bitterness began to divide Democratic
voters from their own elected leaders.

It seemed that almost every question added to the
divisions. One issue involved the location of the
state's various institutions. The government of Oklahoma Territory had established both a university
(at Norman) and an agricultural college (at Stillwater). In addition, Oklahoma Territory had built a
series of normal schools to train elementary school
teachers in several of its towns. Indian Territory
had no such institutions, and the fight to locate
some in the eastern part of the new state caused
bitter feelings. For every town like Ada or Durant,
which came away with a new school, a dozen others
carried away only long-lasting grudges.

One special case involved the state capital. Guthrie had been the capital city of Oklahoma Territory, and the federal organic act had declared that it would remain the new state's capital until 1913. Many felt, however, that the capital should be moved earlier. These included prominent Democrats like Governor Charles Haskell, who disliked the city because it was "a nest of Republicans." Knowing just how good state government could be for business, Oklahoma City's businessmen and civic leaders agreed that a serious error had been made. In 1910 they managed to wrest the capital from Guthrie, and the governor set up shop temporarily in Oklahoma City's Huckins Hotel. The people of Guthrie

Governor Haskell (*right*) with Secretary of State William Cross, both at the new 1910 "capitol"—Oklahoma City's Huckins Hotel.

cried foul and filed a federal lawsuit to void the move under the organic act. The suit failed. Guthrie went into a steep decline. Oklahoma City remained the capital. And the divisions within the Democratic party became that much deeper.

Segregation and Disfranchisement

In the early years it seemed that there was only one question that did *not* divide the Democrats. That was the issue of race. As we have noted, Democrats had firmly endorsed the forced separation of blacks and whites, and their constitution had required separate schools for the children of the two races. Statehood had no sooner been achieved than they added to that a law—the very first law enacted by the Oklahoma legislature—that forced black and white railroad passengers to ride in separate compartments and use separate depot facilities. Such

Jim Crow laws were already common in other southern states where, in addition, most blacks had already been denied the right to vote by various legal provisions and subterfuges.

In Oklahoma black citizens *could* vote—and vote they did. In the elections of 1908 black Oklahomans returned to the polls and to the party of Lincoln and of emancipation. When their votes were tabulated, they had defeated a good number of the Democratic legislators who had approved the offensive act, and their votes allowed the Republicans to elect three of the state's five congressmen.

The official response was not long in coming. In 1910 the state's Democratic officials managed to amend the constitution to eliminate most of the black vote in Oklahoma. A harsh literacy test was their chosen instrument, its purpose was evident because it applied only to black Oklahomans. It, and a subsequent test approved in 1915, effectively denied the right to vote to most blacks—and, of course, to that percentage of Republican voters who happened to have been black.

The deed long remained a stain on the state. At the time, however, it testified to the determination to hold political power without regard to political fairness. Even it, however, could not secure the Democrats' power. Even as they were decimating the Republicans, the Democrats confronted yet another partisan rival to their rule. That opposition came from Oklahoma's surprisingly strong Socialist party.

Sooner Socialism

Oklahomans who note how conservative their state has become may be astonished to learn just how strong Sooner Socialism once was—particularly when they look at it from the vantage point of the collapse of socialism in eastern Europe and in the former Soviet Union. Such comparisons, however natural, are unfair. Oklahoma's early Socialists faced problems unknown to later generations, and they advocated solutions completely unlike those that later failed so dismally in Communist states. These were desperately poor people—people so poor and so desperate that they were ready to replace what they regarded as an evil economic, social, and political system with a socialist alternative.

Especially popular with their rural followers, Oklahoma's Socialists offered a series of "encampments" each summer. These were partly political rallies and partly social occasions. Oscar Ameringer is seated fifth from the right at this 1910 encampment.

A SOCIALIST'S EXPERIENCE IN RURAL OKLAHOMA

Probably the most famous Socialist that Oklahoma produced was Oscar Ameringer. German born and already a Socialist, Ameringer came to the Sooner State in 1907. His orthodox Socialism led him to expect that Oklahoma farmers would provide a poor field for radicalism. After all, were not farmers themselves capitalists? Did not their ownership of land and expensive machinery separate them from the exploited proletariat of Marxist dogma?

Ameringer's experience with Oklahoma's farmers quickly killed such notions. In his autobiography he recorded some of those experiences, and also left us a memorable account of the incredible hardship that many early Oklahomans faced:

I found toothless old women with sucking infants on their withered breasts. I found a hospitable old hostess, around thirty or less, her hands covered with rags and eczema, offering me a biscuit with those hands, apologizing that her biscuits were not as good

as she used to make because with her sore hands she could not knead the dough as it ought to be. I saw youngsters emaciated by hookworms, malnutrition, and pellagra, who had lost their second teeth before they were twenty years old. . . . I saw humanity at its lowest possible level of degradation and decay . . . , as wretched a set of abject slaves as ever walked the face of the earth, anywhere or at any time. The things I saw on that trip are the things you never forget. (*If You Don't Weaken: The Autobiography of Oscar Ameringer*, 232)

For reasons that we will examine in detail in a later chapter, increasing numbers of Oklahoma's farmers faced real want in the early years of statehood. Socialists believed that the state's Democratic officials not only could not solve their problems but added to them. In particular, they believed that the state's political elite had joined hands with its economic elite to force poverty on the masses. In joining the Socialist party, they were in open revolt against that combined elite, the elite that they described as "the parasites in the electric light towns."

Theirs was not a violent revolt. Rather, they

appealed to voters to mark their ballots for Socialist candidates pledged to promoting fundamental changes: for publicly owned cooperatives, state credit for farmers, the forced breakup of great land estates, and the like.

Those appeals fell on fertile soil. In every election from statehood in 1907 to World War I in 1914, the Socialist vote at least doubled in Oklahoma. As early as 1910, Oklahoma had more Socialist party members than did any state in the union, more even than New York, although the Empire State had seven times Oklahoma's population. By the outbreak of the First World War, one out of every five Sooners was voting for Socialist candidates and electing them to the state legislature and to dozens of county and local offices. Particularly in the southern counties (for example, Marshall, Le Flore, Murray, Pontotoc, and Carter), the party was unusually strong. Drawing over one-third of the vote, the Socialists passed the Republicans to become the Democrats' chief opposition in that large section of the state.

The First World War

Socialist discontent with the First World War set poorly with the extreme patriotism that the call to arms awakened in others. These Washita County young men clearly responded to that call as they prepared to leave for the battlefields of France in 1917.

That opposition did not survive the world war. One reason was that the war's demand for farm products briefly pushed prices up to record levels. The temporary easing of the farmers' plight took much wind from the Socialists' sails. The larger explanation, however, was that the war gave state officials the opportunity to blast their vessel from the water. Because many Socialists opposed America's participation in the war, and a few openly campaigned

Sooner Socialists were not alone in experiencing suspicion for alleged disloyalty in wartime. First settled by German-Americans, Washita County's Korn was thoroughly American when this photograph was taken in 1917. Shortly thereafter the community changed its spelling from the Germanic noun to the English equivalent: Corn.

ONE OKLAHOMAN'S MEMORY OF THE GREAT WAR

The extreme patriotism displayed in World War I found other targets besides the politically radical Socialists. Oklahoma's German-born people were particularly suspect during the war fought against their homeland, and many suffered at the hands of their frightened fellow citizens. Pacifists also experienced public scorn for their principles.

So great was the hysteria that it was visited on those who were merely independent—Oklahomans presumed that their independence made them "slackers" unwilling to do their part in the Great War. One of those was Robert Carleton Scott. An evangelist and devout believer in the Scriptures, the Reverend Scott was the grandfather of one of Oklahoma's most famous statesmen: Carl Albert, future

Speaker of the United States House of Representatives.

In his memoirs Speaker Albert vividly recalls his grandfather's fate during the First World War at the hands of Oklahoma's "self-styled patriots":

Grandpa Scott, as independent and as opinionated as any man who ever lived, was no slacker, but the local patriots thought any man so contrary just had to be one. They called on him, demanding that he nail a flag to his house to prove his loyalty. He showed them that he already had one flying from his mailbox. He also showed them the medal that his own father had won as a Civil War soldier fighting for that same flag. Grandpa invited them to nail up all the flags they wanted. They left.

They came back. This time, they wanted him to sign a card swearing loyalty to the president and everything it

took to go into a war. . . . He would sign no card. He would give his country his loyalty. But he would not swear to any man. In fact, he would not swear at all. In his view, swearing violated the Commandments, and that card was the mark of the beast, Revelation's symbol of fealty to the Antichrist.

So they arrested him and threw him in the Pittsburg County Jail. There a gang of patriots, joined by common drunks and thieves, bound him and whipped him, two hundred lashes in all. Grandpa Scott asked the Lord to forgive him and signed the card. He did it with his soul's reservation that he would recant if the Lord asked it of him. The Lord must have understood. (Carl Albert with Danney Goble, *Little Giant: The Life and Times of Speaker Carl Albert* [Norman: University of Oklahoma Press, 1990], pp. 46, 48) against it, their more powerful rivals were able to tar the entire party with the brush of "disloyalty," even treason. This was especially the case after the Socialists became associated with several random acts of violence, as well as an episode known as the Green Corn Rebellion.

In the first summer of America's involvement in World War I, a poorly organized band of farmers in the Canadian River valley took up arms, proclaiming the intent of marching on Washington to force peace on the government. The revolt took its odd name from the rebels' supposed diet as they were to march along the way.

Few ever got beyond their home counties, and their pitiable forces were easily crushed by local sheriffs and the state militia. Still, the audacity of the deed was all that many Oklahomans needed for hysteria. Warmly supported by public opinion, state authorities proceeded to shut down Socialist newspapers and jail the party's leaders—most of whom had no relationship at all to the pathetic rebellion. By the end of World War I, Oklahoma's Socialist party was closed down too.

A Decade of Disorder

The collapse of the Socialist party hardly brought tranquility to Sooner politics. On the contrary, the succeeding decade, the 1920s, was easily the most troubled in the state's entire political history. Before it ended, the state would impeach two successively elected governors and even send a certified lunatic to Congress.

One reason for the political turmoil was the disaffection of the state's former Socialists. Their party had not survived the war, but neither did the high farm prices that the war had produced. In fact, prices collapsed just after the peace, and they stayed low for the entire decade. On top of that, the former Socialists carried a bitter grudge against the Democrats, whom they blamed for destroying their party. Unable to vote Socialist and unwilling to vote Democratic, their first recourse was to vote for the only remaining alternative, for the Republicans.

That opportunity came in 1920. In the first election since the war, the old Socialists repaid the Democrats with a vengeance. They not only carried the

"MISS ALICE" AND "OLD MANUEL"

So great was the Republican landslide of 1920 that it briefly pushed from obscurity to fame two of Oklahoma's most unusual public figures. Although each would serve but a single term in Congress, both attracted considerable public notice.

One was Alice Mary Robertson. Granddaughter of the Cherokee missionary Samuel Austin Worcester, "Miss Alice" ran a cafeteria in Muskogee. A stout opponent of woman's suffrage, she filed for Congress in 1920 from the Second District, at least partially in protest of the recent constitutional amendment that had extended political rights to women. However odd, her position was no more unusual than her forthright platform: "I am a Christian. I am an American. I am a Republican." The last was more than enough to send her, at age sixty-five, to Washington, where she became only the second woman to be elected to Congress— and the only one to date from Oklahoma.

Even more remarkable was the victory of Manuel Herrick in the Eighth District. Raised by his mother to believe that he was the Christ, Herrick was a part-time preacher, perennial office seeker, and occasional patient in the territorial insane asylum. In 1920 he filed as a primary challenger to the Eighth District's six-term incumbent, Dick Morgan. After the filing period closed, forbidding any other candidacy, Representative Morgan unexpectedly died. Herrick thereby became the GOP's official nominee. He won the district's congressional seat by a margin of 8,000 votes and set off for Congress with a self-description of rare candor: "I may be a nut," Congressman Herrick declared, "but I'm a tough nut to crack."

state for the Republican presidential nominee (Warren Harding, whose then record landslide made him the first of his party to win Oklahoma's electoral-college votes), but they also elected a Republican majority to the state house of representatives. In addition, they sent John W. Harreld to Washington as the state's first Republican United States senator, along with five Republicans out of eight members of the Oklahoma delegation to the lower house.

The sudden reversal of party fortunes measured the impact of the postwar political turmoil, and it hardly contributed to placid public policy making. Indeed, the new Republicans in the state legislature joined with a disaffected band of Democrats to bring state government to a near halt. Spending their energies in series of highly charged investigations of Democratic executives, the legislators only belatedly and reluctantly approved a state budget, but they did manage to impeach Lieutenant Governor Martin Trapp, who was acquitted by the Democrats in his senate trial. Republican members in the lower house very nearly impeached two other Democratic officials, including Governor James B. A. Robertson, who escaped formal charges by a single vote. Robertson was hardly the only Oklahoman to breathe a sigh of relief when the ill-tempered legislators finally went home.

The League and "Our Jack"

One lesson from the experience was not lost on the former Socialists: Although voting Republican in 1920 had hurt their old foes, it had not achieved any other purpose at all. For that reason most decided that a better strategy would be to take over the Democratic party itself in 1922. The designated Trojan horse of their conquest was to be Oklahoma's short-lived Farmer-Labor Reconstruction League.

The Oklahoma league drew on similar efforts by disaffected groups elsewhere, most notably in the Dakotas, where the so-called Non-Partisan League already had seized the majority party from its long-time masters. With farmers' prices in full retreat and labor union members reeling from employers' blows, Oklahoma's former Socialists had no difficulty drawing recruits in this state. Meeting at Shawnee in 1922, they launched the league and defined its strategy—which was to place a full slate of their own candidates in the Democrats' August primary election to select nominees for state office. At the top of the slate the league placed the current mayor of Oklahoma City, John Calloway Walton.

Though little known at the time, Walton soon revealed a gift for oratory and campaigning that earned him the affectionate nickname "Our Jack." Never did the misdeeds of Oklahoma's elites loom so ominously, never did the hopes of Oklahoma's poor burn so brightly, as when described by "Our Jack." The regular Democrats never had a chance. Walton won the 1922 Democratic nomination in a landslide and proceeded to defeat the Republican gubernatorial nominee by a then-record margin. A giant inaugural ceremony and barbecue held at the Oklahoma City fairgrounds marked the formal beginning of his term. Impeachment, conviction, and removal marked its end. The two sets of events were separated by a scant eight months.

John Calloway ("Our Jack") Walton—Oklahoma's governor for eight turbulent months.

OUR JACK'S GREAT BARBECUE

Crisscrossing the state, Jack Walton had promised Oklahomans their greatest celebration ever on his inauguration. That was one campaign promise that Governor Walton undeniably kept.

The great festivities began with a parade. Packed with working people, farmers, ex-Socialists, nineteen marching bands, and the entire student body of the University of Oklahoma, the parade stretched for sixteen miles. It took three hours for the last of the marchers to reach their destination, the Oklahoma City fairgrounds.

There the entertainment was nonstop. Fiddlers, clog dancers, and banjo pickers played tunes for the country folk. The more modern danced to the music of fifty jazz bands and ten orchestras.

But it was Walton's promise of a great barbecue that the people had come for, and they were not disappointed. Although federal agents seized forty-two cases of whiskey intended for the celebrants, there was plenty of food for the estimated 300,000 people that ate that day. When the revelers had finished, they had polished off 289 cows, 70 hogs, 30 sheep, 3,540 rabbits, 4,000 chickens, 110 turkeys, 34 ducks, 25 squirrels, 15 deer, 135 possums, and 3 bears—presumably not *the* three bears.

Walton's rule was illstarred from the very beginning. His talent for campaigning was unmatched with any gifts for administration. Attempting to please all, he antagonized most. When the legislative proposals of the league that had elected him went down to defeat under his inept leadership, he desperately attempted to curry favor by rewarding his old supporters with state jobs. Of course, the rewarding of political preference by government employment was hardly new; patronage had long been used to boost political fortunes. No previous executive, however, had used it with the wild abandon of Governor Walton.

Quickly exhausting the traditional supply of state jobs, Walton began to turn even university professorships and presidencies into political appointments. On one occasion he attempted to install a poorly educated ex-Socialist as president of the agricultural college at Stillwater. Meanwhile, evidence began to turn up simpler forms of corruption, including Walton's sale of state favors to wealthy contributors.

As popular opposition to his misdeeds mounted, Governor Walton attempted to regain public favor by recasting himself as the champion of decency and honor. In 1923 he declared war on the Ku Klux Klan.

Sooners in Bedsheets

Across America a reborn Ku Klux Klan rose to great influence after the First World War. Like the original Klansmen in the post–Civil War South, followers of this Ku Klux Klan masqueraded in hoods and robes that in no way concealed their antiblack racism. In a sense, they only supplemented that by adding Jews, Catholics, immigrants, and assorted radicals to their intended victims. Soon, burning crosses, whippings, and tarrings swept across the entire nation, including Oklahoma. However perverse its attitudes and behavior, the Sooner Ku Klux Klan was no force to be taken lightly. Within its ranks were prominent ministers, school leaders, and ambitious politicians. The last included perhaps a majority of the legislature elected with Walton in 1922. In taking on the Ku Klux Klan, the governor was fighting for his political life.

If rather short, the fight turned out to be bitter and occasionally bloody. Responding to Klan outrages—the mutilation of a black man in Tulsa, various whippings in Okmulgee County, and the like—Walton began to issue declarations of martial law. As a result the state militia suspended civilian governments and set up military tribunals to end the Klan's depredations. The governor made declarations that went even further. When the *Tulsa Tribune* editorialized against Walton's high-handed takeover of city and county government, the governor briefly imposed martial law on the newspaper and prevented its publication—a rare, unconscionable violation of both federal and state guarantees of a free press. The attempt to convene a grand jury in Oklahoma City met a similar fate. Declaring martial law on the Oklahoma County courthouse, Walton used troops to prevent the assembly of the grand jury that had been scheduled to investigate his personal misdeeds.

Such extreme actions aroused not only Oklahoma's Klansmen but also most of the state's other citizens. Uncertain of their options, a group of legislators attempted to meet at the state capitol to plan a strategy. They were greeted with barbed wire, machine guns, and armed militiamen. Walton peremptorily had declared martial law on the capitol to prevent their assembly.

"PROMISCUOUS JOY-RIDES AFTER DARK": A KLAN MANIFESTO

Oklahoma's Ku Klux Klan was able to draw the allegiance of many upstanding citizens. Many of them originally saw in the Klan something of a civic-minded organization that would uphold public order and defend traditional values. That tone—which amounted to moral vigilantism—certainly ran through the message that the Ku Klux Klan's "Department of Propagation" had printed in the Cherokee *Republican*:

PROCLAMATION
Cherokee, Oklahoma
January Twelfth
To The City and County Officials and Citizens of Cherokee, Alfalfa County, Okla.

GREETINGS:—
This organization, composed of native-born Americans, who accept the tenets of the Christian religion, proposes to uphold the dignity and authority of the law. No innocent person of any color, creed or lineage has any just cause to fear or condemn this body of men.

To the City and County Officials, we wish to assure you that we are not here to break down constituted authority by any act, word, or deed, but, on the contrary, will uphold the hands of every good officer and citizen in the enforcement of law and order; we expect, however, that every official, elective and appointive, to [*sic*] discharge the duties of

his office, without fear or favor, and to this end, we pledge you our undivided support.

To the fathers and mothers, we suggest that you keep a closer watch over your boys and girls in the future than you have in the past; especially in regard to the promiscuous joy-rides after dark.

To the gamblers, highjackers, bootleggers, dopepeddlers, and other [*sic*] who are constantly violating the laws of God and man—THIS IS YOUR MOVE—500 determined men have their eyes on you—be sure that your sin will find you out.
Cherokee Klan
Realm of Oklahoma
Knights of the Ku Klux Klan

Now thoroughly aroused, the governor's opponents wasted no time in executing a counterattack. Because the legislature was not scheduled to meet until 1925, Walton's foes prepared to amend the state constitution and allow the legislature to summon itself into special session immediately. Knowing the purpose of such an assembly—to impeach and remove him—Governor Walton attempted to prevent an election on the proposed amendment by order-

This Lone Wolf chapter of the Ku Klux Klan had no difficulty in drawing new members to its self-defined crusade for Christian (Protestant Christian, anyway) morality and patriotic Americanism.

ing the militia to close the polls. Except for a few cases, the militiamen ignored the hysterical governor, and the election proceeded in regular fashion with an unsurprising outcome. Oklahomans voted overwhelmingly to allow the legislature's immediate assembly.

Moving quickly to forestall the chief executive's threat to retaliate by opening the prison with a blanket pardon to all convicts, the house of representatives formally impeached (that is, formally *charged*) Walton with twenty-two offenses and suspended him from office. After a more deliberate trial by the state senate, he was officially convicted on eleven of the counts and removed from office.

In addition to ridding the state of an incredibly inept executive, Walton's impeachment had other, more important consequences. Ironically, one was a fatal blow delivered to the Ku Klux Klan. Once the governor was safely out of power, Oklahomans began to come to their senses. Walton's "war" on the Klan, after all, had given publicity to its very worst features: the terror and violence that came easily to men hiding behind hoods. The legislature thereon passed a law forbidding public concealment behind masks or hoods, making the state the nation's first to "unmask" the Ku Klux Klan. Soon, Klan numbers dropped to nearly nothing, and even former members attempted to forget the embarrassment of their parading around in silly garbs beneath fiery crosses.

Another ironical consequence of Walton's impeachment was that it did not mark the end of Our Jack's political career. Running for the Democratic nomination to the United States Senate in 1924, Walton was able to call on enough loyalists to lead a large and divided field in the primary election. Although he took far less than a majority, Walton was able to win the nomination, since state law at the time provided that the candidate receiving the largest number of votes in the primary would be the nominee, even without a majority. Incensed by Walton's unrepentant return, the electorate proceeded to elect a Republican, William B. Pine, to the Senate. Serving during the final two years of Senator Harreld's term, Pine thereby gave the state two Republican United States senators for the first time in its history.

The last election of the 1920s, that of 1928, only added to the GOP's suddenly restored fortunes. Herbert Hoover was that year's Republican presidential nominee, and Alfred E. Smith ran for the Democrats. Not even the most rabid Republican could have designed a better match for the party. Hoover was regarded as a business genius and a political wonder. A self-made millionaire, he had served a succession of Republican presidents since 1921 as secretary of commerce, a position that he had filled with great ability and acclaim. Smith, on the other hand, was the governor of New York, an ally of an infamous Democratic machine (Tammany Hall), a fervent critic of the nation's ongoing "noble experiment" (prohibition), and a Catholic to boot. One needed no great insight to predict the outcome with Oklahoma's predominately rural, moralistic, and Protestant voters. Herbert Hoover won Oklahoma's electoral-college ballots and carried fellow Republicans to victory all across the state.

Among the Republican victors were enough new state representatives and senators to join with a few disgruntled Democrats to give them effective control of the state legislature. They were effective, however, in only a narrow sense. Although the new legislators were remarkably void of ideas of public policy, they were very effective in pursuit of their single purpose: the impeachment and removal of Governor Henry S. Johnston. The hapless Johnston had won office in 1926 but had managed to antagonize many of his fellow Democrats. Unlike Walton, Johnston's faults largely were personal eccentricities, but those eccentricities included the addition of an official astrologer to the state payroll and gubernatorial efforts to seek counsel from the stars on vital state business.

However odd, Johnston's habits hardly amounted to an impeachable offense. Nonetheless, enough Democratic legislators joined the new Republican members to convict Governor Johnston on a single charge of "general incompetence" and remove him from office in 1929.

Henry Johnston's fate may have placed an appropriate exclamation mark on this tumultuous period of state politics. At the time only three state governors had been removed from office in the entire nation's history. Two of those were the successively elected Oklahomans.

Particularly regarding Johnston's fate, not a few Oklahomans agreed with the observation of one of Oklahoma's pioneer statesmen, who observed that "the people have a right to elect a fool, and the best way to cure them of that habit is to let him stay in office." Such was the salty judgment of William Henry David ("Alfalfa Bill") Murray. At the time of Johnston's disgrace, he had been absent from active politics for more than a decade, apparently one of Oklahoma's many political corpses. Soon, however, Alfalfa Bill Murray emerged from the grave to inaugurate yet another colorful decade of state politics. That story awaits a later chapter.

See History for Yourself

Oklahoma's capital since 1910, Oklahoma City is also rich in sites that document the state's history, particularly its political history. Every Oklahoman should visit the State Capitol. Much of our state's political history has occurred within its walls, and the building itself has a rich history of its own. Built during World War I, its original plans called for an external dome. Unable to secure structural steel because of the war, the builders decided to delay the dome. The delay continues, leaving Oklahoma one of the few states to have a domeless capitol. It also is the only state to have oil wells on the capitol grounds—though the last working one stopped pumping a few years ago.

East of the capitol on Twenty-third Street is Oklahoma's Governor's Mansion. Built during the 1920s, it has been the official residence of our state's chief executives since Henry S. Johnston moved in, before moving out after his impeachment. Public tours are available.

South of the capitol is the Wiley Post Historical Building at 2100 North Lincoln. It is the official home of the Oklahoma Historical Society, a state agency charged with preserving Oklahoma's heritage. The building also houses the State Museum of History, which maintains a series of exhibits illustrating life in the Sooner State from its earliest inhabitants through several Oklahomans' travels into space.

Suggestions for Further Reading

Reference

Alexander, Charles C. *The Ku Klux Klan in the Southwest.* Lexington: University of Kentucky Press, 1965.

Burbank, Garin. *When Farmers Voted Red: The Gospel of Socialism in the Oklahoma Countryside, 1910–1924.* Westport, Conn.: Greenwood Press, 1976.

Dale, E. E., and James D. Morrison. *Pioneer Judge: The Life of Robert L. Williams.* Cedar Rapids: Torch Press, 1958.

Franklin, Jimmie Lewis. *Journey Toward Hope: A History of Blacks in Oklahoma.* Norman: University of Oklahoma Press, 1982.

Green, James R. *Grass-roots Socialism: Radical Movements in the Southwest, 1895–1943.* Baton Rouge: Louisiana State University Press, 1978.

Scales, James R., and Danney Goble. *Oklahoma Politics: A History.* Norman: University of Oklahoma Press, 1981.

Related Reading

Ameringer, Oscar. *If You Don't Weaken: The Autobiography of Oscar Ameringer.* 1940. Norman: University of Oklahoma Press, 1983.

Billington, Monroe Lee. *Thomas P. Gore: The Blind Senator from Oklahoma.* Lawrence: University of Kansas, 1967.

Chapter 20: The Economy— the Fat Years

In 1870, Colonel George Washington Miller sold his interest in his family's Kentucky plantation and headed west. With him he took all that was left of his original fortune: 20,000 pounds of bacon. He intended to take it to California, but Colonel Miller never got that far. Instead he traded some of his pork to some Texas cattlemen for 400 longhorns. With Oklahoma's Ponca Indians, he swapped the remainder for a lease on several thousands of acres of grassland. After hiring a few Texas cowboys to tend the herd, Colonel Miller grazed the cattle on his new ranch, which was located a few miles southwest of present Ponca City. Determined to keep his hired hands' minds on their work, Colonel Miller named the ranch for a San Antonio saloon infamous for the headaches that it always inflicted on the slothful and indolent. Thus was born what would become an Oklahoma legend: the 101 Ranch.

The Hundred and One

It was in the first decades of Oklahoma's statehood that the 101 Ranch acquired its legendary status as a "fabulous empire" known to presidents, kings, and more common folk around the world. Although much of its operation was unique, much of the ranch's success derived from elements that were simultaneously shaping less-fabled components of the new state's economy. But, first, the story of the 101.

At the time of Colonel George Miller's death in 1903, the 101 already had grown to more than 50,000 acres, which produced an annual income of $500,000.

Its greatest days, however, lay ahead. Under the direction of the colonel's three heirs—sons Joseph, Zack, and George—the ranch continued to expand, at its peak covering 135,000 acres. By then the 101 was more than a cattle ranch. In fact, by the 1920s it was the world's largest integrated "agribusiness," even though the word had not been invented yet. Decades before giant farming corporations would transform American agriculture, Kay County's 101 Ranch operated as eighteen different departments, each directed by its own manager.

Taken from atop the ranch's headquarters—the "White House"—the photograph shows most (but not all) of the buildings necessary for the 101's many operations.

Cattle raising was but one department, and these cattle were no mangy longhorns. They were some of the world's finest beef cattle, including prize blooded stock that regularly won national championships as the best of their breed. Across the way, the colonel's sons crossbred Arabian stallions with native mares and produced annual crops of excellent polo ponies. These they sold for as much as $1,000 each. Hogs also were produced in typical Miller fashion. From a brood stock of purebred Durocs valued at $75,000, the 101 was processing 20,000 hogs annually in the late 1920s. Huge flocks of geese, chickens, and turkeys added their thousands to annual sales.

Meanwhile, the colonel's early experiments in field crops became a major operation under his sons. The Miller brothers annually planted over 15,000 acres in cereals, and the two major crops— wheat and corn—each recorded yearly yields in excess of 200,000 bushels. Much of the grain was of hybrid varieties developed under Joe Miller's personal direction. So superior were their qualities that the state agricultural college (now Oklahoma State University) required its students to spend two weeks at the 101 observing the growing crops, which were excellent examples of the practical applications of the latest theories taught in the Stillwater classrooms.

Other ranch departments eliminated middlemen to allow the 101 to establish entire industries. A meat-packing plant turned animals' flesh into beef and pork. An adjoining tannery turned their hides into leather used by the saddle shop, which stood beside the tannery. A creamery produced dairy products, which the ranch delivered in refrigerated trucks fueled by gasoline produced at the ranch refinery from oil produced at ranch wells and pumped at the ranch filling station. A steady stream of visitors purchased ranch products at the ranch general store. Others dined on ranch-produced foods at the ranch-owned cafe.

Altogether, total sales from the 101 Ranch industries amounted to more than $1.6 million over the five-year period that ended in 1929. Combined with crop sales and petroleum production, gross income for the Miller brothers' 101 Ranch exceeded $3 million over the same short time span.

That economic success was, however, just one element of the 101's legend. What established its international fame was its Wild West show. Recreating (and considerably glamorizing) western life before manufacturing and modern agriculture—that is, before such enterprises as the 101 Ranch itself—the show featured staged Indian powwows, dances, and buffalo hunts. In carefully swept arenas, immaculately dressed cowboys displayed refined skills as riders and ropers. In time the show toured the entire nation and much of the world. In its peak years

At least one generation of Oklahomans (not to mention others) had their sense of the Old West permanently defined by the Miller Brothers' Wild West show.

STARS OF THE 101

Many of the showmen who performed in the Miller Brothers' 101 Ranch Wild West Show had been actual cowboys before going into show business. Two of the most famous were Bill Pickett and Yakima Canutt.

Like many of the real working cowboys, Bill Pickett was black. Skills that he had developed over years of working cattle and horses provided the basis of his showmanship. One particular talent proved to be his trademark: the ability to ride beside a running steer, throw himself on the animal, and toss it to the ground. As a modern rodeo sport, this is known as steer wrestling, and the 101's Bill Pickett literally invented it. His version, however, was performed with an unusual twist—literally. While twisting the steer's horns, Pickett would also sink his own teeth into the steer's lips, thereby throwing the confused and frightened animal from its feet.

Yakima Canutt was already a rodeo champion when he joined the 101, and

The 101's legendary showman Bill Pickett.

his riding skills made him one of the show's chief attractions. In 1914, while the show was touring England, Canutt and the other performers suddenly found themselves stranded when the British declared war on Germany and confiscated the show's horses for use by the British army. The

Miller Brothers' show disbanded for the duration of the war, and Canutt somehow made his way to Hollywood, where he found work as a stuntman and sometimes as a movie actor. In the latter capacity he became good friends with a former football player for the University of Southern California. Marion Morrison wanted to be an actor too, and he especially wanted to play cowboys in the movies. Unlike Yakima Canutt, however, Marion Morrison had no sense at all of how to ride a horse or even how to walk like a real westerner. It was the 101's Yakima Canutt who showed him how to ride and how to walk with a cowboy's rolling gait, the skills that Canutt had displayed for the Miller brothers.

When Marion Morrison changed his name—to John Wayne—he remembered the lessons. Everyone who has seen the Duke play a cowboy, thereby has been touched by a small piece of the legacy of Oklahoma's 101 Ranch Wild West Show.

during the 1920s, the Miller Brothers' 101 Ranch Wild West Show was adding some $800,000 to the ranch's annual income—and adding immeasurably to the 101's legend and to the public's impression of life in the West.

However unusual—even unique—the 101's story, it does point to several elements that affected Oklahoma's economy during the prosperous first years of statehood. At bottom, both the ranch's and the state's success rested on Oklahomans' imaginative use of nature's resources; wealth first took the form of raw materials wrested from nature's grip. But the real story lay in what Oklahomans did with that wealth. By the time it was fully played out, that story would prove to be as tragic as it had first appeared to be fabulous.

Hereford Heaven

Consider, for example, ranching. The Miller brothers were hardly the only Sooners to use living animals to turn grass and water into food and wealth. Stock raising had been an important part of the area's economy from the time when the earliest Spanish explorers introduced cattle and horses, and several tribal citizens had operated large ranches even before the advent of non-Indian settlement. The change that came in the first years of statehood was that ranching became much more specialized, scientific, and managed. In short, it became much more commercial.

One sign of the change was the swift disappearance of the stock that descended most directly from the original Spanish sources. Scrawny, lean, half-wild longhorns gave way to modern, boxy breeds with fat bellies that barely cleared the ground. Easily the most prominent of the new breeds was the Hereford. Originally a British breed, Herefords began to replace longhorns and other "scrub cattle" just after statehood. By the First World War, cattlemen like J. K. and Henry C. Hitch in the Panhandle raised them almost exclusively. Soon the entire central portion of Oklahoma became known nationally as Hereford Heaven.

One reason for the success of commercial ranching was that nature had blessed large portions of the state with land perfectly suited to grazing. In particular, the short-grass prairie in western Oklahoma was an ideal cowman's country. Its soft, rolling, treeless expanses, covered with native grasses, fed fenced cattle as well as they earlier had fattened roaming buffalo. On the east the lush bluestem grass of Osage County provided some of the best cattle range in the entire world. Little wonder, then, that the county has long been among the nation's leaders in beef production, where the number of cattle always has greatly exceeded the number of humans.

Other regions of Oklahoma proved to be just as hospitable to early economic development. Soils in extreme eastern Oklahoma—especially in the Ozark and Ouachita regions—proved to be slightly acidic and have a high content of clay. In addition, that area's climate tends to be milder than that of the rest of the state, and it regularly receives far more rainfall than does central or western Oklahoma. In those respects eastern Oklahoma is more like the southeastern United States than the Middle West or Great Plains. Indeed, most of its original non-Indian settlers came from southern states like Texas, Arkansas, and Louisiana. In time, they erected in their portion of Oklahoma a new principality in the South's traditional kingdom of cotton.

Of course, cotton had been grown in the area since members of the Five Tribes had brought it with them from their southern homelands. But, as with ranching, the early years of statehood saw a vast expansion of the crop. In 1925, Oklahomans were planting a record high of 5,396,000 acres in cotton—more than a quarter of all the cropland in the state. The proportion climbed spectacularly high in the eastern and southern counties. In fact, during the 1920s only Texas and Mississippi produced more cotton than did Oklahoma.

In that way the old Indian Territory continued to resemble southern states, while much of the former Oklahoma Territory maintained the cast of the Middle West and Great Plains. The soils and climate in central and western Oklahoma shared less with Texas and Mississippi than with Kansas or Nebraska. That region's settlers were also more likely to have come from states like the latter—states in which wheat, not cotton, ruled.

Particularly in north-central Oklahoma, wheat growers were able to draw directly on the experience of their neighbors to the north. By the turn of the century Kansans had learned—through expensive trial and error as much as anything—that the most productive strain of wheat was a hard winter variety known as Turkey Red. The strain originally had come to America from the steppes of southwestern Russia, where it had been grown by German Mennonites who later had immigrated to Kansas as well as to some communities in Oklahoma. In both places Turkey Red proved its superiority, particularly in weathering intensely cold winters during its growing season.

As was true of cotton, wheat production expanded dramatically in the early years of statehood. By 1919—only twelve years after Oklahoma had entered the union—Sooner farmers were cultivating 4,718,000 acres in wheat and harvesting more than 66,000,000 bushels. Only Kansas (which devoted considerably more acreage to the crop) produced more winter wheat for America than did Oklahoma.

The agricultural boom continued through the 1920s. Poor cotton prices in the decade's early years caused some to talk of farmers deliberately holding back production and thereby presumably forcing prices upward. The talk remained mostly that, however: just talk. The reality was that eastern Oklahoma's cotton growers (many of whom did not own their own land) had little recourse but to work even harder to produce even more.

In western Oklahoma, particularly in the three counties of the Panhandle, not even the talk was pessimistic. Seldom was heard a discouraging word as farmers rushed to take advantage of nature's apparent abundance and humankind's latest technologies. Several years of abundant rain combined with cheap new farming implements (most notably, the

By the 1920s wheat waved over (and ruled over) much of western Oklahoma. Even before gasoline-powered tractors became universal, it demanded expensive machinery and heavy seasonal labor.

gasoline-powered tractor and the one-way disc plow) to cause a "great plowup." Every year tens of thousands of acres of native grasses were turned and destroyed. In their place came broad, flat fields bearing tiny seeds that would sprout as waving wheat.

Not all early Oklahomans made their living from farms, but most Oklahomans shared one thing with the Miller brothers—their livelihoods ultimately depended on what could be wrung from the soil. Entire communities across the state existed to service the farms and farmers of their immediate locales. In the cotton belt, in towns like McAlester and Ardmore, cotton gins, cotton presses, and cotton-seed companies depended on the fleecy products of the surrounding countryside. So too did the merchants, whose sales rose and fell with the income earned (and spent) by their cotton-growing neighbors. Likewise, communities like Perry and Woodward prospered as their grain towers and cattle sale lots bustled with the products of nearby fields and pastures. Even Oklahoma City owed much of its prosperity to such businesses as the Oklahoma National Stockyards, the Wilson and Company packing plant, and the Oklahoma Cotton Exchange.

The Oil Boom

Even the wealth produced from the animals and the crops that grew on Oklahoma's soils paled before the income from the oil that gushed from beneath the land's surface. In 1897, only ten years before Oklahoma's statehood, the future state had produced its first commercial oil well, the Nellie Johnstone No. 1. Drilled just northwest of present Bartlesville, the well met an inglorious end when, seeking to warm themselves, ice skaters built a fire on the banks of the nearby Caney River. The fire ignited seepage from the oil well, which perished in a flash of fire and confusion. Unscathed, however, was Oklahoma's passion for oil and the wealth that it could make possible.

Over the next few years that passion was focused on first one oil field, then another; each one discovered seemed to eclipse all the ones before. Just southwest of Tulsa, near the little community of Red Fork, a sizable field was tapped in 1901. It completely erased memories of the ill-fated Nellie John-stone. Four years later, in 1905, the discovery well on the little farm of Ida Glenn opened the fabulous Glenn Pool, a pool large enough to make Oklahoma the nation's leading oil-producing state from the moment that it entered the union, barely two years later.

That was only the beginning. In 1912, Aaron Drumwright opened a pool near the tiny town of Cushing. Others developed the oil field while the original pioneer spent his own energies developing a town to service that field. Oklahoma thereby acquired a new city, Drumwright. By 1919 it also had acquired the fabulous Cushing-Drumwright field, which was producing nearly one-fifth of all the oil marketed in the United States, roughly 3 percent of all that was produced on the planet.

The decade that opened the next year produced the greatest discoveries of all. Oklahoma City, Burbank, Tonkawa, Three Sands, Seminole—every year the 1920s roared with the name of yet another, even more fabulous Oklahoma oil field. During that decade these and other, lesser fields yielded nearly 2 billion barrels of petroleum—1,843,477,000 barrels, to be exact. Oklahoma's natural-gas production over those years equalled nearly 2.4 trillion cubic feet (2,378,014,200,000, for the precise). The official estimate of the value of Oklahoma's oil and gas production over those ten years was $3,587,139,500—a figure precise enough for anyone, and large enough that it equalled roughly one-fourth of all the money earned from American oil and gas during the Roaring Twenties.

Perhaps more telling than such numbers is the

The well drilled on the farm of Mary Sudik was forever known as the Wild Mary Sudik. For eleven days it blew oil uncontrollably. When the wind was right, it sent showers of oil on students making their way to class at the University of Oklahoma, nearly twenty miles south.

THE FABULOUS OSAGE HILLS

In 1872 the United States government forced a deal on the Osages. For the tribe's land in Kansas, the United States would pay $8.5 million. Then the Osages would pay $1 million of that for new lands along the western edge of the Cherokee Nation. It proved to be one of the best real-estate deals in American history, one of the few in which the Indians came out indisputably ahead.

The land that the Osages bought ran from present Bartlesville west all the way to what is now Ponca City. From the Kansas border their land extended south to the Arkansas River and present Tulsa. Totaling 1.5 million acres, its most distinguishing characteristic was its rolling hills. At the time the Osages looked at those hills and saw in them their chief value. "The white man will not come to this land," one of their leaders said. "The white man does not like country where there are hills, and he will not come. This will be a good place for my people."

It proved to be a false prophecy. Whites did come. Initially, they came because of the lush bluestem prairies that covered those hills and fed their cattle. And in time other whites came because their geologists had told them that those hills were classic examples of the synclines and anticlines whose existence suggests incomparable wealth below the surface. The Osage Hills indicated the presence of huge lakes of oil beneath the ground.

The oilmen were right, and the Osages became instantly wealthy. Alone among Oklahoma's Indian nations, the Osages had retained the mineral rights to their allotments as a tribal property, forever inalienable. Although the 2,229 Indians listed on the official tribal rolls of 1906 received the surface rights to individual allotments of 658 acres each, the rights to everything beneath the surface remained as tribal property. Whatever value might lie there was to be divided equally among the 2,229 Osage and their descendants. As individuals, most of the Osages quickly lost their personal allotments as did Oklahoma's other Indians. What they have never lost is the subsurface wealth of all of Osage County.

Particularly in the 1920s, shares in that wealth generated incredible wealth. After E. W. Marland dis-
(continued on next page)

story of a single Oklahoma oilman, one whose personal company was as richly symbolic as the Miller brothers' 101 Ranch.

The Marland Empire

Ernest Whitworth Marland was his name, and he drilled his first successful Oklahoma oil well in 1911 just north of the 101 Ranch. It allowed him to establish his own company—Marland Oils—but that was only the start. Over the next few years his drilling crews opened entire new fields, and his wells pumped ever more thousands of barrels. Some he sold to outside companies (a single deal with Standard Oil of New Jersey yielded Marland $60,000 every twenty-four hours). The rest he refined himself, using his

THE FABULOUS OSAGE HILLS—continued

covered oil beneath the farm of Bertha Hickman in 1920, the rush was on. By the decade's end Osage oil had generated more wealth than all of the Old West's famous gold rushes combined. And much of that wealth fell to a tiny band of Indians.

Oilmen bid millions for "bonuses," paying money up front just for the right to seek oil. Much of the bidding took place on the lawn of the county courthouse at Pawhuska beneath a spreading tree forever known as the Million Dollar Elm. There on June 22, 1924, for example, a crowd that included the princes of American petroleum gathered as auctioneer Colonel E. Walters called for bids to drill on Osage land. Colonel was his name, not his title, and he came from just down the road, at Skeedee, Okla-

homa. When his gavel slammed down for the last time that day, he had sold drilling rights for a total of $10,888,000—for which he received his customary fee, a crisp $10 bill.

The rest went to the Osages, and even more millions were collected as standard royalties when the oilmen's drilling bits pierced the 33-square-mile lake of oil beneath the Osages' rolling hills. Every dime was divided equally among the 2,229 original Osages and their heirs. By 1925 the sum equalled an annual income of $65,000 for a typical family of five. Oklahoma's Osage Indians were suddenly the richest people on earth.

Stories soon spread about the Indians' use of the money. Many were fond of fancy cars, and in 1925 the

most expensive car produced in America cost $8,500— which was not much with $65,000 to spend every twelve months. Stories were told of Indians who would buy a fine car, drive it until it ran out of gas, and then replace it with another. Many such stories certainly were fictions—tales told to discredit the idea that the Osages in any way deserved their good fortune.

Nonetheless, some stories were true. One involved an Osage woman who on a single day in 1927 spent $12,000 for a fur coat, $3,000 for a diamond ring, $12,800 for some real estate in Florida, $7,000 for new furniture, and $600 to ship it to California—$40,000 spent in a single afternoon. On that day, for that woman at least, those rolling hills proved to be very good.

own refinery to produce his own gasoline to be sold at his own filling stations across America.

Ponca City was the headquarters for that far-flung empire, and Marland made it a city worthy of an imperial capital. With Japanese gardeners he planted exotic trees, shrubs, and flowers along wide, majestic boulevards that he laid out. Between those boulevards he built fine homes for his employees, and even finer ones for his executives—his "lieutenants," as Marland liked to call them. He gave the city its hospital, its high school, its library—even its own golf course and polo field. Every church that needed money got it. And when the University of Oklahoma needed a student union and an athletic stadium, E. W. Marland's money bought those too.

In 1928 he launched his grandest building project—

a mansion that would outshine even the one that he already occupied on Grand Avenue in Ponca City. Outside there would be polo stables, polo fields, kennels for hounds imported to hunt imported foxes, three lakes, and a swimming pool that would swallow most houses. Surrounding everything, 300 acres of Oklahoma prairie were magically transformed to resemble the grounds of Britain's Hampton Court Palace and France's palace of Versailles. The interior—all fifty-five rooms, fifteen bathrooms, and three kitchens of it—was designed after Florence's Davansati Palace. The social center of the mansion was a large ballroom opening onto the manicured grounds. Winding across the ballroom's ceiling, a mural depicted the history of Kay County, Oklahoma, from earliest times until (in the very northeast corner) the completion of the mansion late in 1928. It took Vincent Margliatti, an internationally famous artist, over a year to complete the mural with three assistants. Not one of the painters spoke English. But it was money that was doing all of the talking.

Oilman and philanthropist E. W. Marland was also a sportsman. Particularly fond of polo—many Ponca City homes now sit on his old polo fields—Marland was said to have hired and promoted executives on the basis of their skills as horsemen.

And so it was as the 1920s ended. Barely two decades after statehood (and only about two generations after the pioneer settlements) Oklahomans had made the land produce. Indian ceremonies and cowboys trailing ornery longhorns across unbroken prairies—these had been glamorized into commercially successful stereotypes; they were things of the past. The present was cattlemen turning ever larger numbers of livestock on the same land. The present was wheat growers busily plowing up virgin land, killing native grasses, and leaving behind rows of tiny wheat seeds covered with a thin layer of dust. The present was cotton growers plowing more acres behind straining teams to grow ever more cotton. The present was the 101 Ranch. And it was Marland Oils.

In 1929 not many people considered what all that livestock, all that plowing, and all that planting would mean for the future. But then not many people realized that the Miller brothers' 101 Ranch was badly in debt or that E. W. Marland's entire empire—his mansion included—was being built on borrowed money. They thought the future would take care of itself.

It would not. But that story too awaits another chapter.

See History for Yourself

Few Oklahoma communities can match Ponca City for its attractions to students of Oklahoma history. Of particular importance for this chapter is the Marland Mansion and Estate. Now owned by Ponca City and lovingly restored, it continues to display the qualities that made it one of the most remarkable private homes in America. E. W. Marland's original mansion is no shack, either. Also now owned by the city, it houses Ponca City's Cultural Center Museum and contains a wealth of material about the region during its fattest years.

Four miles west of Ponca City and seven miles south on State Highway 156 are the ruins of the Miller Brothers' 101 Ranch. The "White House" and other buildings were destroyed long ago, but a few remnants remain. If you visit the site, continue straight south on the highway until you cross the Salt Fork of the Arkansas. About 100 yards south of the river bridge, a dirt road leads to the left. Take that road to Cowboy Hill, the final resting place of Zack Miller and other stars of the Wild West show. A mile and a half farther south on State Highway 156 stands a rock monument with a white bird at its top. This is the monument to White Eagle, the Ponca chief who granted G. W. Miller and E. W. Marland their original access to the tribe's land and its wealth. It might be worthwhile to stop the car and walk to the monument. At the base of the hill on which it rests is the grave of Bill Pickett, perhaps the 101's most famous performer.

Suggestions for Further Reading

Reference

Collings, Ellsworth, and Alma Miller England. *The 101 Ranch.* Norman: University of Oklahoma Press, 1937.

Forbes, Gerald. *Flush Production: The Epic of Oil in the*

Gulf-Southwest. Norman: University of Oklahoma Press, 1942.

Green, Donald E., ed. *Rural Oklahoma.* Oklahoma City: Oklahoma Historical Society, 1977.

Rister, Carl Coke. *Oil! Titan of the Southwest.* Norman: University of Oklahoma Press, 1949.

Skaggs, Jimmy M., ed. *Ranch and Range in Oklahoma.* Oklahoma City: Oklahoma Historical Society, 1978.

Related Reading

Dale, E. E. *Cow Country.* Norman: University of Oklahoma Press, 1965.

Gipson, Fred. *Fabulous Empire.* Boston: Houghton Mifflin, 1946.

Gregory, Robert. *Oil in Oklahoma.* Muskogee: Leake Industries, 1976.

Hanes, Bailey C. *Bill Pickett, Bulldogger.* Norman: University of Oklahoma Press, 1977.

Mathews, John Joseph. *Life and Death of an Oilman: The Career of E. W. Marland.* Norman: University of Oklahoma Press, 1951.

Chapter 21: A New Society

Almost every family that has lived in Oklahoma over a great length of time has, perhaps in a box buried deep in a closet, a collection of old photographs. Chances are good that a proportion of them date back to the earliest decades of the twentieth century. Many will display an entire family, each member dressed to the very best as he or she stares intently into the camera's eye. No foolishness here, even among the children; all, starched, combed, and polished, stand stiff and unsmiling, their gazes frozen for generations.

"No foolishness here, even among the children; all, starched, combed, and polished, stand stiff and unsmiling, their gazes frozen for generations." A pioneer family in 1890.

"Something Very Real and Very Momentous"

There are reasons why so many such photographs still exist and why they are so strikingly similar. Not many early Oklahoma families could afford their own camera, and so photographs usually were taken by traveling professionals. Each photograph therefore provided a special occasion, one for which a person wanted to look his or her very best. Cameras were special tools, not idle playthings, and their products were treasured documents, pieces of paper that preserved a very special time.

What made it so very special—and what probably accounts for the heirs' careful preservation of those old faded pictures—was not just that an itinerant photographer had happened to stop by the family homestead or house. What made it so special was that these early Oklahomans sensed that they were living in momentous times. In this place, Oklahoma—at this time, the very first years of statehood—these people were part of something that had to be documented. Amid their daily toils, their public accomplishments, and their private sorrows, they were building a new society. Everyone—white, black, and Indian; rich, poor, and middling; women, men, and children—*everyone* was part of something very important. Their daily lives were the stuff of which history was being made, full of events to be preserved and remembered forever.

At first glance the descendants of those early Oklahomans may wonder at the importance that their ancestors placed on such mundane tasks as plowing, planting, washing, and ironing. History, many assume, is something that only great people do, not the daily burdens of simple men and women. Its meanings are measured in wars, treaties, and laws, not fields, kitchens, and neighborhoods.

But our ancestors were right. History is the sum total of everything that everyone has ever done. As they went about the daily business of living, these people were, in truth, making history. And they knew that they were.

Much of the conviction of their own significance was based on Oklahoma's "newness." As one young school teacher put it, "something significant was happening in this new America. If one did not hurry and answer the call, one would miss out on something very real and very momentous." The brand new state offered brand new opportunities. Acting on them, its brand new people could transcend their past, improve their present, and creatively shape their future.

Carrying the Torch

One Oklahoman who did all of those things was Elva Shartel Ferguson. With her husband, Thompson B.

Ferguson, she filed a homestead claim in the original land run of 1889, but they soon sold it and returned to Kansas. When the Cheyenne-Arapaho lands were opened in 1892, they came back to make their permanent home in Blaine County, where they began the *Watonga Republican.*

Even before its beginning, the newspaper was a joint venture. While Elva Ferguson drove one wagon carrying family necessities into the territory, Thompson Ferguson drove the other, which was loaded with cases of type, racks, and an old press. They began the paper in a small, unpainted frame building where they also lived. Thompson Ferguson wrote most of the paper's editorials, and Elva Ferguson filled nearly every other role as reporter, typesetter, subscription agent, advertising manager, and local feature writer. After 1901, when President Theodore Roosevelt appointed her husband governor of Oklahoma Territory, she wrote most of the political news too.

When he left office in 1906, both Fergusons returned to full-time newspaper work. She began writing and printing a entire page in each issue: "Local News Items, Personals, Social Observations and Remarks, by Mrs. T. B. Ferguson." Each column always included her home telephone number. After her husband's death in 1921 she ran the entire paper but continued to feature her personal column. Squeezed among local church and school announcements were her sophisticated views on every political, cultural, and social question of the time. In addition, Elva Ferguson emerged as a political power in her own right. An active Republican, she served on the state party's executive committee, and in 1924 she chaired the Oklahoma delegation to the national GOP convention.

Elva Shartel Ferguson died in 1947. She left behind a remarkable record, faithfully recorded in her own memoirs of her life and times, *They Carried the Torch: The Story of Oklahoma's Pioneer Newspapers.* She also left behind a story so fascinating that the best-selling writer Edna Ferber based a novel—*Cimarron*—on it. Hollywood would turn the novel into a successful motion picture—twice, in fact.

If the lives of few of Oklahoma's early women provided the stuff of novels and movies, many of

ELVA SHARTEL FERGUSON ON *CIMARRON*

Not the least of the ironies in Elva Shartel Ferguson's life was her reaction to the immense popularity of both the novel *Cimarron* and its first motion-picture release in 1931. Not a woman to mince words, she angrily recorded how the book happened to be written as well as her disappointment in it. As an historical document, her reactions should raise questions regarding the relation of her personal viewpoint to the historical accuracy of the novel and movie:

I am writing a true and accurate account concerning [Edna Ferber's] visit to Oklahoma and how she secured her data for Cimarron, beginning with her telegram to me.

WESTERN UNION TELEGRAM
OKLAHOMA CITY OKLAHOMA
MAY 25 1928
MRS T B FERGUSON
WATONGA   OKLAHOMA
I SHOULD LIKE VERY MUCH TO COME TO WATONGA TO TALK WITH YOU ABOUT EARLY OKLAHOMA IF CONVENIENT WIRE ME
          EDNA FERBER

I was thrilled to receive the above telegram from Edna Ferber and answered with an invitation for her to be a guest in my home while in Watonga, which she accepted.

Miss Ferber is a very brisk, business like person and wasted no time in getting at her job. All afternoon and far into the night she worked. I told her of early Oklahoma days, of the trip in wagons from Sedan, Kansas, camping enroute, of the founding of the newspaper by my husband and myself, of the beginning of a town, its social and business foundation, the lives of the folks who were living history. As I talked, she wrote; her fingers flying over the pages of her notebook, pausing only long enough to ask questions or to light a fresh cigarette.

So much for Edna Ferber when she wanted something, but she was an entirely different person after she had gotten it. The foreword in "Cimarron" demonstrates this fact. Her statement that she is indebted to no one person for her data, that her characters are fictitious and not to be confused with real persons or events, etc. True, the

story I told her was twisted and turned in many ways, but the story is there, as everyone who knows of the real experiences of my life realizes. . . . The wagon trip to Oklahoma, the founding of the paper, the description of the town, the events surrounding my family and newspaper were used in my own words as I told her the story. The character of my husband was easily recognized in connection with the early days of the paper.

"Cimarron" is really a work of fiction, but its characters are drawn from living, breathing individuals, who lived in early days in Oklahoma, some of who are still living. Many of these characters became sensational figures by the pen of the author, lending to the book and picture sensationalism and drama, which made this the outstanding work of Miss Ferber. ("The Truth About *Cimarron*," in the Walter Scott Ferguson Collection, box 42, file folder 2, Western History Collections, University of Oklahoma)

them were filled with the same strength, courage, and determination as Elva Ferguson's. Admittedly, most women's lives were greatly affected by their gender. In early Oklahoma, no less than in other parts of America, the lives of men and women tended to fall into separate spheres. It was understood that men would be the breadwinners, pursuing careers outside the home. The home itself was expected to be a woman's chief domain and responsibility, the focus of her creative energies.

The lessons of mothers—including proper social roles—were passed to daughters.

In part, even Elva Ferguson's life reflected that division. After all, it was her husband who drove the wagon loaded with newspaper equipment. Hers was the wagon groaning under a load of bedding, furniture, and kitchen utensils. Thompson B. Ferguson served as territorial governor. Mrs. T. B. Ferguson could not even vote for most of her life.

Though not even Elva Ferguson completely transcended the traditional sphere assigned women, she did transform it. Never repudiating the role of wife and helpmate, she expanded it to embrace matters that went well beyond her home's four walls.

Other early Oklahoma women did the same. A surprising number pursued active careers in their own right. Whether married or single, many worked outside the home. Usually they were in occupations like teaching, nursing, and social work that could be perceived as extensions of women's presumed superior nurturing qualities. That fact, however, should obscure neither the importance of those

Although segregated by law and custom, women of both races excelled in the roles that society provided them, particularly as school teachers.

jobs nor the joy and fulfillment that women found in them.

Women found ways to achieve even when placed in the more traditional roles. Today few things may seem as bleak, cheerless, and unrewarding as being a farmer's wife. Stuck on a 160-acre claim without electricity, without telephones, without modern appliances, but with a large and growing brood of children, farm wives seem to have been prisoners of their gender. Doomed to drudgery and despair, they appear to deserve only our pity.

Most of those women would have spurned such sympathy. They knew that their entire family's comfort and livelihood rested as much in their tired hands as in the calloused palms of their husbands. In Oklahoma's cotton economy, it often was their labor, particularly during the critical picking season, that made the difference between comfort and distress. In the wheat belt their ability to feed a threshing crew put money in the bank or left a crop

E. W. MARLAND'S PIONEER WOMAN

No one knows precisely how or why the idea came to E. W. Marland. Maybe it was the times. The nation was awash in fresh monuments to heroes of the great World War when Marland noted that not one existed to commemorate what he called "the unknown soldiers of the great battle of civilization and the home": America's pioneer women.

Once the idea seized him, he attacked the project in typical Marland style. Inviting the nation's top sculptors to submit competitive designs for a suitable monument, Marland assured all that they would be paid regardless of which design was finally selected.

Six sculptors presented proposals, and Marland insisted that all six designs tour the United States for public examination and appraisal. The final choice was the nation's, since the American people voted by ballot among the competitors.

Five of the six entries included a child with the idealized woman—not surprising, given woman's expected sphere. What may have been surprising was that half of the models submitted featured a woman who carried either an ax or a gun—suggesting perhaps the pioneer woman's transcendence of that narrow sphere.

The winning design was by English-born Bryant Baker. In it a neatly dressed young woman clutches a Bible in one hand while she guides her son with the other. Standing proud and erect, the two stride into the future. Marland ordered that the final statue be placed in Ponca City. There it still stands, perhaps the greatest of his gifts to his beloved community. Not the least of its rich symbolic significance is the forward-striding pose of the figures and the looks on their faces, looks of courage, tenacity, and determination. They look just right in their final setting, just south of Marland's fabulous mansion overlooking the prairie of the old Cherokee Outlet.

rotting in the field. Everywhere, it was what women did for their children, accomplished in their communities, and shared with each other that most directly and decisively molded the future.

Rich and Poor

If gender was one element affecting early Oklahomans' lives, class was a second. Oklahomans liked to claim that the defining quality of their brand new state was the equality of all, but no one could deny that families like the Fergusons occupied a status considerably different from most. Even Oklahoma had its elites—some of whom, like E. W. Marland's crowd, would have been considered upper-class anywhere in America. Though of much more modest standing, at least some in every community were blessed with wealth and comfort that separated them from their fellow residents.

That is hardly surprising. What may be startling is how very poor so very many early Oklahomans were. This was particularly true across the former Indian Territory, where the grafting of land allotments had serious consequences for not only Indians but everyone else as well. One consequence was that a few were able to take control of huge parcels of land. Another was that many were unable to own land at all. Instead, they rented it, usually paying their landlords with part of their crops while keeping only a small share for themselves. What made it especially hard for them is that the crop was almost always cotton (many landlords would not allow their tenants to grow anything else), and cotton prices often barely covered the cost of production.

In no county in eastern Oklahoma did anything like one-half of the farmers own their own land. In many, not even one-tenth did. By the time the sharecropper had paid the cost of ginning the cotton, had given the landlord his share, and had paid off his debts at the local store, he could be left with little, if any, cash income.

You may remember how Oscar Ameringer described some of the social results, including the "youngsters emaciated by hookworms, malnutrition, and pellagra." You also should recall one political consequence: how this large class of the rural

poor provided a fertile field for early Sooner socialism. The end of socialist politics in Oklahoma did
nothing at all to remove the economic and social
crisis on which those politics had fed.

One thing that did ameliorate (if not resolve) the
crisis was the oil boom that exploded across the
state with ever-increasing force. Many of the largest oil fields lay in those parts of Oklahoma that
most needed alternatives to the cotton fields. As
each pool opened, thousands put down their plows,
packed their belongings, put out the fire, called the
dog, and headed for town.

The Boomtowns

By the mid-1920s oil companies were paying their
roustabouts (the semiskilled men who worked the
drilling rigs) an average of $130 a month—more
cash for thirty days' labor than a sharecropper
might see in three years on the farm. It was little
wonder that some tiny communities that lay inno-
cently close to the newest discoveries exploded almost overnight into the latest in a whole series of
Oklahoma boomtowns. Wewoka was but one example. After Robert F. Garland hit oil just outside of
town, the sleepy village of 500 almost instantly became a chaotic city of more than 20,000. Within
three years the same experience was visited on
Cromwell, Seminole, Maud, Konawa, St. Louis, Mission, Earlsboro, and Searight, to name just the ones
affected by a single field.

That was the Greater Seminole field. Centered in
Seminole County, some of its twenty-six separate
pools spilled over into neighboring Pottawatomie,
Hughes, Okfuskee, and Pontotoc counties. Garland
tapped into the first pool in 1923 and struck an even
bigger one in 1926. Within five years other oilmen
had pierced the field with 5,000 wells, wells drilled
to a combined depth of 16 million feet—just about
the distance between New York and Los Angeles.
Add another five years of around-the-clock pumping, and you have $1 billion worth of oil sucked from
the Greater Seminole field in its first decade alone.
Thousands of Oklahoma's poorest farmers greased
their way out of poverty with just part of that money.

Behind them were the cotton fields; ahead of
them were some of the most disorderly cities in hu-

Seminole during the oil boom days—when only mud rivaled petroleum as a natural feature.

man history. It seemed that there was never enough of anything—except mud, which was just one of many unfortunate by-products of the rush to get men and equipment over the primitive dirt roads and into the field. There were not enough doctors, not enough schools, not enough sources of drinking water, not enough houses. Under the circumstances people slept anywhere they could, in tents, in trucks, in railroad cars. One fellow paid a dollar a day to sleep in the only available space—on the roof of a house overflowing with oil hands. That was unusual. What was not unusual was for six men to share one bed, sleeping two at a time over three eight-hour shifts a day. The charge? Five dollars a week per man.

Adding to the disorder were people determined to get their share of the wealth by means more foul than fair. At the peak the total payroll in the Seminole field alone ran to $600,000 per week, and there

As advertised, the beds were new—so was the unpainted lumber—and there was no lack of customers for them in the hastily built "hotel" that sat above this Bowlegs gas station in 1927.

were plenty of places to spend it. One portion of Seminole—Bishop's Alley—was notorious for the options available. Occupying four square blocks along the town's main street, the area took its name from the man who had owned the barn that became the first dance hall. In no time fifty-six so-called "night clubs" had crowded into the area. In any of them a man could get a card game, a drink, some dope, or a woman—or all of them, if he preferred, anytime that he preferred. So riotous was the place that not

HE ROBBED BANKS: PRETTY BOY FLOYD

If any family was typical in eastern Oklahoma, it might have been the Floyd family. The large clan was of southern ancestry—from Georgia—and had come to the old Indian Territory just after statehood. Settling in and near Sequoyah County, most of the Floyds were simple farming folk, cotton sharecroppers who (as one of them put it) "worked the sand hills for a cornbread living." That anyone today has heard of the family owes much to the one who earned his living another way. Charles Arthur Floyd robbed banks.

No one knew just how many banks Floyd robbed in the early 1930s. After being stuck with the nickname "Pretty Boy," he told an interviewer that he could recall robbing thirty-two, but thought the total was closer to sixty. Easily the most audacious was the robbery of the bank in his hometown, Sallisaw.

It seemed that almost everybody knew that Pretty Boy Floyd was going to rob the bank, and even when—November 1, 1932. In fact, his seventy-five year-old grandfather, Charles Murphy Floyd, dressed up in his best pair of overalls and came to town just to watch. After Pretty Boy succeeded in relieving the bank of $2,530, one awed reporter wrote that "it was like the hometown performance of a great actor who has made good on Broadway."

For years Oklahoma's bankers and sheriffs and lawmen in several states tried to hunt Pretty Boy down. None had any luck. The so-called Hoodoo Hoodlum had friends and family aplenty who were willing to hide him. Only when federal agents cornered him out of Oklahoma did they manage to bring Pretty Boy Floyd down.

When Federal Bureau of Investigation agents nailed George ("Machine Gun") Kelly for the kidnapping of wealthy Oklahoma oilman Charles Urschel, he dubbed them "G-Men," and it was G-Men who killed Floyd in East Liverpool, Ohio, on October 22, 1934. His body was shipped home to Oklahoma with money raised from friends of the Floyd family—including a sizeable donation from the Sallisaw bank.

A crowd estimated to number up to 40,000 people attended Pretty Boy Floyd's funeral. The preacher was the Reverend W. E. Rockett, pastor of Sallisaw's First Baptist Church. He was there because twenty-seven Floyds worshipped at his church every Sunday. One of those was Pretty Boy's youngest brother, E. W. Floyd.

E. W. Floyd later campaigned for Sequoyah County sheriff in 1948 on the slogan "He ain't perfect, but he's honest." He won that election, and he kept on winning until he died in office on August 20, 1970.

Charles Arthur Floyd, Sheriff E. W. Floyd, twenty-seven members of the First Baptist Church of Sallisaw—in all its complexity, maybe the Floyd family *was* typical.

even lawmen would enter it alone. In fact, about the only people who would were fellows like Charles Arthur Floyd. Son of some Sequoyah County sharecroppers, he got his start there. Only later, in Kansas City, did he get the nickname "Pretty Boy." In Seminole, there was nothing at all pretty about him or his kind.

The Reality of Race

For all of their disorder and lawlessness, the oil boomtowns offered an escape from rural poverty. Usually, however, the escape was for poor *white* people. The black Oklahomans who needed an escape were even more numerous, but they were less likely to find it in the oil fields. Race—like gender and class—could shape Oklahomans' lives. In the oil fields race meant more-abundant, better-paying, and more-comfortable jobs for the whites. It dictated fewer, worse-paying, and more-disagreeable jobs for the blacks.

Under those circumstances many Oklahoma blacks looked elsewhere. Some, in fact, looked outside the United States. Just as earlier blacks had come to territorial Oklahoma to establish collective communities, others left the state of Oklahoma, again as groups, to establish entire communities elsewhere. For example, sons and daughters of blacks who had fled Texas's Grimes County for Wellston in the 1890s left Oklahoma's Lincoln County for Canada's Alberta province a decade later. There they became the nucleus for the settlement known as Amber Valley, an all-black community of transplanted Oklahomans. Other Oklahoma blacks soon made their way to a similar black community, Maidstone, in Saskatchewan province.

Proving that white Oklahomans had no monopoly on racism, Canadian officials effectively slammed the door to Oklahoma's black immigrants in 1912. Within a year, however, Alfred Charles Sam came to Oklahoma. Claiming to be a tribal chief from Africa's Gold Coast, "Chief" Sam began recruiting state blacks with the promise of transporting them to an African paradise. Hundreds sold everything they had and headed for Weleetka, the staging point for the planned exodus. For a time it looked like entire black communities would be emptied. Their people were leaving everything behind for West Africa—everything, that is, except their hopes. But the colony never happened. Only a few black Oklahomans ever got to Africa, and they failed miserably. A few straggled back to Oklahoma, and with those left behind, they generally dispersed into multiracial Oklahoma cities.

Tulsa was one such city. The former Creek trading post nestled in an elbow of the Arkansas River was well on its way to earning its self-description as "the Oil Capital of the World." Strategically situated amid dozens of booming oil fields, the city's population tripled (to roughly 100,000) between 1910 and 1920. Slightly over 10,000 of that number were blacks. Like the new white Tulsans, they tended to be migrants fleeing from Oklahoma's cotton fields and declining villages. What they were headed for was the state's newest "Promised Land."

In some measure they found it. It was true that Tulsa was no paradise. Usually disfranchised and rarely well paid, black Tulsans knew just where the

---

OKLAHOMA'S BLUE DEVILS

America in the 1920s was said to be in the Jazz Age. With its conscious abandonment of traditional forms and sentimental lyrics, jazz was symbolic of the times. It also was representative in that it bore the markings of Jim Crow. Most of the country's leading jazz musicians were black, and most of them honed their talents playing with other black musicians for black audiences. That was certainly the case of one of the era's greatest jazz bands, Oklahoma City's Blue Devils.

The Blue Devils came together in 1923 and made their headquarters in Oklahoma City's Ritz Ballroom. Mostly they traveled to play at clubs, including white clubs across Oklahoma and surrounding states. The group's greatest popularity, however, was on the old-time Chittlin' Circuit, a string of black-owned clubs that booked black bands for appreciative black audiences. The location of many of those black clubs in Kansas City made that city the nation's jazz capital during the Roaring Twenties.

Kansas City promoters regularly involved the Blue Devils in their famous Battles of the Bands. These were open competitions in which rival bands successively tried to outdo each others' hottest licks. Not infrequently, the Oklahoma Citians bested every big-time band in the region in those competitions.

With the Great Depression of the 1930s, clubs, both black and white, withered; and denied audiences, the Oklahoma City Blue Devils disbanded. Many of their members made their way to Kansas City, where they became the nucleus for a new band directed by one of the Blue Devils' old piano players. That band, the Count Basie Orchestra, continued for decades as America's premier jazz band—a continuing reminder of black achievements behind Oklahoma's walls of segregation.

wall of segregation ran—along Archer Street, not far from Beno Hall, the headquarters for the city's sizable Ku Klux Klan. Nonetheless, Tulsa blacks managed to carve out their own space within the Jim Crow municipality. Black-owned businesses, black-published newspapers, black-built churches—all of these testified to the determination of Oklahoma's African Americans to build a community that nurtured independence and dignity. Its geographical center ran along Greenwood Avenue. Derided by many white Tulsans as the main thoroughfare of "Little Africa," Tulsa's Greenwood was known as something else to blacks everywhere: "the Negro Wall Street of America."

Race War in Tulsa

Greenwood is still there, and at its intersection with Archer one can still see a dim reflection of its former glory. What will probably strike today's visitor is something else. Nearly every building that stands has, somewhere on its exterior walls, a stone that bears the date of its construction. Every stone says the same thing: "1921."

Behind those cold, chiseled stones with their mute digits stands Tulsa's—and Oklahoma's—most disgraceful episode. On the last day of May 1921 two crowds gathered outside Tulsa's county courthouse, which sat across the railroad tracks just northwest of Greenwood and Archer. Inflamed by grossly irresponsible reporting, one crowd, consisting of white Tulsans, was there to see justice meted out to Dick Rowland, a young Negro bootblack who had just been arrested and jailed. According to the afternoon newspaper, Rowland (however improbably) had attempted to rape Sarah Page in broad daylight in a downtown office-building elevator. The other crowd was black, and they were there also to see that justice was done. That hot afternoon had been filled with talk—some of it appearing in the press—of Dick Rowland's imminent lynching.

Soon, hostile looks gave way to ugly words. Words became shots. And a full-blown racial war was the consequence. Two days later every building at Greenwood and Archer (and within a thirty-six-square-block area north of it) was a smoking ruin. Property losses ran into the millions. The number of deaths—

A LYNCHING

Lynching, one of the most disgraceful of human misdeeds, was neither rare nor confined to Oklahoma. At its peak in the early 1900s lynching claimed the life of one black person every three days. The black people who gathered at the Tulsa courthouse in 1921 knew that. They also knew something else.

Only a year earlier, Roy Belton had confessed to shooting a cab driver on the road to Sapulpa, although Belton claimed that it was accidental. As Homer Nida, the cab driver, lay dying, Tulsa's newspapers inflamed the city's passions with daily front-page coverage.

Nida died on the morning of August 28. That night a crowd gathered at the Tulsa jail, removed Roy Belton, and drove him (in Homer Nida's cab) down the road toward Jenks. In an empty field another crowd waited.

In it were members of the Tulsa police force. A lynch mob hanged Roy Belton that night. Afterwards, his body was cut down and pieces of his clothing and the rope that killed him were passed out as souvenirs.

Some said that the police helped direct the traffic home. No one knew if that was true. But they did know that Roy Belton was eighteen. And he was white.

almost all of them black deaths—fell somewhere between a dozen and several hundred. Even now nobody knows for sure.

Among the photographs that document Oklahoma's social history are several taken during the riot and its aftermath. A very famous one shows the burning of Mount Zion Church. Smoke billows through the roof and the windows of the building that Tulsa's black Baptists had completed just a few weeks earlier. All that was left was a shattered hull, an ugly hole—and an $84,000 mortgage that would have to be repaid. The church's insurance policy excluded loss from rioting.

As much as that photograph shows, it does not reveal the most important part of this particular story. In a remarkable display of courage, tenacity, and will, Mount Zion's congregation proceeded to rebuild the church. Not only did they rebuild the

The destruction of Tulsa's Mt. Zion Baptist Church.

structure but they also paid off the original mortgage on the one that it replaced. It took them years to do it—to be exact, twenty-one years, just like the numbers on the building's cornerstone.

Let that serve as our point. Those anonymous black Oklahomans endured and triumphed over momentous times. Like others—nameless roustabouts, oil millionaires, tired housewives, a famous newspaperwoman, even Tulsa's white rioters—their lives were the stuff of which history was made, full of events to be preserved and remembered forever.

See History for Yourself

The home that Elva Shartel Ferguson shared with her husband, Thompson B. Ferguson, still stands in Watonga. Built in 1901, it was Mrs. Ferguson's residence while she edited the *Watonga Republican* until 1943. The *Pioneer Woman* statue remains one of Ponca City's major attractions. Woolaroc, built by oilman Frank Phillips as a private retreat, now provides a wildlife refuge and a museum for the community of Bartlesville. Among the treasures of Woolaroc Museum are all of the entries prepared by sculptors for the contest that Bryant Baker eventually won.

As well as in the wells that are still found in the state, the story of the oil boom of the 1920s is recounted in several Oklahoma museums. One of the most complete is the Healdton Oil Museum, particularly for its materials used in the fields of the time. One of the largest of those fields was the so-called Burbank field in Osage County. Covering thirty-three square miles, it once included 2,000 wells, which at their peak in 1923 constituted the world's largest supplier of petroleum. Because the area was so sparsely populated, several oil boomtowns sprang up only to fade away when the boom passed. One of the most colorful was known to natives as Whizbang (the U.S. Post Office preferred the name De Noya). Although it was once one of Oklahoma's liveliest communities, its only remaining monuments are a few broken sidewalks and weathered foundations. These are found two and one-half miles west of Shidler on State Highway 11.

A more permanent monument is found in Tulsa. Adjoining the campus of the University Center at

Tulsa is the Mable Little Heritage House and Greenwood Cultural Center. The home, which originally stood at the corner of Easton and North Greenwood, was built by survivors of Tulsa bloody race war. Determined that this one would not burn, the original owners used brick, cinder blocks, and very little wood in its construction.

Suggestions for Further Reading

Reference

Crockett, Norman. *The Black Towns*. Lawrence: Regents Press of Kansas, 1979.

Bittle, William E., and Gilbert Geis. *The Longest Way Home: Chief Alfred Sam's Back-to-Africa Movement*. Detroit: Wayne State University Press, 1979.

Ellsworth, Scott. *Death in a Promised Land: The Tulsa Race Riot of 1921*. Baton Rouge: Louisiana State University Press, 1982.

Ferguson, Mrs. Thompson B. *They Carried the Torch: The Story of Oklahoma's Pioneer Newspapers*. Kansas City: Burton Publishing Company, 1937.

Thompson, John. *Closing the Frontier: Radical Response in Oklahoma, 1889–1923*. Norman: University of Oklahoma Press, 1986.

Related Reading

Ferber, Edna. *Cimarron*. Garden City: Doubleday, Doran and Company, 1930.

Wallis, Michael. *Pretty Boy: The Life and Times of Charles Arthur Floyd*. New York: St. Martin's Press, 1992.

Chapter 22: The Great Depression and Global War

In America's history the decade of the 1930s is inevitably linked to an economic disaster so severe that it is called the Great Depression. America and the entire globe associate the first half of the 1940s with another disaster, the Second World War. Both events remind us that the history of a single place is always part of history on a much larger scale. The history of Oklahoma in the 1930s and early 1940s not only affirms that but also points to another obvious truth. Broad national and international events find specific expression as they are filtered through state and local circumstances.

That was certainly the case in the Great Depression. Nationally the depression is said to have begun with the stock-market crash of October 1929. Thereafter the country slid ever deeper in a cycle that began to turn only with the imaginative programs that Franklin Roosevelt introduced after 1933 as part of his "New Deal." Although full recovery remained just over the horizon, the depression's back had been broken by the late 1930s.

However valid that analysis may be for America, each element in it varies when applied to Oklahoma. Entire Oklahoma communities and industries already were in severe depression well before the stock-market bubble broke on Wall Street in 1929. Over the next several years conditions steadily worsened. In part because of some New Deal programs, the very worst of Oklahoma's depression came not early in the 1930s but at the end of the decade.

Symbolic of Oklahoma's experience was the fate of E. W. Marland. We last saw him presiding over the construction of his private palace, its grand ballroom decorated with the ceiling mural recounting the history of Kay County from its beginnings through the fat years.

Marland's mansion was completed in 1928, and Marland moved in with his new bride, Lyde. But only a few months later, E. W. and Lyde Marland moved back out. They moved to a studio left behind by the artisans and craftsmen who had constructed the great house. The great E. W. Marland was broke, so broke that he could not afford the mansion's $800 monthly lighting bill.

In some measure Marland's fall was as singular as his rise had been. Anxious to expand his empire, he had turned to Wall Street bankers—particularly the legendary J. P. Morgan—for loans. The bankers had been more than willing to loan Marland money, but in return they demanded that their representatives take seats on his company's board of directors, taking control of its executive committee. That committee then took control of the company Marland had built. Soon Marland found that the bankers were blocking his plans. The showdown came when Marland wanted to build a pipeline to connect his Ponca City refinery to the Texas Gulf coast. The board refused to approve the move. Instead Morgan's men ousted Marland from his own company and combined it with a small Colorado firm already under Morgan's control. Marland Oils thereby merged with Continental, and the familiar Marland triangles were repainted to bear the name Conoco.

The remade company offered Marland a token and powerless position and a salary of $75,000 a year. There was, however, a condition attached: E. W. Marland would have to leave Ponca City, the city that he had built. Marland refused the offer and thereby became a man without a job.

He was hardly the only oilman in that position. Through the 1920s and into the 1930s the Oklahoma oil fields had erupted in a frenzy of uncontrolled production. Across the Red River even larger fields

OKLAHOMA'S MYSTERY WOMAN

Not even E. W. Marland's story was more poignant than Lyde Marland's.

Born Lyde Roberts, she and her brother George began their lives in the Philadelphia suburb of Flourtown, Pennsylvania. When she was ten and George was twelve, the two came to Ponca City to live with their mother's sister, Mary Virginia Collins Marland. Aunt Virginia was the wife of E. W. Marland, and she and her husband obviously could provide more for them than could their natural parents. Childless for fifteen years, she and E. W. formally adopted both children.

As he planned the great Ponca City mansion, E. W. Marland designed handsome rooms for his two adopted children, each overlooking a formal garden. From George's window the boy could see a life-size statue of himself, dressed in his favorite riding clothes. Lyde's window overlooked a similar life-sized statue of herself in a clinging evening dress.

Virginia Marland died as work on the mansion progressed. Two years after her death, E. W. Marland quietly had a judge annul his earlier adoption of Lyde. When that was done, she and he boarded a train for Flourtown. When they returned, printed notices already had arrived to Ponca City's most prominent citizens: Mr. and Mrs. Ernest Whitworth Marland would be receiving friends to celebrate their new marriage. Lyde, once E. W.'s adopted daughter, had become his wife. He was fifty-four years old. She was twenty-eight.

They were able to live only briefly in the new mansion, although they did occasionally open it for gay formal parties. Decorating the huge ballroom, where couples danced into the cool nights, was an oil painting that E. W. had ordered done. In it Lyde's lovely face appeared on the famous body of Carmen. At the bottom of her Spanish outfit lay a coiled snake, one of E. W.'s little jokes.

Never happy in crowds, Lyde suffered as Oklahoma's shy and reclusive First Lady during E. W.'s governorship. Official visitors often found her with her face hidden behind dark sunglasses. He died soon afterwards, of course, and she lived on in a little cottage in Ponca City, which was all that they had been able to salvage of the once-magnificent estate.

were opened in East Texas and westward in the Permian Basin area around Odessa. Texas, California, Kansas, Louisiana, the Middle East, and Latin America—almost everywhere the crude oil poured forth in record amounts. As it did, it flooded the market, quenching and then drowning the demand. In consequence, the value of black gold dropped precipitously and hopelessly. It was still black, all right, but when its price dropped to twenty-five, even ten

In March 1953 she drove her green 1949 Studebaker out of the grounds with the trunk and seats filled with clothes and some valuable paintings. Her last act in Ponca City was to take the statue of herself to a local monument company, where she ordered its face smashed before her eyes. It was sometime before anyone even knew that she was gone.

In 1955 the Ponca City police officially listed Lyde Marland as a missing person. For all anyone knew, she was dead. Except, once each year, the Kay County tax assessor would receive an envelope. Mailed from various post offices over the years, each one contained a small amount of cash—what Lyde Marland figured was due as taxes on the little piece of ground that she still owned. It was always a little bit too much, so the tax man kept the surplus in a little box, just in case she ever showed up again.

The mansion and grounds continued to deteriorate. The religious order that had bought it was forced to fill in the swimming pool and eventually to sell it to another order. That order could not maintain it either and made plans to let it go. Conoco—the company built on E. W. Marland's ruin— offered to put up half of the $2.5 million asking price if the city of Ponca City would come up with the rest and open the mansion to public tours. The city did not have the money and did not have much desire to raise it.

Not until Lyde Marland returned, broke, to the one thing she still had, the little cottage to which she and E. W. had retreated—the one that she had fled twenty-three years earlier. A few old friends stopped by to visit, learning little. The general public learned nothing at all, except that she thought it a good idea to restore and reopen the place. That the public learned in a letter to the editor that she wrote for the local newspaper. It was her only contact with the media.

The citizens of Ponca City voted a sales tax on themselves. The money (matched by Conoco) reopened the Marland Mansion, and it remains today one of those sights that every Oklahoman should see. Lyde continued to live there, off the publicly owned grounds, in her little cottage shielded by tall cedars. Occasionally, the people of Ponca City would gather on the grounds north of the mansion, perhaps to eat ice cream or watermelon and sing together. Once or twice someone noticed a small, stooped figure, clad entirely in black, sitting off by herself, quietly singing along, especially the old songs, especially the sad ones.

On July 25, 1987, Lyde Roberts Marland died in Ponca City. After her death her statue was recovered and restored. Standing now in the mansion's foyer, the restoration is complete except for a wide scar that runs like a tear down the face. The real Lyde Marland was buried in Ponca City. Only six people attended her funeral. The only flowers came from Conoco.

cents a barrel, it was no longer gold. It was more like a black curse.

Separately, there was little that any individual or single company could do. As long as other companies were pumping oil as fast as their rigs could pull it up, every company had to do the same. One result was that the price kept dropping. Another was that entire fields began to play out. Almost as quickly as they had sprouted, oil boomtowns withered, their easily exploited pools sucked dry. Drilling crews, roustabouts, and roughnecks moved on to start the game all over again someplace else. By the time America had noticed that it was in a depression, Oklahoma's oil industry already had been there for several years.

The Plowman's Folly

The same thing was true of Oklahoma agriculture, and it largely was true for the same reason. Just as uncontrolled production had saturated the market for petroleum, there was a surplus of farm commodities. Every year Oklahomans raised more cattle; every year the price of beef fell. Every year they grew more cotton; every year cotton prices dropped. Every year they harvested more corn and wheat; every year grain prices tumbled. Desperate farmers either took out new mortgages or sank deeper into old debts. As matters grew only worse, repayment became impossible. It was little wonder that half of Oklahoma's farms and ranches were lost to debt in the 1930s. One of those was the Miller Brothers' 101 Ranch.

Of course, farmers and ranchers in every state had the same problems of producing too much for too little income. The difference was that the scenes were acted out in distinctive contexts in Oklahoma. One difference was the prevalence of sharecropping and tenancy in the cotton belt of eastern Oklahoma. As bad as it was for an Arizona cotton grower to see the price of cotton drop to a nickel a pound, it was far worse for an Oklahoman. In all probability, the Arizonan owned his or her own land, and five cents might at least cover the cost of production. But the odds were nine in ten that the Oklahoman did not own his or her land, and the share of the crop that was left after paying the landlord's rent would almost never leave the Oklahoman any cash income at all.

Much of Oklahoma's wheat belt was another very special circumstance. New and inexpensive agricultural technology and abundant rainfall had encouraged farmers to kill off hardy native grasses in the "great plow-up" of the 1920s. In the grasses' place they had sown wheat, and they had sown it according to the prevailing doctrines of "dry-land

THE END OF THE 101

In retrospect, the turning point for the Miller brother's 101 Ranch probably came on October 27, 1927, when Joe Miller accidently killed himself while working on an automobile. A second tragedy came within a year. On February 1, 1929, George Miller lost control of his car on an icy curve outside of Ponca City. When they found him, his head had been crushed under one of the Lincoln's front wheels. Zack Miller, the middle son, was the only brother left, and the national depression was just around the corner.

When the bottom fell out of the stock market in October 1929, the entire empire began to disintegrate. Oil and agricultural prices tumbled, and beef prices fell to their lowest ever. New mortgages briefly blocked the financial hemorrhage, but only temporarily. By the end of 1930 the 101 Ranch was losing $300,000 a year. With no cash reserves remaining, creditors pressing for repayment, and taxes past due, liquidation began in 1931. By 1932 not much remained. Most of that went on the auction block in March.

The last surviving brother did not go quietly. As 3,000 people gathered around the small knot of attorneys and bankers who were now in charge, Zack Miller fired his old shotgun futilely their way. The cops had to haul him off to the Kay County jail.

One of Governor Murray's many declarations dispatched the Oklahoma national guard to the jail and freed Zack Miller. By the time he could get back home, everything was gone except the great headquarters and twenty-two-room family home that the world once had known as the White House. Creditors took it too, with all of its furnishings and all of its contents, in 1936.

Zack Miller, the last of the Miller brothers, died while living with his daughter in Waco, Texas, in 1952. His body rests on a little hill just across the river from the 101's ruins, barely a half-mile from where, thirty years earlier, he had tried to fight off the lawyers and the creditors, regretting that the days had passed when a man could meet his enemies with a gun.

---

farming." Believing that the chief imperative was to preserve moisture in the soil, they had destroyed any vegetation that might compete with wheat for the precious water. They also had left their fields covered with a thin layer of dust—"dust mulch" they called it—to protect the soil's moisture from evaporation.

The result was broad, open fields that stretched as far as the eye could see, fields without the tangled roots that heretofore had held the soil in place, fields just waiting for nature's hand. That hand came not in the soft glove of gentle rains but in the hard fist of drought and wind.

In the mid- and late 1930s rainfall dropped across the entire region. In fact, many Panhandle communities received no rain at all in 1936 and 1937. Dry and dusty towns and fields lay vulnerable as winds swept down the eastern side of the Rockies, picking

Many of the most powerful images of the Great Depression came from photographers who worked for the Farm Security Administration. One of those was Arthur Rothstein, who happened to be in Oklahoma's Panhandle during its very worst dust storm. The result was this photograph—one of the most famous ever taken. Rothstein noted his impressions of the region and its problems on that historic day: "Boise City, Cimarron Co[.], Okla. Thursday   April 23 Very dusty—wind about 25 miles/hr. Went out with Farrel, rural rehab supervisor[,] and photographed a number of rehab. clients and their badly blown fields and farms. Farrel says this is the worst section of the "dust bowl"— An area about 30 sq. miles was originally settled by Missouri & Ohio farmers who plowed up the wrong types of soil and used Ohio farming methods. This section is now a complete desert and is the cause of most of the destruction in the Panhandle. Took 77 pictures. Proceeding to Lincoln, Neb. Arthur."

up momentum and dust as they traveled southward. Nothing built by nature or left by humans stopped them. When they hit the Oklahoma Panhandle, they sucked up dust and dirt and seed, forming huge black walls that roared across the landscape. Nothing—not wheat, not corn, not hope—nothing remained after they passed.

The Okies

Oklahomans could claim to have been hit by depression earlier and harder than the rest of America. That may be one reason why the state became identified with the worst of the Great Depression. The depression seared itself into the national consciousness in a series of indelible images: unemployed men selling apples on big-city street corners, striking workers battling company guards outside boarded-up factories, long lines of people waiting patiently to reach a soup kitchen. None of those images, however, had the power of those that kept repeating themselves in ever-more-depressing forms: uprooted "Okies," driven off the land, fleeing Oklahoma in their old jalopies.

Behind those images were historical truths. Oklahoma lost 60,000 people between the 1930 and 1940 censuses, and most of that loss came after 1937. Drought and dust drove some out, particularly in the extreme western counties. But many more were victims of the collapse of cotton tenancy in the

This family was among the 300,000 people who fled Oklahoma and its neighboring states for California. Whatever their original homes, most were known as "Okies."

eastern regions. The sharecropping system could not survive five-cent cotton. The final blow, ironically, may have come from well-intended federal programs under the New Deal. Hoping to force commodity prices up by paying farmers to slash their production, the New Deal's Agricultural Adjustment Administration paid landowners to take acreage out of production. In areas of heavy tenancy, that meant that landlords pocketed the money, retired their land, and dismissed some of their tenants. Many then invested their savings in new tractors and other equipment that allowed them to get rid of most of their tenants altogether.

Atop these special miseries, Oklahomans also suffered calamities with the rest of the nation. After the stock-market collapse of 1929 banks across the nation collapsed, and they did so in Oklahoma too. Factories everywhere cut back production and dismissed employees, and Oklahoma was part of that. When the national electorate ended years of Republican supremacy in favor of the Democrats' promise of a "New Deal," Oklahomans joined in. In fact, through the 1930s and beyond, the state's Republican party all but disappeared. After decades of bitter partisan strife, Oklahoma became a one-party state. And that one party was the Democratic party.

The effective end of partisan competition did not, however, mean the end of contentiousness. On the contrary, Oklahoma's depression-era Democrats turned on each other with a passion every bit as deadly as the antagonism they had earlier directed toward the Republicans and the Socialists.

JOHN STEINBECK AND *THE GRAPES OF WRATH*

In 1936 a new picture magazine contacted a young novelist living in Salinas, California. *Life* wanted John Steinbeck to write a feature article on a subject that was just beginning to break into public notice, the plight of the migrants, Okies and others, who were flooding into California from the drought-stricken Southern Plains. Steinbeck refused, saying that he did not want to "cash in" on those people and their miseries.

His interest nonetheless aroused, Steinbeck began to visit the migrant camps around Salinas and Bakersfield in the San Joaquin valley. A short series of articles followed—their title was "Their Blood Is Strong"— in the *San Francisco News*. Realizing that the subject was too big for journalism, Steinbeck then began a novel that drew on both his observations and his remarkable literary gifts. The result, in 1939, was one of the most powerful and significant novels ever written by an American.

The Grapes of Wrath was the story of the fictitious Joad family, who were forced out of their homes in Sallisaw, Oklahoma, and followed Route 66 to the fields of California. More than that it was the story of the entire Okie phenomenon, placed in a powerful context of human dignity when it was measured and steeled by appalling conditions. Released the next year as an epic motion picture, *The Grapes of Wrath*, more than anything else, reflected and shaped America's understanding of what had happened to Oklahoma's people at home, on the road, and in California.

Any decent reading of the book, even now, affirms the heroic character of the entire Joad clan, particularly the book's central characters, Tom Joad and his mother. What is surprising, however, is how many Oklahomans reacted to it at the time. Fearful that the book would reflect negatively upon the state, many Oklahomans—particularly those who saw themselves as the state's leaders—rushed to condemn it. Typical was this attack in the Oklahoma City *Times*:

> It pictures Oklahoma with complete and absurd untruthfulness. . . . Goldfish-swallowing critics who know nothing about the region or people pictured in a novel accept at face value even the most inaccurate depiction, by way of regional fiction. No, the writer of these lines has not read the book. This editorial is based upon hearsay, and that makes it even, for that is how Steinbeck knows Oklahoma.

The vigor of that particular attack was matched by politicians, Chamber of Commerce executives, and the like—many of whom had not read the book either.

Ordinary Oklahomans read the book, and many loved it. Some, in fact, lived it. In retrospect, their reading may have been more insightful than the editorialists'. One reader always remembered what happened after a friend loaned her a well-thumbed copy: "When I read *The Grapes of Wrath*, that was like reliving my whole life. I was never so proud of poor people before as I was after I read this book."

Depression Democrats

There were reasons for that. The most important reason was that Oklahoma was really a one-party state. Tensions and disputes that formerly had divided voters along party lines did not disappear. They only moved under the Democratic tent, where they grew no less tempestuous. The result was a period of chaotic politics. The clash of titanic personalities provided what little order there was, although the conflicts were often masked by real or pretended political principles.

"Alfalfa Bill"

Easily the most forceful political personality was that of the man whom Oklahomans sent to the Governor's Mansion in 1930. William Henry David Murray was his name, but everyone called him Alfalfa Bill. For much of the decade Oklahomans divided over his programs, his policies, and (as he might say) his self.

At the time when he was elected as the state's eighth governor, Murray was sixty-six years old with his best political years seemingly well behind him. A major figure at the Sequoyah convention, he had been president of the Oklahoma constitutional convention, where he had left his handprint on many of the constitution's more novel provisions. With statehood he served as Speaker of the First Legislature and later as a member of Congress. He lost his congressional seat in 1916, and an intended comeback in the 1918 gubernatorial race failed miserably. Disappointed with politics, Murray collected a band of would-be pioneers and headed for Bolivia, where he spent most of the 1920s vainly trying to establish a cotton-growing colony. Nearly penniless, he returned to his home in Tishomingo, borrowed twenty-nine dollars from the local bank, and set out to win the governorship.

The campaign provided an omen for his governorship. Murray was a man of strong and unconcealed opinions, some of them outrageous—for example, his proposal to cut costs by pardoning any Oklahoma convict who promised to leave the state. More important than any of his ideas, however, was his personality. Many voters abhorred his crudities, which were often the products of shrewd calculation. More people, however, found it easy to identify with the aging pioneer who had staked everything on the new state's promise only to end up broke. Little wonder that they elected him their governor with a then-record majority.

As governor Murray continued to spew forth opinions and even to make some of them into public policy. He kept his campaign promise to pardon convicts—thereby exporting 2,214 criminals to Oklahoma's less-than-grateful neighbors. Invoking a gubernatorial power rarely used before, Murray also sent a steady rain of executive declarations of martial law on the state. In a famous instance, he commanded the state militia to close bridges across the Red River in a dispute with Texas. Under another

Governor Murray assumes a suitably dramatic pose as he presumably defends Oklahomans from Texas.

declaration, guardsmen shut down every producing oil well in Oklahoma—all 3,106 of them—as the governor ordered an end to the ruinous competition and overproduction. Under the circumstances he might as well have commanded the tide to rise. Prices did eventually improve but less because of Murray's actions than despite them.

Such actions attracted considerable attention (not all of it favorable), but did little to loosen the depression's grip on the state. In 1932, at the midpoint of Murray's term, Oklahomans added their electoral votes to the large majority that sent Franklin Roosevelt to the White House and his New Deal to America. The headstrong Murray would have none of it. Claiming to be the stout champion of the traditional Democratic faith in a weak central government, Murray resisted every New Deal program that came his way. Not surprisingly, that resistance owed less to a pretended philosophy than it did to personality. Fancying himself presidential timber, Murray had campaigned for the Democratic presidential nomination in 1932. The patrician Roosevelt, who was then New York's governor, easily had crushed the Oklahoman's ambitions, pausing only to dismiss the eccentric Murray as something of a hayseed, in fact, as being "as crazy as a bedbug." No one knows the reaction of bedbugs to this slander, but Alfalfa Bill detested Roosevelt and everything for which he stood for the rest of his life. In the resulting clash between their Democratic governor and their Democratic president, Oklahoma's poor suffered most.

Marland's "Little New Deal"

That probably explains why Oklahomans replaced Murray with a governor pledged to do and be something else entirely. E. W. Marland was everything that Murray was not—well educated, urbane, a one-time captain of industry. In 1932 he had entered politics and won the Eighth Congressional District seat, the first Democrat ever to do so. A loyal follower of Roosevelt in Washington, Marland intended to emulate him in Oklahoma City. "Bring the New Deal to Oklahoma" was his single campaign slogan and campaign promise.

No sooner was Marland inaugurated than he attempted to do just that. Drawing on a small corps of intellectuals and other experts, Marland laid before the Fifteenth Legislature a comprehensive "little New Deal" for Oklahoma. The Democratic-dominated legislature wasted no time in laying it to rest. Some members balked at the centralization of power that it would entail. Others resisted creation of the new bureaucratic agencies necessary to administer the ambitious program. Nearly all pointed to the terrific costs involved—Marland put his program's price tag at $500 million—at a time when the state was already nearing bankruptcy. Marland served his four years in the Governor's Mansion as a broken man. When his term ended, he returned to Ponca City. Just before his death in 1940, E. W. Marland sold his one remaining asset. His $2.5 million mansion, which he had lived in only briefly, went to a religious order for $66,000. Meanwhile, the state remained as far removed from the New Deal as ever.

Whatever the opinions of the state's political leaders, most Oklahomans welcomed the new measures coming out of Washington. Under the Works

Progress Administration, for example, thousands of unemployed Sooners got work building public projects, including many local post offices and armories that still stand. Young people earned money working in the forests of southeastern Oklahoma for the Civilian Conservation Corps. Tens of thousands more welcomed both the immediate relief measures and the future promise of a more-secure old age under the Social Security Act.

Red and Reaction

Leon C. ("Red") Phillips, the conservative Democrat elected governor in 1938, was not among those who applauded the New Deal initiatives. Although such programs were too popular for him to condemn them publicly, Phillips could and did condemn most everything else that came out of Washington during his term. Twice, in fact, he declared martial law and called out the national guard to prevent the federal government's construction of dams and water projects, once to block the building of Lake Texoma and later to stop the construction of Grand Lake. The headstrong governor retreated in those instances only when the United States Supreme Court forced him to back down.

Phillips was more successful at preventing in Oklahoma what he regarded as one of the New Deal's major sins—the government's going into debt by appropriating more in spending than it collected in taxes. In 1939, Phillips pushed through an amendment—the so-called balanced-budget amendment—which changed the state constitution to forbid the government from appropriating funds in excess of its tax collections. The provision has been amended itself several times, but it remains in the state constitution, a legacy of Governor Phillips and his war against government spending, whether in Washington or in Oklahoma City.

Phillips's successor as governor left far more substantial monuments. Robert S. Kerr was his name, and he became a legendary figure in Sooner politics.

Bob Kerr and *Oklahoma!*

Befitting a political legend, Kerr was born in a log cabin (now restored) outside of Ada. His family was hardworking and devout, and he inherited those qualities. With a twelfth-grade education (all that was necessary at the time), young Kerr taught at a tiny country school in Beebe, using his small salary to pay for a two-year correspondence degree that he earned from East Central State College. At nineteen he borrowed $350 and enrolled in the law school at the University of Oklahoma. The money ran out after a year, and so did Kerr's formal education. After service in World War I, he returned to Ada, married, opened a small grocery, and intended to settle in. In a few years, however, he lost everything. Twin daughters died at birth. Later, his wife and son both died in childbirth. The final blow was a fire that destroyed his business and left him $10,000 in debt.

Kerr started over. Having passed the bar examination in 1922, he opened a legal office in Ada, married Grayce Breene (the daughter of a wealthy Tulsa oilman), and went into the oil business himself. As his oil interests bloomed, Kerr moved to Oklahoma City. With Dean McGee (an expert geologist whom he hired away from Phillips Petroleum), Kerr launched the series of companies that eventually became the industrial giant Kerr-McGee.

In the 1930s, Kerr moved into politics with the same zeal. Appointed to a series of state positions and Democratic party offices, by 1940 he was Oklahoma's representative on the Democratic National Committee. Two years later he won the governorship of Oklahoma, thereby fulfilling the three ambitions that he had announced to his father many years before. He had a family, he had a million, and he had the governor's office.

Kerr brought to that office insight and found there opportunity. The insight was that Oklahoma politicians had wasted too much energy battling each other and dueling with the federal government. Political embarrassment, disgrace, and humiliation had only tarnished the reputation of a state already shamed by the Great Depression. The time had come to make peace, both among Oklahoma Democrats and with Washington. The opportunity presented to Kerr was that he happened to serve as governor during the Second World War. From a feeble base, America's military spending multiplied several times over after the Japanese at-

THE WAR AT HOME: TINKER FIELD AND MIDWEST CITY

When the Founding Fathers gave authority over military spending to the Congress, even they could not have anticipated the significance of that decision. The eighteenth-century armies of a few thousand souls in scattered outposts gave way in the twentieth century to massive military forces patrolling the lands, seas, and skies of the entire globe. Congress appropriated hundreds of billions of dollars to maintain those forces, and those dollars also sustained entire industries and communities.

In the 1940s this was nowhere more apparent than on the flatland east of Oklahoma City. Still reeling from the twin blows of the Great Depression and the Dust Bowl, Oklahoma's economy sorely needed vast infusions of capital. Its displaced farm and oil-field workers—at least, those who had stayed in the state—needed jobs. The Second World War brought Oklahoma capital and brought thousands of Sooners those jobs because the Second World War brought Tinker Field.

Named for Major General Clarence L. Tinker, a native of Pawhuska and a member of the Osage Nation, Tinker Air Force Base began as one of three regional air depots authorized by the House Appropriations Committee early in 1941 during the battle of Britain. Oklahoma Senators Elmer Thomas and Josh Lee and Oklahoma City's Representative Mike Monroney aggressively pressured both Congress and the Army Air Corps to locate the midwestern depot near Oklahoma City. Their work bore fruit on July 30, 1941, when construction began. The Japanese attack on Pearl Harbor only accelerated and magnified the project, as the Douglas Aircraft Company built a major plant on immediately adjoining land.

Tinker's civilian workforce grew to nearly 15,000 wartime workers, most of whom overhauled B-17s and B-29s. Another 23,000 Sooners labored at the Douglas plant, producing as many as thirteen C-47s per day. Some of those workers commuted 200 miles a day.

Many more, however, found new homes right across the street. After poring over specifications and maps, W. P. ("Bill") Atkinson had become convinced that the new facility could be built only due east of Oklahoma City. Atkinson greeted official designation of the site with his own announcement that he would build a model community—Midwest City—to house its workers.

Peace came to America in 1945. But Tinker Field (which absorbed the Douglas plant) and Midwest City remained. Through the long years of the Cold War that followed, both prospered as part of the permanent transformation of the state's economy.

tack on Pearl Harbor brought the nation into war. Fighting in both hemispheres, the federal government was spending billions of dollars raising troops, training them for combat, and equipping them with weapons. Governor Kerr was determined to get as many of those dollars as possible for Oklahoma.

He succeeded. Burying old disputes, Kerr carefully cultivated the White House, the Capitol, and the new military headquarters at the Pentagon. The consequence was a flood of federal dollars which finally washed away the worst stains of the Great Depression. Soon twenty-eight army installations,

OKLAHOMA'S FIGHTING FORTY-FIFTH

Nearly 200,000 Oklahomans volunteered for military service in World War II, and another 300,000 were drafted into uniform. Those most closely related to the state and its history were the army infantry soldiers of the Forty-fifth Division.

The Forty-fifth's history is longer than the state's. Originally organized as a militia by the first territorial legislature in 1890, the Oklahomans (including troops from Indian Territory) combined with the militia of New Mexico and Arizona territories to form the famed Rough Riders of Colonel Theodore Roosevelt during the Spanish-American War. During World War I, the Oklahoma division joined with the Texas National Guard and served gallantly in the European

trenches. A post–World War I reorganization in 1923 led to the new Forty-fifth Division, based in Oklahoma City and drawing on the state national guards of Oklahoma, Colorado, Arizona, and New Mexico. By World War II its insignia had been fixed: a four-sided diamond (each side representing one of the four states) with a golden Thunderbird stitched on a red background.

In peacetime most of the Forty-fifth's members were store clerks, teachers, farmers, cowboys, and oil-field hands—just about everything and anything. Ever ready at time of crisis (or, during Governor Murray's reign, at a gubernatorial whim), the guardsmen maintained their civilian lives, trained in summers, and hoped that war would never

come. When it did in 1941, the Thunderbirds were among the first to go.

By 1943 they had fought in North Africa, Sicily, and Anzio. At the war's end in June 1945 they were in Munich. In between, they had fought 551 days, crowning their glory by liberating the prisoners held at the Nazi concentration camp at Dachau.

Along the way one soldier, Bill Mauldin, became known to every American soldier as the cartoonist who drew the beloved Willie and Joe characters for *Stars and Stripes*, the serviceman's newspaper. Eight soldiers earned their nation's highest honor, the Congressional Medal of Honor. Others were among the 6,500 Oklahomans slain and 11,000 wounded in World War II.

at Fort Sill and elsewhere, were vastly expanded and welcomed tens of thousands of new recruits. Thirteen naval bases—the largest on the prairies at Norman—sprang up hundreds of miles from the nearest ocean. Huge air bases consumed miles and miles of poor farmland and put thousands and thousands of Sooners in well-paying jobs. British and Canadian pilots trained at Miami and Ponca City. The government even built prisoner-of-war camps to house enemy prisoners (Germans for the most part), who found themselves transported from North Africa and Europe to sit out the war in Tonkawa, Chickasha, Alva, Tipton, or Okmulgee. Every one of these brought money to the state, jobs to its citizens, and at long last, an end to Oklahoma's Great Depression.

The Oklahoma that came out of that depression

and the world war to welcome peace in 1945 had been remade by both experiences—not to mention by all of the other events that had befallen it since 1907. At the time, *Oklahoma!* was still enjoying a remarkable run on Broadway. In fact, Governor Kerr was one of its proudest fans, having seen the musical more than a dozen times. But as Kerr and others left the theater humming "Brand New State . . . ," those were only words to introduce the title song of the musical. Oklahoma was no longer new. Two world wars, decades of booms and busts—all of this and more had left Oklahoma much older. It remained to be seen if it was any wiser.

See History for Yourself

Among the physical legacies of the Great Depression are the public buildings built under the federal government's Works Progress Administration (WPA). One of the New Deal's many efforts to reverse the economy's downward spiral, the WPA hired unemployed workers to build needed public works. In Oklahoma fifty-six armories were built by WPA workers. Thirty-four are still used for that purpose, and there is quite possibly one in your community. Other major WPA projects include the county courthouse at Wagoner, the school at Westville, and Tucker Tower at Lake Murray.

One WPA program hired unemployed artists to decorate public buildings. In that way thirty-one Oklahoma post offices acquired original art as murals for their walls. Many survive, including those at Cordell, Marietta, Nowata, Bartlesville, and Weatherford. The mural that adorned Edmond's old post office was removed when that building was destroyed, and it was restored in the new city building. Among the most interesting of the surviving post-office murals are those in the post office at Anadarko. These were done by three of the artists already famous as the so-called Kiowa Five, whom you will soon meet.

The state's rural areas often have facilities built by another New Deal program, the Civilian Conservation Corps. Among them are Beavers Bend State Park, the Holy City Easter Pageant grounds in the Wichita Mountains, and the rock walls that line Horse Thief Canyon along the Talimena Drive. Connecting Talihina, Oklahoma, to Mena, Arkansas, along the crest of the Winding Stair Mountains, the Talimena Drive is itself one of our state's most beautiful assets. It should be seen, particularly in the fall, when the change of seasons adds charm to geography's splendors.

Suggestions for Further Reading

Reference
Bonnifield, Paul. *The Dust Bowl: Men, Dirt, and Depression.* Albuquerque: University of New Mexico Press, 1979.

Bryant, Keith L. *Alfalfa Bill Murray.* Norman: University of Oklahoma Press, 1968.

Fossey, W. Richard. "Talking Dust Bowl Blues: A Study of Oklahoma's Cultural Identity during the Great Depression." *Chronicles of Oklahoma* 55 (1977): 12–33.

Gregory, James N. *American Exodus: The Dust Bowl Migration and Okie Culture in California.* New York: Oxford University Press, 1989.

Logsdon, Guy. "The Dust Bowl and the Migrant." *American Scene* 12(1971).

Morgan, Anne Hodges. *Robert S. Kerr: The Senate Years.* Norman: University of Oklahoma Press, 1977.

Stein, Walter J. *California and the Dust Bowl Migration.* Westport, Conn.: Greenwood Press, 1973.

Worster, Donald. *Dust Bowl: The Southern Plains in the 1930s.* New York: Oxford, 1979.

Related Reading
Guthrie, Woody. *Bound for Glory.* New York: E. P. Dutton, 1943.

Hendrickson, Kenneth D., Jr. *Hard Times in Oklahoma: The Depression Years.* Oklahoma City: Oklahoma Historical Society, 1983.

Stanley, Jerry. *Children of the Dust Bowl: The True Story of the Weedpatch Camp.* New York: Crown Publishers, 1992.

Chapter 23: **The People of Oklahoma**

If you have learned nothing else about history by now, there are two things that ought to have become obvious. First, history—whether it is the history of a nation, a state, or another entity—is always about the same thing: it is about people, who they are, what they do, and why they do it. Second, history is an interwoven tapestry: threads prominent at one point may recede for a while but often reappear later. The constant coming and going of each thread as it crosses and weaves among others is what makes history a seamless web. In history, one person or event is always related to others.

The life that each of us lives today is somehow related to the lifes of those who have gone before us. That is why history is important: because others' lives can be every bit as important to us as our own, history is by definition interesting to us.

This chapter illustrates both of those principles. It considers a group of Oklahomans (or, in one case, a person who considered himself an Oklahoman) and shows what each did in Oklahoma's early history that affected others in the state's later history. Among the "others" is someone whose life was closely related to that of an earlier individual. Thus the accounts were written in pairs. But make no mistake about it: the "others" include all of us too.

The "Kiowa Five"

When Plains Indian culture was at its zenith, one symbol of its power was the remarkable art that

By the time this photograph was taken Louise Bou-ge-tah Smokey had left the Kiowa Five. James Auchiah took her place in the group of artists. Shown here are (*left to right*) Monroe Tsatoke, Jack Hokeah, Stephen Mopope, University of Oklahoma Professor Oscar Jacobson, Spencer Asah, and Auchiah.

emerged from nearly every tribe. On the Southern Plains the Kiowas were noted especially for their calendars. Known as winter counts, these were elaborate series of pictographs composed and executed collectively to record the tribe's history through the seasons and the years. Individuals also displayed on hides their personal history and notable exploits with elaborate and colorful images. So striking was the tribe's use of art, that some people said that every Kiowa was a natural-born artist.

After the American army defeated the Indian warriors and destroyed their nomadic cultures, their art assumed a different role. In 1875 tribal elders reluctantly designated more than seventy of their young men for punishment for the tribes' raids against whites. Federal authorities transported these Kiowas and others far from their homes to a prison in Fort Marion at Saint Augustine, Florida, where they remained until 1878. Captain Richard H. Pratt (who later founded Pennsylvania's Carlisle Indian School) headed the prison. He recognized at once that his pathetic prisoners were energetic painters. Providing them paper (lined army ledger books), pencils, and paints, Captain Pratt suggested that they create art for sale to the white tourists who often stopped by to see the "wild Indians." More than 600 drawings and paintings resulted. Known as ledger art, these were not like the tribal displays of the past; instead, they were the private expressions, often painfully autobiographical, of individual Indians. Many even signed their paintings with their private mark. When they returned to Oklahoma, their people called them by a word previously unknown in most Indian tongues, "artists."

Few white people recognized the significance of the work created by these Indians and those inspired by them. Determined to root out all traces of Indian identity, the superintendent of Anadarko's Indian school forbade it when he found some young Kiowa children devotedly sketching and painting. He protested that "they should have been trying to become white men rather than wasting a lot of time with drawing." One of the few who thought otherwise was Susie Ryan Peters.

A native of Tennessee, Mrs. Peters had come to Oklahoma Territory in a covered wagon. In 1916 she went to work as a field matron for the Kiowa agency in Anadarko. Uninterested in teaching young girls to clean house, she was convinced that her charges—both girls and boys—included several natural artists. In 1918 she arranged for an art instructor from Chickasha to come to Anadarko and teach them, paying the artist's salary herself. Although those informal classes lasted only three or four months, Susie Peters persuaded Saint Patrick's Mission School in Anadarko to accept the most promising of the students. At the school, Sister Olivia and Father Al enthusiastically added to the students' preparation.

The budding Kiowa artists were neither average students nor stereotypical "savages." Several were the sons and grandsons of famous war chiefs and holy men, and most came from important Indian families. All were close to the leaders of their people, for whom ancient traditions remained vivid memories. Many continued themselves to participate in rituals that dated from long before the whites' arrival.

In 1923, Susie Peters and Father Al asked the University of Oklahoma to admit some of the Kiowa artists, but none had the necessary scholastic background or the money for tuition. Although they never enrolled as students, Oscar B. Jacobson, head of the university's School of Art, invited them to live in Norman, where they could paint in the university's studios under his supervision. In 1927 five young Indians arrived to great excitement. Collectively they were to achieve fame as the "Kiowa Five": Monroe Tsatoke, Stephen Mopope, Spencer Asah,

Jack Hokeah, and Louise Bou-ge-tah Smokey, who later was replaced by James Auchiah.

They were almost instant celebrities. Awed by their quickly developing gifts, Jacobson mounted a university exhibit of their work within weeks. In November 1927 they gained national recognition when the American Federation of Arts exhibited their paintings at its national convention in Denver. Soon the world learned of the Kiowa Five through their exhibition at the First International Art Exposition in Prague, Czechoslovakia. In 1929 a prestigious French publisher issued a beautiful folio of some of their more-important works.

Imaginatively combining color and detail in a highly stylized format, the Kiowa artists launched an entire school of instantly recognizable Indian art. In some measure they may even have influenced the U.S. government's policy toward Indians. The enthusiasm for rediscovered Indian traditions, sparked in part by the Kiowas' brilliant work, found one expression in the Indian Reorganization Act of 1934. One of the New Deal's reforms, this was the law by which Washington finally abandoned its determination to assimilate Indians into white society through the calculated destruction of their separate cultures.

In Oklahoma the Kiowa Five continued their work through the 1930s. In particular, several found employment when the New Deal hired unemployed artists under the Works Progress Administration. Later they went their own ways, some continuing as painters while others took up more pedestrian employment to support themselves and their families. Still, even today, a few of Oklahoma's older public buildings display the murals and other projects that they created. Their legacy, however, is much, much more than that.

Jerome Tiger

Eufaula, Oklahoma, takes its name from an appropriate source: an Alabama Creek town and a Creek word which means "they split up here and went to other places." At the end of a dirt road that runs three miles west of Oklahoma's Eufaula stands the West Eufaula Baptist Church. Like all Creek baptist churches, it faces east. For more than 150 years the

church has provided not only a center of Christian worship but a site for Indian stickball games, ribbon dances, and other traditional Creek activities. In a weather-beaten four-room house on the church ground, one of Oklahoma's—and America's—most-acclaimed twentieth-century artists spent the formative first ten years of his life.

Jerome Tiger's grandfather, Lewis Coleman, was the church's pastor. Like the Reverend Coleman and his wife, Hettie, Jerome Tiger's parents, Lucinda Coleman Tiger and John Tiger, were bilingual. English was used with whites, but all were more comfortable with the Creek that they spoke at home and in church. Because other Indian families moved in and out of the other houses on the grounds, young Jerome lived not only amid an extended family but in something approaching a traditional Creek communal village. Daily he was surrounded by the living traditions of his fellow Indians.

But these were modern times, and Lucinda and John Tiger left Eufaula for Muskogee. Lucinda took a "white" job, pressing clothes at Teel's laundry. John did too, beginning to drive fifty miles to Tulsa and his job at the Douglas Aircraft plant. For the first time Jerome and his brothers attended predominately white schools—Edison Elementary, Alice Robertson Junior High School, and Muskogee Central High.

School was not particularly hard for Jerome Tiger, but neither was it much fun. He spent most of his spare time with Indians his age and other lower-income boys whom other students regarded as hoods. His chief interests were an odd combination of violence and sensitivity—boxing and art. Bored with school, he quit after his junior year, served a two-year hitch in the United States Navy, and returned to Muskogee. He hoped to enroll in Bacone College.

The little college had begun as a Baptist missionary school for Indians. Although many (even in Oklahoma) had never heard of it, it had been a national treasure for years because of its art department begun by Acee Blue Eagle. Blue Eagle, also a Creek, had studied art at the University of Oklahoma, beginning there just after the Kiowa Five had left. While Blue Eagle headed Bacone's art department from 1935 to 1938, he had established national reputations for both himself and the college. Subsequently, Woody Crumbo, of Creek and Potawatomi ancestry, took Blue Eagle's place and, like him, further developed the Indian style and enhanced the college's fame in art circles. He too had studied under Oscar Jacobson (and Susie Ryan Peters). When Jerome Tiger returned to Muskogee, Dick West, a Cheyenne, headed the legendary Bacone art department. Unfortunately for Jerome Tiger, he could not be admitted to the college, since he lacked a high-school diploma. His older brother, Johnny, however, was a student there, and through him, Jerome learned the conventions and styles of Indian art.

No one had to give Jerome Tiger his talent. From his boyhood onward, he had spent hours drawing scenes inspired by events around him and from his imagination as it had been shaped by his elders' stories and tales. Naturally right-handed, he also could draw amazingly well with his left hand. In fact, he once did four drawings simultaneously—one with each hand and one with each foot!

Returning to his grandparents home in Eufaula, Jerome Tiger married, had the first of two children, and began to work seriously at his art. Soon his paintings came to the attention of Nettie Wheeler, owner of the Thunderbird Shop. Located north of Muskogee on Highway 69, the little shop sold tourist trinkets and doodads. Stashed amid the prevailing disorder were priceless original works of art, for Nettie Wheeler was an expert on and patron of Indian artists. Recognizing Jerome Tiger's genius, she began to promote his paintings and entered two of them in competitions at Sante Fe and Tulsa, where both won prizes. She also encouraged Tiger to take advantage of a new program of vocational training offered by the Bureau of Indian Affairs. Jerome, his wife, and his daughter moved to Cleveland, where he studied at the famous Cooper School of Art.

Cold and crowded, Cleveland was utterly unlike any place where Jerome Tiger ever had lived. Other than the Major League baseball team, there were few Indians in Cleveland, and most of them were Navajos, with whom Tiger regularly fought. He did like the Cooper School, however, even accepting for the first time the discipline required in formal art training. He might have stayed at the school if he had not happened to wander by a professor's office one day. Standing unseen in the hallway, he overheard one teacher tell another that, although the young Oklahoman certainly had talent, "by the time we get through with him, he'll be just another Indian that bit the dust."

Jerome Tiger had other plans for his life. He left Cleveland and the Cooper School behind, returned to Muskogee, and polished and perfected his craft. In little time he developed a style so personal that his works were instantly recognizable. Although based on the conventions and themes pioneered by the Kiowa Five and furthered by others, his works were unlike anything ever seen in Indian art before. Clean and uncluttered, their fine lines and exquisite colors seemed to flow together to suggest movement and emotions as much as they did objects and people. Amazed to learn that he was largely self-taught, critics pronounced him a "painter's painter." His works, whether based on traditional Creek ways or illustrating the humor and the poignancy of contemporary Indian life, completely fulfilled the mandate that his grandfather had given him. "Put on paper what the Creek has in his heart," old Coleman Lewis had told him. Jerome Tiger did that better than anyone else ever had.

Tiger created an amazing number of paintings. By the hundreds they poured from his home in Muskogee. Working primarily in a corner of his bedroom, he painted whenever and as long as the inspiration moved him, sometimes working all night and into the next. Some he gave away to friends and family. Others he sold, often for as little as thirty or forty dollars. For many purchasers, his work provided their introduction to Indian art, or, for that matter, original art of any kind. Outside his immediate surroundings, Tiger's paintings regularly won national prizes and took his fame across America. They did not, however, take him. He mailed his paintings to competitions around the country, but Jerome Tiger never traveled outside of Oklahoma again.

The fame that came to him did not change Tiger. He kept up his boxing, one year winning the Oklahoma Golden Gloves championship as a middleweight. He continued to participate in Indian dances and consult with honored Creek holy men. Surrounded by his old friends (some of whom had no idea of his national stature), he played pool, drank beer, and played around with firearms. He was doing the last in the early morning hours of August 13, 1967. After a stomp dance in Eufaula, he piled into his brother's car with some other friends. Pulling into an all-night restaurant and service station, the group was ready to break up when a deafening explosion shook the car. Jerome Tiger's .22 pistol had discharged accidently, sending a bullet into his brain.

When he was buried three days later, the funeral brought television crews, nationally famous artists and critics, and scores of simple mourners to the West Eufaula Baptist Church. That is where it all had begun not much earlier. Jerome Tiger was twenty-six years old.

Woody Guthrie

Fate decreed that his life would be a tragedy, but Woody Guthrie made it a joyful song. His tragic fate was inherited, but not from his father. Charley Guthrie was not much different from many Oklahomans. Born in Texas, Charley had come to eastern Oklahoma back when it was still Indian Territory, finally settling in Okemah. While pursuing a brief political career (as a Democrat, of course), Charley dabbled in real estate, buying, selling, and swapping land. When oil was found in the vicinity, Charley plunged deeper, rose higher, and fell flatter than most. He was dead broke.

But the tragedy that his eldest son inherited came from his mother, and it was worse than mere poverty. Nora Guthrie was a strange woman, sometimes given to uncontrolled, jerky motions of her body and odd facial contortions. No one knew the cause: Huntington's chorea, a disease as rare as it is hideous. Its victims have it from the moment of their conception, but it manifests itself only when they are in early middle age. Gradually and inexorably, slight nervous twitches and tremors become convulsions that lead to insanity and the wasting away of their bodies. Death comes after the brain literally rots. By the time they know they have the disease victims of Huntington's chorea usually have borne children, and each of those children has exactly a fifty-fifty chance of inheriting the disease. Woody Guthrie was born with Huntington's chorea.

No one—not even Woody himself—suspected that. What they knew was that he had something of his mother's gift for music. From her he learned old ballads like "Barbara Allen" and mournful new ones like "A Picture from Life's Other Side," by Hank Williams, Sr. He added to his musical heritage from every source—bAlack music and Indian, coal miners' tunes, and prisoners' laments. After his mother's death at the state asylum in Norman, he took off for the Texas Panhandle, married the first of three wives, and joined a cowboy band. In the mid-1930s he left West Texas for California. He was one of thousands of refugees from the region's Dust Bowl, and he became the balladeer and chronicler of them all.

In California, Woody teamed up first with his cousin Jack Guthrie, who is best remembered for his recording of one of Woody's early songs, "Oklahoma Hills." Soon, Woody had his own show on Los Angeles radio station KFVD. With his new partner, Maxine ("Lefty Lou") Crissman, he sang old songs and constantly made up new ones. Many in his audience were migrants. Okies and others daily crowded around their hissing radio sets to hear Woody's funny stories and latest songs about dust and dirt and hard travelin'.

In no time he was off to the East Coast, where he became an instant celebrity. Sophisticated New Yorkers had heard about Okies, and many had read John Steinbeck's *The Grapes of Wrath*. But here was the real thing. Woody's unmistakable Oklahoma twang rang out everywhere from concert halls to union halls. In Washington, Allen Lomax heard him. Lomax and his father, John, had spent years traveling America's back roads to collect authentic folk songs in prisons, fields, and shipyards. Woody Guthrie knew almost all of them; even better, he could make up new ones that were at least as good and usually better than any the Lomaxes had discovered.

Convinced that he had discovered a "Shakespeare in overalls," Allen Lomax brought Woody to the Library of Congress, stood him in front of a microphone, and recorded hours of playful banter, poignant autobiography, and twenty-eight songs both old and new. Lomax next took his discovery to Victor Records, which recorded and released a two-album, twelve-record set of Woody's original compositions.

The title of the collection was *Dust Bowl Ballads,* and it included songs still sung today: "I Ain't Got No Home," "Do Re Mi," "So Long, It's Been Good to Know You," and "Dust Can't Kill Me."

Inevitably, such songs carried a political message. That message was proudly radical and thoroughly defiant. In songs like "Jolly Banker," Woody heaped scorn on the rich, whom he felt were despoiling his kind of people. Seventeen verses of "The Ballad of Tom Joad" turned Steinbeck's *The Grapes of Wrath* into a rousing anthem for a poor boy who battles the big men in the name of starving kids. In Guthrie's song of the same name, "Pretty Boy" Floyd became a social bandit, a modern-day Robin Hood who stole from the rich and gave to the poor. "They Laid Jesus Christ in His Grave" made the Savior a rural radical who rallied working people until "the bankers and the preachers and the rich men and the soldiers" nailed Him to a tree.

Such sentiments hardly won Guthrie a following among those who thought of themselves as the better element of society. When not dismissing him as a hick, his critics claimed that he was a Communist, which he may have been. Certainly, he was brutally honest. Woody's friend Pete Seeger said of him that he was like Popeye—he was what he was and that was all that he was.

No one could deny that what he was included a phenomenal talent. He had a gift for lyrics, never better expressed than in a song that he first scratched on the back of a piece of paper on February 23, 1940:

This land is your land, this land is my land.
From California to the New York island,
From the Redwood Forest to the Gulf Stream waters
This land was made for you and me.

At the bottom he placed his credo: "All you can write is what you see."

"This Land Is Your Land" remains one of the best-known songs ever written by an American. In the 1960s it became popular enough that some suggested that it replace "The Star-Spangled Banner" as our national anthem. Everyone from the Mormon Tabernacle Choir to Country Joe and the Fish recorded it. As royalty checks poured in, Woody Guthrie, for the first time in his life, suddenly was rich.

He did not know it. In the 1940s he had first displayed the early signs of Huntington's chorea. In 1956 he had entered Greystone Hospital, a state institution in Morris Plains, New Jersey. He spent the next eleven years dying.

He left behind "This Land Is Your Land" and more than a thousand other songs for which he will always be remembered. That memory should include these words, for they capture the triumphant determination not only of his own life but also of his native state and its people at the worst times in their history:

> Ya know, we been held down, nailed down, beat down, shot down, shut down, set down,
> drove down, shoved down, and pushed down, talked down, chained down.
> We been blowed down and showed down, chopped down and hoed down. . . , left ragged, hungry, broke, Disgusted, busted, and not to be trusted.
>
> But in spite of all this and many other things, we ain't down yet!
> Naw, WE AIN'T DOWN YET!

Merle Haggard

One can imagine Jim and Flossie Haggard among the Okies who listened to Woody Guthrie on KFVD out of Los Angeles. Except for the poetic appropriateness of their last name, they were just about as typically Okie as you could get. Back in Checotah they were hard-working people whose luck all ran

out in 1935. Their barn burned down, and their crops failed in the drought. Like thousands of others, they packed up everything they had and headed for California. At the end of the long road their nine-year-old Chevrolet pulled into Bakersfield. Already overcrowded with so many Okies that some said that it was Oklahoma's third-largest city, Bakersfield is where their son was born two years later. They named him Merle.

Merle Haggard grew up part of a generally despised minority. Most Californians looked down on Okies, saying they were poor, ignorant, lazy, and stupid. Perhaps for that reason, or because his father died when he was only nine, Merle Haggard was a rebellious teenager. In and out of reform schools for stealing, fighting, and drinking, he hopped his first freight train when he was ten. At fourteen he hitchhiked to Texas, bought his first cowboy boots, and served his first time in an adult jail. Eventually sentenced to San Quentin, he "turned twenty-one in prison" (to quote a song of his), serving three years for burglary and an escape attempt.

When Merle Haggard left prison, he was a changed man. He may have noticed that California had been changing too. The military spending that had helped pull Oklahoma out of the depression had been even greater in California, and it continued through the 1950s and 1960s. Thousands of Okies had moved out of migrant-labor camps and into factory jobs and suburban neighborhoods because of defense work.

Still, they had not left their past completely behind them. One thing that still set them apart from others was their fondness for music, particularly that known as country music. Many had been musicians of a sort themselves (both Merle Haggard's father and grandfather had been fiddlers back in Oklahoma), and they kept their interest alive through both bad years and good. Some had done quite well with it. Oklahoma's Gene Autry became a California millionaire several times over as America's first "singing cowboy." Whenever Bob Wills left his base in Tulsa to perform out west, the crowds went wild when Bob cut down on "Osage Stomp," "Red River Valley," or "Take Me Back to Tulsa." Wills's Bakersfield crowds often included young Merle Haggard, who put on hold his errant ways to see the performer whom he regarded as a hero. After all, Haggard later recalled, "it was like he brought some of home with him" when Bob Wills played in California.

At the time Merle Haggard returned to Bakersfield, it was the center of a booming country-music industry. The city supported a variety of radio programs, a daily television show, and several small record companies. Most important, Bakersfield was the home base for a rising superstar. Buck Owens, himself a migrant from Texas by way of Arizona, was the hottest thing in country music at the time, and Merle Haggard jumped in right behind him. He made his first record in 1962, hit the country Top 40 charts in 1964, and signed with a major recording company in 1965. By 1969, Haggard not only had released thirteen albums and as many hits but also had married the former Mrs. Buck Owens—Bonnie Owens, who was herself an Okie migrant, from Blanchard.

Most of Merle Haggard's early songs derived from his past and his rowdy ways. "Sing Me Back Home," "I'm a Lonesome Fugitive," "Branded Man," and "Mama Tried" were all painfully autobiographical. All drew on a tradition that was old in country music: the laments of prisoners and convicts who see too late the error of their ways, a theme perfect for Merle. Soon, however, his music had an overtly political tone. "I Take a Lot of Pride in What I Am" was first, followed by "Working Man's Blues." Both were best-selling tributes to the American working class, and both expressed a significant new theme for country musicians.

By this time, out in California, back home in Oklahoma, all across America, country music was becoming identified less with region and more with class. Originally the music of the American South and Southwest, country music became the voice of a blue-collar America. One was as likely to hear it in a Polish working-class bar in Chicago as in an all-night truck stop in Chandler. Not least it appealed to conservatives who felt threatened by a bewildering variety of social changes. Many of these were represented by a stereotype that was part caricature: the long-haired, dope-smoking, flag-burning, campus-rioting college student. In 1969, Merle Haggard put all of the enmities into one unforgettable song.

Touring with his band, someone noticed a sign that showed the distance to Muskogee and laughingly said, "I bet they don't smoke much dope there." Though he had never even visited it, Haggard had heard of Muskogee all of his life. It was near Checotah and, as his comment about Bob Wills suggests, part of that Oklahoma that he considered home. Suddenly inspired, Merle Haggard hammered out a song in twenty minutes, "Okie from Muskogee."

That song—right from its first lines, "We don't smoke marijuana in Muskogee / We don't take our trips on L.S.D."—suddenly elevated Merle Haggard from mere singer to political troubador. People who had never taken country music seriously bought the record. President Richard Nixon wrote him a personal letter of tribute and invited him to perform "Okie from Muskogee" at the White House. When he followed it with "The Fighting Side of Me," critics pronounced Haggard to be the "poet laureate of rednecks."

For all of the political fuss over his songs, Merle Haggard was himself nonpolitical. Rarely did he vote, and he even turned down the president's request. Perhaps because he was surprised that what he had written in a few light-hearted moments was taken so seriously, he began to explore his people's heritage. In the same year that "Okie From Muskogee" drew so much attention, he released a little-noticed song, "Mama's Hungry Eyes." Its images were as powerful as anything ever photographed by the Farm Security Administration or written by John Steinbeck.

A canvas-covered cabin in a crowded labor camp
    stands out in this memory I revive.
'Cause my daddy raised a family there with two
    hard working hands
And tried to feed my mama's hungry eyes.

He dreamed of something better there,
    and my mama's faith was strong.
And us kids were just too young to realize that
    another class of people put us somewhere just below.
One more reason for my mama's hungry eyes.

"Mama's Hungry Eyes" was followed by an entire series of songs collectively referred to as the "Dust Bowl Ballads." "Cotton Fields," "Tulare Dust," "They're Tearing the Labor Camps Down," and "The Roots of My Raising" never approached "Okie from Muskogee" in sales or in public acclaim. What they did do may have been even more important.

Merle Haggard brought to a close the experience of the Okies who had survived the burdens that Woody Guthrie's original Dust Bowl ballads had described. The pride that they now felt in one of their own was pride that they had in themselves. They had endured, and they had triumphed. In poetic images of people who had overcome adversity through fierce determination, Merle Haggard completed the story of these Oklahomans in exile, people tough enough to affirm that they still were not down yet.

Edward Preston McCabe

On the second floor of the Oklahoma State Capitol are portraits of some of Oklahoma's most-prominent citizens. Sequoyah (the Cherokee who gave his people literacy) is there with Jim Thorpe (the great Indian athlete) and Robert S. Kerr (Oklahoma's governor and United States senator)—all in larger-than-life paintings. Speaker of the U.S. House of Representatives Carl Albert also is there along with Dr. Angie Debo, whom you will meet later in this chapter. Off on the side, away from all of these, hangs a portrait smaller than any of the others. This is the portrait of Edward P. McCabe. Even if segregated and diminished, McCabe is one of only a few black Oklahomans so honored. It is time that you got to know him better.

Although he was born in 1850, McCabe never experienced slavery. His parents were free African Americans who lived in Troy, New York, when he was born. His restless family relocated to Fall River, Massachusetts, and Newport, Rhode Island, during McCabe's boyhood. Apparently, he inherited some of that restlessness himself. While still a teenager, he set out on his own for Chicago, where he picked up some formal education in the law. April 1878 found him in Nicodemus, Kansas.

Nicodemus has an interesting history. Named for the disciple who cared for Jesus's crucified body, the community had been founded by Exodusters, that is, blacks who fled the South after Reconstruction's end. In relocating west to Kansas, they had intended to establish whole towns—cities, even—that would be all black. There African Americans would be free to build their own schools, publish their own newspapers, write and enforce their own laws, and live their own lives—all without the constant threat of racist persecution. Although Nicodemus was never very large (it still exists as a small all-black town), in the 1870s it was a magnet that drew blacks like Edward McCabe.

McCabe practiced law in Nicodemus and also entered politics. Like nearly all African Americans at that time, he was a Republican. The votes of his fellow blacks, and of many of the county's white Republicans too, won him the clerkship of Graham County. In 1882 he sought higher office still. Because Kansas's Republican's depended so heavily on the Exodusters and other black voters, the party placed him on its ticket as its nominee for state auditor in 1882. Defeating a white Democrat, McCabe won that election. Except for those who had served during the brief experiment of southern Reconstruction, he was the first black person to hold a statewide office. Performing well, he won reelection to a second two-year term in 1884.

By 1886, however, the racial climate of Kansas had worsened. As more and more African Americans had poured into Nicodemus and other black settlements, white Kansans began to fear a black takeover. Although blacks were still so few that those fears were absurd, they did have results. Many whites bolted the Republican party in favor of the Democrats, who were not known for any noticeable sympathy for blacks. One casualty was McCabe, who lost his job to a white Democrat. Losing again in 1886, McCabe knew that Kansas had no future for him and not much for his people.

Even as prospects in Kansas were fading, the land immediately to the south was booming. Nowhere was Boomer fever hotter than in Kansas, and whites were not the only ones to feel it. Blacks did too, and especially Edward Preston McCabe. With other black Kansans, McCabe began to push for the Oklahoma land's immediate settlement.

Many black Kansans joined the Oklahoma Immigration Association. Based in Topeka, its officers included Green I. Currin and W. L. Eagleson, and the association claimed to have agents in every major southern city, agents who expected to send 100,000 African Americans to Oklahoma as soon as it was settled. Eagleson expressed their reasons for emigrating when he addressed "the Colored People of the South," telling them: "There never was a more favorable time than now for you to secure good homes in a land where you will be free and have your rights respected. The soil is rich, the climate favorable, water abundant. Make a new start. Give yourselves and your children new chances in a new land."

When the Oklahoma lands finally were opened in 1889, a good number of black people did seize the opportunity to claim "new chances in a new land." Among them, of course, were McCabe, Currin, and

Eagleson. McCabe believed that his own opportunities were especially great. There was talk that President Benjamin Harrison would appoint him Oklahoma's first territorial governor.

McCabe had at least as much political experience as any other likely candidate. Both of Kansas's Republican United States senators endorsed him, as did influential party workers in Ohio, Indiana, Illinois, New York, Pennsylvania, and Massachusetts. His supporters, however, did not include Oklahoma's white homesteaders. As had been true in Kansas, whites feared a black takeover in the new territory, particularly if an African American became their governor.

Although Edward McCabe would never be Oklahoma's governor, as a black Oklahoman he was determined to help himself and his people, and one way to do that was with political power. Appointed auditor of Logan County, he happily saw his friend Green Currin elected to the territorial legislature from that county. With W. L. Eagleson he developed a strategy to further secure their race's position. All-black towns—maybe an entire series of them—could complete the vision that the Exodusters had carried to Kansas. The first and most important was Langston, which McCabe and Eagleson founded twelve miles northeast of the capital at Guthrie.

Within months of its founding, Langston had a population of 2,000, every one of them black and proud. To secure its future, McCabe, Currin, and others persuaded the territorial legislature to place one of Oklahoma's first four colleges there. That college (now Langston University) was devoted to the education of black Oklahomans. One of the nation's most-successful black-owned newspapers, Eagleson's *Langston City Herald* never tired of reminding its readers that the city of Langston, the college at Langston, and the people that supported both would prove to the world the worth of Oklahoma's black Americans.

In time that was true. But it was not in the way that McCabe had intended. As you have learned, Oklahoma's promise for blacks soured with statehood. For decades most black people were not even allowed to vote. The constitution and statutes thoroughly segregated blacks from whites in everything from schools to telephone booths. In one of his last public acts, Edward McCabe attempted to file a federal suit to strike down such laws as violations of the federal constitution. It got him nowhere. Just as he earlier had given up on Kansas, he eventually gave up on Oklahoma—and on America. In 1908, Edward Preston McCabe emigrated to British Columbia, Canada.

Langston—both the city and the college—remain. The dream that McCabe and others based in them remains too.

Roscoe Dunjee

The college at Langston opened for its first classes in 1898. The first catalog listed eighty-one enrolled students. One of them was Roscoe Dunjee, whom the catalog identified as from the little community of Choctaw.

Roscoe Dunjee had been born fifteen years earlier in a place significant in black history, Harper's Ferry, Virginia, where John Brown had tried to arm and arouse the slaves, only to be hanged as a traitor in 1859. Later Roscoe Dunjee's father, the Reverend John William Dunjee, a former slave who had escaped to Canada, worked for a small college there and published a newspaper. As a missionary for the American Baptist Missionary Society, one of the nation's largest black organizations, the Reverend Dunjee moved his family first to Minnesota, then in April 1892 to Oklahoma.

Roscoe Dunjee later recalled that his first Oklahoma home was a dugout, which was soon to be replaced by what the boy then regarded as a "palatial mansion." In retrospect he realized that the "mansion" was not much more than a shed, although it was unusual for its time and place. Not only was it permanent, but it was filled with books—some 1,500 of them—which his father had read and collected over forty years.

As the son of an educated man, Roscoe attended one of the territory's earliest elementary schools. It was Dunjee School, named for his own father. Afterwards he went to Langston, studying at the college and learning the printing trade while working for the *Langston City Herald*. After his father's death Roscoe Dunjee left Langston, settled in Oklahoma City, and eventually purchased a small printing press. On November 5, 1915, he printed and released the first issue of what became one of America's most significant newspapers, Oklahoma City's *Black Dispatch*.

The *Dispatch* first appeared at a critical time for black Oklahomans. Since 1910 few had been allowed to vote, and nowhere in Oklahoma were black people permitted to attend schools with whites or, for that matter, do much of anything else that might imply their equality. A violent race riot lay just over the horizon.

Under those circumstances even the earlier black achievements were being erased. The city of Langston still existed, but it was one of the few all-black towns that survived, and it barely held on with a population of a few hundred. Most of them would not have been there were it not for the college, and even the college was withering in the heat of ascendent racism. White politicians had just forced out the school's first president, Dr. Inman Page. The accepted explanation was that Dr. Page, a graduate of Brown University, took too seriously the task of preparing black students to compete with whites. It was much better, some thought, to keep them in their place by training the boys to be farmers and the girls to be housekeepers and laundresses. Out of that philosophy had grown a new reality: the school called itself a college, but of the more than four hundred students, only about a dozen were enrolled in college-level classes. Half of the rest were taking elementary classes, and the remainder were in secondary or vocational courses.

That was just one of the things that Roscoe Dunjee was determined to change. Every Thursday, when his weekly *Black Dispatch* hit the stands, more than 20,000 readers eagerly turned to the editorial column, and they were never disappointed. His fiery but literate editorials demanded change and demanded it now. One demand was that, if white Oklahomans insisted that black Oklahomans could go only to Langston for college, then they should let Langston *be* a college.

Although the legislature never gave Langston anything like its fair share of funding, it did start to give it more. Elementary and secondary classes disappeared. More college programs replaced them, and they were good ones. Even if the professors never earned as much as white professors in the state's other colleges, Langston was able to build a nationally known music department. Over in the English department, Professor Melvin B. Tolson taught literature. When not teaching, he wrote poetry and was recognized as one of America's greatest living poets. In such ways Langston came to symbolize not the inferior facilities to which Oklahoma assigned its black citizens but a proud example of what those black Oklahomans could do with them.

Roscoe Dunjee was certainly a proud man. Although the law said that he could not sit in the front of buses, he did. Neither could he lawfully ride beside whites on railroad cars, but he did. When Governor "Alfalfa Bill" Murray decreed that black people could not live north of a certain street in Oklahoma City, Roscoe Dunjee found some black citizens who needed homes and personally rented two houses for them—both on the north side of the street.

Dunjee also recognized that such personal acts had to be extended. After the National Association for the Advancement of Colored People (NAACP) was organized in Springfield, Illinois, in 1910, Dunjee was one of the first to join the Oklahoma branch started in Oklahoma City. In 1931 he forced all of the state's local branches to combine into a single state-wide conference and prepared that conference for battle. The contest was over the rights of black Oklahomans—of black Americans, in fact. Dunjee's weapons were lawsuits filed by courageous plaintiffs, argued by impassioned attorneys, and financed by nickels and dimes if need be. Not infrequently those lawsuits brought Oklahoma before the nation's ultimate authority—the United States Supreme Court.

In case after case, the state lost. It lost the power to exclude blacks from juries (*Hollins* v. *Oklahoma*, 1935). It lost the chance to single out blacks for literacy tests (*Guinn* v. *United States*, 1915). It lost the ability to refuse to register black voters (*Lane* v. *Wilson*, 1935). It lost the authority to force black students out of the state for professional education (*Sipuel* v. *Oklahoma State Board of Regents*, 1948). It lost the right to put ropes around black students in white classrooms (*McLaurin* v. *Oklahoma State Regents for Higher Education*, 1950). Every one of those cases produced a landmark decision by the United States Supreme Court. Most of the lawsuits were masterminded by Roscoe Dunjee. In each the state of Oklahoma lost. And in each the people—all of the people—of Oklahoma won.

In time the victors became even more numerous. Based on the principles laid down in such Oklahoma cases, the United States Supreme Court eventually dismantled the entire system of Jim Crow segregation, not just in schools but in every part of society, not just in Oklahoma but everywhere. During that process in the 1950s and 1960s America became a different country. That was due at least in part to the dream that Edward McCabe had carried to the prairies of Oklahoma Territory, the dream that Roscoe Dunjee had refused to let die.

Kate Barnard

Even as a grown woman, Catherine Ann Barnard barely stood five feet tall and never weighed more than ninety pounds. To a generation of Oklahomans and Americans, however, this tiny lady was known as "Our Good Angel, Kate."

She was born in Nebraska in 1875 and lost her mother when she was two. Her father, John Barnard, then took her to Kansas, where he lost most of his money. In 1889 he and young Kate came to the new Oklahoma Territory, buying a home in south Oklahoma City. The neighborhood was a poor one, and in it Kate Barnard had her first taste of something new, urban poverty. Although she had known poor farm families before, this was something different. Particularly heart-wrenching were the children not much younger than herself. All of her life, Kate Barnard would remember those children, "peaked and poor and thin and sallow . . . little children who drifted around, hungry, cold, uncared for, unloved."

As a young woman Barnard devoted her life to helping such people. With other concerned women, she formed clubs to collect food and clothing for the needy. Realizing that no amount of private charity would solve their problems, she urged the working men and women to organize labor unions. To help, she and women like her promised that they would buy nothing unless it was made with union labor.

Ultimately, Kate Barnard knew that her crusade would have to go beyond such things. Poor people needed shorter hours and safer working conditions. Their children needed to be learning in schools instead of sweating in factories. Orphans and other dependent people needed secure and sustaining surroundings. All of that meant that laws would have to be passed and enforced. That is why Kate Barnard went into politics.

When she chose a political career, women were allowed neither to vote nor to hold office in Oklahoma Territory. Those unfortunate circumstances did not even slow her down. With her friends in the labor unions she met with farmers in Shawnee in 1906 at the joint meeting of the Indiahoma Farmers' Union and the Twin Territorial Federation of Labor. Kate Barnard spoke to the assembly, and her delicate but firm hand was visible behind several of the resulting twenty-four demands, especially those aimed at shaping a state constitution that would protect the poor. The great majority of the delegates who were elected to the Guthrie convention endorsed every one of her demands.

Because she was a woman, Kate Barnard was not able to vote or run in the election of delegates to the constitutional convention, but that did not mean that she could not attend. She did, and in fact, she was one of the few nondelegates invited to address the all-male assembly. Everything she asked for she got: an eight-hour day for state employees, prohibition of child labor in mines and factories, health and safety legislation for workers—and more. To oversee such provisions and others, the delegates even created a state office, that of the commissioner of charities and corrections. It was the only office open to citizens "of either sex." The insertion of those three words—the only place in which they appeared in the constitution—had one reason: everyone knew that Kate Barnard would be the state's first commissioner.

She was. Receiving more votes than any other person running for any office, Kate Barnard became the first woman to hold a statewide office in any state in the union and the only one to do so before women were allowed to vote in federal elections in 1920. In the big parade that carried Oklahoma's new public officials to the inauguration ceremonies, she rode in an open carriage, smiling and waving broadly at the adoring, applauding crowd.

She went about her work, however, with a grim determination. Convinced that the new constitution's provisions needed sharp teeth, she drafted a series of bills, took them down to the legislature, and cornered the male lawmakers. Not many could resist. Those who did she wrote off as enemies of Oklahoma's working people and children. When re-election time came around, most of them discovered that a tiny lady from the capital had made it a point to visit their districts and tell the voters that she needed their help to do her job—and that their current representative was no help at all. Most of them lost. Kate Barnard won, drawing over 72,000 votes, more than anybody else, and about half again as many as the new governor had gotten.

By then some said that she was the best politician in the state. But it was her humanity that had taken her into politics, and it was her humanity that guided her always. One day she heard that there were three "wild" children living near Muskogee. She went there and found three small Indians sleeping in an old tree. Gently awakening them, she cut the matted hair from their heads and listened as they told her how they lived. They had been drinking from a stream. Their food had been what little they could steal from nearby farms. The abandoned children tore at her heart. She was incensed when she learned that each starving child owned valuable land, land that was producing thousands of dollars in oil money. Every penny had been stolen by the children's guardian. The same man apparently had looted the estates of at least fifty-one other Indian children.

You earlier read about grafting. This was one of the worst examples, but it was far from isolated. Commissioner Barnard learned that there were 60,000 other potential cases. These 60,000 Indian minors had been allotted lands worth at least $155 million. Since the Indians were all underage, each had been assigned a guardian whose job it was to see after the child's property. Many such guardians robbed the children, as we have seen, and they could do that because they answered to no one except Oklahoma's county judges, only forty of whom served in the former Indian Territory. The judges could not do the job, and no one else seemed much to care.

Kate Barnard cared, but there was nothing that she could do about it unless the state passed a law giving her the authority to protect the children's allotments. This the legislature would not pass and the governor would not sign. Without the law, she acted anyway. She began to write and speak, spreading the story of Oklahoma's shame across the country. Many were moved. But in Oklahoma, much of the movement was in anger. Kate Barnard was disgracing the state. She had to be stopped.

The members of the legislature—more beholden to the grafters than to the children—launched an investigation of Barnard's office, the Commission of Charities and Corrections. The investigating committee found not a single significant misdeed; nonetheless, the legislators recommended that the entire office be abolished. Because it had been established under the constitution, they could not eliminate it. What they did was refuse to appropriate the money necessary for Kate Barnard's work.

From outside of Oklahoma, some people sent money, voluntary contributions, to keep the office open. But Kate Barnard was broken, first in spirit, then in body. Although she was not yet forty years old, her health had failed so badly by 1914 that she could not endure another campaign. Her political life was over. Grafting continued, worsened even, as the Indian minors' lands were discovered to be rich in oil. But no one paid much attention to that. Neither did they pay heed to the frail woman who soon died. It had been a long time since "Our Good Angel, Kate," had smiled and waved at an adoring, applauding crowd.

Angie Debo

One of the people who had stood and applauded Kate Barnard on inauguration day in 1907 was a seventeen-year-old girl from a small town about twenty miles north of the capital. She had taken time out from teaching in a little rural school because she knew that history would be made that day. Angie Debo already knew a lot about making history.

Angie Debo was born on a farm near Beattie, Kansas, in 1890. In 1899 her father went down to Oklahoma Territory and bought a farm near Marshall, in Logan County. He returned and packed up

the family—Angie, her mother, and her brother—
and they moved to Oklahoma. All of her life Debo
would remember their covered wagon's arrival on
November 8, 1899, a "warm, sunny day, the lively little town, and the greening wheat fields we passed as
we lumbered slowly down the road to our new home."

Life on the Oklahoma frontier was hard, particularly for a person like Angie. Marshall had no library. Nobody in town received a magazine. The
only books in the Debo home—aside from a well-
worn Bible—were those slowly collected as each
child received a single book every Christmas. It was
some time before there was even a school in Marshall. When it finally came, it was not much, but
Angie Debo rushed to its one room as soon as it
opened. After that there was no secondary school
until the town got around to funding the first year
of high school. When it did, Debo rode her pony
three and one-half miles each day to school until the
one year ended, then she waited around some more.
Finally, the village worked its way to having a four-
year high school, and Angie Debo graduated in its
first class. She was twenty-three years old.

After teaching in rural schools to earn money for
tuition, she went to the University of Oklahoma. By
then there was no doubt what she wanted to do with
her life. She would write and teach history. To do
that, she would have to go on to graduate school,
and in 1923 she went to one of the best in the country at the University of Chicago. A college teaching
job in Texas came her way, and she taught there
while working on her doctoral degree. Dr. Angie
Debo was forty-three years old when she finished
her education, and she was unemployed. It was the
middle of the Great Depression, and there were
hardly any jobs to be had. It did not make much
difference that her dissertation had been published
and was awarded a top prize by the American Historical Association. Times were hard—and especially
hard for a woman. At the time the history teaching
field was locked and barred to women.

So Angie Debo staked her life—literally staked
her life—on her ability to write history, to write it
so well that she could support herself back in Marshall, Oklahoma. Her chief subject would be the
fate of Oklahoma's Five Tribes. Everyone knew about
the Trail of Tears, but no one had ever bothered to

learn and record what had happened since. In the 1930s no one cared to remember.

Months turned to years as Debo traveled to Washington, to Oklahoma City, to dozens of county courthouses, poring through dusty records, turning brittle pages, carefully collecting evidence on small, handwritten sheets in ink. Satisfied that she had the story right, she wrote it under the title *And Still the Waters Run: The Betrayal of the Five Civilized Tribes*.

Debo told the story that you have learned in this book—the story that included grafting and fraud and deceit. It was lost until Angie Debo recovered it. In stunning, irrefutable detail, she restored the record, not even hesitating to name the names. Was this man a powerful politician? Here is how he got his start. Was this one a wealthy oilman? He made his money from Indian minors' allotments. Was this family prominent in social circles? Their money came from land stolen from Indians. Whatever happened to Kate Barnard? This is what happened, and this is why.

It was powerful stuff. Fearful of retribution against the university, she let the University of Oklahoma withdraw its contract to publish the book. When the book finally found a publisher, Princeton University Press, hardly anyone in Oklahoma read it or even heard of it. The state historical society refused to announce or review it in its journal—but then the name of the president of the society was one of those that appeared in her book.

Angie Debo kept writing. When she wrote an essay on Oklahoma's history for the Works Progress Administration's guide to the state, someone decided to drop it, substituted a tamer one, and published it in her name. No one had bothered to consult her. But she kept on. Dozens of articles, scores of reviews, and thirteen books poured from her bedroom in the little frame house in Marshall. The last, a biography of the Apache warrior Geronimo, was published when she was eighty-six years old in 1976.

By then no one could ignore Angie Debo. Although she had never held a permanent college teaching job, she had won nearly every major award for historical scholarship.

As a citizen Debo was equally fearless and equally effective. When Marshall's Methodist minister went to World War II, she pastored the church. Active in Oklahoma's American Civil Liberties Union, she lived to see its annual award named for her. When oil was discovered on Alaska's North Slope, Angie Debo launched a one-woman crusade to secure the rights of Alaskan Native Americans. As a result an act of Congress did for Alaska's natives what Kate Barnard had tried to do for Oklahoma's. Debo also helped rescue the homes of the Havasupais who dwell on the floor of the Grand Canyon. At nearly ninety, she took up the plight of the Pimas and their neighbors in central Arizona in a fight that produced a comprehensive water policy for the American Southwest. She had worn out several typewriters, but she had guaranteed that the history that she had recovered and recorded would not be repeated.

When Angie Debo died, a Tulsa newspaper announced the news in a story that began with this sentence: "Dr. Angie Debo died unexpectedly today at age ninety-eight." Everything she had ever done had been unexpected.

It may be that everything every one of these Oklahomans had done was unexpected. But why should it be so? Why should greatness of character and great deeds not be found among our own people?

See History for Yourself

Some of the best work of the Kiowa Five can be found in the murals of the State Museum of History at Oklahoma City. Tulsa's Gilcrease Museum—one of the nation's premier art museums—is famous for its collections of western art in general and Indian art in particular. Several of Jerome Tiger's works are on display there. You also should visit the campus of Langston University. While in the area, drop by the Edmon Low Library at Oklahoma State University. There you will find a special Angie Debo Room, furnished with materials from Dr. Debo's home in nearby Marshall.

Suggestions for Further Reading

Klein, Joe. *Woody Guthrie: A Life*. New York: Alfred A. Knopf, 1980.

Tiger, Peggy, and Molly Babcock. *The Life and Art of Jerome Tiger: War to Peace, Death to Life*. Norman: University of Oklahoma Press, 1980.

Unit 7: **MATURE OKLAHOMA**

Introduction

U nless you are new arrivals, your parents' generation and your own are the two most recent generations of Oklahomans. These Oklahomans have shared a history at once entirely different from and strangely like that of earlier generations. None of us arrived here at the end of a Trail of Tears or for the start of a land run. The old frontier has closed. If Oklahomans are unlikely ever to see another oil boom like that of the 1920s, neither are they likely to experience another Okie migration like that of the 1930s. Only a few of us depend directly on the soil and the weather for the money that we earn and spend.

Still there is much that we share with those who have gone before us. We share the movement of people into, out of, and around the state. We share the experiences of different races and different peoples living a common history. We share the effort to find economic security in an environment of change and uncertainty. We share the hopes that we have entrusted to our politicians, and sometimes we share the disappointments with the results. In sum we share the things that always have made Oklahoma's history, that continue to make it, and that always will.

What follows is that history as it moves from the past to the present tense on its way to the future.

Chapter 24: **The Politics of Maturity**

It was not difficult to see that Oklahoma's politics changed considerably after the Second World War. The old cast of characters, whether they were dramatic or comic, gave way to entirely different public figures. They no longer stormed and strutted before the electorate, expecting that the public would mistake their thespian talents for political wisdom. Oklahoma's days of one-party rule had passed, likely never to return. Issues may have been less divisive, but neither were they so simple.

Recall, if you will, some of the political leaders that Oklahoma had produced in the past. One year Sooners sent to Congress a woman opposed to woman's suffrage and a lunatic temporarily out of the asylum. They then elected "Our Jack" Walton and Henry S. Johnston their successive governors, grimaced at their antics, and generally applauded when the legislators promptly impeached and removed them. Then there was old "Alfalfa Bill" Murray. His outrageousness began with his nickname and did not end until he had most of the state under martial law. In nearly every election citizens confronted monstrous ballots, many several yards long, liberally sprinkled with the names of dead poets, dead generals, dead presidents, and living charlatans.

Recent Political Changes

Those days are probably behind us forever. It is true that in 1954 the state elected a lieutenant governor named Cowboy Pink Williams, and in 1974 Hamp Baker became a corporation commissioner. The latter had made his own name famous by putting it on hundreds of crudely painted old car hoods telling motorists, "Hamp Baker Says Drive with Care." The Cowboy and Hamp were, however, aberrations. It is more revealing to note that in every year except one since 1947, Oklahoma was represented in the United States Congress by at least one Rhodes scholar, Representative Carl Albert and/or Senator David Boren. No other state offered the nation such distinguished intellectual leadership. Like those

THE SPEAKER FROM BUG TUSSLE

Bug Tussle's most prominent son and the Oklahoman who has risen highest in national politics: Carl Albert, forty-sixth Speaker of the United States House of Representatives.

In 1914 a horse-drawn buggy pulled up in front of a two-room school in the little settlement of Bug Tussle. The buggy carried the Honorable Charles D. Carter, United States Congressman from Oklahoma. Included among the sixty or so students in the school was an unusually small first-grader, the son of a coal miner and farmer. When Representative Carter addressed the students, he told them that ours was a great country, one in which any little child might one day grow up to be a congressman from that very district. Hearing those words, Bug Tussle's smallest student was certain that the congressman was speaking directly to him. Carl Albert would one day go to Congress.

At the time anyone except a child would have been sure that that was impossible. Albert's family was not prominent or wealthy. Neither of his parents had more than a few years of schooling. Bug Tussle was

two, most of the modern state's political leaders were well educated, if less colorful than in the past.

Another difference is that today's politicians are likely to include, far more than in the past, representatives of Oklahoma's many peoples. Kelly Haney, a full-blood Indian, is a nationally recognized artist in the tradition of the Kiowa Five and Jerome Tiger. Since 1987 he also has been State Senator Haney, representing a predominantly white district. In 1991, Susan Loving became Oklahoma's first female

a poor, backward community, its only distinction its peculiar name. Its one school went no higher than the eighth grade. Surely, one would think, such lowly circumstances could never produce an important person.

Bug Tussle did produce Carl Albert, and Carl Albert became one of Oklahoma's and America's most-important public men. One reason that he did so was that he defined early what he wanted to do with his life and worked long and deliberately to make it possible. He became the first person in his family to graduate from high school. He was the first from Bug Tussle to graduate from college, the University of Oklahoma, where he won every top honor, including one of thirty-three Rhodes scholarships awarded in the nation. That scholarship sent Carl Albert to England's Oxford University, where he earned a law degree before he returned to Oklahoma and unemployment during the Great De-

pression. When he finally found a good job, it took him out of state, and soon the U.S. government took him out of the job and sent him to the Pacific Ocean as a private in the United States Army. He returned from World War II wearing a lieutenant colonel's eagles and a Silver Star. Finally ready to run for the office that he so long had prepared for, Albert filed in the Democratic primary for the Third District congressional seat in 1946. He won by 330 votes.

Over the next decades fourteen more elections came and Carl Albert won them all. After the 1946 race none of the contests was even close. His fellow congressmen recognized at once his intelligence, his dedication to work, and his devotion to the House of Representatives. In 1954 they named him as the Democratic party "whip," the third-ranking post in the majority party's leadership. By 1962 he had moved up to number two, House

majority leader. In 1971 he became the forty-sixth Speaker of the United States House of Representatives, the highest government position yet held by an Oklahoman.

Speaker for six years, Carl Albert presided firmly but fairly over the greatest constitutional crisis since the Civil War—the House impeachment inquiry into President Richard Nixon's misdeeds in the so-called Watergate affair and other matters. In 1977, his reputation only enhanced by thirty years of public life, Carl Albert retired as Speaker and Third District Congressman. He returned to where it all had begun and where he always felt most at home, to a piece of land that had been part of his father's Bug Tussle farm. Just over the hill lay the two-room building where, more than a half-century earlier, a visitor in a buggy had dared a little boy to make his life count for something.

attorney general and one of the few women to serve any state as its chief legal officer. After Logan County sent A. C. Hamlin to the legislature in 1908, it was the mid-1960s before another black man served there. Since then every legislative session has included black men. Black women, too, held prominent positions, including Oklahoma Secretary of State Hannah Atkins and State Senators Vicki Miles–Le Grange and Maxine Horner.

Gone too are most of the raw conflicts that bedeviled Oklahoma politics in the past. The Ku Klux Klan became as much a relic of Sooner history as the Socialist party. Modern candidates appeal to a broad spectrum of voters rather than just to the discontented. Campaigns feature slick television spots and radio ads, not vicious attacks on other candidates' ideas, accomplishments, and ancestry. Officeholders spend more time building coalitions and less energy fighting each other. One of the characteristics of the new political style is that it is much more urban than in the past.

Rural Oklahoma's Domination

Through most of our state's history politics was dominated by representatives of Oklahoma's small towns and rural communities. Originally that made sense because that was where most of the state's early population lived. Over generations, however, Oklahomans moved away from farms and villages. If they did not leave the state entirely, they tended to go to cities like Tulsa and Oklahoma City. This was particularly true during and after World War II when tens of thousands left places like Eufaula and Tishomingo for jobs at Douglas Aircraft or Tinker Field. Yet that did not change rural Oklahoma's control of political power; it only created a new tension as rural forces clung to their power against the rising tides of metropolitan Oklahoma.

One reason why rural politicians held on for so long was that the state legislature remained firmly under rural Oklahomans' control. When Oklahoma became a state, it divided its house and senate districts so that the members of each chamber represented roughly the same number of people. The 1907 constitution also instructed future legislatures to redraw legislative districts to take account

Although many Oklahomans regarded the legislature's long refusal to reapportion itself as a clear violation of the state constitution, their attempts to end rural domination yielded no effective results. Even this imaginative effort to "bury" legislative malapportionment beneath a casket load of popular petitions counted for nothing until the federal courts intervened.

of population changes after every succeeding federal census. The legislators proved to be poor students. Only to a slight extent did they do as told after the census of 1910. After each of the next five censuses the legislature did nothing at all. Thus in the early 1960s, when nearly half of the state's population lived in or near Tulsa or Oklahoma counties, those two counties still had only two seats in the state senate and not many more in the state house. For that reason one voter in Beaver County carried as much weight on election day as did eighty citizens of Oklahoma County.

The long rural domination of state politics had consequences for state policies. More than the governor, the state legislature dictated what the state would do, and usually it did what rural Oklahoma and its representatives preferred. Because rural Oklahomans tended toward conservative moral views, the state continued to prohibit the sale of alcohol. Urban (and other) Oklahomans drank, but they did so illegally and hypocritically, buying their liquor from bootleggers who openly advertised their prices and services, including home delivery. Because rural Oklahomans included many farmers who were ineligible for federal Social Security in their old age, Oklahoma provided ample state pensions— pensions so numerous and so generous that no state in the union spent more on public welfare. Because rural Oklahomans always needed jobs, the legislature functioned as an employment agency that jealously guarded the right to hire and fire almost all state employees, regardless of their merit or their

LEGAL LIQUOR OR NONE AT ALL

Although its fifty-two-year history demonstrates that many Oklahomans took seriously their state's prohibition of the sale of alcohol, not all did. Bootleggers did, in fact, advertise their wares and services, including brand-name prices and home delivery. Because violation of federal liquor laws was a serious offense (unlike the weak and poorly enforced state laws), the illegal sellers even purchased federal liquor stamps, making their names available to any determined state prosecutor. Apparently, none were determined enough. As for Oklahoma's voters, Will Rogers once declared that Sooners would vote for prohibition as long as they could stagger to the polls.

In 1959, Governor J. Howard Edmondson and his young commissioner of public safety, Joe Cannon, determined to change that. Employing units of the state's highway patrol and special task forces, Cannon also insisted that local sheriffs do their jobs—enforce the state's liquor laws. Well-publicized raids closed even such well-known watering holes as the private country clubs that served the state's elite in Oklahoma City and Tulsa. Out in the country, one local editor expressed shock when he wrote that even "Spavinaw is dry."

Oklahoma voters were plenty dry when the time came to vote for the amendment repealing prohibition. It passed overwhelmingly, perhaps because Sooners finally were not able to stagger to the polls.

need. Thus Oklahoma maintained a Confederate Veterans' Home long after the last surviving Confederate had died in order to provide jobs for one state senator's friends and family. Because rural voters depended on county roads and bridges, the lawmakers turned over a large portion of state highway money to the county commissioners back home. Many commissioners simply put it in their own pockets.

For years after World War II the resulting tensions defined much of state politics. The most successful postwar governors recognized the facts of political life and acted accordingly. Governor Roy J. Turner, who served from 1947 to 1951, continued much of the progress begun under Governor Kerr, but no more than Kerr did he dare confront the rural lions in their legislative lair. Raymond D. Gary, the state's governor from 1955 to 1959, won great praise for dismantling Oklahoma's system of segregated schools, but the former senator from Madill likewise allowed his old rural allies to dominate state affairs.

Ironically, one of the few governors to question rural domination was himself the son of one of Oklahoma's most countrified statesmen. Johnston Murray—Alfalfa Bill's boy—served from 1955 to 1959, between governors Turner and Gary. At the end of his term he was so frustrated with the state's rural domination that he moved to Texas and joined the Republican party. Governor J. Howard Edmondson, whom urban voters elected in 1958, may have had a worse fate. Although he was able to force the repeal of Oklahoma's prohibition laws (largely by giving Sooners the choice of legal liquor or no liquor at all), his other attempts to reform state administration usually ended with his head bloodied by powerful rural forces.

In time the rural domination of Oklahoma politics finally ended. The time was long in coming, and when it came it came not from Oklahoma's politicians. Federal judges played the most important role. In 1964 they ordered Oklahoma's legislature to redraw both its senate and its house districts on a "one-man, one-vote" basis. When the stubborn lawmakers failed to do so, the judges did it themselves, finally restoring equal representation and breaking down the citadel of rural power.

The Commissioners

Other political changes also came from outside the state. In the 1980s federal prosecutors began to file criminal charges against county commissioners for abuses that had gone on for decades, perhaps even to the early years of statehood. Commissioners routinely had taken 10 percent kickbacks on everything they bought with state tax money. Not infrequently commissioners and suppliers took 50 percent cuts for each by billing taxpayers for items that were never even delivered. Nearly everyone knew about such practices, but no one had done anything about it. One reason was that Oklahoma's county commissioners paid the salaries of the state's county attorneys, the very officials whose responsibilities included prosecution of such crimes.

Under those circumstances it was not surprising that real changes would have to come from outside the corrupt system itself. When they did, the only shock was how extensive the corruption was. By 1984 federal prosecutors had secured convictions against more than 200 people, including 110 of the then 231 incumbent county commissioners and 55 former ones. Sixty of Oklahoma's seventy-seven counties saw their local leaders leave the court-

YOUR CHEATIN' HEART

Even if the county commissioner scandal of the 1980s were the only example, Oklahoma politics would still be tarnished with an image of endemic corruption. That scandal was one of the biggest and longest-running episodes of systematic corruption in any state's politics in this century. Unfortunately, however, it was far from a single, isolated example. Thirty years before the crooked commissioners made national headlines, *Time Magazine* already had written that there always was an "Aroma in Oklahoma" around state politics, and the stink continued right on through the years. Between 1977 and 1987 an astonishing total of 246 Oklahoma public officials were convicted of federal crimes, and countless others were convicted of state offenses.

During the entire postwar era since 1945 the smell reached into every corner of state affairs. At the federal level one Oklahoma congressman (Victor Wickersham) was voted America's "Worst Congressman" in large part because of his ethically dubious practice of operating a private real estate business out of his Capitol office. Another (Mickey Edwards) was revealed to have been one of the worst abusers in the congressional check-writing scandal of the 1990s.

Within the state, several governors were connected to criminal investigations, and one (David Hall) left office to serve time in a federal prison for his attempt to bribe the secretary of state. Legislators also had their troubles with the law; their convictions ranged from drunken driving to narcotics trafficking and indictments for bribery and extortion. Even the judiciary had not been immune. In the mid-1960s federal courts handed down bribery convictions and federal prison terms to a former state supreme-court judge and two sitting justices.

The explanations for the widespread and odious lapses ranged all the way from simple bad luck to Oklahomans' supposed proclivity for corruption. In the end no one could offer a certain cause. Most agreed, however, that no small element was that Sooner voters somewhere had lost their capacity for outrage at such behavior.

There probably was something to that. After all, the corrupted commissioners generally justified their misdeeds to themselves by saying not only that everyone did it and everyone knew it but also that everyone expected it, too. In fact, outsiders were particularly appalled when one convicted commissioner's friends and constituents hosted a big going-away party as he prepared to head for prison. Folks turned out to wish their departing official well. A hired country band played "Your Cheatin' Heart" while the crowd shared tears and beers and barbecue.

house for the Big House, usually the federal prison at El Reno.

A Two-party Oklahoma?

Another of the state's recent political changes owes more to Oklahoma circumstances. For most of its history Oklahoma had been pretty much a one-party state. Until after World War II, Republicans rarely carried the state for their presidential or senatorial candidates, and they did so always under

unusual circumstances. Until well after the war the
state had never elected a Republican governor.
Most voters had not taken Republicans seriously.

A careful observer might have noted that things
began to change just after World War II. Harry Truman won Oklahoma's electoral votes in 1948, but he
was the last Democrat to do so for sixteen years.
Dwight Eisenhower comfortably carried Oklahoma
in both 1952 and 1956. Richard Nixon did so as well
in 1960. In 1964, Lyndon Johnson added Oklahoma's
vote to his near-record total, but afterwards state
Democrats had little cause for joy. Richard Nixon

Gleeful Sooner Democrats
watch the election returns
roll in during their 1964
sweep. They had no way of
knowing that it would be the
last such celebration for at
least three decades.

(in 1968 and 1972), Gerald Ford (in 1976), Ronald
Reagan (in 1980 and 1984), and George Bush (in 1988
and 1992)—every Republican presidential candidate since Johnson carried Oklahoma, usually by
big margins. Between 1952 and 1992 only Arizona
was more consistently Republican than Oklahoma
in presidential elections.

Oklahoma's elections for the United States Senate
became almost as one-sidedly Republican as the
presidential elections. After serving as governor,
Democrat Robert S. Kerr went to the Senate in 1948,
and Mike Monroney (at the time a Democratic congressman) joined him there in 1952. After Kerr's
death in 1963, however, Republicans won six of
Oklahoma's senatorial contests, twice as many as
they had won in the state's first sixty years. Henry
Bellmon retired Monroney in 1968 and won a sec-

ond term for himself in 1974. Dewey Bartlett's 1972 victory briefly gave the Republicans both of Oklahoma's Senate seats for the first time since the early 1920s. Because of failing health, Bartlett did not seek a second term, and Bellmon turned down a third term in 1980. The Republicans, however, kept the seat because Don Nickles replaced Bellmon, the first of Nickles's three easy victories. In fact, the only Democrat to win a full Senate term in recent years was David Boren, who won his first in 1978.

Gubernatorial politics changed, too. As late as 1958 the Republicans could not deliver a single Oklahoma county for their nominee. Then in 1962 the party easily made Henry Bellmon Oklahoma's first Republican governor and the first Republican to govern a southern state since Reconstruction. Just as Dewey Bartlett would later follow Bellmon to Washington, he followed him then to the state capital, winning the governorship in 1966. In 1986, Bellmon came out of retirement at his Billings farm and gave the Republicans their third gubernatorial victory in twenty-four years, only the third Republican gubernatorial win in the state's entire history.

Students of state politics do not have to look far for the sources of the recent Republican resurrection in Oklahoma. Whether in presidential, senatorial, or gubernatorial races, the party was the beneficiary of two remarkable trends. One was that, on the whole, the Democratic nominees were perceived as being more "liberal" than the Republicans. This was particularly true at the presidential level, where Democratic presidential contenders had to win over several liberal constituencies (labor-union members, blacks, and other minorities, for example) to get their party's nomination. In Oklahoma, Republicans running for nearly every office generally wrapped themselves in the banner of conservatism while trying (often with great success) to pin the liberal tag on their Democratic opponents. That habit, not to mention its results, testified to the increased conservatism of Oklahoma's electorate.

The other cause of the Republican revitalization was less visible but more powerful. The Republican party increasingly became the instrument of the state's large and growing number of metropolitan voters. In a half century only two Democrats (Harry Truman and David Boren) carried both Oklahoma

For much of Oklahoma's history it was inconceivable that the state would elect Republican governors or United States senators or give their electoral votes to Republican presidential candidates. Beginning in the 1960s and 1970s, however, a new era emerged. Three beneficiaries were (*left to right, excluding the obscured figure*) Gerald R. Ford, Henry Bellmon, and Dewey Bartlett.

and Tulsa counties in an important race. So great was the Republican advantage in those two big-voting counties that they several times gave the party its margin of victory as it was losing in the remaining seventy-five.

Both of those trends shared a common explanation. Oklahoma's major cities and their surrounding suburbs were crowded with predominately white voters who held white-collar jobs and owned their own homes. Typically well educated (a large percentage held college degrees), they tended to be relatively well paid, too. Such voters had come a long way from the depression generation that had worshipped at the shrine of Franklin Roosevelt and his liberal New Deal. They were even further removed from the dispossessed sharecroppers and workers who had provided the sinews of Sooner Socialism. These urban voters were people basically content, or at least they were content until something threatened their pocketbooks with higher taxes or threatened their values any number of ways. These voters thought of themselves as conservatives, and they did have much to conserve. Everywhere such voters gave the Republicans their greatest strength. In Oklahoma they gave them their post–World War II victories.

Political Persistence

Although it is easy to document and possible to explain the development of Oklahoma's new two-party system, it is very difficult to be certain about its effects. Governors may be Republicans, or they may be Democrats. Legislators may represent small towns or pieces of large cities. Either way, no governor can do more than the constitution allows him (or her), and legislators cannot spend money that they do not have. In Oklahoma (as everywhere) those important conditions have been remarkably immune to any changes at all.

For one thing, the Oklahomans who left their air-conditioned homes in foreign automobiles for office jobs a generation after World War II were still governed under a constitution written by farmers for a horse-and-buggy age. Old Bill Murray and his friends at the "Con Con" (as the constitutional convention was called) had been dead a long time, but the constitution that they wrote back in 1906 and 1907 remained very much alive. Because it did, Oklahoma's governors remained relatively feeble compared to the chief executives of other states. Alfalfa Bill and his crowd feared too much power in the governor's office, and so they bound it tight with constitutional chains. Nothing in the succeeding decades at all corroded those bonds; in fact, an accumulation of subsequent constitutional amendments and state statutes strengthened them.

The original Oklahoma constitution boldly declared that the governor would exercise "the Supreme Executive power," but even as the ink in those words was drying, their authors were adding other clauses, paragraphs, sections, and articles. These sapped the governor's presumed powers by grafting onto the executive branch a briar patch of other elected executive officials, each of whom was given power that otherwise would have been the governor's. By the time they had finished, the "supreme executive power" was not the governor's at all. Rather it had been parcelled out everywhere and nowhere.

None of Oklahoma's political history since 1907 substantially changed that situation. It was true that subsequent constitutional amendments gradually reduced the length of Oklahoma's ballot. At the same time, however, still other constitutional amendments and legislative acts were creating what amounted to a fourth branch of government: a tangled undergrowth of independent agencies, boards, and commissions. Oklahoma voters used to elect twenty-one state executive officials. In 1990, when they elected David Walters their governor, they selected only eight other executive officials. The governor, however, shared executive authority with not only the other elected officers but also no fewer than 246 executive agencies, none of them directly under his immediate authority.

Some of those boards and agencies were trivial. No one particularly cared that the Santa Claus Commission, not the governor, selected Christmas gifts for the children in state homes and hospitals. It did, however, make a difference that the State Regents for Higher Education, not the governor, controlled Oklahoma's twenty-six state colleges. It made a difference that the Highway Commission, not the governor, decided when and where roads would be built. It made a difference that the state Human Services Commission, not the governor, controlled Oklahoma's welfare program, which was the state's most expensive activity and the largest employer in Oklahoma.

Fearful of strong governors, the constitution's writers had spread power about and guaranteed that no one person could govern too poorly; however, they and their descendants may have created a situation in which no one could govern very well either. Oklahomans expected much from their governors, but they gave them few tools to achieve much.

The legislature's power was not unlimited either. Although the constitution generously provided Oklahoma's lawmakers with abundant powers, no constitution, no amendment, and no act could repeal the basic laws of politics.

Modern government (in Oklahoma and elsewhere) was chiefly a service industry. Oklahomans looked to the state government to build and maintain the highways upon which they traveled and the schools in which they learned. When necessary, state government prosecuted and imprisoned their criminals, just as it fed, clothed, and sheltered their needy. Everything Sooners expected from the state—everything from bridges to textbooks to prisons—cost money. It was the legislature's major responsibility to raise that money by taxes and spend it through appropriations.

Taxing and Spending

With regard to raising revenue, the legislature's powers were very much limited. For one thing, the constitution and statutes earmarked many of the state's tax collections: the money raised from a given tax was dedicated to a specific program, usually one that had been favored decades before. Although the need for later programs might be more compelling, they could not draw on those funds. Many programs that the state administered also involved federal monies. Washington always sent its checks with conditions attached, conditions that again circumscribed what the legislators could and could not do, not only with the federal dollars but with the state's also. The final limit to the legislature's actions was the most obvious. Whether they were Democrats or Republicans, whether they answered to voters in Beaver County or in Oklahoma County, legislators could not spend money they did not have.

Ours is not a wealthy state. Although the Great Depression had long since gone, Oklahomans still earned less, on the average, than did citizens of most other states. That alone provided the chief limitation on the government services that Oklahomans could buy. Below the national average in personal income, Oklahoma also sat below the national average in nearly every category of public spending.

Other limitations were self-induced. For example, Oklahomans preferred that their taxes be kept low, and their politicians generally granted them their wishes. After World War II most states raised their tax levels to take advantage of the nation's renewed prosperity. They rode the waves of that prosperity to provide their citizens new and improved services.

Oklahoma did not. For more than twenty-five years after World War II, Oklahoma's legislators (and governors, too) promised to hold the lid on state taxes. That was a promise that they kept. Between 1945 and 1970 the single increase in Oklahoma's general tax rate was a twenty-five-cent rise in the cost of a driver's license. Because other states were increasing their rates, Oklahoma's taxes kept dropping relative to other states. Economists estimated in 1960 that Oklahoma's overall tax effort placed it twenty-eighth among the nation's fifty states. Measured again in 1971 and 1975, the state had drifted to last place in both years.

It did not take a professional economist to predict the results, but economists did measure the effects

OKLAHOMA IN THE NATION

No study of a state's politics should be done without an awareness of how that state compares with others, particularly when one studies a state's economy or its government's taxing and spending. Merely to know, for example, how much Oklahoma raises in taxes means little until we have some idea of how much other states raise. Economists and political scientists ask those larger questions, often expressing their findings through statistics and rankings. The results can be a chart similar to the one below, which compares how much Oklahomans earn, how much they tax themselves, and how they choose to spend some of their tax dollars, with the average of the figures for the other forty-nine states.

	Per-capita Income, U.S.	Per-capita Income OK (rank)	Per-capita State/Local General Tax Revenue, U.S.	Per-capita State/Local Tax Revenue, Oklahoma (rank)	State/Local Tax-Effort Index U.S.	State/Local Tax-Effort Index Oklahoma (rank)	Per-pupil Public-Education Spending, U.S.	Per-pupil Public-Education Spending, Oklahoma (rank)
1960	$2,222	$1,876 (33)	$281	$280 (26)	100	94 (28)	$375	$311 (38)
1970	3,966	3,387 (34)	643	575 (31)	100	68 (50)	783	540 (46)
1975–76	6,399	5,707 (33)	1,193	992 (37)	100	79 (50)	1,578	1,261 (36)
1980	9,521	9,116 (28)	1,688	1,505 (32)	100	71 (48)	2,094	1,798 (33)

Note: The state and local tax-effort index is calculated by averaging the rates for each tax collected by the fifty states and their local jurisdictions. That average is assigned the value of 100. Each individual state's actual revenues under each tax are then totalled and compared to the average collected by all states and assigned an index number. Any number above 100 indicates that, on the whole, the state and its localities tax their citizens *more than* the national average. Any number below 100 indicates that their taxes are *less than* the average of all states. Thus Oklahoma's index of 68 in 1970 means that its citizens were paying only 68 percent as much in taxes as they would have paid had their taxes been set at the level of the average state's.
(David R. Morgan, *Handbook of State Policy Indicators*, 3d and 4th eds. [Norman: University of Oklahoma Bureau of Government Research, 1978 and 1982])

of Oklahoma's low taxes. In 1960 only four states invested more of their personal income in elementary and secondary education; in 1976, forty-seven did so. In 1960 only ten states had given more aid to their needy old people; in 1976 only four gave less. In some respects, Oklahoma's decline was more than relative. Even though in 1975, Oklahoma had more colleges, and more students in them, than it had in 1968, the state's real spending on higher education dropped by 10 percent over those seven years.

A modest series of tax increases sponsored by

Governor David Hall (who served from 1971 to 1975) did not even slow the retreat. Under Hall's two successors, David Boren (governor from 1975 to 1979) and George Nigh (who served two terms, from 1979 to 1987), thirteen separate tax cuts rolled most people's taxes back to or even below earlier rates. This was possible because the Arab oil sheiks had artificially raised world oil prices, and Oklahoma's tax collections increased from the state's tax on the value of crude-oil production. That consumers in other states ended up paying most of that tax made it all the sweeter.

When the oil bubble broke, the state was left high and dry. Even though the legislators had no choice but to raise taxes in both 1984 and 1985, Henry Bellmon began his second term as governor in 1987 with the state facing a $350 million crisis. That figure (equal to 17 percent of the state's existing budget) represented the continuing downward slide in tax revenues. Over strenuous protests—protests from urban legislators and rural ones, Democratic lawmakers and Republicans too—Bellmon stopped the tide with a series of modest tax increases. A second round of bitterly contested tax increases followed. These were dedicated to improving the state's deteriorating public school system.

In one sense the immediate consequences were hard to detect. Four tax increases in the 1980s still left Oklahoma's overall tax effort one of the nation's most feeble. Even with the new taxes devoted to education, the state's per-pupil spending for education ranked it forty-third in 1991, about where it had been (thirty-eighth) back in 1960. In fact, its average teacher's salary had dropped from twenty-eighth nationally in 1960 to forty-eighth in 1991.

Another consequence of the modest tax increases was easy to see. Angered by the legislators' rounds of tax hikes, Oklahomans began the 1990s by hammering two new amendments to their lengthy constitution. The first limited future state lawmakers to no more than twelve years legislative service in their lifetimes. The second required that almost any subsequent tax increase would need the voters' direct approval before taking effect.

No one knew the effects—if any—that these changes would produce. What they did know was that Oklahoma's political future would rest partly on the outcome. Whatever the future bore, it was certain that it would share one quality with the past. That is, Oklahomans would get just the government that they deserved, no better and no worse. Nothing before or after World War II had, or ever would, change that.

See History for Yourself

Befitting their status as two of Oklahoma's foremost public men, Speaker Carl Albert and Senator Robert S. Kerr have been honored in several ways. The University of Oklahoma maintains the Carl Albert Congressional Research and Studies Center, the nation's only academic center devoted to the study of Congress and of representative government in general. Among its resources is an exact replica of Speaker Albert's office in the Capitol at Washington. Ada recently has restored the log cabin of Senator Kerr's birth and placed it alongside his grave. Six miles southwest of Poteau stands the home that Senator Kerr built two years before his death. A portion of it is used as a museum showing materials related to Kerr's life and that region of eastern Oklahoma.

Suggestions for Further Reading

Reference

Benson, Oliver, et al. *Oklahoma Votes, 1907–1962.* Norman: Bureau of Government Research, University of Oklahoma, 1964.

Benson, Oliver, Alan Durban, and Asoke Basu. *Oklahoma Votes for Congress, 1907–1964.* Norman: Bureau of Government Research, University of Oklahoma, 1965.

Morgan, David R., Robert E. England, and George G. Humphreys *Oklahoma Politics and Policies: Governing the Sooner State.* Lincoln: University of Nebraska Press, 1991.

Related Reading

Bellmon, Henry, with Pat Bellmon. *The Life and Times of Henry Bellmon.* Tulsa: Council Oaks Books, 1992.

Albert, Carl, with Danney Goble. *Little Giant: The Life and Times of Speaker Carl Albert.* Norman: University of Oklahoma Press, 1990.

Chapter 25: **The Strains of Social Maturity**

Not even the lingering celebration of America's recent victories over Germany and Japan dispelled the gloom that hung over the regents of the University of Oklahoma at their December 1945 meeting. The entire state, the university included, was in something of a continuing psychological depression as intense as the recent economic depression. True, the dust storms of the 1930s were things of the past, but would they return in the future? Nobody was writing novels or songs about the Okie migrants, but people were still leaving the state every day. At the university morale had not yet recovered from the budget cuts that had slashed faculty salaries into the bone in the 1930s. The legislature's recent threats to fire liberal professors had only worsened the sour mood. As if things were not bad enough, football coach Dewey ("Snorter") Luster had just resigned. "Ill health," he said, though everyone knew that the cause of his terminal illness was the inability to beat Texas and a humiliating 41–0 loss to Oklahoma A. and M.

Just the Thing!

A suggestion by regent Lloyd Noble pierced the gloom. An Ardmore oilman and a towering force behind university affairs, Noble observed that the state's high schools were about to yield a fine crop of graduating seniors. Fast, lean, and hungry, those boys were just the stuff to build a fine football team. If someone could add a few men to them—say, returning servicemen ready to start college—why, that was the stuff that could make a *great* football team! Just the thing the university needed. Just the thing the state needed. Something to give Oklahomans back their pride!

One month later, the University of Oklahoma replaced Snorter Luster with Jim Tatum, a young, aggressive coach who had headed the football program at North Carolina until the war took him into the navy, where he coached sailors' teams. In his one year at Norman, Tatum demolished A. and M. (72–12) and played a powerhouse Army team to a standstill on way to an 8-and-3 season and a Gator Bowl championship. Tatum then left—his good health taking him to the University of Maryland. He left the OU program in charge of a young assistant who had worked with him on the navy teams before coming to Oklahoma as one of Tatum's assistants. When he was barely thirty—not much older than some of his players—Bud Wilkinson took over the

Starting only his second season as OU's head coach, Bud Wilkinson (*third from left*) already was building a Sooner legend.

Sooner team in 1947. Over the next sixteen years, Coach Bud made every bit as much Oklahoma history as any mere discoverer, president, Indian chief, governor, or oil millionaire ever did.

Coach Bud and His Boys

A stern disciplinarian and brilliant strategist, Wilkinson perfected the split T offense. His "three-four" defensive alignment (three down lineman supported by four standing linebackers) became known as the "Okie three" years before the pro teams got around to using it. With a smile that could melt any mother's heart and a grip that let every father know he was in the presence of a man, Bud became a hero to every boy, turning the part of America that lay within a 300-mile radius of Norman, Oklahoma, into his private recruiting preserve. Dozens—hundreds— of quick, fast, strong boys descended on the campus from every town in Oklahoma as well as outlying areas like White Deer and Olney, Texas, and Hobbs, New Mexico.

The result was recorded on college football scoreboards. After winning seven games and a conference crown in his first season, Wilkinson's Sooners reeled off thirteen more consecutive conference championships. Into 1959 they had played seventy-four straight conference games without a single defeat. Nationally, his Sooner teams were 6 and 2 in bowl competition, winning national championships in 1950, 1955, and 1956. When his teams rolled over

Few Sooner victories are ever as sweet as those over the Longhorns of the University of Texas. In the Wilkinson era they came with a regularity that was never monotonous. The 1953 game—won by Oklahoma 49–20—was only one.

thirty-one consecutive opponents, they established an astonishing record winning streak. More incredibly, after a loss to Notre Dame in 1953, his Sooners took a deep breath, tied Pittsburgh, and immediately began another streak. That one ended only in 1957—forty-seven straight wins later. Since never even approached, that may remain one of the few untouchable records in American athletics. After an 8-and-2 1963 season, Wilkinson left coaching to run for the United States Senate, suffering one of his few defeats. At the time no one thought that his overall record would ever be equalled.

"THE ONLY ONES WHO NEVER LOSE"

November 16, 1957, was fifty years to the day since Oklahoma had become a state. It is likely, however, that the record crowd of 63,170 fans who jammed into Owen Field that day were thinking of a different kind of history. Nearly fifty fall Saturdays before, the Fighting Irish of Notre Dame had last visited Norman, where they had broken the Sooner's record thirty-one-game winning streak. Now they were back again, carrying a 4-and-2 record and ready to avenge 1956's 40–0 loss at South Bend.

Oklahoma took the ball first and promptly marched to the Notre Dame 13. It was to be the Sooner's deepest penetration of the day. From then on the two teams struggled near the field's midpoint. Neither was able to crack the other's determined defense.

Not until the game's closing moments. Then, beginning on its own 20, Notre Dame ran up the middle repeatedly, smashing down to the Oklahoma 12 before fumbling. The referee's signal that Notre Dame had recovered unleashed 63,170 groans from the Sooner faithful. With 3:50 left to play, Notre Dame sat on the Sooner 3. It was fourth down with a record to go. As the Big Red defense effectively jammed the middle of the line, Notre Dame's quarterback tossed the ball to Dick Lynch, who scooted around the Sooner's left end. Notre Dame scored on that play, finally ending Bud Wilkinson's incredible forty-seven-game winning streak.

As a hushed and stunned crowd crept toward the exits, Jack Ogle, the stadium's public-address announcer, instructed the crowd: "Come back next Saturday, folks. That's when the new streak starts."

It would not—not for Oklahoma and probably not for anybody else, ever. That is one reason that Coach Bud's words proved to be more prophetic. "The only ones who never lose," he told a tearful squad in the postgame locker room, "are those who never play."

Those records are sports history, but another kind of history was what regent Noble had anticipated, and more so: more than anything else, the remarkable athletic prowess of their postwar athletic teams restored Oklahomans' pride in their state and faith in themselves. And it must be said that Bud Wilkinson was not the only one building that pride. Up the road at Stillwater, Oklahoma A. and M. (after 1957, Oklahoma State University) was building records nearly as brilliant as Wilkinson's at Norman. Myron Roderick was maintaining the international powerhouse that Ed Gallagher had begun in wrestling. Coaches Henry Iba and Labron Harris kept their teams at the top in collegiate basketball and golf. In fact, for all of the attention paid to the University of Oklahoma's football teams, it was Oklahoma State University that entered the 1960s with more national championships in more sports than any other school in the National Collegiate Athletic Association (NCAA).

While the school was still known as Oklahoma A. and M., Coach Henry Iba led the 1945 and 1946 Aggie teams to the first consecutive national basketball titles in the history of the sport.

If one were an athletic fan—and not many Oklahomans were not—it was a good time to be alive. Whether clad in crimson and cream or in orange and black, Oklahoma's "boys" (and "girls," too) could do just about anything.

OKLAHOMA'S GREATEST COACH

Coach Teague with her 1933 Byng, Oklahoma, basketball team. There would be thirty-six winning teams after that.

Until very recent times women had little place in competitive athletics. State colleges rarely had women's athletic teams. When they did, they lavished on them nothing like the attention (and the money) devoted to men's athletics. In Oklahoma's large metropolitan and suburban high schools, few considered it appropriate for female students to do more than lead cheers for the boys' teams.

Perhaps surprisingly, some of the few cracks in that otherwise impenetrable so-

In fact, it looked like Oklahomans as a whole could do just about anything and everything. Across the state, people moved into communities like Edmond, Moore, Broken Arrow, and Jenks, transforming sleepy villages into bedroom communities for the wideawake metropolises of Oklahoma City and Tulsa. New shopping centers opened, almost daily, it seemed. Consumers took their billfolds, checkbooks, and credit cards into bright, shiny new stores and loaded up with the latest appliances—automatic washers, dryers, dishwashers, and perhaps most important, air conditioners. Out in front of their miraculously cooled new homes sat gleaming hunks of Detroit iron with eight cylinders ready to roar into life and the turquoise paint shining bright in the Oklahoma sun.

In the summer teenagers drove those cars to amusement parks like Bell's in Tulsa or Oklahoma City's Springlake. The latter was famous for its penny arcade, the mammoth swimming pool, and its

cial barrier were to be found in Oklahoma's very smallest schools. Perhaps because their student numbers were so small that to field any kind of team in any kind of sport was something of an accomplishment, several of Oklahoma's smallest school systems fielded excellent athletic teams with young women who enjoyed the thrill of competition and their town's acclaim. Outside of those towns, however, few—even in Oklahoma— paid much attention.

Perhaps that is why so few people have even heard the name of Oklahoma's most successful coach in any sport, ever. This was not Bud Wilkinson, Barry Switzer, Henry Iba, or Ed Gallagher. Instead, it was a first-grade teacher in Byng, Oklahoma, who doubled as the coach of the Byng Lady Pirates basketball team. She was Bertha Frank Teague.

Although she had never played the game herself, she agreed to coach a bloomer-clad team that practiced on a dirt court in Coal County in 1927. When her husband, Jess, took a teaching job in Byng the next year, she went with him and began a four-decade-long career. Over that time, her team lost 115 games—but they won 1,157. Coach Wilkinson's teams won 47 straight.

Coach Teague's teams once won 98 in a row. The Sooners did not lose a conference game in twelve years. The Lady Pirates did not lose one in twenty-seven years. Wilkinson, Switzer, Iba, and Gallagher won several championships. Bertha Frank Teague won thirty-eight conference championships, forty district crowns, twenty-two regional titles, and eight state championships.

Bertha Frank Teague was, quite simply, the most successful athletic coach that Oklahoma has ever had. How many of you ever had heard of her? What does that tell you?

giant roller coaster, the Big Dipper. During the school year kids in the Oklahoma City area rushed home to turn on the television set and laugh with Ho Ho the Clown's cartoons and Tom Paxton's high jinks, and to learn that there was no problem that 3D Danny and Foreman Scotty could not solve in

AFTER-SCHOOL TV

Believe it or not, there once was a time when there was no television. TV's basic technological prerequisite, the cathode ray tube, was not invented until 1929. Nobody saw a television in Oklahoma until 1939, when the *Daily Oklahoman* and WKY radio sponsored a five-day demonstration before an awed audience at Oklahoma City's new Municipal Theater. It was ten years after that before Oklahoma's first TV station went on the air with regular broadcasts. WKY-TV (Channel 4) made its debut on June 6, 1949.

Americans already remembered June 6 as D day, the day that Allied forces invaded Europe to end World War II and change the world forever. In a sense this June 6 is every bit as important because on that day life in Oklahoma began to change in ways impossible to imagine in 1949. It also was something of a D day itself. A featured performer on WKY-TV's very first program (the "Gizmo Goodkinds Show") was a young man named Danny Williams. He played Spavinaw

3D Danny (Dan D. Dynamo)

Spoofkin, "Chief Spoof Spinner of Gizmo Goodkin Land." If your grandparents or parents were raised in central Oklahoma, it is almost certain that they know him as 3D Danny.

An entire generation of central Oklahomans were raised with the adventures of Dan D Dynamo. Many were Unicorpsmen, signed up in his Universe Science Corps—and some probably still have their thunderbolt shoulder patch to prove it. There were enough of these in the Oklahoma City area that "The Adventures of 3D Danny" beat the pants off ABC's "Mickey Mouse Club"

in the 4:00 P.M. time slot—Annette notwithstanding.

Star status also fell on Steve Powell, who perfected the character of Foreman Scotty and entertained two decades of children after school with his broadcasts from the Circle 4 Ranch.

In the early days of television there were not dozens of cable channels, including MTV and VH-1, as there are now. Instead, a generation of Oklahomans huddled around flickering black-and-white TV sets every afternoon, sure as shootin' that science would solve all of our problems if we only held fast to the cowboy's code.

You probably know some of these people now that they are in their middle age or older. They may not be quite so sure of science's promise or of a cowboy's virtue—or of anything else, for that matter. But if you want, you might ask them who Bazark was (3D Danny's robot, of course!) and speak the magic word, "Nix-O-Billy." To an entire generation, that was what would summon Foreman Scotty's Magic Lasso. Say it now; it may yet summon magic.

thirty minutes, including the time wasted on commercials. In Tulsa some said that, if you touched your TV while Oral Roberts was preaching, you could get cured of everything except insanity.

Jim Crow Must Go!

The pride that Oklahomans placed in their athletic teams and their material progress might have been better focused on dealing constructively with troubling social questions. None was more vexing than the ancient issue of race. Particularly in the 1950s, when the United States Supreme Court decreed that segregation must end, Oklahomans rose tall and strong to meet the challenge. Other states—including Oklahoma's eastern neighbor, Arkansas—met federal court orders with hostile defiance. In 1957 federal paratroopers armed with rifles and bayonets had to patrol the streets of Little Rock and the halls of its Central High School to be sure that a handful of black students could exercise their right to attend school with whites. In other states, particularly in the South, the troops were unnecessary— but only because no blacks dared to assert the rights that the Supreme Court had said were theirs. In some places troops were unneeded because defiant whites greeted orders to integrate their public schools by closing them instead.

Oklahoma had it different, and Oklahoma had it better. The high court's original 1954 decision (*Brown v. Board of Education of Topeka*) outlawing segregated public education had been based squarely on earlier lawsuits filed by black Oklahomans and masterminded by Roscoe Dunjee. Perhaps because it was prepared, the state met the Supreme Court's declaration with quiet acceptance. In fact, Governor Raymond Gary, himself a politician from Oklahoma's "Little Dixie," personally led the drive to amend the state constitution in 1955 to put Oklahoma and its schools in compliance with the court ruling. As he explained, as a Christian he could not do otherwise.

Oklahoma's private citizens—both black and white—joined together in the cause of change. In Oklahoma City, Clara Luper launched what later became known nationally as the sit-in movement when her Douglass High School students went to the

Before sit-ins became nationally known as a weapon in African Americans' fight for civil rights, young students of Oklahoma City's Douglass High School were successfully using the technique to integrate downtown lunch counters.

downtown Katz Drug Store and patiently sat waiting to be served at the all-white lunch counter. Patience had its reward when Katz agreed to drop its color line, not just in its Oklahoma City stores but in its entire national chain. Later demonstrations led to the peaceful integration of Springlake and other previously whites-only private facilities. In Tulsa blacks and whites—many of the latter were active in that city's surprisingly powerful All Souls Unitarian Church—staged similar protests with similar results.

Year of Wonders: 1955

On the whole, Oklahomans had good reason to feel good about themselves. Take just one year, 1955. In that one year Chevrolet introduced its new high-compression V-8 engine, put it in a completely redesigned, streamlined body, and sold thousands to Oklahomans. Many bought their cars with paychecks earned at Midwest City's Tinker Field or Tulsa's McDonnell-Douglas plant, which both were fattening payrolls with military contracts. In 1955, Governor Gary called on Oklahomans to do the right thing. They did, and the Oklahoma governor was telling America that the all of the South would one day integrate its public schools. Looking at Oklahoma, some dared to believe him.

In 1955 a team from Douglass High School met and defeated a Capitol Hill football team. Ten thousand fans packed the stadium that night, and thousands more saw it live on Oklahoma City television. They were watching the first integrated football game ever played in the state. In 1955, Bud Wilkinson's team came from behind in the second half to win the Sugar Bowl, complete a second consecutive perfect season, and win the national championship. The Sooners' victim was a fine Maryland team coached by Jim Tatum.

In 1955, Hollywood released the movie version of *Oklahoma!* At last Oklahomans could see for themselves what had been thrilling New Yorkers since 1942. All things considered, 1955 was just one year in which Oklahomans were proud to sing out, "O, what a beautiful morning!" It seemed that Oklahoma was enjoying a lot of beautiful days.

The Color That Counts

As things have a way of doing in Oklahoma, many of the best recent changes made their way onto the football field. The star player in the Douglass–Capitol Hill game had been a lightning-quick halfback named Prentice Gautt. As a high-school student he and his friends had sometimes ridden the interurban down to Norman, where they climbed the big fence surrounding Owen Field and walked with awe-filled steps across the green grass and chalked stripes. Once a Norman resident had encountered them on the streets and reminded them that they had best be out of town by six o'clock.

In 1956, Prentice Gautt enrolled at the University of Oklahoma, put on his pads, and reported for practice. With those acts, Prentice Gautt became the first black to play football for the University of Oklahoma. This time no one reminded him of the Norman custom that required blacks to leave town before sundown. No one cared about that anymore. The only color that counted was Sooner red.

Prentice Gautt, OU's first black football player and now a Ph.D., came to the university on an academic rather than an athletic scholarship.

Because freshmen were then not allowed to play on varsity squads, Gautt became eligible only in 1957, the same year that Notre Dame broke Bud's winning streak and Oklahomans' hearts. In 1958 the hated University of Texas Longhorns beat Bud's Sooners 15–14—the first Cotton Bowl loss for Oklahoma after seven straight wins. As a senior Prentice Gautt made All-American in 1959, but the Nebraska Cornhuskers ended the conference-game winning streak that same year. After that Oklahoma football fell on hard times—by its standards, at least. No one forgot those standards, however. Starting in 1973, the Sooners rose to match them again.

The Bootlegger's Boy

In that year OU named Barry Switzer its new head coach. Like Wilkinson, Switzer had been a Sooner assistant coach. Like Wilkinson, he was an offensive genius. His wishbone offense rolled up yardage records unseen since the days of Bud's feared split T. Like Wilkinson's, Switzer's best teams coupled offensive firepower with defensive tenacity. But the most important quality that Barry Switzer shared with Bud Wilkinson was his magic as a recruiter. Surveying the talent that he amassed, some dared whisper that he was an even better recruiter than the master had been. One thing was sure: Barry Switzer was a different kind of recruiter.

One difference was the consequence of technology. Jet air travel stretched indefinitely Wilkinson's three-hundred-mile recruiting radius, and Barry Switzer made the entire nation his recruiting field. Oklahoma and Texas still provided the largest numbers of large bodies, but every team had stars from Florida, California, Louisiana—everywhere. Another difference was that a large proportion of those recruits were stunningly gifted black athletes.

After Prentice Gautt's arrival black players were standouts on every subsequent Sooner team. Their numbers were small, but it remained unusual that they were even there at all. Incredibly, the ten schools of the football-mad Southeastern Conference (including the universities of Alabama, Florida, Mississippi, and Tennessee, as well as Louisiana State and Auburn) did not field a single black player until 1968. Neither the Arkansas Razorbacks nor the Texas Longhorns, OU's most immediate recruiting rivals, had a black athlete on scholarship until 1970.

Through the 1970s and beyond OU did not have quite a monopoly on recruiting black talent, but it did have the advantage, and Barry Switzer made the most of it. One Switzer team, in fact, had three future stars of the National Football League rotating at the same position—all of them black. Ferocious black linebackers, rabbit-quick black quarterbacks, explosive black running backs—every Switzer team added an incredible array of black talent to the athletic gifts of white kids from farms and small towns in Oklahoma and everywhere.

College scoreboards recorded the uncanny results. On the New Year's night when Switzer's 1985 team destroyed Penn State to give the coach his third national championship (the others had been in 1974 and 1975), Switzer's record became exactly identical to Bud Wilkinson's at that point in the coaches' OU careers. Of 153 games played, each had won 125, each had lost 25, each had played 4 ties. Each had won three national championships, two of them back-to-back. No wonder a popular bumper sticker—as likely to be seen on oilmen's Cadillacs in Tulsa as on farmers' pickups in Sayre—announced, "It's Hard to Be Humble When You're a Sooner." Many found it downright impossible.

Once again, the athletic success of Sooner football had counterparts at the state's other comprehensive university. At Oklahoma State the basketball program remained strong, and the baseball teams became perennial powers. Joe Seay, the new coach that athletic director Myron Roderick brought in to restore the luster of Cowboy wrestling, returned NCAA national championship banners to Gallagher-Iba Hall after a long drought. Under Jimmy Johnson and Pat Jones, Cowboy football fortunes soared to approach, if never quite equal, the wins that were fanatically expected down in Norman.

In the Switzer era a series of black backs ran with abandon. Some—like Joe Washington—apparently could fly.

The Terrible Years

Oklahoma athletic fans (that phrase may be redundant) had reason to proclaim again in the 1980s that those were beautiful mornings, but the darkness fell swiftly. In a single six-week period starting in December 1988, Switzer's football program was socked with several bad blows. First, NCAA penalties were imposed for a series of recruiting abuses. Then the state rocked with headline-making news from Bud Wilkinson House, the Sooner athletic dormitory. One player wounded another with a gun. A young woman from Edmond filed rape charges against several players. Federal agents arrested the starting quarterback for drug-dealing. Altogether, five players left the dorm under state or federal criminal indictments. *Sports Illustrated,* the nation's leading sports magazine, ran a full-color cover photograph of law enforcement officers removing a Sooner player to jail, his hands cuffed behind him. He wore not the familiar crimson and cream but a convict's standard-issue orange coveralls.

Not much later, NCAA officials came down hard on Oklahoma State, hitting its football program with heavy sanctions for recruiting violations that exceeded even OU's. Joe Seay left Stillwater in disgrace, and the wrestling program was stripped of every single scholarship. In 1990 the state legislature even called OSU President John Campbell on the carpet, demanding to know why he personally had ordered several football players readmitted to the school although each had flunked out. The legislators (and others) were mightily embarrassed, in no small part because Dexter Manly, one of those who had taken Cowboy football to glory, had recently told Congress that he had successfully completed four years as an Oklahoma State University student-athlete, leaving as he had entered, unable to read.

Under heavy storm clouds, Barry Switzer resigned his coaching job and authored a book. *Bootlegger's Boy* was a proud defense (some said an arrogant offense) of what he had done at OU. It was a national best-seller, nowhere more avidly read than in Oklahoma.

Switzer's side of the story was but one piece of evidence in Oklahomans' painful reassessment of where their society had gone since World War II. Bud Wilkinson and Barry Switzer had built programs that gave the state pride. But had that pride all along been misplaced? How important was it, after all, to push an oblong ball across a rectangular surface? Was it not true that outsiders who once had scorned Oklahomans for their poverty were now ridiculing them again, this time for being people who found surrogate social status in the achievements of a few burly late adolescents?

Oklahomans were used to outsiders' criticism, but (except among the most fanatical) this time the criticism came from within the state, too. Many noted that frightfully large percentages of the athletes recruited for sports teams at both universities had failed to graduate. This was particularly the case among the black athletes. Many of them had been poorly prepared by schools in the urban ghettos and came to OU or OSU for just a few months of glory. Except for the few who went on to the pros, many had ended up none the better for the experience. Some black Oklahomans were particularly resentful, although admitting that the same situation all too often prevailed at other schools in other states. It was somehow worse when it happened to poor black kids whose sole worth seemed to be their ability to entertain the predominately white and middle-class fans who packed OU's Owen Field and OSU's Lewis Field on a few Saturdays every fall.

And what about the other things that had given Oklahomans such pride? Both state universities were nationally noted for sports—but only for sports. Their football, basketball, wrestling, baseball, and other teams regularly won Big Eight championships, but in nearly every other category—spending per student, average faculty salaries, size of the library, and the like—one school was invariably seventh, the other invariably eighth in the conference. Come to think of it, even the athletic glory tended to fall only on young men. Although there were exceptions, most of the state's women had no real outlet for their athletic gifts. This was particularly the case in the state's largest school systems, where cheerleading and pom-pom routines were the most important activities open to girls. Many welcomed it, but more began to wonder if that was enough. When Edmond's Shannon Miller returned from the 1992 Olympics weighted down with gymnastics medals, the final answer seemed to be that it was not.

Similarly, the suburbs that had given so many Oklahomans both their homes and their identities came under reexamination. For every Moore and Broken Arrow that had blossomed, had not dozens of Gotebos, Garbers, and Konowas withered? There were gleaming shopping centers in the metropolitan communities, but out in rural Oklahoma merchants were boarding up their stores, doctors were closing their hospitals, and superintendents were padlocking their school doors. What did it mean to be a teenager with nothing to do but hang out at a dimly lit hamburger stand or, for that matter, in a brightly lit shopping mall? Some believed that they found partial answers to those questions in the alarming increase in teen drug and alcohol use as well as in teenage pregnancies—one of the few social categories in which Oklahoma regularly led the nation.

Contemporary Oklahoma suburbs have exploded in population, but smaller communities, particularly in the state's western portion, have had a different experience. There it may be boredom that leads to the effacing of official signs—or it may be an expression of the desire to leave town as soon as possible.

Later events disrupted even Oklahomans' complacency over their indisputable crowning social achievement of the early postwar era. They had ended peaceably and quickly the legal segregation of the races, but racism itself proved to be a hardy and adaptable monster. The phenomenal growth of the suburbs and their school systems had left many inner-city schools just as black and just as inadequate as they ever were. No laws prohibited black people from buying homes wherever they wanted, but that did not mean that they could afford what they wanted or that they would be welcomed by their neighbors.

Thus it was that a modern visitor to Tulsa's Greenwood district would notice but one major change since 1945. Most of the business buildings were closed. The black-owned establishments had become casualties of the continuing poverty of their still all-black neighborhoods. In Oklahoma City, Springlake had finally opened its gates to the black people who lived in the neighborhoods that surrounded it, becoming one of the last Oklahoma private businesses to integrate. Then on Easter Sunday of 1971 the park erupted in a fury of racial rioting that it took half of the Oklahoma City police department to quell. Never recovering, Springlake soon closed permanently, bulldozers knocking down the rickety skeleton of the once-proud Big Dipper.

None of those problems was Oklahoma's alone. Every state and every community had their own versions of them, and therefore Oklahomans had no reason to see their society as a singular failure. It was neither singular nor a failure, but neither was it quite as young or quite as vigorous or quite as sure of itself as it had been earlier, say back in 1955. In Oklahoma life at last had come to imitate football. In both, the assuredness of adolescence had given way to the self-assessment of later years.

After all, is that not what maturity is all about?

See History for Yourself

Even those who are not sports fans should attend a football game at Owen Field and a basketball game at Gallagher-Iba Arena. At a minimum they will leave the experience knowing that something special and powerful has happened—even if they know not what or why.

Suggestions for Further Reading

Reference

Bischoff, John Paul. *Mr. Iba: Basketball's Iron Aggie Duke.* Oklahoma City: Western Heritage Books, 1980.

Cross, George Lynn. *Presidents Can't Punt: The OU Football Tradition.* Norman: University of Oklahoma Press, 1977.

———. *Blacks in White Colleges: Oklahoma's Landmark Cases.* Norman: University of Oklahoma Press, 1975.

Keith, Harold. *Forty-seven Straight: The Wilkinson Era at Oklahoma.* Norman: University of Oklahoma Press, 1984.

Related Reading

Luper, Clara. *Behold the Walls.* Oklahoma City: Jim Wire, 1979.

Switzer, Barry, with Bud Shrake. *Bootlegger's Boy.* New York: William Morrow and Company, 1990.

Chapter 26: **The Economy's Maturation**

For all of its history, Oklahoma's economy has been intimately related to other aspects of its people's lives. The generation that survived the Great Depression to fight and win the Second World War certainly had every reason to know that. When they had left their homes for the battlefields of Europe, North Africa, or a dozen Pacific Islands, they carried with them vivid images of big-city unemployment, small-town decay, and rural despair. They returned to a state that they may not have recognized.

Oklahoma's two major industries—oil and agriculture—had experienced painful wartime self-corrections. If no one expected to see again the giddy boom times of the 1920s, neither did they want to repeat the busts of the 1930s. Rain falling from the heavens had refreshed dried ponds and restored devastated fields, breaking the longest drought in memory. Checks descending from Washington had restored old industries and allowed new ones to bloom, breaking the worst depression in history. Happily, the early postwar years continued the prosperous trends of the early 1940s.

Modern Agriculture

Oklahoma's farmers and ranchers were in no mood to see a repeat of the depression's grief, and they did not experience it. It was true that droughts returned over several years of the 1950s, but they were nothing compared to those of twenty years earlier. Crops and grasses withered in the fields, but they did not completely die off. Several summers saw ugly cracks appear in the red clays of central and western Oklahoma, but the soil did not turn to powder, and it did not blow away.

The biggest change owed less to nature than to government. During the 1930s the federal government had begun a series of experiments to secure farm prices through deliberate government actions. These included setting production limits on major crops (a move that would reduce the surpluses and thus increase crop prices) as well as paying subsidies that put taxpayers' dollars directly into farmers' pockets. At the time many protested such steps, thinking that they saw in them the first stages of some form of government socialism. By the 1950s, however, the programs had proven their worth, if not to the taxpayers then to farm-state voters and to the politicians who answered to them. The cries of "socialism" weakened and disappeared, and the Congress and the White House saw to it that such experiments became both permanent and larger.

Such programs partially obscured fundamental changes that were occurring in Oklahoma's agriculture. Every year fewer Oklahomans made their living from farming. Every year agriculture accounted for less of the state's total income. As late as 1950 one in five Oklahomans was a farmer, and farms accounted for 14 percent of state income. By 1970 only one Oklahoman in twenty was a farmer, and agriculture gave the state but 6 percent of its earned income.

Although it attracted nothing like the attention riveted on the great exodus of the 1930s, Oklahoma continued to lose farmers after World War II. Between 1950 and 1960 the state lost 219,000 of its citizens, more than had left during the Dust Bowl years of the 1930s. The greatest portion of these emigrants were farming people, particularly from the state's southern and western regions. Nearly every county in those areas lost population every year after 1950. Between 1950 and 1975 the counties suffered declines that on average removed one resident of every five. Many ended up in California, just like the Okies before them. Even if they stayed in the state, they did not stay in Johnston or Harmon counties, and they did not stay in farming or ranching. The odds were that they went to Oklahoma City or Tulsa, where they worked in defense plants or in retail stores.

The ones they left behind may have stayed on the land, but their lives changed too. Their bodies were on farms (certainly, their hearts were there), but they needed other sources of income to support their farming habits. If they still planted crops, it likely was only a few acres. If they kept cattle, it probably was only a few cows and calves or some yearlings. The few dollars that they earned by selling a truckload of melons here, or a cow there, did not support them. Instead, they found jobs—full-time jobs, in fact—in surrounding small towns. They might also draw government pensions or state relief grants. The only ones still able to make a living from agriculture were those with enough luck or enough wisdom to invest in land and expensive equipment.

Neither fortune nor foresight count for much unless they are accompanied by capital. Postwar agriculture became an expensive proposition. It took tens of thousands—hundreds of thousands—of dollars to buy land, fertilizers, herbicides, tractors, combines, harvesters, and the rest of the necessary

Modern Oklahoma agriculture is a capital-intensive industry. Only a few farmers, such as this Kickapoo Indian, can call for outside assistance. In his case the Bureau of Indian Affairs helped finance expensive irrigation equipment.

materials. In the Panhandle, to give one example, wheat returned as a major crop, but only for those able to buy all of those items plus the center-pivot irrigation pumps that sucked water up from the Ogallala aquifer at a cost of thousands of dollars each. The total value of a modern family farm easily could run over $1 million. Everywhere, those who could not afford the game left the table. Those who

TODAY'S COWBOYS: HITCH ENTERPRISES

Economic change can seem vast and impersonal until it is reduced to a single operation. Consider the changes in Oklahoma's agricultural industry as they are reflected in a single family and firm.

James K. Hitch settled in Oklahoma's Panhandle when it was still "No Man's Land." In 1884 this native of Tennessee began grazing longhorns close to Coldwater Creek, near present Guymon. After statehood the operation grew slowly as herefords gradually replaced the longhorns. On James Hitch's death in 1921 his son Henry continued the investments in more land and better cattle. Those investments allowed the Hitch operation to survive the very worst years of the Panhandle's history—the "dirty thirties," when the howling dust storms blew so many others away.

After World War II, Henry's son, H. C. ("Ladd") Hitch, Jr., joined the business and began drilling deep irrigation wells to tap the Ogallala aquifer. Water pulled from the wells enabled the Hitch fields to become a secure and steady source of grains. Those grains allowed the family to enter the feedlot business.

Today the Hitch cow herd is around 1,200 head. The Hitch feedlots, however, hold up to 158,000 cattle on any given day. They are brought there by the Hitch Cattle Company, the family-owned firm that buys them from smaller producers. Much of what they fatten on is grown by Hitch Farms, Inc., the family's 10,000-acre farming operation. Those not sold to packing houses are processed by Booker Custom Packing, the family-owned meat company. Underwriting every phase of the business is Hitch Ag Credit Corporation.

All of those companies together constitute Hitch Enterprises, Incorporated. This modern, multimillion-dollar corporation is just about as far away from the romantic world of the lonely cowpuncher as Oklahoma is from those days.

remained knew that it was a high-stakes gamble, and the stakes kept getting higher and the odds kept getting longer.

Modern Petroleum

Oil, the state's other major industry, experienced the same sorts of changes in the immediate postwar years. Oilmen, like farmers, learned to avoid the frightful calamities of excessive production and ruinous prices. For them too government was no small part of the solution. Hardy individualism of the rugged variety had become a luxury that oilmen could not afford—even if some of them found it hard to quit talking about it.

State proration laws (assigned limits on crude-oil pumping) continued right on from the 1930s through the 1940s and beyond. These were direct parallels of the government programs to benefit farmers by controlling their production. In addition, the federal government clamped tight quotas on the amount of oil that could be imported from abroad. The declared purpose was to secure America's energy independence from unstable foreign sources. If that was one effect, another was to keep domestic oil prices artificially high, since producers in Oklahoma (and elsewhere) did not have to compete with the cheaper foreign suppliers. The latter consequence was neither unknown nor undesired by Oklahoma's oilmen and the politicians whom they helped keep in office.

Within the state the oil industry settled comfortably into its new ways. Looking back, economists noted that Oklahoma had reached its peak of energy production way back in 1927. Fewer people shared in the industry. Every year after 1927 the number of oilfield and refinery workers dropped, as did the number of working wells and the volume of their production. By the 1970s the production of oil and gas and their refining accounted for just about 5 percent of the state's total employment and the same small share of its total income.

If some people missed the excitement of swapping leases beneath the groaning rigs of the latest boom field, most found it pleasant enough to set long-range corporate plans in air-conditioned offices and hatch a few deals over rounds of golf or drinks at the local country clubs. With their days of frenzied growth well behind them, communities like Seminole, Wewoka, and Healdton settled down to an existence that was both orderly and dull.

The Chief Industry: Government

Behind many of the changes in Oklahoma's agriculture and oil lay the hand of government, which held both the dollars and the reins. Not many protested the second as long as there was plenty of the first. In fact, government at all levels expanded enormously in the postwar years. Although few people noticed it or pondered its implications, government—not farming, not ranching, not oil, but government—became Oklahoma's number-one industry.

As early as the 1970s one dollar in every five that Sooners earned came to them as government paychecks. That was one trend that continued without

During the oil boom in the late 1970s even old fields found new activity. One was the Oklahoma City field that includes land near the state capitol. That oil boom would bust, but the economic importance of government only continues.

significant change. Readers of the state's official almanac for 1991–92 might have noted that great space was given over to the importance of agriculture and energy to Oklahoma. They hardly could have missed the beautiful color photographs of oil wells, refineries, and various rustic scenes. Only those who turned to the back pages and looked closely would have noted that of the state's fourteen largest employers eight were government agencies of one kind or another. Those eight included every one of the largest seven employers.

Another way to see the significance of government to Oklahoma's economy was to look at only one of the many government activities at one of its many different levels. In Oklahoma higher education was almost entirely the responsibility of state government and far from its biggest responsibility at that. Yet by the 1990s there were more people enrolled as students at either the University of Oklahoma or Oklahoma State University than there were full-time farmers all over in Oklahoma. Tulsa still thought of itself as the Oil Capital of the World, but Tulsa Junior College enrolled five times as many students as there were refinery workers in the entire state.

College enrollments only suggested the impact of government on the state's economy. After all, college students did not make much money. (We can assure you that their professors did not either.) Collectively, the people who worked at Midwest City's Tinker Air Force Base or Oklahoma City's Federal Aviation Administration (FAA) center did earn good wages. Collectively, the people in every county who worked for the State Department of Human Services or the Department of Health did bring home full-time paychecks. Collectively, the thousands of school teachers who worked for the hundreds of local school districts did earn a living. The money that such government employees earned was easily the largest source of Oklahomans' personal income, equal to at least four times that earned either in farming or in oil.

Bringing Home the Bacon

Although the figures varied from state to state, something like the same was true almost everywhere. What set Oklahoma apart from many other states was that much of the government spending was due not to accident but to design. This was particularly true of the federal government's expenditures. Especially in the 1950s, 1960s, and 1970s, a remarkably talented and powerful delegation served Oklahoma in the Congress. Since Oklahoma was one of the nation's less populous states, its delegation was always one of the smallest. Many, however, regarded the Oklahomans as "pound-for-pound" the strongest force in the entire Congress.

From his election in 1948 to his death in 1963, Oklahoma's Senator Robert S. Kerr contributed many of those pounds—in more ways than one. Weighing in at up to 270 pounds, the Oklahoman was known as the "uncrowned king of the United States Senate." From his place on the Senate Finance Committee, Kerr saw to it that every tax bill treated Oklahomans kindly—particularly those Oklahomans who (like him) made their living from oil. From his perch atop the Senate Subcommittee on Rivers and Harbors, he also saw to it that Congress was unusually generous with public works for Oklahoma.

Kerr's sometime colleague Senator Mike Monroney headed the Senate's Aviation Subcommittee until he lost his seat in 1968. That fact should answer any question why Oklahoma City has a huge FAA center—or why it bears the name of Senator Monroney. Over on the House side, Speaker Carl Albert (from Okla-

When President John Kennedy committed the nation to a space race in the 1960s, Senator Robert S. Kerr was ready to do his part—and ready to see that Oklahoma got its part too. Heading the Senate Aeronautics and Space Committee, he anticipated a twentieth-century economic boom for Oklahoma that would overshadow even the land runs of the nineteenth century. Although that did not happen, Oklahomans like Shawnee's Gordon Cooper (one of America's first astronauts) did benefit.

homa's Third District) and Representatives Page Belcher, Ed Edmondson, and Tom Steed (from the First, Second, and Fourth districts, respectively) looked over every bill with their powerful eyes, keeping Oklahoma's interests always in sight.

At the peak of their influence these Oklahomans' work in the Capitol's corridors had powerful consequences for cash registers back in Oklahoma. Add the dollar value of federal spending at Oklahoma's many military bases, throw in the dollars spent at the civilian agencies, total the worth of the dozens of dam and other water projects, and do not forget the money spent on federal highways or under Social Security. Sum all of these, and one has the remarkable equation that for every dollar that Oklahomans sent to Washington as federal taxes they received $1.22 back as federal checks.

The deaths, defeats, and retirements of men like Kerr, Monroney, Albert, and the rest had their effects, as did the gradual realignment of Washington's priorities. Still, the next generation of Oklahoma politicians might campaign on the need to cut the fat from federal spending, but when they got to the Capitol they always remembered to send the bacon back home. They kept government a major player— *the* major player—in Oklahoma's economy and one of the few economic activities that guaranteed Sooners a return on their investments.

Except for lingering grumbling about so-called

wasteful government spending, many Oklahomans overlooked the economic impact of government on their lives. Oklahoma's people still liked to think of themselves as independent spirits. The symbols of that independence remained not the 8:00-to-5:00 government bureaucrat but the self-contained cowboy, the risk-taking farmer, and the free-spending oilman. Such mythology counts for something, and for a few heady years it seemed to account for too much.

The cowboy culture, if only as a commercial symbol, remains strong in Oklahoma. Ford Motor Company, for example, used it to promote the sale of automobiles in the 1970s.

Boom Times Again

From the mid-1970s through the early 1980s a series of events released an intoxicating new aroma in Oklahoma, one that many had forgotten and others had never known. It was the smell of money. A meat shortage drove beef prices higher, putting coins in cattlemen's pockets and ideas in their heads. If they kept and bred their heifers instead of selling them for slaughter, they soon would have more cattle for sale at the better price. When enough did that, the first effect was to further reduce meat supplies. The second effect was to drive prices up higher still. The third effect was to encourage even more stockmen to hold their own heifers off the market. The ultimate effect was a sudden upward spiral of beef prices to levels not seen in decades.

At about the same time a series of crop failures abroad and massive U. S. grain sales to the rapidly decaying Soviet Union drove Oklahoma wheat prices to record highs and Oklahoma farmers into the nearest banks and implement dealers. "Plant wheat from fence row to fence row," the secretary of agriculture had told them, and they intended to do just that. As prices kept climbing, the more optimistic among them set more irrigation wells, pumped more groundwater over their fields, and bought more expensive machinery. Credit usually financed the machinery, and it almost always underlay the purchase of more land, for which prices headed toward an unheard-of $2,000 an acre. The bankers were anxious to loan money, the implement dealers were anxious to get it, and the farmers were anxious to spend it. After all, prices kept going up, approaching $6 a bushel for wheat.

All of this stunning new prosperity paled before that gushing from Oklahoma's oil industry. During the Arab-Israeli War of 1973, the Arab-led Organization of Petroleum Exporting Countries (OPEC) suddenly shut off the spigots that supplied oil to Israel's western allies, including the United States. Already the United States had ended its quota policy on oil imports, so thirsty was it for oil in what had become a very tight market. Deprived of foreign supplies, angry consumers stood in long lines for precious gasoline. In states like Oklahoma the lines consisted of oilmen making a beeline for the fields, turning up old wells and drilling new ones as the price of crude suddenly soared.

Although the 1973 war was not long lasting, its effects were. The restoration of peace did not mean the restoration of abundant and cheap oil. On the contrary, having tasted power, the OPEC oil sheiks grew fond of it, clamped tight lids on their production, and boldly announced a series of increases in the prices that they would demand and the world would have to pay. Twelve-dollar-a-barrel oil went to twenty dollars, then twenty-five, thirty, and thirty-five dollars. Over the horizon, many oilmen went to sleep with visions of forty- and fifty-dollar sugarplums dancing in their heads.

Because their oil commanded the same stunning prices, Oklahoma's oilmen rarely bothered even to sleep. Old rigs pumped around the clock, sucking up crude oil almost as fast as its price was rising. New wells dug deeper and deeper, tapping pools that never would have been profitable at the old price levels. Gas producers shared in the abundance, driving pipes miles beneath the surface of the Anadarko Basin to break the earth's seal on millions of cubic feet of natural gas.

During the height of the energy boom massive and expensive rigs such as this tapped vast quantities of natural gas buried miles deep in Oklahoma's Anadarko Basin.

Entire communities and whole industries remade themselves to take advantage of the new situation. Out in Elk City and up at Woodward, developers bulldozed over cottonwoods and ceders, leveled the terrain, and threw up houses, waiting for the flocks of oilfield workers sure to roost there soon. Investors unable to wait opened motels as overnight lodgings for the landmen, lease hounds, and speculators who showed up every night and every day. Car dealers suddenly found it easy to sell Cadillacs—gold ones being especially popular. Jewelry dealers stocked up on Rolex watches. Banks loaned money as fast as they could; none faster than Oklahoma City's Penn Square Bank, (it was said that one bank official often celebrated his latest deal by sipping champagne from his Gucci loafers).

And Bust Times, Too

And then it all ended—all of it—as fast as it had begun. When meat prices crested the hill and started slipping downward, ranchers rushed to get their cattle to the market. More cattle at the sale lots meant lower prices, lower prices meant cutting back herds, cutting back herds meant even more beef for sale, and that meant even lower prices. The upward spiral had became a downward one, drilling Sooner cowmen.

At about the same time the United States announced that it would suspend Soviet grain sales as punishment for the Communists' recent invasion of Afghanistan. The benefits for the people of Afghanistan were dubious. The effects for wheat growers in Alva and Alfalfa County were certain: disaster. Grain prices tumbled and kept right on tumbling. Wheat that had sold for $5.60 a bushel brought $2.70. Unable to service their debts at that price, farmers began missing payments. Swiftly, many lost everything they had. Implement dealers, finding their lots overflowing with repossessed tractors and combines, counted themselves lucky if they could get ten cents for every dollar still owed on them. Bankers repossessed land, sold it at auction, and felt fortunate when they got $600 an acre for it.

And then, in 1984, the oil bubble burst. The OPEC nations broke rank, and world oil prices began a mad retreat. Oklahoma oilmen gave up their dreams of forty and fifty dollars a barrel. Instead they suf-

The oil boom became the oil crash, and oilfield equipment yards became cemeteries of rusting rigs and hopes.

fered nightmares as crude prices slipped down an oily slope past thirty-five, past thirty. The rout was on. In a matter of weeks crude prices fell from $27 to $13. Developers suddenly wondered what they would do with all those empty homes and vacant rooms. Car dealers took back their fancy cars, their metallic gold paint covered with Oklahoma's unforgiving red mud. Jewelers shipped Rolexes back to Switzerland, and Penn Square Bank closed. Belly up, its fall probably hurt the champagne business, not to mention the trade in Italian footwear. Far worse, Penn Square's fall began a train of bank failures that brought down dozens of Oklahoma banks and did not end until Chicago's Continental Illinois (the nation's fourth largest bank) went under with them. For a while the nation's entire financial structure was in jeopardy.

These rapid-fire disasters were every bit as dramatic as those that had befallen Oklahomans almost exactly fifty years earlier. As before, their impact went beyond mere economics. Here was the reason that state tax collections tumbled so disastrously, setting off the rounds of necessary tax hikes. Coupled with the scandals surrounding the state's athletic programs and the county commissioners, they contributed to an atmosphere of psychological gloom.

A Mature Economy

Still, the final effects did even approach the depression of the 1930s. Agriculture and oil still provided Oklahomans with powerful symbols, but few Sooners any longer depended on them for their livelihood. Even those who did kept their sense of humor intact. "Lord, Send Me Another Oil Boom. I Promise Not to Blow This One" was the lesson another popular bumper sticker offered on events.

The real lesson ought to have been something bigger. Oklahoma's economic health no longer depended merely on what the individual could grow, pump, or sell. Even the symbols of rugged individualism ultimately depended on what cowmen across the country did, what politicians in Washington chose to do, and what Arab oil powers could get away with. The cowboy, the farmer, the oilman—all of them

ZERO BOMB SHOWS THE WAY

Many economists say that the worst thing about Oklahoma's economic boom in the late 1970s and early 1980s was not that it busted but that it ever boomed at all. The reason, they say, is that the brief burst of farm and oil prosperity diverted Oklahomans' attention from the best path away from their chronic economic difficulties. The best course is away from the production of raw commodities like crude oil, wheat, and livestock, and toward diversified manufacturing. Several Oklahoma companies already have blazed that trail, usually with great success.

Consider, for example, the Zero Bomb Company. Originally, the Tulsa-based company produced explosives used in the oil fields—always a risky place for any kind of business, whether explosive or otherwise. After World War II, however, it shortened its name and turned its energies to the manufacture of a small, inexpensive item that is used by millions. Perhaps you have one—a fishing reel that bears the brand name ZEBCO.

were every bit as dependent on others as were government employees who depended on taxpayers and the citizens who depended on government services.

The awakening realization that there were limits to the sovereign individual, that each person's well-being depended on the well-being of others, was a lesson painful to learn. The acceptance of that lesson was another measure of Oklahoma's maturity.

See History for Yourself

One Oklahoma company that has continued to prosper through good times and bad in the oil industry is Duncan's Halliburton Company. Started by Earle P. Halliburton in 1924, the company is active in every major oil development around the world. Understandably, the Stephens County Historical Museum devotes considerable space to documenting the company's history in Oklahoma and internationally. You should also visit the Tulsa Port of Catoosa/Arkansas Waterway Museum in Catoosa for an idea of the impact that government has had on the state's modern economy. Tours are also available at Fort Sill and may be arranged at Midwest City's Tinker Air Force Base. These remind us of the powerful impact that military spending has had—and continues to have—on the Sooner economy.

Suggestions for Further Reading

Reference

Ezell, John Samuel. *Innovations in Energy: The Story of Kerr-McGee.* Norman: University of Oklahoma Press, 1979.

Green, Donald E. *Panhandle Pioneer: Henry C. Hitch, His Ranch, and His Family.* Norman: University of Oklahoma Press, 1979.

Lage, Gerald M., Ronald R. Moomaw, and Larkin, Warner, *A Profile of Oklahoma Economic Development, 1950–1975.* Oklahoma City: Frontiers of Science Foundation, 1977.

Lobsenz, Norman M. *The Boots Adams Story.* Bartlesville: Phillips Petroleum Company, 1965.

Yergin, Daniel. *The Prize: The Epic Quest for Oil, Money, and Power.* New York: Simon and Schuster, 1991.

Related Reading

Singer, Mark. *Funny Money.* New York: Alfred A. Knopf, 1985.

Zweig, Phillip L. *Belly Up: The Collapse of the Penn Square Bank.* New York: Fawcett Columbine, 1985.

Chapter 27: Oklahomans Look Forward and Backward

As we finish *The Story of Oklahoma*, our world approaches the twenty-first century of the modern era and our state approaches the second century of its modern history. As we have learned, Oklahoma's total history stretches back much further than that—back five or more centuries to a time when its residents thought of themselves as the First People. The First People are gone now, and we strain to recapture pieces of the history that was theirs. We do so because it also is part of our history.

The things that have happened since are other parts of our common history. It is long—probably much longer than you anticipated when you began your study with us—and it is important. Not always has our history been positive. The record contains too much blood, too many tears, and too much tragedy to be recalled with uncritical pride. But it holds much that is inspiring too. It is the story of human beings placed in an environment that is frequently beautiful, often hostile, and occasionally deadly. It is the story of people who have confronted changes that were not always of their own making. They met their challenges as best they could, shaping what they could change and accepting what they could not, always trying to do what was necessary to maintain human dignity. Our history has stories of cruelty and of justice, of greed and of glory, of folly and of wisdom. The history has been made by saints and by scoundrels, by geniuses and by fools, by malcontents and by visionaries. In other words, this is a universal story of humanity made by the universal elements, humanity itself.

What difference does it make that this history happened in the corner of the world that we now share? What difference does it make that its particular twists and turns have occurred in this state?

One difference is that this history defines us. Sometimes it does so individually. Consider, for example, Robinson Risner. An Air Force colonel, Risner had been in combat in Vietnam less than a month when his plane was shot down and he was captured by the North Vietnamese. He spent the next seven years as a prisoner of war, much of the time locked in leg stocks and fed stale bread and foul water. Although physically abused and weak, Colonel Risner knew that the real challenges that he would face would be mental—to keep his sanity amid nearly impossible conditions.

One of the things that enabled Risner to survive was the careful recollection of his own personal history. When he was six, Risner and his family had moved to Tulsa, where the family lived in the same house all through his growing-up years. Although living in a city for the first time, the family kept a spotted horse in the backyard for the boy and his sister to ride. They joined a church—the First Assembly of God—and young Risner made his first close and his most-lasting friends in its youth group. When he was sixteen, he got a part-time job with the Tulsa Chamber of Commerce. He learned welding at school and occasionally picked up a few dollars doing odd jobs around town.

Because Risner's dad ran a used-car lot, he spent every Saturday washing and waxing cars, giving them a shine to reflect the string of lights that hung over the lot at night. He early learned that his father had two forbidden topics. No one could criticize either the Risner children or President Franklin Roosevelt. The second prohibition may have been even more powerful than the first. One day he stopped his own daughter's teasing him about his love for FDR by telling her, "If you ever vote Republican, I hope to live to see the day that you go hungry!"

Around such nuggets as these, Robinson Risner reconstructed the history of his own life. Doing so, he filled his days with meaning and his nights with hope.

Something like that happens all across Oklahoma in the last days of summer. Near Ponca City caravans of cars descend on the fields at White Eagle every Labor Day for the annual Ponca powwow. Families set up camp and exchange greetings. Dancers repair their costumes, and honored elders break out their drums. When those drums begin to beat, the heat of the day (and much else that belongs to that day, too) begins to melt away.

On the same weekend nearly three hundred miles away, Choctaws gather around their old tribal capital at Tuskahoma. They play stickball and offer up prayers—many of the prayers in Choctaw. They may have had to buy it in a grocery store and they may prefer to eat it barbecued, but many families dine on buffalo meat that weekend.

To outsiders, much of this may seem terribly unauthentic, "un-Indian." Cars? Nylon tents? Store-bought food? Gas charcoal grills? The participants know better. As one explains, "Being an Indian doesn't depend upon how you dress or whether you have an old Ford or a young pony. Indians in bright cars and neat suits are still of the eagle race; and as the people of the eagle race, we are still a proud people who have kept alive a great spirit."

As students of history, you should be able to recognize what is going on here. What keeps the spirit of the eagle race alive is its consciousness of its own history, a collective history that brings some to White Eagle and others to Tuskahoma. What kept Colonel Robinson Risner alive was the same thing. His own life's history was, after all, a history that countless Oklahomans have shared. Like his family, theirs have moved to the cities. Like his, they try to keep alive the ways of their rural past. Like the Risners, they join churches and polish cars and turn their times and skills to dollars. In not a few cases, neither do they brook criticism of Franklin Roosevelt, either.

That is the difference that Oklahoma's particular piece of human history has made. This is the portion of human history that most directly affects us. This is the history that happened where we live, the history that happened to people like us. This is the history that we have made, and it is the history that has made us.

Whatever their origins, whatever their times or reasons for coming here, all of Oklahoma's people (right and facing page) have built a tradition to be known, understood, appreciated, and preserved.

Many who will read this book are of Native American descent. It is our hope that now they will know a little more about their people and their history—and how important that history has been to others. Others share experiences more like the Risner family's. Although few will ever have to remember their past in circumstances as difficult as those endured by Colonel Robinson Risner, all can use our shared experiences to cast their lives into the larger net of history that gives identity and meaning to each of us and to others we know.

At their best, Oklahomans always have known that. One who did was Senator Thomas Pryor Gore. Like other Oklahomans of his day, he came from elsewhere—Mississippi by way of Texas, in his case. Like others, he came to Oklahoma when it was still a territory, fresh and green and full of promise. Like some, he prospered, earning honors that in other places or other times would have been unavailable to men like him. The son of poor farmers, Gore was largely self-educated. By adulthood, he also was totally blind. Nonetheless, Oklahomans

sent him to the United States Senate in 1907, making him (with Robert L. Owen) one of our original two United States senators. Defeated in 1920, he returned to win another term in 1930. In 1936 he lost his reelection bid, his last chance for public service.

Returning to Oklahoma with no apologies for his personal past and no illusions about his personal future, Thomas Pryor Gore looked to his state's past and his state's future. Speaking his last words to an Oklahoma audience, his sightless eyes looked both forward and backward to see the relationship between past and future. They saw the whole point of *The Story of Oklahoma*:

> I love Oklahoma. I love every blade of her grass. I love every grain of her sands. I am proud of her past, and I am confident of her future. . . . The virtues that made us great in the past can keep us great in the future. We must march and not merely mark time. We must solve new problems, must meet new conditions with new measures, but they should be met with the same resolve and courageous spirit as of old.

If we keep alive that great spirit, we shall all be of the eagle race.

See History for Yourself

Summer time brings Native Americans together for fellowship and celebration at powwows all across Oklahoma. Visit one near you.

Suggestions for Further Reading

Risner, Robinson. *The Passing of the Night: My Seven Years as a Prisoner of the North Vietnamese.* New York: Random House, 1974.

Wallis, Michael. *Way Down Yonder in the Indian Nation.* New York: St. Martin's Press, 1993.

Illustration Credits

The help of the following institutions and individuals is gratefully acknowledged for illustrations on these pages: **5, 11 left, 16, 22, 27, 56, 113, 139, 176 top, 178, 180 top right, 187, 188 top, 193, 202, 212, 213, 215, 221 right center and bottom, 251, 254, 262–71, 279, 281, 285, 288, 293, 297, 300, 301, 302, 304, 312, 313, 316, 323, 325, 336, 343, 345, 346, 347, 350, 353, 359, 360, 364, 366, 369, 372, 376, 380, 385, 395, 398, 407, 413, 420, 426, 430, 453, 454, 461, 463,** Western History Collections, University of Oklahoma; **20, 42, 53, 54, 111 right, 114, 120, 133, 137, 153, 155, 156, 162 right, 164, 173, 176 bottom, 177, 182, 188 bottom, 190, 195, 197, 198, 204, 208** (photograph by William S. Soule), **209, 211, 221 top left, 232, 244, 249, 253, 255, 257, 315 bottom, 331, 423, 439, 443, 458, 460, 470, 473, 476, 486 top,** Archives and Manuscripts Division, Oklahoma Historical Society; **3, 13, 17, 69, 74, 131, 161, 163, 221 top right, 223,** W. David Baird; **35, 36, 41, 43 bottom, 44, 108, 111 left** ("Tulloc-chish-ko & Ball Play Dance of the Choctaw Tribe," in Catlin sketchbook), **119 bottom,** Thomas Gilcrease Institute of American History and Art, Tulsa; **134, 151, 159, 180 bottom, 183, 184, 277, 299,** based on John W. Morris et al., *Historical Atlas of Oklahoma,* 3d ed. (Norman, 1986), maps 20, 23, 24, 28, 33, 63, 52, and 48, respectively; **49, 59, 61, 77, 82, 97, 103,** George Catlin, *Letters and Notes on the Manners, Customs, and Conditions of the North American Indians,* vol. 2 (New York, 1841), Western History Collections, University of Oklahoma; **11 right, 87, 93, 466, 479,** Hal Adamson, Edmond; **139, 141 left, 174 left, 240,** in Thomas L. McKenney and James T. Hall, *History of the Indian Tribes of North America* (1836–44), Western History Collections, University of Oklahoma; **29 top, 436, 445, 475,** Carl Albert Center, University of Oklahoma; **57** (National Anthropological Archives), **141 right** (painting by John Rubens Smith, National Portrait Gallery), **180 top left, 242** (Museum of Natural History), Smithsonian Institution; **37, 45, 58,** Oklahoma Museum of Natural History, University of Oklahoma; **81** (Geography and Map Division), **152** (painting by Charles Fenderich, 1842), **174, 394,** Library of Congress; **171** (Brady Collection), **174 right, 315 top,** National Archives, Washington, D.C.; **39, 43 bottom,** Don G. Wykoff and Dennis Peterson, *Educational Aid for the Spiro Mounds: Prehistoric Gateway, Present-day Enigma* (Norman, 1983); **119 top, 121,** James R. Lockhart, Office of Historic Preservation, Georgia Department of Natural Resources; **160, 162 left,** *Chronicles of Oklahoma* 29 (1951–52): 444 and 318, respectively; **6,** Sinclair Pipeline Company, Tulsa; **8 left,** Franks Griggs Collection, Bartlesville Public Library and History Museum; **8 right,** Parker Drilling Company, Tulsa; **9,** based on Kenneth S. Johnson et al., *Geology and Earth Resources* (Norman: Oklahoma Geological Survey, 1972), Educational Publication 1, p. 8; **29 bottom,** U.S. Army Corps of Engineers, Tulsa District; **91,** Hynes Fine Art and L. and J. Celic, Chicago; **93,** Geoffrey Goble, Norman; **94,** Thomas Nuttall, *A Journal of Travels into the Arkansas Territory During the Year 1819,* ed. Savoie Lottinville (Norman, 1980); **98,** Missouri Historical Society, Independence; **128,** Oklahoma Planning and Resource Board, Oklahoma City; **144,** in John R. Etling, ed., *Military Uniforms in America* (San Rafael, Calif., 1974), print 4, courtesy of Company of Military Historians; **206,** Fort Sill Museum, Fort Sill; **247,** in Joshua Giddings, *The Exiles of Florida* (Columbus, Ohio, 1858); **361,** Bailey C. Hanes; **390,** Marland Mansion and Estate, Ponca City; **410,** Peggy Tiger, Tahlequah; **416,** photograph by Ann Mull, courtesy of Merle Haggard, Hendersonville, N.C.; **456 top,** Oklahoma State University Special Collections and University Archives, Stillwater; **456 bottom,** Mrs. Omiga Johnson, Byng; **478,** Parker Drilling Company, Oklahoma City; **487,** Guy Logsdon, Tulsa.

Index